ANTONINA

A Byzantine Slut

(REVISED)

By:

Paul Kastenellos

D1596389

An illustrated introduction to
Byzantium can be viewed on the
publisher's website:
apuleiusbooks.com.

This novel is a work of historical fiction. Any resemblance to modern persons is coincidental.

This edition is essentially the same as the first in content. There are, however, many minor corrections in phrasology and punctuation, a revised map of the battle of Dara, and a very few footnotes (in addition to the afterword) to appease scholars concerned about historical accuracy.

Published by:

Apuleius Books

PO Box 234

Garrison, N.Y. 10524-0234

The cover image includes a photo of the Aurelian Wall - Sentry Passage near Port Metronia, made by Joris van Rooden on 01/03/2006. All images are from Wikipedia or J.B. Bury's *Later Roman Empire Of The East* and have been modified by the author.

SAN: 920-0517

ISBN: 978-0-9839108-2-4

Library of Congress Control Number: 2012936004

apuleiusbooks.com

Well behaved women seldom
make history.

    ... Laurel Thatcher Ulrich

MAIN CHARACTERS

More details are given in the appendix, together with notes about other persons mentioned. Glossaries of terms and places are also provided in the last pages of this book; as is an afterword filling in some details that are not in the novel itself, and indicating where the story elaborates on the historical record.

Antonina - Our heroine; the wife of General Belisarius and confidant of the Empress Theodora.

Belisarius – Perhaps the noblest man ever to lead great armies in battle and one of the most successful.

Chosroes - King of Persia during the Second Persian War, also called Nushirvan the Just.

Callista - Antonina's daughter and the wife of Ildiger, born before she met Belisarius.

Gelimer - Vandal king of North Africa. He imprisoned and later had the rightful king murdered.

Ildiger - As the husband of Antonina's first daughter, Callista, he was Belisarius' son-in-law. He was Sent to Libya after Belisarius' victory there. Later he joined Belisarius in Italy where he was a loyal subordinate. He prevented a Gothic entrance to Rome through an aqueduct and was responsible for saving Bloody John at Rimini.

Joannina - The only child of Belisarius, Theodora wanted to have her nephew marry Joannina, allegedly in order to acquire Belisarius' wealth. It is not known whether these lovers married after Theodora died.

John (Bloody John) - A thorn in the side of Belisarius during the Gothic Wars; nevertheless he was an aggressive leader of men. He has been charged with caring more about looting easy districts in Italy than achieving strategic success. It was difficult for Belisarius to control John, especially since he was friends with the grand chamberlain Narses.

John the Cappadocian - Praetorian Prefect. Although John had an excellent legal mind and oversaw the commission that codified Roman law, he is best remembered for his zeal in raising revenue for Justinian's projects. Antonina brought about his downfall.

Justinian - (Born 483, Emperor 527-565) One of the world's great historical figures. More details of his reign are given in the afterward and notes to this volume.

Kobad - Kobad was the Persian king when war broke out on the Armenian frontier and Belisarius had his first experience of warfare. He was still king throughout the first Persian war. On his death peace was arranged and it more or less held until Chosroes assumed the Persian crown.

Narses - The eunuch grand chamberlain was a rival of Belisarius. Late in life he completed the conquest of Italy begun by Belisarius.

Perozes - The Persian commander at Daras.

Photius - Antonina's son, born before she met Belisarius.

Procopius - The private secretary of Belisarius and his biographer. His book, *The Wars*, recounts Belisarius' exploits but his *Secret History* repeats every slander of the time.

Silvarius - Silvarius was elected pope over the objections of Theodora who favored the archdeacon Vigilius. Silvarius refused to confirm Anthimus as the Monophysite patriarch of Constantinople. Vigilius, she thought, would be more flexible toward the Monophysites. He wasn't.

Sittas - General and friend of Belisarius. His wife was Theodora's sister. Sittas and Belisarius had campaigned together as young officers on the Armenian frontier.

Theodatus - The king of the Goths at the time Belisarius invaded Italy. A cultured man, he was also a coward who for a time offered his throne to Justinian. He was deposed by the Goths after the fall of Naples and was shortly thereafter killed by a personal enemy.

Theodora - Justinian's wife and empress. She shared power with her husband. Some of her early life as a porn star before meeting Justinian is quoted from Procopius in the afterword.

Theodosius – Belisarius' godson and Antonina's paramour.

Totila – King of the Goths during the Second Gothic War.

Vigilius. Pope - He succeeded Silvarius. Theodora had always wanted him as pontiff because she considered him malleable. Yet as pope he did not support Justinian's attempt to reconcile orthodox and heretical sects within his realm by formulae that he could not accent to on theological grounds.

Witiges (Vitiges) - King of the Goths through most of the first Gothic war after Theodatus was dethroned and killed.

Zabergan, Bulgar khan - He crossed the Danube, pillaged the Peloponnese, and threatened Constantinople. Then he met the aged Belisarius in one of the general's smallest but most important engagements.

Maps: Pages 58, 72, 92, 160, 184,

Afterword: page 299

Notes: page 315

Names: page 345

Places: page 365

AUTHOR'S INTRODUCTION

German and Roman cavalry charged each other; or more exactly, Gothic lancers met ax-wielding Herulian foederati from Scandinavia, and mounted Hun and Arab mercenaries, the finest light cavalry in the world.

The Goths were German but the "Romans" were allied tribes and mercenaries in the pay of the sixth century empire, still nominally the Roman empire but soon to be known to history as the Byzantine.

If the battle went the Roman way the commander would reward his men with plunder from the enemy: captured arms, gold jewelry, and male and female slaves, the latter being the families of deceased Gothic warriors. For these they would get cash from merchants who followed the army.

The emperor of the polyglot "Romans" still spoke Latin and that was the language of imperial edicts, but Justinian would be the last emperor to do so. Greek had always been the common language in the eastern part of the empire and it was about to become the only language, save for the barbarian patois of its soldiers. Roman law continued but the imperial religion was Christianity. A few feeble remnants of paganism survived in outlying districts but all formal worship was of the Christ. The old temples were falling into decay or being put to other purposes.

The great Roman roads would continue to carry troops throughout the shrunken empire's Byzantine phase but they had not seen an infantry legion in one hundred years and the cavalry that moved along them were at best from Greece or Asia Minor and more often were barbarians. These foreigners thought of themselves not as Roman soldiers so much as professional warriors, allied to what was still the greatest single state in Europe.

The city of Rome itself had long since been ceded to barbarians, in fact if not in theory. Visigoths, Ostrogoths, and Vandals had invaded Italy and it had been, or soon would be, threatened by Franks, Lombards, and Burgundians. However, after long occupation of the western part of the empire, the foreigners who settled in Italy could be nearly as cultured as the citizens of the eastern empire's capital at Constantinople and they still nominally acknowledged an imperial hegemony.

Of course, the battle might not go the Roman way, not merely because the enemy were excellent horsemen and infantry archers, but because the so-called Romans were themselves unreliable. Each troop owed allegiance to its own barbarian warlord, not to the imperial general in overall command; and each warlord's loyalty was self serving and could be bought. They felt little patriotic duty to a far-off sovereign and what loyalty they felt to the Byzantine general in command depended entirely upon his character, charisma, and most important, his ability to bring them loot. If the loot was insufficient he might not survive the barbarian politics.

Either way, the farms and fields not only of the enemy but of the empire could be set afire by a disappointed army. Then only a large bribe and a new commander might possibly restore some loyalty to the crown. There would also be slaughter after the battle itself. Priests, aging wives, and children too young for slavery could die for no other reason than that they were there. If an imperial city was taken by the enemy, in all probability it would be plundered, burned, and women of all ages and status raped.

It was not only the barbarian mercenaries and allied foederati whose loyalty was variable. History has borrowed the term Byzantine politics from an empire where each aristocrat thought himself fit to rule, and each general had an army of personal retainers loyal to him alone. Furthermore, these were the best troops available, the backbone of the armies that were charged with keeping the great Persian empire at bay on its eastern frontier; those barbarian tribes who had not yet been incorporated, safely beyond the Danube; and the state itself from further spinning out of control in a succession of civil wars.

But this was the army with which a noble young man of Thrace would defeat the indomitable Persians and reconquer much of the western empire. Flavius Belisarius was certainly the finest office ever to lead such rabble to victory, and beside him would ride the one-time prostitute Antonina, surely one of the most remarkable women of the time.

CHAPTER 1

565 AD
THRACE

The grim day had come, as at last it must to all who are born of Eve.

It was a pleasant warm spring afternoon on their Thracian estate and Antonina, now an elderly *grande dame* of nearly seventy, knelt beside her husband's deathbed. To the last she would remain at his side as she had, and he by hers, since they had first met so many years and campaigns ago.

Antonina would have much to fear when her own death came. Would it be the bright angel of a merciful God who would come to carry her to paradise, or a dark angel of justice come to throw her soul to the devils below? Antonina wished that she had faith in the absolution of the priests; she had more trust that her husband would intervene before Christ's throne on her behalf.

She had not been a good woman, while her Belisarius was the finest man who ever lived, save for Jesus himself. She knew that he would have nothing to fear in the hours ahead when he slipped away to eternity. True, he had been a soldier and had dealt out death his whole career, but that was in warfare and war was the way of the world. Her own sins had been political or in petty retribution. He had saved the Roman world from the Persians and reconquered much of the empire from the barbarians; but he had always spared life when able to. She feared for her own soul but not for that of the dying man.

"I love you, my lord."

"I know."

"No, I love you. I just did not know how much until now."

"I know."

In time Antonina had come to regret the infatuation she had once had for Theodosius. He'd been fun to be sure; but like every other officer under her husband's command he'd had his own agenda. He had used the general as he had used her, and she him. She hoped it had not been entirely a calculated thing but he had advanced because he was Belisarius' trusted son in Christ.

Theodosius had long years ago faced Christ's justice for their sin. One day soon she also would have to. Dare Antonina ask a favor of her husband that she dared not ask of Christ herself: "When you are with Our Lord, please pray for our godson and for me." Belisarius squeezed her hand with something still of the iron grip with which he had held a sword. Then he left this earth.

The old widow wept for three days and nights but on the morning of the fourth day while she looked out across the Sea of Marmara, she was at peace. In her heart she no longer just felt, but now knew that he had been blessed. In Belisarius she had seen and known and loved a reflection of the Divine Mercy. She had betrayed him and he had forgiven her. Yet in her way she had loved him as deeply as he had loved her. As Edward Gibbon wrote: "She reigned with long and absolute power over the mind of her illustrious husband; and if Antonina disdained the merit of conjugal fidelity, she expressed a manly friendship to Belisarius, whom she accompanied with undaunted resolution in all the hardships and dangers of a military life."

This author chooses to believe that Antonina was less to be faulted than successful businessmen and gossips. She was just unimpressed by the hypocrisy of those who make much of the seventh commandment while ignoring the others. Antonina had boldly sinned in the sunlight. She had not hidden her sins in the dark, and Belisarius was so secure in himself and their marriage - a marriage firmly founded on a lifelong friendship, not male rights of property over her - that he would forgive her anything and defy any man to call him cuckold. This, his jealous and cowardly secretary, Procopius, dared only after the general's death.

Antonina wept for three days and nights but on the morning of the fourth day while she looked out across the Sea of Marmara she was at peace.

511 AD
CONSTANTINOPLE

We must begin our story fifty four years earlier. Antonina's father had won the trophy at the hippodrome, the race course of Constantine's city - the New Rome - assuring him a continued income for some time to come. There had been celebrating late into the night until, at last, the now quite drunken charioteer came home to his family. He was still excited:

"By the mother of God...."

"Don't use the Theotokos' name like that or you'll go to hell," Antonina's mother yelled back.

"Then by Diana's big tits I'm still the best; and the Blues will pay for a lot of wine and meat for us so long as I keep winning." Antonina's father was referring to one of the two factions in the hippodrome, the Blues and the Greens, who make modern sport rowdiness pranks by comparison.

They regularly killed each other and murdered for profit, rioted in the streets and could even threaten the throne. Indeed they were at least as much political and criminal as athletic factions, and as deadly enemies as the Chicago gangs of the nineteen-thirties.

His wife went to bed. After eating some bread to soothe the queasiness that too much wine had left in his stomach, the drunken man found his child asleep in bed. As he was wont to do, he lay beside her only intending to hug his child for a few moments. It would have been better had he fallen into a stupor instead. The author would like to draw a curtain rather than describe fully and unnecessarily what happened next and would affect Antonina all the days of her life.

Very soon there were other men. Antonina developed into a beauty sought by all and available to any who would please the child with some bauble. She had long strong legs, deep blue eyes and light hair. She had a waist as narrow as her bosom and hips became full. There was a lilt in her voice and on her lips bright repartee to match. This emphasized her intelligence. Sometimes she would sit and talk with the more learned whom she met. From them she learned not only a bit of philosophy and theology but also to be patient; that a few little lies would please a dignitary even when he knew that she was lying; that power was available to a girl who used cunning and flattery so long as she never showed her iron back.

I do not mean to blacken her. After all, Antonina was perhaps no more than twelve or thirteen and surrounded by particularly poor role models: cutpurses and even cutthroats among her father's Blue supporters. Even among those who were not guilty of crimes, the pettiness of a hardscrabble life had necessarily left them without much learning and with little regard for those who had. Antonina had as yet no wish to harm others. However, she saw no reason why she should not accept the little advances in society that book learning or being friends with a senator could provide. Roman society in the sixth century was stratified but not without opportunities for the ambitious and clever.

Antonina's father had not been made rich by his victories. He was lauded as much or more than a modern athlete. His name was placed on a monument at the hippodrome. He was wined and dined to excess. He had women. But as with modern boxers he was surrounded by thieves. When he passed his prime those pimps and frauds whose comradeship he had purchased with his winnings faded away from him with excuses. Like lice they attached themselves to new winners. Then he died.

In time, like any young person in her situation, male or female,

Antonina developed a hard shell to hide a troubled soul. She had no thought of where she was going, much less where she should go. Far ahead is difficult for any child to more than dream about. There was only the now. If someone showed any honest care for her she would always respond in the only way she knew. She wanted to be nice to him but knew no other way than to share their body heat and, for that moment, forget altogether that the world is a cruel place.

Antonina's next years were awful. She was not much more than a child when her mother put her on the stage, which is to say more or less officially prostituted the teenager. After all, there was no money coming in anymore. "It was good enough for me," she'd say to others, "and look at me: I married a charioteer. Antonina is pretty. She could do as well, or even better. Already she knows some men of wealth who might like to put her up in a place of her own and pay her bills. Lord God, she does have bills. The girl likes nice things ... and why shouldn't she? She's pretty."

To Antonina her motherly advice was simple: "I don't say ignore what the priests say; but you must live for yourself and not for others. What have any of your cushy friends ever done for you that wasn't for themselves? Let a guy think you love him, that will make him guilty if he's a decent sort. If not, take what you can before he drops you. Try to get something against him too; you'll need it when you're older."

Practical advice, but cold. At first Antonina did just as her mother advised, and she did well. She even became known beyond the slums and the hippodrome. By seventeen she could sometimes be seen early in the morning returning from one of the city's better districts. In the evenings she entertained. She quickly learned that there was a better life than that of a whore and cheap dancer for the crowds that thronged the hippodrome and the theater. She found direction. By age eighteen she'd begun to study by day and at night assume something akin to the role geishas performed in medieval Japan: a cultured entertainer who could sing and play the lyre, dance prettily with her clothes still on, chat a bit about Homer and Aeschylus, and choose her own consorts, not the other way around. Still, a feeling of self worth does not necessarily accompany success. While still quite young, Antonina had born a daughter and given her up to be raised by nuns. Antonina showed herself more caring - or maybe more fearful for her soul - than others in her position. In her day baby girls born to whores did not always survive.

In her later teens Antonina was to be seen very often in the company of a man of senatorial rank, one Anthemius Antonius. He was the scion of

12

an old family, not wealthy but with a certain prestige; the type of man for whom some dignified employment would always be found by family or friends more successful than he. Could Antonina have done better? Possibly. But Antonius was the type of solid person that a working girl, very aware that she was no longer the child type that gentlemen seemed to desire, might choose. He was unmarried, a widower. He would provide for her, and if she behaved herself, would likely keep her. They could age together. He wasn't exciting but Antonina looked about and decided that excitement just meant late hours. It also meant being the excitement and she was getting a bit sick of that.*

---

* See the afterword, pg: 308 - 309.

The reader is advised that the two footnotes refer to possible "spoilers" in the afterword and may want to ignore them until the end of the narrative. Aside from these arguable concessions, made to advance the story, the author has tried to remain as close as possible to the known facts.

CHAPTER 2

516 AD
ALEXANDRIA

The citizens of sixth century Alexandria were more late Hellenistic than either Roman or Egyptian and they were proud of it. Of course, they were also proud of Egypt's Pharonic heritage but the era of pyramid building had been uncounted centuries past. Even the dynasty of the Grecian Ptolemies, though it had ruled Egypt in recorded time, was a distant memory. Besides, all these worthies had been pagan. Alexandria was a proudly Christian city.

For six hundred years Egypt had been a Roman province that had fed the empire from the fertile fields that filled the Nile delta; yet it had never truly adopted Roman ways. Alexandria was the seat of a learned and Hellenized patriarch and had been since the time of the apostles. Before the persecutions, St. Mark the Evangelist had founded a church in Alexandria. Alexandrians felt free to look down upon the upstart patriarch in Constantinople who had only sat on that throne since Constantine the Great founded the eastern capital less than two hundred years before. Of course they dared not also look down upon the Roman government centered on Constantinople, but Egypt had outlived all the world's conquerors and empires and with God's help would outlive this one too.

Old Rome was of no importance anymore; it was in the hands of Gothic barbarians; but Constantinople had become a great city in its own imperial way. It and Antioch and Ephesus and a few other cities were fine places to visit. So too were some of the cities of the Greek Peloponnese. Athens and Corinth still possessed great works of art in their streets. pagan philosophy would still, for awhile, be studied in Athens; and though they had lost their prestige these ancient cities were interesting in an antiquarian way. Thessaloniki was a metropolis in Macedonia. These places and the people from them had to be respected.

But Alexandria was special. It had the great lighthouse, the tallest building in the world and with nothing elsewhere to match its unique mirror that reflected the sun thirty five miles to sea. Alexandria also had by far the world's greatest library to which for hundreds of years scholars had come from east and west, even from Persia and sometimes India. It had famous churches which the citizens believed to be the finest, richest, and most beautiful anywhere.

Alexandria also had fanatics. Like all Greeks, these descendents of Alexander the Great's veterans loved to quarrel. That may have been the reason that the Monophysite dispute was centered upon that city rather than elsewhere. Monophysitism pitted Christian against Christian in angry debate about the nature of Christ. Was he of one Divine nature only as the Alexandrian Monophysites held, or of a Divine and a human nature perfectly in accord as had been declared at the Council of Chalcedon sixty five years before? The dispute pitted the city's Monophysite monks against orthodox imperial soldiers in bloody street riots. For Alexandrian monks theological disputation could be even more satisfying than self-flagellation.

It was to this city that Antonina, now a young woman of eighteen, traveled with her new friend, the senator Antonius, late in the year 516 of the Christian era. Antonius would represent the emperor at the city's council and his family's financial interests in the gold market. Antonina would travel as his wife. though few would believe that the girl who was always at his side could be other than a courtesan or concubine - for she would hold his arm in her small hand and look at him as though he were a god.

"Antonina," he had said when they lived together in Constantinople, "you must see Egypt: the pyramids, the great sphinx, and the animal temples, the library in Alexandria. You wouldn't believe how much sand there is in Egypt. It's far more than in the Syrian desert, even more than in Arabia. A person could travel for weeks and never see anything but sand. But he'd die first since there is so little water. There are so many great things though. The Copts have built beautiful churches and there are wonderful beaches at Alexandria." With honeyed words Antonius lured Antonina to Alexandria. It had not been very difficult and possibly he had not intended to be dishonest.

For two years Antonina lived with Antonius in Egypt. For a much shorter time she was happy. At first she had time to study and learn. She tried to forget Constantinople where her mother still lived in the world of the race course with its vulgarity, its flashy pimps, and the stink of animal shit. Her mother still loved it when chariots crashed together spilling horses and charioteers, with the charioteers occasionally under the hooves of the horses; Antonina no longer did. Not that Egypt was a constant joy but at least there was little in Alexandria to remind her of a home she wanted to forget. She knew no one at the race track there. The pimps were Arab not Greek, and the whores more often than not were from Abyssinia: tall voluptuous girls with smooth black skin. She had nothing in common with them for only a few could speak more than a few words of street Greek and none could speak Latin, still the official language of the empire. So she just avoided the hippodrome area. Then too, by virtue of living with Antonius

16

she was respectable. She began to enjoy wearing stylish but demure clothing and behaving in a wife-like fashion. She rarely wrote home but she did send money.

Alexandria was indeed pretty with the mansions of its wealthy merchants planted among groves of fruit trees. But if there were wealthy homes in Alexandria, there were gawd-awful slums too, worse than in Constantinople. Still, there was the Church of St. Mark built by the Alexandrian Patriarch, and the great library which by virtue of his imperial office Antonius and Antonina were permitted to visit.

Such sites of the city were quickly seen and needn't be seen again, and the downside of the city could not be ignored. In Alexandria there were more camels than Antonina had ever seen and more than she'd ever wanted to see or smell. In the close confines of the city's narrow streets the stench of a caravan could be worse than the hippodrome in Constantinople. Sometimes she'd escape to the beach and kick sand to cool her frustration.

Whatever Antonius' promises, he and Antonina never traveled far from Alexandria. She saw sand but was never to see the pyramids much less the Pharonic temples at Luxor and Thebes. Antonina's life was secure but a bore. Antonius drank too much. He was conservative and not inclined to be Antonina's liberator. When her pregnancy came in 517 she lost all chance for travel and adventure.

Then she lost her babies. Was it a curse from God that she bore twins instead of a single child as He had intended for humans? This much should be said for Antonius: that he kept assuring his concubine that God would not do such a thing, no matter what ignorant and superstitious people might say. Besides, earthly life had been theirs, if only for a few days. They had received baptism and were now with the saints. Antonina should pray to the infants instead of lamenting their deaths. Did he believe it himself? Perhaps.

519 AD
ANTIOCH

Antonina knew little but boredom and depression. Then late in the year 519, by our Gregorian calendar, Antonius was reassigned to the city of Antioch. It was in that year too that God relented and Antonina bore a healthy baby boy whom she named Photius, meaning light.

Like Alexandria, Antioch was wracked by the religious disputes between the orthodox Catholic faction which held to the doctrine proclaimed by the Council of Chalcedon and numerous Monophysites sects who stubbornly refused to give up their belief that Jesus was not a man at all but of one nature with the Father only. According to them God had simply passed through Mary as through a canal, or his human nature had been fully absorbed by the Divine: a man had not died on Calvary hill, only an image. The dispute was not limited to academia; every man and woman in the street had an opinion and would share it as readily and with as much anger as a modern might share his opinion of the president of his country or the chances that his favorite team might win this year's championship. Disputation regularly boiled over into fights at the wine shops and in the streets. Finally, in the same year that Antonina arrived in Antioch, the newly made emperor Justin determined to put an end to it.

At that time the patriarch in Antioch was one Severus, himself one of the foremost Monophysite champions. The comes (count) Irenaeus was dispatched from Constantinople with a troop of Imperial soldiers to arrest him and bring him to the capital to answer charges of heresy. Arriving in Antioch, Irenaeus ordered Antonius to accompany him together with other local dignitaries so as to intimidate the patriarch's supporters. That failed. There were riots and in the confusion Severus made his escape to Alexandria. Antonius went home to his family.

"Gone to our old home town, has he?" Antonina was speaking to her consort while diapering the infant Photius who had been born only weeks before.

"Yes, the Lord help him. But I think no one will dare to lay hands on him in Alexandria. His friends are too strong there and the Alexandrian authorities are sick of trying to compromise their faith with the cowards who prevailed at Chalcedon." Antonius poured himself a large cup of wine.

Like the long-suffering mate of fans everywhere, Antonina made no answer. *Monophysites or Catholics, Chalcedon or antichalcedon; who cares?* At least Antonina did not have to work outside the home; only be Antonius' servant day and night, supervise their few slaves, and listen to his ranting.

"Keep the kid quiet. I'm going to sleep."

522 AD
ANTIOCH

Three years later, Antonina's world, such as it was, fell apart. Antonius died suddenly leaving her with a young child to care for. The physician gave a convoluted explanation. His humors had been out of harmony. The bad temper he had shown for weeks had resulted from an excess of Choleric bile. That could mean anything. It didn't matter anyway; he was dead. Antonina and the city authorities saw to his funeral but she was not legally his wife. As his consort she was quietly allowed his readily available funds in the city but she had no call upon his estate. So that was the end. Antonina would soon be in extreme poverty. If life with Antonius had been dull at least she had only had to deal with one drunken man. What choice had she now but to return to full time whoring? She could go back to Constantinople and do that. She was twenty four now so the pickings would be poor. She could survive, but what of Photius?

Maybe if Photius had just been born.... She knew many a prostitute who had killed her child at birth, but the boy was past three now. He was far too old to leave outside a convent or orphanage as she had done when she gave birth as a teen; but the thought of bringing him with her and raising him among the dainty ladies of a whore house was depressing. For some months Antonina mulled her few options while she hoarded what money she had been given. None were good.

Then in the spring a miracle happened which if it did not immediately improve her situation, at least it lifted some of the gloom in her life and was eventually to change her life.

War with the Sassanid dynasty of Persia was threatening again. Rome and Persia had been at war on and off for centuries. This time it was over the disputed allegiance of the Lazi, a tribe on the east coast of the Euxine (Black) Sea. Their ruler had turned against his suzerain lord, the Persian king of kings, and allied the Lazi with Constantinople. Persian troops might raid the Roman frontier in retaliation. A small troop of cataphracts, the Roman heavy cavalry, had taken up quarters in Antioch to reinforce the garrison. *Maybe I'll stay awhile in Antioch*, Antonina thought. She might do some business with the officers.

"Yes sir."

"Yes sir."

"No sir." Antonina was worried about her boy, in a foul frame of mind, and in no mood to answer questions.

"Look sir, I was an actress; you know what that means; and I was raped three times before I had breasts. Twice by a priest and once was by my dad when he was drunk. Oh, he was so apologetic. Said he'd never drink again. But he did. He tried to do me again too, but ma threw a pot at him. Is there anything else you'd like to know?"

She was speaking with a young guards lieutenant; a tall guards lieutenant with piercing eyes. Those dark eyes were the eyes of a man who missed nothing despite his youth; no more than in his late teens and certainly a lieutenant only by virtue of family prestige. Antonina wasn't the kind to shrink before a child soldier, and why should she? His face was the face of a predator but a young and friendly predator: a cat's face. Although he had stopped her he had addressed her in a pleasant and respectful way, inquiring her business instead of demanding it or assuming it with a teenager's leer. Was that because Antonina was clearly his senior by more than a few years? She was an attractive woman and still not old enough to be his mother; not quite anyway. Old enough to be his teacher though.

Now why did I tell him that? Her mood was improving with the banter for this lieutenant was cute and not looking to do business.

The business the lady was about was indeed that of an actress: which is to say a prostitute looking for a new sugar daddy between jobs on the stage; and jobs on the Antioch stage weren't much more respectable. They were usually such soft porn as the censors still allowed. The most an actress might aspire to was to be a courtesan, or if really fortunate, a concubine to someone with enough money to support a working girl. She'd done it and she'd hated it.

Those days had gone with the death of Antonius. Boring though they'd been Antonina was far from certain of her ability to do as well again. She no longer had much girlish chatter on her lips nor the freshness of pubescence in her face. Yet her skin was fair and still unblemished by the sun. Despite her pregnancies her waist was nearly as narrow as it had been ten years before. Life with a senator had even taught her how to act stately if she thought to. She could now affect a calm cold demeanor to match her natural intellect, and had acquired enough learning to associate with her betters without causing discomfort for herself or them. She might yet snare one of the merchants who would soon be arriving to provision the Roman frontier army. Of course, she would have to stop beginning conversations with a recitation of her father's sins.

And what about Photius?

A grim smile began to soften Antonina's countenance. If she could not find a man to support her maybe she could open a shop and sell pots. *Oh God, pots. Well, why not? Not just pots of course; pretty pots. I know some sailors. I could import from Libya and also sell some of the better glassware being made locally. It would be better than hawking fish, and Photius can help when he's older.*

The tall guardsman had not dismissed her with the detached arrogance of sentries, nor did he seem particularly interested in her "talents." Might he be some sort of reform-minded teen from a family of priests who thought to save a slut from her life of sin? Was he going to offer to her in its stead the poverty of the workhouse with its drudgery: spinning and weaving? There'd be time for that soon enough when she'd be too old for anything better. *Better to sell pots*, Antonina said to herself and almost laughed.

Belisarius stood back with a slight and unexpected bow and Antonina started through the city gate. For a moment she looked back and thought to add something more - something both witty and cutting. She stopped herself. Her mood had improved substantially. The guardsman hadn't acted righteous. He had not actually suggested anything. It could be that he was just a nice young man. *Hah!,* she thought momentarily. *There are such guys - but not many.* She determined to be friendly: calm, reserved, and friendly. When he looked at her she made herself smile a weak smile. There was still some slight chance of her again becoming a well-to-do guy's trophy. She should practice smiling more; people had always said she had a pretty smile.

That was their first meeting: Belisarius, the young guards lieutenant on temporary assignment to Antioch, and Antonina, the no longer young prostitute. It was also the beginning of a love story. After a few chance meetings Antonina found herself finding excuses to pass his post and exchange greetings with him. There was no longer any question of cutting remarks; friendly was more fun.

Belisarius enjoyed the banter. Though Antonina had just turned twenty five she had not entirely lost the pleasure younger people have in testing each other with words. Nor had she lost the urge to tease a young man in other ways: eyelashes batting she'd smile over a shoulder, her bottom turned to him with her tunica pulled tight. Sometimes she would chastise herself for it. *Antonina, you are too old to be enjoying this so much. Antonina, you're wasting time. You should find a nice elderly widower and settle down and pet cats. Antonina, stop this now!*

And Antonina would have stopped teasing and forced herself to be as serious as Belisarius, except that he did not wish it. He was smitten. She was so much more forthright than the crowd around the palace in Constantinople. Not rude - well occasionally - but entirely outspoken. Who at the palace would have begun a conversation with a stranger by reciting how she'd been raped by her father? No one of course. That was what one might expect from some fishwife or, yes, a slut; but this street-girl said it without bitterness or expecting any pitying response. For once in her life

Antonina wasn't looking for anything. The rape had simply been a part of her life, no more or less a part than when she had poured wine for a drunken old man, or discussed with some senator the meaning of lines in a Hellenic play.

To Antonina, Belisarius seemed virginal; with ideas of honor and romance and duty that are rarely found in elderly widowers looking for a trophy. She had to admit to herself that she found him more than interesting. Belisarius was one of those rare men to whom come naturally all the qualities necessary to excel. She could see how even veteran soldiers looked to this teenager for leadership not because he was an officer but because his decisions were thought through and right, He already had an excellent mind. True, his ideals were those of many young aristocrats: honor, duty, and loyalty; but in him they weren't simply the silliness of untried youth. They were solid and certain. *Strangely,* she found herself thinking, *in him they are quite reasonable.* Antonina saw that the only virtue lacking for a very successful career (if lacking be the word) was cunning. A trait that she herself could supply. *Antonina, no. He's eighteen.*

But if one is no older than he feels, in his presence she felt no older than he. Antonina had always enjoyed young men; and as an actress had known quite a few. But they soon bored her with their ignorant and simple solutions to the world's problems. They would make her recall that she was getting older in a business that valued youth above everything else. In the company of Belisarius it was different. She felt young, not like his mother. Her speech was young and her thoughts were young for he brought out in her the desires of a teenage girl; desire for his strength and beauty to be sure, but also for his bright laugh which roused an innocent humor in her that she had thought to be dead. She admired his intellect which complemented her savvy, and for the confidence in himself which she knew instinctively was not merely the bravado of youth but well-founded in solid character. In short, she valued his character. She could hardly believe it herself. Of course, Antonina had not suddenly become so saintly-minded as not to admire his muscular charm too ... *and those eyes.*

I'll wager there isn't a blemish on him yet. Stop! Stop, Antonina! But she could not stop. Even had she been willing to go away Belisarius would have chased her through every alley in Antioch and he would have found her.

"Antonina, it is good to have you to talk with."

"Thank you." She was teasing. It was a dumb answer to a sweet statement. That was as Antonina intended it.

"Really, Antonina," said Belisarius, "There aren't many people back in the Great Palace that I can talk freely with. And here all my friends are guys from the barracks."

She took his hand and they walked awhile along Antioch's fortifications on the Orontes River. Belisarius noted some weakness where the river bank was too far from the city wall. Boats could land there and men put ashore near a minor gate which the soldiers on guard used to gain access to the stream for swimming. It might not have been a problem if the river there were full of rocks, but the water was clear and the sand beneath quite visible. Nothing could be done about the wall unless the city's engineers decided it, and access to its fresh cool water was a nice touch for troops who had spend a hot day or dreary night on duty. Still, some sort of obstruction could be dropped in the water to prevent boats from landing; rocks, or masonry from one of the city's more dilapidated buildings.

Antonina brought Belisarius' thoughts back to her by stopping and standing stark still directly in front of him, her head a full foot lower than his so that she had to look up at Belisarius in a perky way. Then she stood on tiptoes and grinned a wide and girlish grin directly at him.

"Lets gossip. Is it true that Justinian has a girl friend?"

"I don't discuss such things." Justinian was the emperor Justin's nephew and heir to the throne. He had already been raised to the rank of consul and as such was second in importance only to Justin. He was also in much better health, well educated, and more competent.

Belisarius deliberately stood even more erect than usual, so that even on tiptoe Antonina could not look him in the eye without backing off a bit.

"Is it true she's a street girl?"

"If you mean the lady I think you mean, and if our next emperor does know her; no, she's not. She's a good friend of Senator Hecebolus."

"A concubine, you mean. Gee, I'd love to be a concubine again."

Belisarius was taken aback, but then he remembered that since the death of Antonius such a position would be a step up for Antonina. He preferred not to think about it.

"I think it would be great if Justinian had a girlfriend from the streets though. Everyone would think it great. It would make him seem more human. People are so stuffy in the palace; or so I'm told. Behind their masks they must have secrets though. Yeah, an emperor with a street girl ... eh, a courtesan as a girlfriend. They might even marry. I might even have known her back when. What's her name?"

"You're fantasizing, Antonina, but it's Theodora."

The two walked on, chatting like puppies who've just met. The usually cool-minded lieutenant mused that the Orontes that day was as pale as some rare beauty's eyes; not that he'd ever looked into the pale eyes of a rare beauty. The air was fresh. He was happy.

Antonina felt clean. She hadn't blown a man behind some wine shop in weeks and she didn't want to.

Photius? He was four now. Should she tell Belisarius about him? *No, no. I can't. I should have told him from the first. I can't spring a kid on him now. Besides we can't go on like this. There's no reason to tell him.*

It would be pleasing to write that Antonina told Belisarius about Photius and that the three of them ran off to live happily ever after. That could not be. Antonina liked young men and was beginning to love the young lieutenant; but Belisarius had many responsibilities. Besides, he had been raised a good Christian so concubinage was out of the question. He knew that he loved Antonina but also he was of age to find a wife, and to marry her was equally impossible. There was their age difference to consider, and the difference in family status. Belisarius had been born into a rural but rich and noble family on the Thracian - Macedonian border. Descended from one of the Slavonic invaders of that part of the empire, his family had for many generations been a bulwark against other waves of barbarians. He had been raised to command. He had been brought up to wealth and honor, but also to duty, and he would one day have power. How could he possibly chat with the patriarch, and with the monks that surrounded the imperial presence, while keeping a low-born one-time actress at home?

Eventually the dilemma was settled for him. He was called back to Constantinople by the ailing Justin, who recruited him into his personal bodyguard to serve his nephew and adopted son, Justinian, who already effectively ruled the empire on a day-by-day basis. That action foreclosed any further meetings with the girl that he had fallen head over heels in love with.

Should Belisarius have lived in Constantinople with a courtesan and one-time street walker, seven years his elder; a denizen of the city's subculture? It could not be. He was a good Christian and it would have been a sin as well as slanderous and an insult to his parents. Still, it was sad. He had come to care deeply for Antonina, and Antonina truly wanted to better know this cute young man who hadn't wanted to jump into the nearest bed at the first fluttering of her eyelashes.

24

She was not used to that. She didn't quite know how to handle such a friend. She thought to go to Constantinople and observe him from afar. That would be painful though. She would be just another old whore there, mooning over the unattainable like the peasant girl in some fairy tale. Well she was a peasant, an entertainer, the child and grandchild of rude charioteers, and she knew she was not good. Though she had attained some respectability as something akin to a common law wife of Antonius, she'd been raised as a slut. She'd spent her youth "doing" men at the city's race course. Life around the hippodrome in sixth century Constantinople can be compared to the London of Dickens, or to Eighth Avenue at the bus terminal in present day New York. There were male and female hustlers, con artists, petty thieves, drunkards and addicts of all descriptions. There too were the poorest children of God: forsaken, rejected, weak, and oppressed beyond their strength. All harbored hostility, and while still children had learned to value cunning. By the time they were old enough to know right from wrong the two were so melded in them that it did not matter. These children were expert manipulators from the age of five or six. They hardly knew when they were lying, and they did not care. As they grew older their only concern was to get things, survive and get stuff in anyway they could. It was a lesson that Antonina had learned well - even if, for now, her thoughts were far from such selfishness. Belisarius had no place in that world, nor she in his.

She also did not want to bring Photius into the world of the hippodrome and raise him as her mother had raised her. Instead she began to query some old friends about the wisdom of opening a shop. There were plenty of places to buy pots in Antioch, but not so many with blown glass and pretty earthenware from Libya. Maybe Belisarius could put her in touch with an upscale manufacturer in Constantinople who could use a distributor in Antioch. No, she must try to forget him.

Life goes on. Antonina put aside thoughts of the young man, though she would not forget him. For awhile he had been a bright light in her life. He was good, very good but without the impossible saintliness of the monks. Being near him had made her cheerful for a time, truly cheerful without the giddiness of the depressed drunkards in the slums from which she came. He had simply been Belisarius, quiet and gracious at all times and yet forceful, with a self-assurance that brought forth trust in all who knew him. It was as the scriptures say: *Better is the patient spirit than the lofty spirit.* (Eccl 7:8)

CHAPTER 3

525 AD
CONSTANTINOPLE

The emperor Justin, who was already elderly when he assumed the purple, informed the senate that he would raise his nephew and adopted son to the imperial rank of caesar, and later would make him an augustus and co-equal ruler. Afterward Justinian, who already bore the title of consul, spoke to a favorite guardsman, the one with intelligence. He was sitting on a marble windowsill of the Great Palace. Belisarius had not prostrated, for Justinian had not yet been raised to such a dignity. Instead he was standing in something resembling the modern "parade rest" position. That was their concession to imperial formality. Of course, Justinian normally acted more regally even when with friends. He would also lose most of them. But this friend was different and would be treated differently. Though there were twenty three years difference between them, rumor had it that the Guards lieutenant had some experience in the matter which Justinian wished to discuss and he wanted to put him at ease.

"Flavius, what do you think?"

"Your Excellency?"

"You know. The whole city knows. What am I to do? I love Theodora; we've been together three years. Only now, I am to be a caesar and she lived with Hecebolus in Libya. She's the daughter of a whore and a bear keeper. Everyone remembers her filthy act on the stage. They can't forget what she once did to earn a living, or forgive her sins."

The obvious solution would not pass Belisarius' Christian lips. The obvious solution was to wed a lady of high birth and marry off Theodora to some ambitious and malleable nobleman. Then see to it that he owned a villa not far from the Great Palace.

"The empress won't hear of our marrying, neither would the priests. She is the daughter of a bear keeper and a stripper from the hippodrome."

"Excellency, be patient."

Like the old emperor, the empress was ill and elderly. Justinian knew what Belisarius meant but would not say. What Belisarius did say was not at all what he expected. "The power of the throne doesn't finally rest upon the priests or nobles, Sir. Your success or failure as ruler will lie with the crowd outside these marble walls. Ask, what would your people think?"

"That I'm a romantic and a fool. Wait! If I were to be a romantic but convince them that I am not a fool, that would surely please them."

"Yes, Excellency."

In the following weeks Justinian easily forgot that Belisarius' suggestion was not his own idea; and Belisarius did not think that patience applied to his own situation ... *unless of course ... unless, unless.*

Belisarius was studying at the palace school of strategy and tactics when war broke out with the Persians. It looked to be only a frontier skirmish and Justin determined to give Belisarius and Sittas, another promising young officer, more experience than they could acquire in an infinity of years guarding the palace.

It is not known exactly how they came to be appointed to combat command. Both Belisarius and Sittas were of noble birth but that alone would not have sufficed as the Romans took the defense of their frontiers seriously. Both showed promise but especially Belisarius. Family had certainly helped him acquire a commission in the personal troops of Justinian, and family wealth would provide him with a retinue of armed retainers, his bucellarii, as he advanced in rank; but only ability really mattered otherwise. He had a keen intellect and was decisive without being rash. He had no false modesty but no false pride either. Such pride as he showed was displayed only as the reward for long hard work in the guards and at his books.

He had already shown tact in handling situations with the civil population of Antioch. He had not badgered or intimidated them to demonstrate his authority He was popular with his own troops and with his superior officers. He was well liked even by quite senior officers though they may have worried that he would one day surpass them in rank and in Justinian's estimation.

Then too, this bright young man was from a rich, warlike, and powerful family, the very kind of man whom Justinian wanted to bind to himself. Such a man must either be a friend or be eliminated - otherwise he would be a threat. Belisarius' abilities and sense of honor spoke in favor of promoting him and keeping him as a close friend, but still one to be watched.

THE PERSIAN FRONTIER

Belisarius kept his eyes on his troops en route to the front and closely observed their behavior. *Esprit de corps* had only been touched on in school. He had noted, however, that the best of ancient commanders had

28

been those who not only best understood the capabilities and limitations of the officers under their command, but did not allow themselves to be distanced from the men who would do the fighting. No soldier ever willingly risked death for an officer who did not share the danger of a campaign and no officer ever commanded the love and respect of men whose comfort, sorrows, and joys he did not consider his first responsibility.

It was a long trek along the Anatolian peninsula to Armenia and Belisarius also had time to consider matters of a personal nature. He knew that he should be considering marriage sometime soon lest he gain the reputation of being a would-be monk, or worse. No doubt many of the court ladies would be outstanding consorts but they were all *oh so genteel....* Not at all like Antonina whom he could not forget. *Of course they are much younger. Yes, proper little princesses who never go beyond the palace walls except in palanquins surrounded by guards in perfect uniform.* If he were to follow his heart, his heart belonged to a give-'em-hell lady who compared very favorably with the very proper women of Justin's court. His first and, as yet his only love could not help his career; only bring pain and slander to his family. Belisarius sighed. Sittas looked at him.

"A long ride. Hard on the butt."

"Yes", Belisarius replied, "A long ride with lots of time to think."

"You gave Justinian some advise about women, did you not?"

"Yes."

"It's easy to give advice to others, yes?" Sittas paused. "But you were right."

Belisarius and Sittas reached the Armenian frontier unopposed. Easily skirting the Persian guards, they fell upon the province with the ferocity of the inexperienced. Local levies scattered before the heavily armed and armored Roman cataphracts and the two officers were quite pleased with themselves. They gathered captives by the score and retired back across the frontier. There they celebrated their easy victory while dining at a small frontier post. They congratulated each other exuberantly and decided to repeat the victory and bring more captives back to the capital, not so much to laud themselves as to embarrass some of the old guard who had not seen a victory in years. They failed. This time the Persians were not caught unprepared and the two friends had to retreat with their troops before experienced heavy cavalry. They lost everything that they had taken on the first raid.

It was a humiliation and Belisarius and Sittas feared for their careers. They were saved by the cowardice of the Roman commander at the fortress town of Dara who fled before a threatened Persian counterattack without even giving battle. Next to him Belisarius and Sittas looked good. At least Belisarius had led from the front asking no more of his cataphracts than he himself risked. Sittas too had acquitted himself with honor. It had been a minor incident and they had proven their bravery and lost their cockiness. Justinian sternly lectured the two, then promised Sittas another opportunity soon to prove himself. To the shock of Belisarius, Justinian appointed him to replace the disgraced commander of the Roman force at Dara.

526 AD
ANTIOCH

In Antioch someone knocked over a lamp or failed to carefully attend a cooking fire; the reason was never determined. The city's slum district was aflame and the fire, though eventually contained, could not be extinguished. The city's garrison did all they could and several soldiers surrendered their lives trying to save children; but as quickly as one group of shanties was pulled down the fire would spread down another alley. Eventually it reached the wharves and warehouses along the river.

Displaced slum dwellers gathered in makeshift shelters made of branches and old cloth without any facilities at all for sanitation or cooking. There were more small fires in the camps and the troops were spread thin trying to contain these along with the main blaze. In truth, the devastation was never completely controlled before the city was struck by a second and worse calamity, an earthquake. Now the wealthier districts which had been spared by the fire began to topple house upon house.

Antonina had been fetching water when the first shock hit. She was not a panicky female from the nobility. She grabbed Photius and lay face down over him in an open square with her hands over her head. She tried to pray. She felt guilty that she was asking for God's help now and at no other time and did not dare to make him any promises that she knew she would not keep if she lived. She just asked his mercy and reminded Christ that he was good and kind. In a moment between bouts of fear for Photius' life and her soul she prayed that God would get her respectable employment far away from Antioch, maybe in one of Constantinople's many rich villas or, better still, find herself a husband.

When the first shocks subsided Antonina returned to the reality of her life. She didn't really want a job waiting upon her betters, nor did she want another demanding man. But now they'd be no need for pretty pots to decorate the homes of Antioch for some time to come; so that half formulated plan was null. Whoring wasn't great either but it was far more likely.

In temporary quarters outside the city proper Antonina began to pace in an unsettled manner. She could not shake off the realization of how short life could be. It would be stupid to continue just living day-to-day. Corpses were being found and excavated all around her. The very young were a particularly sad business but their deaths did not have the same horror of mortality and damnation about them that the deaths of women near her own age did. Young women who'd had no opportunity to repent their sins; who, like her, had likely given no more than formal ascent to religion and had then been so suddenly taken to be judged. Antonina decided that she didn't want to go back to giving blow jobs to rich men, and anyway, there weren't many men looking for her skills in a city that still shook from time to time. Although it never occurred to her that she might be alive because for a moment she had turned to Christ, she took up nursing the injured and cooking for the other aid-givers. It didn't pay but for once there was purpose in her life. She and Photius ate and she felt better than she had since Belisarius had left, and that was what she wanted.

The shocks were felt even in Constantinople. Fast imperial couriers soon brought the news of Antioch's total devastation along the coast road through Anatolia to the capital. Within two weeks, help from Constantinople began trickling in. Justin had pledged massive assistance and chosen sackcloth over wearing the imperial purple. The co-emperors appeared to the city's populace in this simple attire, asking for those with medical experience to board one of the relief ships headed for the devastated city. They pledged financial aid and imperial workmen to help in the rebuilding. Though aged and in ill health, Justin led the services in the cathedral of Hagia Sophia. Even so, he could not forget the Monophysite heretics of Antioch and suspected that the hand of God had been involved.

"Most merciful God who sent an earthquake that the jailer of Paul and Silas might listen and believe, accept the repentance of thy people in Antioch and save that city from the fate of heretics. Be merciful also to us thy obedient servants; let our aid ships fly quickly to Antioch. In anticipation of thy mercy we here pledge to rebuild thy churches there in a manner greater and more fitting than they were hither-fore, and likewise to provide for the orphans and widows of that city, and assist with our own gold and silver in the rebuilding which must be done. Remember thy city of

Antioch where Peter and Paul preached and where thy people were first called Christian. Do not destroy it for its heresy, we pray."

Justinian listened to his uncle and was moved by Justin's sincerity. He promised himself that he would not wait until he was near death to do the sort of things that Justin had pledged in his last days. Many of the churches which great Constantine had built throughout the empire two hundred years before were now in disrepair, he would rebuild or replace them and give glory to Christ. The priests would bless him and posterity would remember him for his sanctity.

527 AD
CONSTANTINOPLE

Although childless, like other usurpers Justin wanted to found his own dynasty to improve on those that had gone before. He himself was an illiterate swineherd who'd become a soldier and risen in rank to command the palace guard. Then purely by virtue of being in the right place at the right time and with an army behind him, he was elected emperor. Soon afterward he became aware of his nephew Justinian's administrative ability. As was a common Roman tradition, he adopted Justinian as his own child to be his heir.

The aged emperor's health, and his wife's, had declined rapidly in the year proceeding the border skirmishing with Persia. They were dying and knew it. Before that could happen Justin raised Justinian, now forty five, from the minor imperial dignity of caesar to augustus, a full co-emperor with himself in name as he had long been in practice. The succession settled, in his last weeks Justin was able to concentrate on prayer, lament the wrongs he had done, busy his mind with aid for the stricken of Antioch, and hope to continue life with his wife in heaven.

His wife, the empress Euphemia, had died not many weeks before the earthquake. She had opposed a marriage between Justinian and Theodora, but after she died Justinian was able to convince his adopted father that a marriage to the commoner he loved would show fellowship with the masses that he would rule as God's elect. Wasn't that important and wasn't it the Christian way? At that time Justin was more concerned with the Christian way than he'd ever been before.

"It is," the emperor agreed. " I'm an old man, my son. I'll soon be leaving you in charge of a very troubled world. We have enemies. Marry your Theodora if you really want to.

"But remember: there are many who would wear your crown if they could get it, therefore there are three things you must always remember: Powerful friends are actually your enemies. Never let a soldier be more popular than you. Your throne is secure if the people love you, no matter who else doesn't. Thereby I became emperor and have held it against many others." These words reminded Justinian of Belisarius who was powerful and a soldier. He'd forgotten that what Justin said of the people echoed the very advice Belisarius had given him.

"One more thing. This Theodora whom you care for, I'm told that she has an old acquaintance in Antioch. Young Belisarius moons over a lady that he met there of the same name. It is possible ... well look into it. To bring an aspiring young officer his heart's delight would weld him to your side. Not to mention that it would be a nice thing to do for them." Since Justin was not known to be of a romantic nature, he delivered the last sentence as a mere throw away line and in a gruffer voice than necessary.

Justin lived long enough to see his son very happily married. Besides assuring Justinian's popularity there was another reason that he was glad to have Theodora as a daughter-in-law. Neither he nor she were intimidated by the alleged superiority of the "well bred." Justin had been born a poor peasant who rose to be a troop commander. He had taken the throne by intimidating the senate in Constantinople when his predecessor died. Theodora had been a popular porn star in the theater and a prostitute before rising to the status of concubine to a respectable aristocrat.

Justin was not an educated man but he had been a strong ruler with an instinct for survival and, from the first, Justinian had been at his side. His nephew was certainly very intelligent and had all the benefits of a Constantinoplean upbringing that he himself lacked. If education, sophistication, and ability could keep him on the throne he would surely be secure. But of course they couldn't. A wife who had risen from the city's grubbiest streets to become a concubine for a senator and had then been able to seduce the affections of the co-ruler of the Roman world must surely possess cunning and a will of iron. She must also have the strength his son had not needed with a powerful uncle to hold the throne for both of them. *Ah, what princess would have such traits?* It seems that Justin was not so senile as his enemies averred. He was happy to bless the union.

He was also pleased that Justinian could now father a child to continue the dynasty. Justinian was forty five and, though no child bride, Theodora, at twenty nine had a decade or so of child bearing years before her.

The final years of Justin's reign had seen the beginning of far reaching changes in the Roman world, but much that was begun in his name was actually conceived of by Justinian. After the old emperor's death these things came to fruition. As soon as possible after assuming sole rule, Justinian set in motion some plans he had been nursing for years. The empire had become tattered. No emperor since Theodosius had felt justified in building a triumphal arch. But when he thought upon Rome at its height he could see no reason why it should not again be ruler of the whole world. Over the years barbarians - some friends, some enemies - had assumed real, if not theoretical, rule over large parts. Northern Africa which Scipio had secured from the Carthaginians was now under Vandal control. Spain too was Vandal. Italy itself was in the hands of Goths who ruled only in theory under his auspices. Gaul - which great Caesar had conquered - was in the hands of the Burgundians and the Franks, and Britain was long gone to German invaders.

Almost as important in Justinian's eye, public buildings were aging and no longer impressed anyone. Many of the greater churches dated to the time of Constantine the Great one hundred and fifty years before; they could use remodeling and extension with new mosaic decoration to replace the aging originals. Other towns and cities were insufficiently adorned to reflect the glory of Christ's empire on earth. He dreamt of gold domed houses of worship where now more simple churches had to meet the needs of the people. Certainly, nothing could bring simple people to faith better than glorious ritual in splendid surroundings raised to the glory of God by their emperor.

There were other things that should be done. For the moment he dared not cramp the corrupt system of taxation if he wished to carry out his other plans, but he could reform the courts. The law codes of Rome had become an unwieldy collection of contradictory precedents. Justinian ordered that they be synthesized, simplified, and brought into conformity with Christian ethics. He assigned the task to the brilliant but venal jurist Tribonian. He knew that Tribonian's judgments had a price but he also knew that the jurist truly cared for the law so long as he himself was not involved. His solution was to remove Tribonian from the courts and shut him up with other scholars until the work was completed.

"Your Serenity," Tribonian was prostrate on the marble floor before his emperor. Even so there was a hint of aloofness in his voice.

Illustrious Tribonian, I have assigned to Cappadocian John the duty of reconciling the laws of my predecessors and of the Republic with our duty as Christ's holy empire."

34

"Your Sovereignty, there are far too many conflicting decisions for a bureaucrat to deal with – occupied as he is with many things. Besides, John is a worthy executive but he is not well versed in all the subtleties of the law."

"Which is why you are here." The emperor made no move to put the jurist at ease. "John is only to deal with the details of the operation and to bring anything irreconcilable to me for reconciliation. He will seek out the best legal minds in the empire and bring them here. His office can weed out obvious duplication and prepare briefs for you where opinions have differed. You will do the hard part. I am not asking anything new of you. That shall be the emperor's concern so do not set precedents unless you speak to me about them first. What I have need of is an incisive legal mind to find common threads and to apply Christian principles where appropriate."

"What you ask would mean a lifetime of study, Serenity...." Justinian cut him short.

"Which we don't have. That is why I am getting you all the help you may wish. I'm told that there are fine jurists in Antioch and Thessaloniki and I've asked the pope to send experts on both civil and canon law to us. I only hope they are not simple antiquarians, for the law must be a living thing. Just as the body remains the same person even as it matures, so too must the law."

That was it. The palace academy was a very pleasant prison in which Tribonian had the constant company of like-minded intellectuals instead of defrauders, assassins, rebels, and their sleazy lawyers. It was a good life for seven years and the result of Tribonian's work became the foundation of western law. It was also the last major imperial production in Latin as Justinian was the last emperor to use that language. Thereafter Greek predominated in imperial edicts as it always had in the daily life of the eastern part of the empire.

About the same time, the emperor closed the schools of Greek Philosophy in Athens. These represented one of the few smoldering remnants of paganism in the empire and Justinian was determined to destroy them. "Besides," he said to Belisarius, "It's all repetition. Those learned men haven't had a new thought in centuries. Aristotle would be ashamed of how little curiosity or analysis they encourage. Plato would hardly approve of them either. They don't challenge his wisdom but only repeat it; and the worst of them have created a new religion of mysticism in the name of his philosophy."

The angry teachers tried to respond, sending long missives with many quotations to Justinian and anyone else in Constantinople who they thought might influence the emperor. They received no reply. There were demonstrations but these quickly petered out. It was as though a modern college president were to eliminate the arcane study of Latin or Greek to make room for Chinese language studies. Regrettable, but not terribly upsetting to anyone save students of the classics. In fact Justinian's action caused hardly a stir among the intellectuals of Constantinople who preferred to study the fathers of the Church. Besides, though these decadent pagan schools were ordered closed, the study of the original sources and myriad commentaries was still encouraged throughout the empire. Many a learned bishop still admitted to a guilty affection for classical philosophy and tried to accommodate it to his Christian beliefs.

It is hard to know who was a friend with who in Justinian's court. Alliances lasted so long as they were beneficial to both parties, It is hard to say what was best for a military man of ability and ambition. If he returned successful from the battlefield he would have wealth and status at court, but a high profile would put him near the top of the ladder with mastiffs nipping at his feet. If he remained on campaign for more than a few months the rumor mill would always paint his expedition as bathed in corruption, which it probably was; and disloyalty, which it only sometimes was. No matter how useful a man might be when the empire was at war against an ancient enemy like Persia, in Constantinople it would always be rumored that he was of the meanest and basest sort .

One of the meanest and basest sort around the throne was not himself a professional military man however. Justinian's grand chamberlain, the eunuch Narses of Armenia, was responsible for disbursements from the privy purse. At this time he was forty-three years of age. He would live to be ninety five. His demeanor was described by Agathias Scholasticus, who wrote: "He was a man of sound mind, and clever at adapting himself to the times. He was not versed in literature nor practiced in oratory, but made up for it by the fertility of his mind" Agathias also gave a physical description of Narses. "He was small and of a lean habit, but stronger and more high-spirited than would have been believed." Put in the language of today, he was a talented and power hungry lackey; Justinian's right hand but not to be trusted by anyone else. Justinian and Theodora understood the man, as would Antonina. Belisarius understood his type just well enough to keep his head down and at as great a distance as possible. He did not fear Narses; Belisarius feared no man, not even Justinian; but he didn't like him and it were better if that not show.

Narses was far more knowledgeable about affairs of state than might be expected of a person from rural Armenia. He would have initially been unfamiliar with the Byzantine court which he had only joined as a young man. But he was a quick learner and he quickly learned to make alliances that would bring him advancement. Later he would delicately walk away from any that compromised a new position. He bought some creeps with favors and found it useful to protect other creeps from their enemies. Justinian did not care. He was already in his middle years when Justin died. The only thing he cared about were results.

"My days are swifter than a runner. They speed by without seeing happiness." Justinian was feeling sorry for himself this morning. Perhaps Theodora was in one of her famously foul moods. He was speaking informally to the Praepositus of the Sacred Bed Chamber, his grand chamberlain, and quoting from scripture as he often did. Narses, not usually known for his knowledge of literature or scripture, managed a quote from Seneca: "Life, if well lived, is long enough." He was quite proud of himself but decided it best to quit the game while ahead. The emperor had a classical education and was deeply immersed in the bible and church fathers. He wasn't. "Your Serenity, exactly what do you most want to accomplish before Our Lord takes you to himself?"

"That is a difficult question. There are so many things."

"But are there, Basilios? There are many, many details certainly; but can they not all be placed in a few categories, as Aristotle would have?" *Great; he'll love that reference,* Narses was thinking. Justinian was a bit surprised too that his chief Advisor would drag out the old philosopher. Narses was smart but entirely of a practical mind. They had met years before, even before the emperor had married Theodora. In those days they had partied together. He trusted the eunuch so far as he trusted any man.

"The Persian frontier is weak. I can strengthen it. That is one thing. But do what I can there, it is purely defensive. I want to be remembered for all that I can accomplish for the empire, not just for holding some line in the desert."

"Then you will need money. The caesars of old are remembered for their building projects. Beautify this city. That is two categories."

"I would be known for justice. I have already begun a compendium of the law."

"Which is three things. Like Solomon, let your wisdom shine in your edicts."

"That is enough for any one man."

"No, emperor. There is one other thing if you wish to be remembered. Advance the frontiers of your empire. Make the barbarians fear you."

Narses was friends with several ambitious army officers. One of these was another John, an aristocrat derided by Belisarius' secretary, the historian Procopius, as "Bloody John." Whenever there was an opportunity he would intercede with Justinian to advance John in the service. It was not that John did not deserve advancement; ability was necessary to advance very far in the Roman Empire and Narses would never attach himself to some idiot. Yet Narses' friendship with John would be disastrous. In time their selfish ambition would cause endless difficulties for Belisarius and wreak havoc throughout Italy.

Narses nurtured other friendships with the military. He himself probably knew more about strategy and tactics than many of them for he spent hours with the instructors at the military academy. Most of them were elderly generals of merit who liked to show off their knowledge to the emperor's favorite adviser over a cup of wine. Other acquaintances were active officers. Men who would serve under Belisarius: Armenian John, Bessas, and Bouzes. They were more than pleased to have the emperor's favorite as a friend and confidant. They had no intention to do other than to loyally serve but it could not hurt to have a political friend close to Justinian. The empire was at war, or clearly would soon be at war on several fronts. There would be attrition and with it opportunities for advancement.

Then, as now, more actual work is often done over a pleasant dinner with friends than in conferences. Narses, who was in fine health his whole long life, would often (too often) begin by lecturing a younger acquaintance on the merits of different foods.

"In the morning you should drink milk, fresh milk, and eat nothing else until that is digested. Then chicken eggs, not goose, and eat them raw or only a little cooked." His guest, who was probably looking forward to a dinner of fat, would then have to listen to the benefits of fresh fish for dinner – but not all fish, preferably mullet and bass, this to be served with whole wheat bread and leafy vegetables.

"Consider our holy emperor. Is he not the healthiest of men, with more energy than anyone we know? He eats sparingly and never eats sweets. He only drinks wine in moderation."

Narses' guest would be glad when the conversation turned to war and war plans. He might ask whether the country could afford Justinian's expansive dreams, and Narses would answer in a long lecture that actually said nothing. Then he would feel out the officer across from him as to what he would do in specific situations.

"How would you deal with the Persians?"

"Is the navy reliable? Could it support an expedition in the west?

"Can the road to Palestine be cut?"

"This man, John, is he as good a soldier as he seems?"

Many of Narses' dinner guests would answer that last question evasively. "John is a bold troop commander; I'd not want to face him. He seems a bit aggressive, however. He needs someone with more strategic sense to reign him in."

"Yes, someone like that other young man, Belisarius. What do you think of him?"

"Justinian has faith in him. So it doesn't matter what I may think. He's a good staff officer but if he loses another battle that will be the end of his career. Justinian is not a fool."

"No," Narses would answer. "He is no fool, and neither is Belisarius. You would do well to keep close to both. Justinian has need of smart young officers like Belisarius and yourself." If the young officer had made a good impression on the Praepositus of the Sacred Bed Chamber, the application of honey would begin.

For all of this military talk, Narses gave the impression of great piety. He tried to mirror his master, Justinian, who always affected a mild and venerable manner in public. He was often to be seen in prayer before an image of the Virgin Mary. He constantly sought council from the Queen of Heaven and accorded her the credit for successes. Was he truly pious? Superstitious? It was in his interest that credit be given to her rather than some subordinate or rival.

CHAPTER 4

427 AD
Dara

Constantinople was the capital of the world, but not the only city of importance. One of those who studied in the provinces was a young scholar of Caesaria in Palestine. Like many officials of the Byzantine era, Procopius was a eunuch.* His pious parents had found an excuse to have him castrated at a young age so that he could devote his entire energy to study without distraction. He had no regrets about it, only some curiosity. He had a phenomenal memory and committed much of classical literature to memory before he left Caesaria to seek his fortune in the capital. There he studied some law and found employment in that field. He quickly learned that in the courts of Constantinople knowledge of the law was less important than connections. All power lay within the gates of the Great Palace, so he attended banquets and complimented those whose friendship was useful. He negotiated the personal affairs of mid level officials and did not reveal them to others. He gossiped and listened to gossip, always being careful not to offend or reveal anything of actual importance. Mostly he observed and made himself useful. He heard more and more about the young Belisarius who seemed by reputation to be a man of honor in an otherwise corrupt military system.

To learn more, for a time he offered his services as an imperial courier. It was a minor post but he could see opportunities. To be a courier it was far from sufficient that he be able to ride a horse. He would be in daily contact with those who formed policy. He would acquire many bits of information including many items best hid from public view. He had to be both intelligent and discreet. Many a courier who kept his nose clean had entered the household of a man of wealth and distinction and had received the rewards appropriate to his loyalty.

When Belisarius took command in Dara he was in need of both a secretary and legal adviser. He simply had no time to deal with polite letters and he knew enough about the infighting among the aristocracy to know that he had to protect his flank if he was to have a career near to the throne. This was entirely probable. Before his appointment to Dara he and the young emperor had struck up a friendship; at least as much a friendship as

---

* See the afterword, pg: 304-305.

Justinian's caution and imperial position would allow. Justinian had already shown ability as Justin's day to day administrator; unfortunately he had also shown another side. He could be gracious one day and petty the next. Worse, he was jealous and fearful. One might say, that was no more than prudent in a ruler, but it was unattractive all the same. It was not so much Justinian's wrath or anxiety that concerned Belisarius however, as it was others near to the throne: aristocratic families, ambitious generals, and palace eunuchs who schemed to promote their relatives and might turn the emperor against him. Belisarius would need someone knowledgeable about the law and a bit slippery; a man who could outwit schemers if necessary, but also a man who could be trusted to watch his master's back; a man who would not aspire to higher position than he could achieve by loyalty to a successful general. And, of course, a man who could not be bought. But if that last was unlikely to exist in a person with the other qualities, Belisarius' family wealth would bind him as effectively.

Damn! I'm being as devious as the man I need to hire. What I need is a well educated man, someone who can throw a proper classical or biblical allusion into a letter; someone who doesn't know one end of a lance from the other but does know how to tie a sash.

Gawd! I need a wife too.

Antonina?

No, no, no.

She's the only girl I want.

She couldn't prepare a really nice phrase if the world depended upon it. How could she fit in? No, no, no. She couldn't talk with stodgy aides to Justinian, or to diplomats. No, she'd never be accepted.

But Justinian married Theodora.

That's different; he's the emperor. Besides, Theodora might not like me having a mate who reminds her of where she came from.

For awhile Belisarius had to remain a bachelor but the aide appeared. Procopius arrived at his headquarters in Dara, bearing with him a message from the emperor about some trivial matter; for no matter was ever too trivial for Justinian. It was a pleasant summer afternoon and not an overly busy one, so he and Belisarius fell to discussing some of the lighter matters of the day: athletes and court gossip. As they spoke over a local wine it became clear to Belisarius that this man had many of the attributes he wished for in an *aide de camp*. He was knowledgeable, but cautious without appearing so. Though Procopius spoke easily about many things he actually revealed nothing that was not already known - a blarney-man the Irish would call such a person in later centuries, but one with a classical education. Belisarius decided to test him. His test was to send Procopius

42

back to Constantinople with a bit of gossip of his own, then sit back to see if the rumor he might be starting returned to Antioch. It didn't and shortly thereafter Belisarius sent for him and offered him a position. That was that, so far as the young officer was concerned. So long as Procopius remained discreet he would be a useful addition to the staff.

Belisarius had his aide and the eunuch his hero. Those who had observed Belisarius in the palace military academy thought him a brilliant young strategist and staff officer. Justinian had been expanding his army and Belisarius was the rising star of the empire's rebuilt military. It was clear that Justinian intended to use them both. It was also possible in the opinion of many that one day the young officer might take the throne himself should an emperor falter. That was a common enough occurrence in the Roman Empire and even supported by the theory of government. The emperor was the elect of God to rule the Roman world; but should he prove unworthy that mandate would pass to another who raised the flag of rebellion in the name of Christ. Of course, if the rebel failed, God's elect would exact savage retribution against the sacrilegious usurper.

Yes, Procopius had his star and would attach his wagon to it and wait. He knew instinctively, as he did many things about human nature, that this general would not be impressed by a fawning yes-man. That was good; Procopius had played that part and did not relish it. It would not be necessary anyway; Belisarius' had real abilities and needed no garnish. His virtues and abilities were obvious. Besides his day-by-day duties, Procopius began to envision a literary work. If Belisarius were to have as bright a future as Procopius thought in view of his family status and the unsettled Persian frontier, then he would memorialize the general for posterity. Barring some curse of the gods that might smash him, like disgrace, or death in battle or from disease, all the clerk would need to do would be to report honestly the truth about him, merely omitting the inconvenient. A successful war against Persia would be historic, and it was rumored that Justinian dreamed of rebuilding the empire in the west. His own reputation as a biographer would be made. That was what Julius Caesar had done for himself in Gaul and Xenophon had done in Persia. Their memoirs were still a part of a military education and Procopius had studied them in detail. His book might also be studied in centuries to come.

But that was for the future. For now Procopius would have the opportunity to demonstrate his classical education when he prepared reports and speeches for Belisarius. The general had entered upon a military career very early in life without the fullness of a classical education. He regretted that his speech did not demonstrate a more liberal training than he had actually acquired. This is not to say that Belisarius was in the least uncouth, but he came from Thrace not Constantinople. His way of expressing himself was that of a soldier, like Julius Caesar, forthright and without flourishes. It was not the language in the rarefied atmosphere of those raised to wait upon royalty. Procopius could help. The general summoned his aide.

"There will probably be war. Kobad is itching for a fight and so is His Sovereignty. How do I say to Justinian that I need more troops if we're not to be driven out of Asia? If I just say that I'll look like a pleading fool making excuses for weakness or cowardice."

"Certainly General. So don't say that." The letter that Justinian received over the general's signature spoke of glory. It spoke of retribution for the pain the Persian monarch had caused in years past. It quoted Herodotus: "'Some men give up their designs when they have almost reached the goal; While others, on the contrary, obtain a victory by exerting, at the last moment, more vigorous efforts than ever before.' For Your Sovereignty to attain glory with a victory over an ancient enemy will require nothing more than the efforts of a few thousand fresh cataphracts, as Kobad believes our position to be weak and will flee before a concerted counterattack."

"Good, Procopius. I'd have said it in fewer words."

"And I in more, were it not a simple dispatch. If it were to be read to the senate, for example, I could have dragged it out for an hour or more." The two men gave each other knowing grins, then Belisarius went out to enjoy the night air and think of Antonina."

Procopius also understood finance and could be Belisarius' discreet financial adviser. Success in battle would bring not merely riches but also the opportunities which are thrust upon the very successful to increase their wealth. There was nothing to be ashamed of in that, any more than there was for an admiral in the British navy of the Napoleonic wars to receive the lion's share of the profit from French ships seized by subordinates as prizes of war; and to invest those profits in companies making war materials.

Most important, he could lend a late-night ear when Belisarius needed to vent the day's problems and the discouragements which accompany command. Procopius would be happy to be the commander's camp-wife in all but the bedroom affairs which occupied so much of the attention of otherwise sensible men. He'd not have refused that either if the chief had been so inclined, but Belisarius made it plain that he had no interest in such very unchristian and very illegal locker room antics. With a proud tight grin he'd said that he was Thracian not Hellenic or Macedonian.

The next time that Belisarius met the Persians in combat it was again the result of a border incident. He had been promoted by Justinian and ordered to refortify the town of Mindon not far from Dara. Mindon lay in the no-man's land between the two empires. Kobad, the aging Persian monarch, Padishah, Shahanshah, and king of kings. sent a lieutenant who haughtily demanded that Belisarius cease the work and dismantle what he had already accomplished. Whatever the merits of the Persian demand, Belisarius was acting under straightforward orders. Justinian was augustus now and he had an agenda. Instead of continuing the wasteful military incursions which each side frequently made into the territory of the other, he would neutralize the threat that the powerful Sassanid empire poised on Rome's eastern frontier by acting decisively to heavily fortify the border. Belisarius had his orders. His answer to the king of kings was a sixth century equivalent of General McAuliffe's "nuts" at Bastogne, and the on-again off-again war between the two most powerful states west of China was on again.

The news of Belisarius' defiance of Kobad reached Antonina in earthquake-ravaged Antioch and a sense of pride in him gripped her heart and held her. She also thought of the life she had and the life she wanted. They differed substantially. Antonina's life was no better than her mother's had been. It had been little but a succession of fights with a drunken man and then to bed for some wearisome sex; then up again in the middle of the night when the baby cried; an unending cycle of a man, a baby, and nothing more. Now even that was gone. For the present she supported herself and Photius by aiding the craftsmen sent by the emperor to rebuild the city. That could not last long. Would she have to be a whore again? Even if she could find a merchant to care for her it would probably be no more pleasant than life had been with Antonius. The pot shop began to look attractive, especially since she was about to turn thirty.

Wanting more news of Belisarius, she would leave her son with a friend who actually enjoyed motherhood to hear what she could hear. She hung on every word in the marketplace even though she knew that they were only rumors. *Flavius, Flavius! Why did I have to be a woman? If I were a man I'd not be sitting around waiting for something ... anything to happen. I'd be fighting the Persian dogs beside you. Flavius Belisarius.* She dared to fantasize it: *my Belisarius.*

Justinian had not merely intended to fortify Mindon. Belisarius and the Romans were bait. The Persians would attack and he and his small force were to hold Mindon until reinforced by two other commanders who would sail from Constantinople. Coutzes and Bouzes weren't incompetent but they were patricians with pedigrees that went back centuries. Though young Thracians themselves, they were jealous of another upstart commander from the hinterland, one who had the ear of the emperor and was already known for his savvy. When they should have joined together with Belisarius they attacked alone and their troops were slaughtered unit by unit.

When Belisarius heard what had happened he was pissed. Not only had these officers endangered his own force and denied it victory, their narrow self-importance had cost the lives of many good men under their command. "It's one thing to lose men when you must," he muttered to Procopius while pacing about like an angry animal. "That's war. But for good men to die because an officer doesn't give a damn about their lives is unforgivable, and I hope Justinian cashiers them both." That would not be necessary; Coutzes had been captured and Bouzes was retreating in disgrace.

The enemy were Persian saravan from the ancient aristocracy already confident of their own military prowess. In truth they were better cavalry than the Romans, so, lacking the promised reinforcements, Belisarius was forced to retreat behind the walls of Dara. The saravan dismantled Mindon and attributed success to their noble birth rather than Roman infighting. "Pride goeth before a fall" seemed their motto. Their smug superiority would cost them dearly in later battles but for now they gained further confidence.

Ordered back to Constantinople, Belisarius mulled his second defeat. It had been the fault of others but that was a fact of life which had to be lived with. Excuses would not offset defeat and Kobad had to be contained. His secretary watched how Belisarius learned from the defeat; afterward he would always work to obtain consensus before battle. This was not out of any indecisiveness on his part but to assure unity in an age when battles were lost because each lordly aristocrat or commander of a foederati unit of Ephthalite Hun or Sythian archers considered himself autonomous.

Two battles, two losses. Not good, Flavius. Belisarius returned informally to the palace school and began to query each old general teaching there about the areas each knew best. Over and over he was given the same advice: "Trust no-one."

But how could he achieve victory if he could not trust in other commanders? The old men were too cautious. It seemed to him that they feared defeat more than they valued victory. The record did not lie however,

46

and he spent more and more time studying the history of warfare and the character of each victorious leader. He spent yet more time getting to know each promising young officer in the army at Constantinople. He would discuss tactics with them until the wine began to flow and nothing more could be accomplished than speculating on the bust size of passing girls. He sought to learn how each one thought; which ones were overly cautious and which were overly eager. In the years to come he would watch each one's career progress to confirm or modify these first impressions. It would be necessary to know how a subordinate or superior might be expected to behave in battle when dust or dark hid him from view. He also came to know that most of them were very political. Victory in battle was important, certainly, but the politics of the capital was at least as important. *Damn it; the old generals may be right after all, "Trust no one."*

When they'd returned disgraced to Constantinople after the defeat at Mindon, Bouzes had been dismissed though his career was not ended. Belisarius was merely reprimanded, then actually promoted. He was the youngest of the three commanders - still in his early twenties - but he was learning quickly. He did not defend himself before Justinian by blackening the other leaders, but detailed the failures in tactics. Justinian was an astute man and the adopted son of a successful troop commander. He could imagine the jealousy which had resulted in uncoordinated attacks without that jealousy being pointed out to him. He was impressed by the willingness of Belisarius to shoulder blame without excuses, even valid ones; and by his cool analysis of the defeat. The next time Belisarius would be sent into battle any Roman officers sent from Constantinople would be clearly instructed by the emperor himself that Belisarius - still young though he was - would be in sole command on the battlefield regardless of their long beards or high positions back at court. They would not want to answer for insubordination. Such cooperation as that could only be hoped for in the barbarian foederati however. The obedience of barbarians would depend upon Belisarius being able to deliver victory, honors, and booty, not some abstract oath of loyalty to an emperor.

Of course, even for the Greek generals, were the "sole commander" to stumble all bets would be off. Each would want to be the one who "could have won had he been in charge."

CHAPTER 5

528 AD
ANTIOCH

In the sixth century plague and childhood illnesses doomed most infants; Antonina's twins had died before they were three days old, Even the best of parents learned not to become too attached to the weak squalling things until they had lived a few years.

If a baby didn't die naturally it still might be exposed if born to a poor parent. Other poor parents sold their children while still young to brothels - girls and boys alike - knowing that there they would at least eat regularly.

Photius was not Antonina's first child; nor was he the only one to survive infancy. She had born a daughter while still in her early teens. She had been unable to smother the pretty little thing. Even her mom had not advised that. Instead, she'd left her to sleep off her mother's milk outside a nunnery. Antonina had not murdered her daughter and had not needed to even consider it with Antonius' son. Antonius was no saint, but he was a Christian and would never have wanted that on his conscience. Also, although he had not been wealthy, he'd had money enough that while he lived Antonina had not had to work outside the home; just raise the boy. For these blessings she was grateful though she'd rather have not become pregnant at all.

Boys who survived infancy could be put to work at age six. Antonius was dead now and Photius was ten. Antonina felt that he was certainly old enough to work. He could be apprenticed to some family with a small business. So it was that she went to a man who had known Antonius. He was not a patrician like the boy's father but that might have been just as well. Being a patrician's bastard was not particularly honorable in a city that valued Christian chastity more than Christian charity. But he was a good man with a good wife. Photius went to live under their roof and learn carpentry. He only saw his mother on Sunday afternoons. As the months passed Antonina seemed more like a beloved aunt than his mom. She would bring sweets.

Antonina was still in Antioch when the second earthquake struck. The first had largely devastated the city two years before; that is, devastated what remained of it after the great fire of the year before that catastrophe.

Poor Antioch. But by 528 citizens and visitors alike had begun to return and were enjoying the fine weather of this city on the Orontes river when their fun-filled days and cool exciting evenings were again shattered. On and off, the earth shook wildly for a full hour then continued to move for days afterward. Antonina and Photius were unhurt as were the boy's master and his family, but those who had taken shelter in their strong houses often died there. Those who fled into the streets more often survived. The poor survived the shaking itself better than the rich. Cheap shacks fall like cards but at least they don't weigh like marble. It was another matter afterward. What professional medical care was available could be bought but not if one was poor. Nearly five thousand souls perished. A few of these were friends of Antonina but there was no leisure to mourn their passing. It must be admitted that the city's many monks and priests, orthodox and Monophysite alike, tried to aid everyone without regard for their wealth. This was the first time many had done so with good will for only the wealthy could support the monasteries and churches. But in times of crisis the clergy can rise to heroics just like everyone else and recall why it was that they entered Christ's service. The local dux sent troops to help retrieve the injured from the rubble and prevent looting. Retrieving decaying bodies was not a first priority however, and deaths from disease soon followed deaths by trauma.

Antonina again helped the wounded but this time she would not stay to watch the rebuilding. Photius was safe and his master's business of making simple furniture was intact. Coffins were necessary and soon refurbishing would begin. Antonina needed money but there was little way for her to earn any in Antioch. Antonina had to face the reality of her situation; Photius was better off with his master than with her, at least until she could raise herself out of the gutter again..

"Photius, momma must leave you here for awhile. I have to earn some money and I cannot do that in this city."

"Yes momma. Can't I go with you. I can help."

"I wish that were possible." Of course, Antonina did not say why her son could not help. He knew nothing of her life before Antonius.

"Be good, so that I can be proud of you."

"Yes, momma." Photius hugged his mother.

"When you finish work each day, try to help your mistress all you can. She is a very good woman and will take good care of you until I get back.

There were tears.

"Say your prayers. Kiss your momma."

That was that. With a heavy heart Antonina turned from her son and his mistress who was kneeling beside the boy with her arm around him. She went to the shelter where she was lodging with some women who'd been widowed by the quake. It was nothing but some tents next to a church. There the ladies were fed by the priests and, in return, did the heavy work of moving rubble. She began looking for cheap transportation to the capital: a caravan maybe, where she would be safe from bandits on the long trek through Anatolia. But fate had been cruel enough to Antonina; her luck changed.

Once the emergency was past she was invited by a friendly old senator to accompany him and his escort back to Constantinople. He had been sent to Antioch by Justinian to oversee the distribution of imperial largess. He was a fatherly soul; a Christian with a wife in Constantinople and several grandchildren. Antonina did not have to seduce him or pretend to be seduced. He arranged a carriage for them to share and separate quarters where they stayed each night, often at military sites or posts of the imperial courier service. He watched over her as a fond father might.... *Not as my own father might have*, Antonina mused, and her mood grew a strange mix of contentment and resentment. She did not mention Photius. Photius was safe and had a sure future with a good Christian family who would help him along in life. She would probably be selling herself in the capital. But the day was fine. There was nothing she had to do. She was free. She loved the son she was leaving behind. It had been hard to leave him, but for months they had not been in each others company for more than a few hours a week. His free time was filled with friends of his own age. *Anyway, it will not be forever. We will visit when he is older.* For awhile Antonina would think only of tomorrow.

It took three weeks for their party to cover the eight hundred miles along the Roman road that passed through innumerable villages along the Mediterranean coast and then north through the barren wastes of central Anatolia. There hermit monks lived in cells cut from the lunar-like landscape. Others, slightly more sociable, dwelt underground in veritable cities dug long centuries before for protection from invaders. These were mostly deserted now but not quite. Besides the monks at prayer, other religious services would sometimes be held underground, such as memorial services for the entombed dead. On a more practical level, food was stored lest the rooms again be needed for shelter. Of course, Antonina could not stay with the monks. To a man they would have shooed her away; but they did steer the travelers to comfortable lodgings and a few sites along the way.

These were the poor remains of Hittite cities, but all the monks could tell them was that they were old places whose inhabitants had died in Noah's flood.

At last the caravan reached the Hellespont, the modern Dardanelles. There, Antonina and the senator took passage on a naval dromon returning to Constantinople for the short last leg of the trip home. The mild Aegean winter was well past and the few days at sea were warm and sunny. There was little privacy on the dromon but little was needed. Antonina slept comfortably on a hammock slung on the after castle and the ship's master readily loaned her his cabin when asked. She could easily imagine herself as a fine lady here. He poured her a wine that he'd been saving to entertain some lady.

"The wine is so cool. How do you manage that in such warm weather?"

"It is the best thing for the wine, mi-lady Antonina. I keep it below the waterline in damp sand. That way it never gets very warm or attracts worms." The master refilled Antonina's cup without any improper expectations. She was traveling with a man who outranked him as the sun outranks the moon.

A part of Antonina did not want to return to Constantine's city with its grubbiness, but another part did: the part which had begun to want to be a lady and a friend of Belisarius. Antonina allowed herself a daydream: Belisarius was still unmarried and they could be friends without causing scandal, just like Justinian had been with the lowborn Theodora for years before they married. She dared hope for nothing more. A friend, just a friend; a friend with friends who cared about things other than sex and themselves. Maybe Belisarius even knew the nice gentleman with whom she was traveling. *Maybe.*

As for Theodora, the empress? Indeed, Antonina knew her. She also knew that it would be unwise to impose on her. Most likely she would not appreciate acquaintances of her youth pestering her. They had never actually been friends anyway, though Antonina recalled meeting the future empress a few times at parties. She also remembered that Theodora had been oh so nice with her rich clients, but a bitch otherwise.

The dromon traversed the Hellespont under oars, for the current from the Black Sea hampers any sailing vessel trying to beat its way north. But on the third morning the crew was able to rest as a rare breeze from the south took them quickly across the Propontis, the Sea of Marmara. Taking advantage of the breeze, they sailed all night and reached the capital of the

Roman Empire late the next day where they tied up at a naval shipyard on the Golden Horn. Antonina began to thank her host for the seventh time since they'd left Antioch but he brushed it aside with a question.

"What will you be doing here, Antonina?"

"I don't know. I really don't; but I grew up in the city. I have friends here." Antonina's smile was forced but she really did not want to impose any further on the old man. Had he been someone else she'd probably not have been so unselfish. She could hardly believe it of herself that she was passing up an opportunity to get close to someone important. "My husband died some years ago. His brother lives here too."

"Antonina, you're a terrible liar." No one had ever said *that* before. Antonina was an excellent liar and knew it, but the old man was perceptive.

"Why don't you come to meet my family. We can find you someplace to stay until you get settled. I dare say your relatives here are not expecting you." He did not say they would not welcome Antonina with open arms, but had she been on good terms with them she surely would have said something earlier about looking forward to seeing them.

Of course that offer which Antonina had not solicited was irresistible. She summoned her best classical Latin though she knew it wasn't much better than the street Greek she usually spoke. "Honored sir, most excellent of men, I could never fit into your household. I cannot say why but my presence would surely embarrass you and your wife. Do not worry about me though, I am skilled in survival." She turned to leave knowing that the good man would not allow it.

"I suspect you've had a hard life. Have you not?" Antonina nodded, not looking back at him. "Let me tell you, that is no barrier among my friends so long as you care about people. Did not our holy emperor himself wed the daughter of a bear keeper, not to mention her.... Well, you know. I understand that you nursed the dying after the first earthquake and again these past few weeks. That means more to us." Antonina was looking at her sandals now. Why had he offered her passage to Constantinople and why was he offering her asylum now?

"Come Antonina; we can take a carriage to my home." That was something rare for her. When first she'd met Antonius he'd sometimes sent a carriage or palanquin to pick her up. But not for long; not after she'd moved in with him. Such transport was expensive and she was no lady. She could walk.

"Besides, mi-lady," - The senator was using rather formal language himself now. - "though my family goes back to Great Constantine here, and even to old Rome itself, we've never been snobs.... Well, not as snobbish as some anyway." He smiled. "My sister married into Thracian blood. When I mentioned you in a letter home my nephew indicated some desire to meet with you. That is why you are sitting here beside me now."

CONSTANTINOPLE

Meanwhile, despite a less than stellar beginning as a field commander, Belisarius was quickly becoming the most important young strategist in the realm and he was often in one of the military buildings within the palace. When Senator Appius arranged a luncheon meeting for the three of them, Antonina flew to him and he to her. He was so proud of her. "You are a cubicularia now; who would have thought it?" At the Divine Liturgy she dared to pray that he'd realize that he wanted a helpmeet by his side, not some idle daughter of some courtier with no ambition for herself or him. She wanted him for herself it is true, but she also wanted to be his. He needed her. She could help him. Of course she knew that it was probably a forlorn hope. Belisarius was farther above her in family and wealth than the stars are above the mud. His family would not permit it. Still, so many good things had happened in the years since last they'd met; couldn't one more good thing happen? Couldn't love mean something too?

Antonina's senator secured her a minor position waiting - along with clouds of other cubiculariai - upon the grand dames who actually surrounded the empress. Now she could live in the palace complex and have status such as the charioteer's daughter would never have dared dream of before. No longer was she Antonina the actress, Antonina the daughter of a chariot driver, Antonina the concubine, Antonina the aging slut, or more respectfully, Antonina the refugee nurse from Antioch.

Antonina slowly found her way around the extensive buildings, courtyards, and chapels of the Great Palace. More than one official wondered who the new but no longer young lady-in-waiting was. They found out that Senator Appius had found her nursing the injured of that city's multiple disasters. She had been without family; maybe they had lost their lives in the quake. That was enough: the displaced last member of some provincial aristocratic family for whom honorable employment had been found by a caring old man. The palace was full of women and no one cared to delve deeper.

One of the dignitaries that Antonina met was the eunuch Narses. In a way they were much alike. Though Narses was a high official and confidant of the emperor and empress themselves, he had come from rural Armenia and was a bit uncouth by Constantinoplean standards. He had latched onto Justinian's coat tails while Justinian was only his uncle's assistant. He knew human nature and used that knowledge to his advantage. Antonina, too, knew human nature and if she had not used Senator Appius, she had used others and was aware that to be trusting in the palace was foolish and unwise. Respect and advancement came to those who could play the game.

Narses appeared a loyal Catholic, spiritually much more devoted to the Mother of God than Antonina was. But he was also as much a realist as Antonina so they could on occasion be found escaping together when they tired of listening politely to the priests, bishops, and amateur theologians around Justinian's throne. Antonina didn't actually like him. She didn't trust him, but they did understand each other and he was a power to be cultivated. After vespers one evening, she started to worry: Narses, Bloody John, and men like them might become jealous of her Flavius and delight in any misstep he made. Antonina knew herself to be more clear eyed about human nature than Belisarius would ever be. As a soldier he would often be on campaign and far from the seat of power. A palace functionary like Narses could help him or hinder his ambition. Narses would definitely have to be humored. So she joked with him, and laughed when he made some snide remark about one of his palace enemies.

"Did you hear any good gossip lately?" Thus Antonina would often begin a conversation. It would not take long before the Praepositus of the Sacred Bed Chamber was spilling out long streams of information which, of course, Antonina promised not to reveal to anyone. And she didn't; she wanted his trust.

"War with the Persians is almost certain. That idiot Bouzes and his brother pretty much guaranteed that. We looked weak at Mindon."

Antonina looked worried.

"Don't worry your pretty self, Antonina. By the way, did you hear about Bishop Kerykos and his boyfriend ...."

The palace precincts were home away from home for numerous clerics including bishops from all parts of the empire. The nation was torn by religious disputes, the most important being that between those who held to the orthodox Catholic position enunciated at the council of Chalcedon in 451 and those who espoused the heretical doctrine of the Monophysites. Publicly the emperor was a convinced Catholic; but as emperor his first responsibility, as he saw it, was to Christian unity on earth, not eternal truth.

That was for bishops immersed in obscure Greek analysis. He tried to bring the sides together, hatching formulas of conciliation throughout his reign, but to little avail.

It was well known that Theodora sympathized with the deposed Bishop Severus of Antioch. Justinian may have honestly sought religious peace and conciliation, but with such powerful people as he and Theodora holding to different views, those only concerned with victory saw triumph as possible for their more extreme positions. The city and empire were rent with dissension. Of course, Justinian may equally well have wanted to fuel that and use it to control his political enemies. He could affirm Chalcedon; but when Monophysite support of the throne was needed, Theodora would be their champion who could mollify the emperor.

To Antonina it didn't matter. She tried to avoid discussion of theology for she'd had enough of that with Antonius. This made her valuable in the eyes of Theodora. The empress had enough partisan flunkies around her. What she needed was a loyal assistant who didn't give a damn. When she heard rumors of Antonina's past she summoned her. Theodora immediately remembered Antonina, but since her new cubicularia made no mention of their past she put aside any fear that Antonina would impose on her out of some mistaken assumption of sisterhood.

After the formalities of speaking with an empress - in which Antonina had been quickly tutored in the basics - Theodora dismissed all but one guard. "Lady Antonina, you can relax now."

Antonina could not relax. Here she was in the presence of the most powerful woman in the world and one who might not like having a former hippodrome hussy nearby to constantly remind her by her presence that she had once been one too. Besides, Antonia did not feel that she belonged in the palace. She was still not accustomed to being called "lady."

"Lady Antonina, the empire is torn by religious feuding. There are hardly two persons around the throne who share the same opinion in matters of theology. We have learned from Senator Appius that you have no runner in that race. Is that so?"

"My former employer Anthemius Antonius was a Monophysite, so I was too. But, Mi-lady, I know little of these things." Antonina had perhaps chosen her words too carefully and that did not pass Theodora's notice.

"Your employer? Oh yes, he died while you were still in Antioch. He was a fine man I'm told, though I'm sure we never spoke more than a few words at some gathering or other. There is much to be said for the Monophysite cause, and the orthodox Catholic, and the Arian cause, and the dozens of other opinions that presently divide our realm. You can speak freely; every one of them has supporters around my throne."

56

"Truly, your serenity. I left such matters to Antonius. To be frank, I was keeping house." Antonina did not mention that she had also been raising a child. Theodora gave no hint that she knew, so hopefully Senator Appius didn't either. *Should I tell her? Would a whore hiding a ten year old be sent packing? Probably yes.*

But Theodora's near-permanent scowl settled it for her. It dawned upon Antonina with a clarity that could not be denied that should her mistress discover her secret it would be worse than if Belisarius did. Theodora knew much about Antonina's life in Alexandria. She might already know about Photius. She would never again trust Antonina if her cubicularia did not volunteer the information to her.

"What should I do, mistress? I have kept it a secret from everyone here, but I have a son living in Antioch. He doesn't know what I do here but he does know that I live and work in Constantine's city. I cannot even face my friend Belisarius with it, or Senator Appius. I should have told them from the beginning. They know nothing. They, at least, should have known from the beginning."

"Your discretion and your pain is noted, Lady Antonina." Theodora took a sip of spiced spring water, then continued rather coldly: "I don't care what you tell or don't tell others about your personal life, but with me you must be forthright." The empress paused as though considering whether to continue, and Antonina wondered if she had been wise in disclosing that she had a son in Antioch. However, the empress had dismissed the matter with no more than the wave of her hand. Finally Theodora added sharply, "Look, lady, I'm surrounded by a bunch of prissy intellectuals and pseudo intellectuals; most of whom hate me. I known damn well that you're smarter than you're letting on, but you are of no use to me if you're going to be as slippery with me as they are. Go to your quarters and think about it."

As Antonina began to withdraw as gracefully as she could, Theodora stopped her. She had something to add: "Lady Antonina, I'm not scolding you. I'm telling you that you've a future here if you'll just grab it. Study and listen. Now get out."

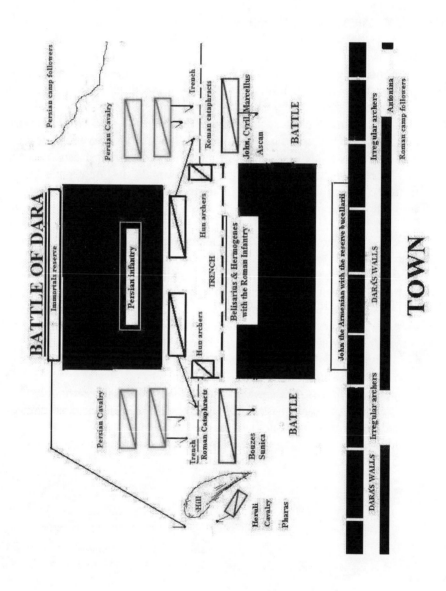

BATTLE OF DARA

Persian camp followers

Persian Cavalry

Trench

Roman cataphracts

John, Cyril, Marcellus
Ascan

BATTLE

Immortals reserve

Persian infantry

Hun archers

TRENCH

Belisarius & Hermogenes
with the Roman infantry

Persian Cavalry

Hun archers

Trench
Roman Cataphracts

Bouzes
Sunica

BATTLE

Hill

Heruli
Cavalry
Pharas

John the Armenian with the reserve bucellarii

Irregular archers

Antonina

Roman camp followers

DARA'S WALLS

DARA'S WALLS

Irregular archers

TOWN

58

CHAPTER 6

530 AD
CONSTANTINOPLE

The war against Persia continued without much success. Peace negotiations were initiated but failed. Now Justinian desired to end the stalemate with a decisive victory and decided upon a unique honor. Until now Belisarius had only failed on the battlefield, yet – like Ike Eisenhower at Army War Plans in the nineteen-thirties - he seemed to have a better grasp of what was needed than the other generals at court. Justinian determined to appoint him as Magister Militum Per Orientem – Master of Soldiers For The East - a theater commander, and send him to the frontier. Belisarius was being appointed over the heads of more senior commanders with the understanding that he was being honored because the emperor wanted others to know that it was ability alone that would be important in the future. He had better show some. With him Justinian would send Hermogenes, a soldier-diplomat, to make one more attempt at a peaceful solution with the enemy. If that were not possible they were to fight.

Antonina and Belisarius had met early on a Sunday morning, before there was anything of importance for either of them to do at the palace. For a few hours they could take the air and enjoy the imperial gardens. The air was damp and the grass was cool. Agatha, an elderly friend of Antonina who had taken her under her wing, was hurrying through the winding foliage as quickly as her elderly legs permitted.

"Antonina! Belisarius! I just heard a wonderful rumor. Belisarius, you are to lead our armies against the Persians." Antonina blanched. Her first thought was of the danger he would be in. Her second thought was of how her friend from Antioch would be leaving so very soon after she had found him again.

As for Belisarius, his thoughts immediately turned to what Justinian might intend. Would it be another holding action or an outright war of conquest? How many troops would he be leading? Who would be commanding the units under him?

But that was compressed into but a few seconds. He quickly dragged his thoughts to the awkward little cubicularia before him with her hair curled and wearing the prettiest of silk stolas that fell in folds over a simpler tunic which touched her toes. Her face was drained of blood. He finally and clearly knew what he wanted even more than to be a victorious soldier. He wanted Antonina. He drew her behind a wall where Agatha did not follow. His fingers were in her hair, quite ruining it. "Wait for me."

It was with some sadness he had not felt before that Belisarius took ship for the east. He was leaving behind his Antonina. However he had no time for much sadness. The general concentrated on the details of getting to sea. Most of these were competently handled by sailors and dockyard workers, but he still had to watch his cataphracts, for many were landlubbers who had never been aboard a boat before. On land they were fearsome cavalry but on shipboard they were no more than passengers. Mounts would be waiting for them at Antioch, to which they would march from the coast en route to their destination, Dara.

Antonina wished she were in Antioch with Photius. She watched, waving, as Belisarius boarded a dromon, and was a bit peeved at how quickly he turned his full attention to duty. It was a feeling shared with the wives and girlfriends of soldiers and sailors from time immemorial.

Why must I just wait here?

Dara

When Belisarius returned to Dara, he wasted no time. His regulars numbered only ten thousand while the approaching Persian host totaled forty thousand, many of them heavy cavalry. Locals were quickly drafted into the defense of their city. They would be infantry, of course; rather poor infantry. In the short time available to train them, there was no possibility of their becoming competent with axes or swords. But any strong farmhand could hold a pike before him and most had some experience hunting with the bow. Nor were they unwilling; Dara was a Christian city while the proud Persians worshiped Ahura Mazda in the form of fire.

The frontier had been disputed as long as Rome and Persia had existed as the most powerful states in the western world. Phalanxes of Greeks and Persians had competed to determine which culture would dominate the eastern Mediterranean. This was just another round in the war their ancestors had fought. There was pride in that connection and so long as Belisarius did not ask the impossible, each man and teenage boy determined in his own mind that he would not disgrace himself before his lifelong friends. Belisarius knew how to encourage his frightened but determined irregulars.

"When we meet the enemy, our cataphracts would like to have the field to themselves, but I'll not allow that. They have a duty to defend the

60

frontiers of Christ's empire. You citizens have the right to defend *your* hearth and home and city; *your* wives and girlfriends and sisters; *your* children, *your* kid brothers. They might like to have the field to themselves but they are outnumbered. Brave and competent though they are, without *your* help they might lose the battle. They need you more than they like to admit. So too do your families behind Dara's rather weak walls. I do not need to encourage you to be brave. You are brave. I merely remind you of the consequences should the Persians occupy Dara."

Belisarius' personal guards, his bucellarii, trained the recruits as well as they could in the few weeks they had. These were all hardened troopers, the kind of soldier that young men could respect; not the spit and polish officers of Constantinople but men who knew how to kill. As important, they knew how to stay alive and keep their men alive in battle.

"Steady, legionaries. Steady there on the right."

In Constantinople, Antonina was impatient. Every day she would leave the palace and go with the kitchen servants. She got little pleasure out of gossiping with other women but she wanted news and Antonina knew markets and market gossip far better than she could decipher the rumors at court. Soon there would be a battle. Who would win? Would *her* Belisarius even survive? When she went to church she prayed.

There was no time to train in maneuvers but there was just enough for Belisarius to weld the infantry into a force able to support each other in close combat. Friends were kept together and steady old regulars were mixed into the formations to give them courage. Belisarius himself trained afoot with the infantry whenever possible. They were mostly teens who trusted the young general because he did not disdain foot soldiers.

"Steady. Persians are only flesh and blood. Oceans of pagan blood, as you'll find out if you do your work well. .... Steady."

When word reached Dara that the enemy was but a week's march away Belisarius ordered a blacksmith to fashion an iron standard with the imperial eagle like the ancient legions had borne before them. He presented it to the infantry with great ceremony. He called them legionaries and spoke of other battles long ago when Persians had fled the field before their ancestors.

Then it was time to wait. The Romans would stand on the defensive before the city wall. The days passed. Belisarius stood with his infantry: "Steady, steady."

The inhabitants of Dara - the women and those males too old or too young to fight - stood atop the battlements like Trojans of old. The scene could have been from Homer except that this time it was Greek infantry who were trying to hold a city in Asia and foreigners who would be attacking. Well, not quite; there were the cataphracts. It was not Belisarius' intention to pit his untrained infantry alone against Kobad's mounted and armored heavy cavalry; his own ten thousand lancers would hold each wing. His infantry in the middle and directly below their relatives on the walls numbered only another fifteen thousand. It was a far weaker force than the Persians were committing, but at least he had the advantage of the tactical defensive and his young troopers would be fighting under the eyes of their mothers.

Experienced lieutenants echoed the general's constant refrain to the boys of Dara: "Steady, steady. If every man stands put beside his friends we will win; if not you will be slaughtered like sheep. Steady, steady."

"We could use a Hector about now." One of the more junior officers from Constantinople said, looking at the battlements and thinking of Troy.

"Why? He lost." That was all the old veteran next to him said. *Young idiots; they think that war is a game. It's only a game to kings and emperors. The worst they ever have to fear is being captured and being treated like honored guests until enough poor farmers pay enough taxes to ransom their hides.*

In the days remaining before the Persians would arrive, Belisarius put his cataphracts to work beside women, children, and old men digging trenches and hauling dirt. The farm boys in his new infantry were too busy learning their trade to dig. Cataphracts alternated between resentment that they had to do the work of peasants and the reality of those peasants needing all the training they could get in the little time remaining. *We'll try to protect the boys*, each of the better sort thought, *but God help them if Persian saravan get through to them. All the training in the world won't help infantry under the hooves of war horses.*

His cavalry were too badly outnumbered to face the Persian veterans in a man-to-man frontal clash. Riding full tilt kneecap to kneecap against each other was the kind of warfare both his cataphracts and their Persian adversaries loved, but his outnumbered lancers could not win such a battle. He would have to draw the enemy into initiating some action that they could not win. When the ditches were dug and several thousand stakes driven into the ground, Belisarius set his infantry to building wooden bridges across the trenches. If necessary his cavalry could cross the ditches and regroup behind his infantry.

Who were these cataphracts? They wore scale armor to their knees, a helmet with a visor to cover their faces, and carried, besides their cavalry sword, the spathion, both a light bow and an ax. At their core were Belisarius' bucellarii, hand picked by him and his most trusted lieutenants. These were men who would die for him and sometimes did. But then he would die for them too; as he would for the emperor, the empire, or the church. That was what he had vowed when he joined the imperial guards. In years to come when things were bleakest he would remind himself: *I took an oath.* At times he may have ruefully wished he hadn't, but if so he never let on.

Except for the bucellarii, there were few Hellenes, Thracians, or Macedonians in his cavalry. The bulk weren't even heavily armed and armored cataphracts, but Ephthalites, so-called White Huns from the Steppes of Asia, and ax-wielding Heruli mercenaries from Scandinavia. The Ephthalites though lightly armored were excellent mounted archers and in the coming battle Belisarius would place them on the infantry's right and left wings, between the boys of Dara and the heavy cataphract lancers who would hold the flanks. There they could at least help slow a Persian advance. If Perozes, the Persian commander could be lured into charging the infantry and these stinging Ephthalite wasps, the cataphracts would close around him and the battle would be over quickly. That was unlikely. Perozes was an experienced commander and it would be miraculous indeed were he to fall into such an obvious trap.

What then was the trap? Or was there one? Did Belisarius intend to simply slug it out?

"Steady."

Finally the enemy arrived and spread out their camp within a few bow shots of Dara's walls. The day before battle was to be joined Belisarius wrote to Perozes. His letter, as well as Perozes' reply have been preserved.

The first blessing is peace, as is agreed by all men who have even a small share of reason. It follows that if anyone should be a destroyer of it, he would be held responsible by his whole nation for the troubles which would come. The best general is that one who is able to bring about peace from war. But you, when affairs were well settled between the Romans and the Persians, have seen fit to bring upon us a war without cause. The counselors of each king are looking toward peace, and our envoys are already present nearby. They will settle all the points of dispute when talking over the situation together. Lead away as soon as possible your army to the land of the Persians, and do not stand in the way of the greatest blessings lest at some time you be held responsible by the Persians, as is probable, for the disaster which will come to pass.

Perozes replied: *I should have been persuaded by what you write, and should have done what you say, were the letter not from Romans for whom the making of promises is easy, but the fulfillment of the promises most difficult and beyond hope. We, therefore, despairing in view of Rome's past deceptions, have been compelled to come before you in arms. My dear Romans, consider that from now on you will be obliged to do nothing else than make war against the Persians in this place. For here we shall either die or grow old until you accord justice to us."*

Again Belisarius wrote as follows: *O excellent commander it is not fitting in all things to depend upon boasting, nor to lay upon one's neighbors reproaches which are justified on no grounds whatever. For we said with truth that Rome's envoy was not far away, and you yourself will know this soon. But since you are eager for deeds of war we shall array ourselves against you with the help of God, who we know will support us because of the peaceful inclination of the Romans. He will rebuke the boastfulness of the Persians and your decision to resist us when we invite you to peace; and we shall array ourselves against you, justified for the conflict. In testimony of our just intentions we shall fasten the letters written by each of us on the top of our banners.*

The last message from Perozes put an end to all correspondence: *"Neither are we entering upon the war without our God, and with his help we shall come before you. I expect that on the morrow God will bring the Persians into Dara. Let a bath and lunch be in readiness for me within the fortifications."*

Belisarius affixed copies of the letters to the Roman standard. Then he knelt to pray for his men – briefly, for there was little time and the enemy was gathering.

From his letters one might think that Belisarius was anxious to avoid combat because of the relative weakness of his forces. If Perozes thought so maybe that would make him overconfident; but in truth Belisarius never fought a battle that could be avoided, nor slaughtered a defeated enemy. He was a soldier but a Christian soldier. He had a duty as a Roman officer to defend Christ's empire. He also had a duty as a Christian to be charitable to those whom he had to kill and maim in defense of that empire.

An attack on the Roman center would have been easy. It is easy to fall into a trap and for a brief time it seemed that the Persians might. Their heavy cavalry, disdaining the Roman trenches, lined up facing the Roman line with their weakly armored infantry and archers in a mass between them. It seemed that the Persians intended to charge the whole Roman front so that Belisarius' split cataphract force could not combine. The peasant infantry of Persia would be allowed to finish off the Dara infantry and loot their bodies; work too undignified for the nobles.

But Perozes would not fall into the trap he saw. Clearly, he must have thought, the young Roman in command lacked finesse if he were so naive as to expect him to make a simple frontal assault on the Roman middle and be enveloped and trapped. Instead he would ignore the infantry and Ephthalite archers to direct his cavalry only at the flanking Roman cataphracts. He expected to entangle with them before the Roman archers could seriously impede his heavily armored horsemen. If he could drive these back against the walls of Dara, they would be nothing but a confused mass of men and horses, pinned against their own walls to be shot down by Persian bows in the hands of experienced saravan or impaled on their lances. The Roman infantry could be expected to flee the field when they found themselves squeezed between two armored columns.

But Belisarius, himself, was with the infantry, a shield resting against his thigh, his spathion in his right hand, and a simple infantry pike in the other. He had sent his horse to the rear. He stood at the head of his young men. Foolish? Perhaps; perhaps not. Beside him one of his best recruits held the eagle aloft so that Perozes would know where the Roman commander was.

He sent a message to his cataphracts under Bouzes and Pharas, encouraging them but also reminding them of the shame of their previous loss to the Persians. His words have been recorded and probably improved by the rhetoric of Procopius: *"Persians are not invincible, nor too strong to be killed. You know that, having taken their measure in the previous battle. You were superior to them in bravery and in strength of body. You were defeated only by reason of being heedless of your officers. This you cannot deny. You now have the opportunity to set right that defeat, for while the adversities of fortune cannot be set right by effort, reason may easily become a physician for the ills a man caused himself. If you heed orders you will win in battle, for the Persians come against us basing their confidence on nothing else than our previous disorder. As for the great numbers of the enemy by which more than anything else they hope to inspire fear, despise these men. Their pitiable infantry is nothing more than a crowd of untrained peasants who come into battle only to dig through walls, despoil the slain, and to serve the real soldiers."*

Again, the scene somewhat resembled Troy. The days of single combat were generally a thing of legend by then, but on that day a tall and powerful lord rode out from the Persian ranks and taunted any "Greek" to single combat. One of the Roman regulars, a bold man named Andreas, who in civilian life had been a wrestling coach in Constantinople, took up the challenge and speared the Persian in seconds. Another noble challenged the Dara defenders. The low born Andreas also laid him on the ground. The omens were bad for his saravan and Perozes delayed a day.

———————————

The next day the opposing armies resumed the same positions as on the previous. Unbeknown to Belisarius, Antonina was standing with a group of women and tradesmen and merchants on a section of the the city's walls that they had appropriated. She looked across the thin desert grasses that separated the Roman army and Belisarius from the Persians. There was nothing she could do but watch: watch and wait and worry. Antonina had come to Asia again but she was no longer the girl who had accompanied Anthemius Antonius to Antioch. For the last year she had lived in the household of a Roman senator, something like a guest and something like a family member; then, in a little room of the Great Palace itself. She was experienced now not only in the vices of the Roman empire which she had seen from birth, but also in the more proper behavior of those who directed the state, sometimes with larceny but sometimes by the very same men with virtue and nobility. Today would see the latter.

She had taken the road through Anatolia to Dara, avoiding Antioch. En route she had seen first hand the bloody business of empire. Along the frontier soldiers too badly injured to travel were being cared for in monasteries and villages. These were the veterans of Mindon and other skirmishes. She noted that the villages had been stripped of young men; they were with Belisarius now. Food was scarce for those who remained, having been requisitioned for the army. There was no starvation but there was hunger.

Now she felt useless but consoled herself with the thought that after the battle she could help the injured using the knowledge of wounds she had acquired while treating the maimed of two earthquakes. For now she would watch and hope *her soldier* would survive the horror about to unfold on the field below. He did not know she was there and would have had no time for her had he known.

Almost out of sight from Dara's walls, behind a dust cloud raised by the Persian horde, there was another group of camp followers watching from a hilltop and praying to Ahura Mazda, and to his prophet Zarathustra.

Had he the time, her husband might have spared a thought for the enemy women, but that was not in Antonina's makeup. She stood alert and watched only the Romans. She tried to look confident and strong to the others gathered around her; that much she could do for her side. Just for a moment she considered taking charge and hushing the nervous clatter of the wives and washerwomen and prostitutes. *No,* she thought, *they can no more be silent than a child would be on his first day at school. Let them jabber away if it helps them.* The Arab money changers were more serious. If the battle turned against Belisarius and the Romans, as seemed likely, they would simply slip through some unguarded gate before the town could be looted. If it went in their favor there would be Persian loot to purchase from the victorious Roman soldiers at a fifth of its value. In the Antioch bazaar they would resell swords, rings, and gilded Persian armor.

The Persian attack came at noon heralded by trumpets. Dara's women hurried to the battlements of the town along with old men and boys. The men and boys strung bows while the women prepared to take the wounded to safety. Antonina, with the camp followers, had never seen a battle but she was not afraid of every movement the enemy made. The Persians were fearsome to be sure, but so were her Romans. She felt that today was not going to be a standoff like yesterday or a skirmish from which both sides would emerge slightly bloodied and each claiming victory. There is such a thing as days of decisive battle and both armies on the plain of Dara were intent that this would be such a day.

Belisarius had been busy for weeks preparing his soldiers, but he knew that once battle was joined there was little that could be done by the commander. Like Antonina and the camp followers, Belisarius would not be able to do much more than watch the troopers and their junior officers at the bloody work of slaughter; possibly slay a Persian or two if they attacked where he stood. That and pray. It mightn't bring victory but it couldn't hurt. Besides, the wounded and dying on both sides would want prayers.

There was an exchange of archery directed at the all-important cavalry and each side covered themselves with their shields as best they could until most of the arrows had been fired. Belisarius again stood with the infantry. He knew his officers from their months together in Constantinople, and knew they could be relied upon to lead the Roman cavalry. He'd stay with the infantry. His farm boys and the young men of Dara were proud, for the general himself was with them. Today the weak and despised infantry of the sixth century Byzantine Empire were determined to hold their ground for him. More, they would support the haughty cataphracts instead of merely taking up space to divide the wings of the Persians and spread them far apart. Indeed were it not for the steady commands of Belisarius the infantry would have charged from their trenches to attack the opposing Persian infantry who, as it turned out, would not even be committed to battle.

Throughout the lines, the various lieutenants of infantry repeated Belisarius' constant refrain: "Steady, steady."

Now the enemy cavalry could be heard gathering in formation. These saravan were the scions of proud aristocrats whose own fathers and grandfathers and great grandfathers had fought the fathers and grandfathers of Romans for generations. Their own sons would do the same if they survived this war to father any. They were proud. Just as Belisarius' local boys had determined to hold their ground, not one Persian nobleman would be so craven as to flee without orders, however frightened he might be. Should he do so his family would lose everything they owned and be shamed forevermore. Better to die bringing down a Roman than to flee.

The solid front of Persian cavalry divided and charged the Roman cataphracts on both flanks of Belisarius' infantry and light Ephthalite cavalry. At first the battle seemed to go their way as the cataphracts were pushed back. Yet arrows from the Ephthalites and also from the city walls were taking a toll at the trench. Just as bad was when the Persians managed to advance near to the battlements and found their broken front could not panic the foot soldiers between their two thrusts. A line of Roman pikes held against one attacking column on the right and another on the left. It was unheard of that saravan cavalry were unable to squeeze Roman infantry. Fire continued from both the Ephthalite horse archers stationed with the infantry and from old men on the battlements. Moreover, the Roman heavy cavalry were showing themselves braver than expected. It was the Persians who were becoming worried and confused. The Roman cataphracts had not broken as they'd retreated toward the city wall. They turned, and under the command of John, the son of Nicetas on the right and Bouzes on the left, they pushed back. Now Belisarius ordered the mounted Ephthalite archers to attack both Persian prongs in their rear while their vanguard was still engaged at the wall. Persians on the Roman right could only break west like fluid from a ruptured bladder. Even this escape was denied them on the Roman left for Belisarius had stationed his Heruli reserves behind a small hill and he now sent a message to Pharas who had asked the honor of that command. He ordered Pharas to release these fresh ax-wielding Swedes and close the box on that side.

The Persians left eight thousand dead on the battlefield including many of their immortals. These were the picked shock troops of Persia who tried in the last hour of battle to save the day by counterattacking the Herulian horse. They failed and retreated, a thing almost unknown until that day. Pharas and the young Bouzes could barely contain their joy. This time Bouzes had obeyed the orders of Belisarius and victory was theirs. The cloud over him since Mindon had dissipated

When the enemy fled the field, the Romans would have followed them, hooting, cursing, and slaughtering comfortable cavalrymen and poor infantrymen alike were it not that Belisarius forbade it. It would have been poor tactics. The Persians were not cowards. If they could regroup they would still have outnumbered what by then would be his equally disorganized Roman army. There was another reason too: mercy.

It was the first defeat Persia had suffered at the hands of the despised Romans in decades. Kobad was learning that the Byzantine cavalry were becoming as good as his own. He was also learning that Byzantium had bred a new kind of general, a man willing to delegate the honor of responsibility for his primary forces to trusted lieutenants while himself remaining afoot with half-trained peasant pikesmen. That day at Dara he stood with the Roman infantry and gave them the confidence to provide a solid wall which the proud enemy could neither penetrate nor confound. In the Persian capitol of Ctesiphon Kobad considered whether it might not be best to negotiate.

As night fell Belisarius began his most hated duty but it was one he would not shirk. He had sent scouts to watch the retreating Persians and with a priest he now returned to the field of carnage. The dead of both sides were all about. He had ordered that the Persian bodies be given a proper funeral. The saravan would have wanted to be exposed for the birds to devour as was Mazdan practice but there were far too many and the danger of pestilence so near the city was too great. A Mazdan chaplain was found. He had come of his own volition to do his duty by his god and countrymen. Indeed a holy man, he performed the rites and begged Ahura Mazda to forgive the Roman desecration of fire. While the Christian soldiers stood apart, the bodies were cremated. The Roman dead were buried near the battlefield, while priests sang masses that God would forgive them the slaughter they had wrought for the good of his Christian empire.

The wounded of both sides had been brought within Dara's walls and were being tended to in its hospices and churches. Romans had preference but both were cared for as the Persians would have cared for fallen Romans had the field been theirs. War was for kings; the wounded soldiers were brothers now. Many would not see the next dawn; maybe they were the lucky ones. Crude surgery would save some lives but the shock of amputation or the gangrene which followed merely increased and prolonged the death-agonies of many more. Once, when the empire had been pagan, a spiked roller drawn across the battlefield had provided the *coup de grace* to badly wounded friends and foes alike. Soldiers wondered if that had not been a better way, but it was forbidden by the church. *God is merciful,* Belisarius though, *but theologians at their books who have never seen a battlefield.... Oh, what's the use. The world is what it is.*

Inhaled hashish and mandrake mixed in wine were used as anesthetics when available but they worked poorly and could kill. They were reserved for surgery on those not strong enough to endure much more pain but who yet had a chance of survival. All night the saws and knives did what swords and axes and arrows had left half finished. All night long there were screams. The next day there were fewer. Belisarius came again - he owed his men that - and took time to speak with those Romans who were conscious:

"Yes, I will see that a letter is sent home. I will write it myself."

"No, your wound will heal." He hoped he wasn't lying.

"Rest your head on my hand. Let us pray together."

"You have saved Dara, young man. Your mother is here; your father too. He was on the wall and saw you fight. He says you were very brave."

Then the general had to return to his staff. The enemy had been defeated and was retreating. but they might turn and attack again. There were plans to be made. He tried to look confident. He tried to look cheerful. A woman who had kept her head covered and her back to him, seemingly busy with unpacking bandages, watched him leave with a feeling of pride mixed with a sense of horror. The man she loved had ordered and overseen this butchery.

En route to Dara Antonina had not stopped in Antioch to see her son. She feared she might not have been able to leave again. She dared it going back. There was a kindness about Antonina now which Photius had rarely seen in his mother before. Of course, she did not mention Belisarius except as the commander of the Romans. She only indicated that she had been near Dara as a servant. Though Photius was old enough to doubt that lie, he noticed that for the first time there was pride about his mother, and happiness too. She spoke of the honor of Belisarius and of his men. Rarely before had she spoken of honor.

70

"Many men had to die, my baby." Antonina was gently speaking to her child; "but they died for a great cause. They were men, great men. Even boys who were no older than you were shooting from the walls to save their city. Their older brothers were with Belisarius himself. Imagine, teenage boys armed only with pikes held off armored cavalry. Of course, our cataphracts will claim the victory for themselves but without the youth of Dara they would have failed. I am sure of that." The boy began to think that he might want to be a soldier. Perhaps he could some day be an officer and fight alongside Belisarius.

Meanwhile, the local infantry had returned to their fields and shops with stories to tell of fighting an ancient enemy and of a young general who fought afoot with them and seemed unafraid of anything but failure.

"You should have seen the general, Dad? He was dancing like a girl when the immortals turned tail."

"You are safe, son. Go to the priests and pray."

Of course, when seeing their sons returning safely, the first thoughts of all the parents were not always so religious, but most of them probably mumbled a prayer to some favorite saint.

"Your brother, is he safe?"

"Yes."

"Thank God, The Persians will be back though. They've been humiliated. They'll be back."

"Then Belisarius will kick their asses again."

"We love you."

There was much hugging and kissing, and the proud young warriors were unashamed to be mothered in front of their friends. For a moment each tried to forget the horror he had survived … and the stench of battle for which there are no words.

Not all the defenders of Dara would return to their previous lives of course. Some had been killed, others were too badly wounded to be of much use for a long time, if ever. Justinian had sent whole chests of coin to help their families, and Belisarius had made it clearly understood that the gold must be fairly distributed. Any officer or clerk found suddenly rich would be executed. After several were, the distribution went ahead most scrupulously.

The Roman - Persian Frontier

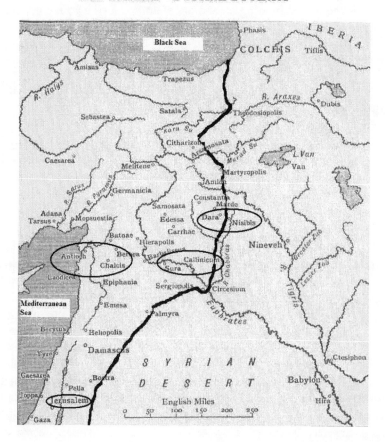

CHAPTER 7

530 - 531 AD
ANTIOCH

Though Kobad entertained emissaries from Constantinople he was now eighty one and looking toward his legacy. He was not quite ready for peace. Rather than negotiate from a weak position he would try again to push Justinian back from his western frontier. He would subdue proud Antioch while, if possible, avoiding battle with the sharp young general who had sent his fine cavalry reeling homeward with their tails between their legs. Belisarius had not even pursued them. To both King and soldier his mercy seemed disdain, for they had been denied an opportunity to regroup and redeem themselves.

To the east of Antioch lay the sands of the Syrian desert, empty save for Bedouin tribesmen. These men did not fight for the honor of any nation; they fought for cash. Some tribes supported Persia, some Rome. They were worthy scouts and skilled raiders but only light and unreliable auxiliary cavalry in a pitched battle. Their prophet had not yet come to give them any sense of mission and at this time most would change allegiance as circumstances promised profit. Nonetheless, the tribe of the Hira had remained loyal an old man's lifetime to the Persians and regularly fought beside them. For fifty years the Hira had raided Roman territory, killing, burning, and enslaving even when Persia and Rome themselves were temporally at peace. Their chieftain, Alamoundaras, had long ago become a trusted adviser to the Sassanid monarch. He knew the Romans and he knew the desert. He advised Kobad not to attack the garrison at Antioch by the easy road from Amida on the Tigris. Kobad did as he advised. He sent a force of fifteen thousand heavy cavalry under the general Azarethes, along with Alamoundaras with his Arabs and a large body of Persian infantry directly through the desert to outflank Antioch's defensive outposts. They crossed the supposedly impenetrable desert without opposition and came to within a hundred miles of Antioch. The prospect of revenge for the Persians, and of loot for the Arabs, inflamed the allies' passion for battle.

When word of the Persian approach finally reached Antioch many citizens panicked. Antonina who was still there was frightened too but did not show it. She would protect Photius with her life if the enemy reached the city, and would leave a letter to Belisarius so that he would know her feelings for him and how because of him she too had determined to live life with a bit of honor. Even if that might mean the losing of it. She was scared. At Dara she's been near him and unafraid. *I'd not feel this way if I were with him; if I could see him. Then I'd be strong like him.*

My dearest Belisarius, she began. *I have never dared to call you dearest until now, but if you see this letter you will know that I have been killed here in Antioch. This is where I lived with Antonius so it is not a bad place for me to die. From you I have learned that the Persians are not dogs, as people say, but soldiers doing their duty just as you must. Forgive the man who kills me, for the sake of my soul if not his.*

I have loved you since the first day we met - when I told you all about my mother and my wretch of a father. But I should not say such a thing about him when I am about to go to God's judgment as he already has.

I have a confession. I never told you that I have a son. His name is Photius. He is apprenticed to Cyril, the carpenter, here. But he wants to be a soldier like the noble Belisarius. If you can, please look after him because he's a terrible carpenter.

I love you.

She and Photius did not die in Antioch and Belisarius never received the latter. Kobad underestimated Belisarius. He had been wary of the young general but not wary enough. He assumed that Belisarius was immobilized in Dara; that surely Belisarius would not leave the Mesopotamian frontier undefended lest the Persian thrust at Antioch was merely a feint. Belisarius would not dare move to intercept his army moving across the desert until it was too late to prevent the occupation of Antioch. Then Justinian would have to yield Dara to get back Antioch.

Wrong; Kobad had misread the Roman commander. Belisarius did just what Kobad was sure he would not do. Kobad expected Belisarius to be as cautious as he would have been. Belisarius could be cautious but not when he knew that his enemy expected it. His motto that day could have been the French army's: *avoir de l'audacité, toujours l'audacité, encore une fois l'audacité.* By forced marches he reached the desert town of Chalcis with twenty thousand infantry and cavalry including two thousand fresh Isaurians from Constantinople. He was waiting in fortified positions when the Persian armies passed on their march to Antioch. Roman scouting parties struck hard at Persian scouts who quickly retreated. Belisarius prepared to engage Azarethes and Alamoundaras in the morning.

The Persian generals now saw the flaw in Kobad's plan. At Dara, Belisarius had been fighting far from reinforcements, here it was they who would be without help. If necessary Belisarius could fall back upon the fortifications of Antioch and stand a siege. Its armories, granaries, and stables were full and it could be reinforced by troops moving up the gorge of the Orontes river. At the Persians' back lay only the rocky desolation of the Syrian desert. A victory in the morning would be meaningless; a defeat would be disastrous. Azarethes and Alamoundaras chose the course of safety.

The raid on Antioch was ended before it could begin. Without drawing a bow or setting a lance the Byzantines were entirely victorious - in previous years they would have been satisfied to eke out a draw. The threat to Antioch was raised, and Azarethes and Alamoundaras retreated with their armies toward Mesopotamia. There they would have to answer to Kobad for the humiliation of turning away without loosing a single arrow. Belisarius moved his forces in pursuit, shadowing them as they retreated, and each evening occupying the enemy's campground of the previous night. Of course Belisarius would not follow too deeply into Persian territory where his communications with Antioch could be cut, his force surrounded, ambushed, and annihilated in a hostile land - the very fate his enemy had feared. For Azarethes and Alamoundaras, retiring with an unwanted Roman tail would be humiliation enough. The Persian king would be both fearful and embarrassed. The despised Roman infantry and the mounted barbarian rabble which had stopped his elite immortals at Dara, might soon be knocking at the door to his realm.

The frontier was secure and Belisarius was moving too quickly into enemy territory for Antonina to follow. Besides, it was obvious that before long he would force a truce on the haughty Persian monarch: Padishah, Shahanshah, and king of kings, so it was time to think of returning to Constantinople. Was it also time to tell Photius what her job was there? She almost did. But would she then still have a job? Photius was a fine young boy, but at thirteen totally unprepared for the life at court. An uncouth carpenter boy would certainly be treated with disdain by the other youths. He might even be an embarrassment. Until she were more secure it might be best that Photius continue to live in Antioch. She would soon be able to provide him with such opportunities as she had never imagined before. For now she left his master with a purse of coins and instructions to give him the best education available in Antioch. He would certainly not be a carpenter now and would one day need all the learning he could get when he did come to Constantinople.

Belisarius was about to make a mistake. In April he let himself be forced into battle against his own judgment. He allowed himself to be swayed by the fervor of his troops despite being unconvinced. Procopius tells us what happened:

"The Romans had passed the night in the city of Sura, and, removing from there, they came upon the enemy preparing to depart their own camp. The feast of Easter would take place on the following day and though the Roman army had fasted the entire day in preparation, it was anxious to celebrate the holy day with a victory over the pagans." Belisarius wished to persuade them to give up this idea. He called the whole army together and Procopius has preserved his address to the troops:

"'O Romans, whither are you rushing? What has happened to you that you are purposing to choose for yourselves a danger which is not necessary? There is only one victory which is unalloyed, namely to suffer no harm at the hands of the enemy, and this very thing has been given us in the present instance by fortune and by the fear of us that overpowers our foes. It is better to enjoy the benefit of our present blessings than to seek them when they have passed, for the Persians undertook an expedition and now, with everything lost, they have beaten a retreat. If we compel them against their will to abandon their purpose of withdrawing and to come to battle with us, we shall win no advantage whatsoever if we are victorious for why should one rout a fugitive? But if we are unfortunate, as may happen, we shall be deprived of the victory which we now have - not robbed of it by the enemy, but flinging it away ourselves. Then we would have to abandon this land of our emperor's and it would lie open to the attacks of the enemy. Moreover this also is worth your consideration, that God is always accustomed to succor men in dangers which are necessary but not in those which they choose for themselves. Apart from this, Persians who have nowhere to turn will fight bravely and the obstacles before us are many for a large number of you have come on foot and all of us are fasting.'

"The army began to insult him, loudly and without concealment. They came shouting before him, and called him weak and a destroyer of their zeal; and even some of the officers joined with the soldiers in this offense, thus displaying the extent of their daring."

Belisarius felt that he had no choice. If his own subordinates were to join a mutiny not only might the army be destroyed but he would indeed be shown as weak whether the engagement were lost or won; and he was certain that thus fought it would be lost. At least with himself in overall

76

command it would not be fought by jealous subordinates and federate tribal leaders each out for glory. Therefore he turned to praising the soldiers for their aggressive spirit and drew up the hungry army as best he could under the circumstances.

"He formed the phalanx with a single front, disposing his men as follows: On the left wing by the river Euphrates he stationed all the infantry, while on the right where the ground rose sharply he placed some Saracen mercenaries. He took the center with his cavalry. When Azarethes saw the Romans gathering in battle line he exhorted his men with the following words: 'Persians, many of you are bound to die, either gloriously at the hands of the enemy or shamefully, led to punishment by your king. It is extreme folly not to choose what is better instead of what is most shameful. Therefore, I consider that it befits you all to bear in mind not only the enemy but also your own lord and so enter this battle.'

"Azarethes, in command of the Persians and their Saracen allies stationed his phalanx opposite his opponents, assigning the Persians the right wing and the Arabs the left. Straightway both sides began the fight. The battle was fierce. Occasionally, as of old, a champion would take his place between the armies and make a display of valor. The arrows, shot from either side, caused great loss of life in both armies but the Persians were felled by the arrows in greater numbers. Their missiles were incomparably more frequent, since the Persians are almost all bowmen from birth and they learn to make their shots much more rapidly than any other race; but the bows which send the arrows are weak and not tightly strung. A missile hitting a corselet, perhaps, or helmet or the shield of a Roman warrior, was often broken off and had no power to hurt the man who was hit. Roman bowmen are always slower but as their bows are extremely stiff and very tightly strung, they easily slay much greater numbers of those they hit than do the Persians.

"When two-thirds of the day had passed and the battle was still undecided. the Persians gathered the best of their cavalry and advanced to attack the Roman right wing where the Saracen allies of the Romans were stationed. These unreliable mercenaries broke formation and moved apart betraying the Romans to the Persians. Before the enemy had even reached their lines they beat retreat. The Persians broke through the damaged Roman line and circled to the rear of the cavalry. Now the Romans, who were already exhausted by the march and the labor of the day and with fasting were assailed by the enemy on both sides, They could hold out no longer. Most fled to an island in the Euphrates which was close by, but some remained on the field and performed deeds both amazing and remarkable against the enemy. Among these was Ascan, a friend of Belisarius, who, after killing many of the notables among the Persians, was gradually hacked to pieces and finally fell, leaving to the enemy abundant reason to remember him. With him eight hundred others perished after showing themselves brave men in this struggle."

Not all who did not flee to the island were brave. "Almost all the Isaurian cavalry and their leaders fell without even daring to lift their weapons against the enemy, for they were thoroughly inexperienced in this business having only recently left off farming for the rewards and perils of warfare. Yet these were the very men who had been most furious for battle and most reproachful of Belisarius, charging him with cowardice."

If the fleeing and dying Isaurians had dared to take a moment to look behind they would have been shamed by the man they'd called a coward. Belisarius "remained in the thick of the battle with the few men who remained. As long as he could see Ascan, and his men holding out, Belisarius and his companions held back the enemy; but when some of Ascan's troops had fallen, and the others had turned to flee, then at length he was forced to join some infantry who were still fighting, although most of the infantry had by now fled too. He gave up his horse and commanded all his men to do the same thing and on foot with the infantry to fight off the oncoming enemy. Those of the Persians who had been following retreating Romans returned and rushed upon the infantry and Belisarius and his dismounted cavalry. The Romans turned their backs to the river so that no movement to surround them might be executed by the enemy, and as best they could defended themselves. Again the battle became fierce although the two sides were not evenly matched in foot soldiers. Some few of the Roman infantry were forced to fight against the whole of the Persian cavalry.

"Nevertheless the enemy were not able either to rout them or in any other way overpower them. Standing shoulder to shoulder they kept themselves constantly massed in a small space forming with their shields a rigid, unyielding barricade so that they shot at the Persians more conveniently than they were shot at by them. Many times the Persians would advance against them determined to break up and destroy their line. But they always retired unsuccessfully from the assault, for their horses, annoyed by the clashing of the shields, would rear up and make confusion for themselves and their riders. Thus both sides continued the struggle until it had become late in the day. When night came the Persians withdrew to their camp and Belisarius accompanied by some few men found a boat and crossed over to the island in the river while the other Romans reached the same place by swimming. On the following day many freight-boats were brought to the Romans from the city of Callinicum and they were conveyed thither there. The Persians, after despoiling the dead, departed homeward. However they did not find their own dead less numerous than the Roman.

"When Azarethes reached Persia with his army, although he had prospered in the battle he found Kobad exceedingly ungrateful. It is a custom among the Persians that when they are about to march against a foe, the king sits on the royal throne with many baskets before him. The general who will lead the army is also present. Then the army passes before the king, one man at a time, and each of them throws one arrow into the baskets. Afterward they are sealed with the king's seal and preserved and when the army returns each soldier takes one weapon out of the baskets. They are then counted. In this way it becomes evident how many have perished in the war. This law has stood from of old among the Persians.

"Now when Azarethes came into the presence of the king, Kobad inquired of him whether he came back with any Roman fortress won over to their side, for he had marched forth with Alamoundaras against the Romans with the purpose of subduing Antioch. Azarethes said that he had captured no fortress, but that he had conquered the Romans and Belisarius in battle. Kobad bade the army of Azarethes pass by and from the baskets each man took an arrow The king rebuked Azarethes for such a victory and thereafter ranked him among the most unworthy."

Sura had certainly been a defeat for Belisarius and Roman arms, but no victory for the proud Persians.

––––––––––––

With the Persian threat lifted, the city of Antioch began to return to normal; if the business of rebuilding after two earthquakes and a citywide fire can be called that. Antonina knew that she must soon return to Constantinople and make excuses for her long absence. Before leaving she had simply told senator Appius' wife that she had to finalize some affairs of Antonius' in the east. Probably nobody believed that lie anyway. At the palace she was hardly missed among the hundreds of twittering cubiculariai. The only one to know the truth was Theodora to whom Antonina dared not lie.

How stupid of me, Theodora thought. *Why did I not see that those two are in love.*

Before leaving Antioch, Antonina would enjoy a last long walk along the river with her son and the lady who had taken him into her home.

There they saw some Roman officers who were arriving ahead of the main army. Among them were officers assigned by Belisarius to arrange provisioning and housing for his troops. They would commandeer private houses but the owners were to be properly compensated. Belisarius sent his secretary along with the advance guard of officers. Procopius was a well educated man and an aristocrat but these were the very people most likely to try enriching themselves by service in the army; not every aristocrat had Belisarius' personal fortune to fall back on. With care and luck an illustrati's fortune could be rebuilt, particularly in time of hostilities. Some things which today would be considered graft or fraud in the West were as much a simple fact of life in the Roman empire as in the urban politics of nineteenth century America or twenty first century Afghanistan. Belisarius understood and usually allowed the respectable tradition of looting an enemy. He could even turn a blind eye to a bit of minor misappropriation. But stealing from those they had been sent to protect, or chipping at the emperor's largess intended for poor families who had given their breadwinner in service to the nation was another matter entirely. Procopius had learned at Dara that his master would not tolerate fraud in these affairs.

Antonina watched the group who approached along the riverside. She did not know any of them but clearly three were officers. From his beardless face it was obvious that the fourth was a eunuch. That would not have excluded him from service in the army; even his lack of uniform did not mean anything. He could simply be an officer in mufti, doubling in the civil affairs of the province. It was his relaxed gait which gave it away. The other men walked as one, obviously accustomed to marching with troops. Their steps were long but loose from years of pounding the imperial highways. Procopius' walk was sloppy by contrast. He was a newcomer to the military.

But if his bearing was nonmilitary it was still that of a man sure of himself; certainly not a merchant or clerk. It was not that sloppy. Possibly he was one of the city's scholars who had remained in Antioch to study the effects of the earthquakes. Or he could be a civilian official sent from Constantinople.

It did not matter. The four men looked at the women and boy without any particular interest. That pleased Antonina. She had come to like not being immediately noticed by men. Since she'd lived with Antonius she had given up her whore-walk and the clothing styles which marked her as a slut. Of course she was not wearing court dress either, just a simple tunic that fell from shoulder to ankles. Now the two women stood aside just lifting a bit of scarf to partially cover their faces while they waited for the men to pass. Photius, however, wanted to know all about the great battle for

Dara and hurried up to the men to query them.

"Are you from Sura? Were you in the battle? Do you know General Belisarius? Were you at Dara?"

They listened then answered the boy. They all knew Belisarius. The three experienced officers had fought beside him at Dara and at Mindon and in the ill-conceived engagement near Sura. The eunuch, though he hadn't fought beside him, was now attached to the general's personal staff. The three experienced officers were polite and enjoyed playing the part of stalwart heroes; The fourth was less so. He was Belisarius' secretary, Procopius, whom Antonina had not yet met. He was in a hurry and said so. His abruptness made Antonina bristle.

Still, the others had been polite and helpful. Antonina tried to concentrate on that. She knew that Belisarius would have instructed them to be friendly with the residents, some of whom would have to put up with housing his rough cavalrymen for weeks. The older officers knew the importance of good will, though Procopius had not yet fully gotten the message.

Antonina spent her last evening in Antioch with the carpenter and his family. She was glad to be with Photius, and he to be with his mother for a few last hours. She had brought him sweets but the lad had proudly told her that he had foresworn them as childish. She was hurt and perhaps hurt even more when he obeyed his master's wife and apologized for his rudeness. Should she have gathered up the boy in her arms and taken him with her to Constantinople? He was happy here and she would continue to provide for him. Her future was still unsure but as an unwed mother she dare not bring him to the palace ... not yet, she told herself. Theodora mightn't care but others would.

It had been three years since the last time that she had hugged him and gone away, and the youth felt a strangeness and awkwardness that he knew he should not. His mother had done all she could for him. Perhaps the best thing she had done was to leave him though he hated to make that admission. She loved him, he knew. After all, she had sent money for his education by the priests and apprenticed him to a fine family. Still, he felt a sort of guilty relief when she left him the next morning; a relief that Antonina felt as well though she too would not admit it to herself.

At thirteen Photius was no longer a boy, if not yet a man. He did his carpentry diligently but without the skill to ever do more than rough building. His hands were unfit for fine detail and his master was glad to have the money that Antonina had given him to provide the boy a fine education. He had also begun to consider another reason to release him from his contract. Photius might be suited to a life in politics or the church, or he might become a lawyer. He also showed an aptitude for the military. His master, who knew nothing of Antonina's position at court except that she had a position, probably minor – a laundress or cleaning woman perhaps - considered whether it might be best for Photius to follow some such career. If his hands were unsuited for cabinetry they might be better able to wield a pen or a sword. The Persian raid had awakened the city authorities to Antioch's vulnerability. Now, from childhood, all boys would be required to gather in a city square to practice the use of arms; just as English youths in later centuries would gather to practice with the long bow. Photius was not as strong as some others but he was not incompetent with an ax or a sword. He showed as much spirit in mock battles as any youth his age. He was also intelligent.

The war was over, not so much because the aging Persian monarch wanted peace as because he died in a timely way and his son, Chosroes, who was facing a family feud for the throne, chose peace. Justinian, for his part, wanted to free his army for other enemies and signed an "eternal" peace with Persia. It would last ten years.

While Antonina was in the east, Theodora had arranged a stipend to cover her expenses in Constantinople until she was settled. This time, when she returned to Constantinople, it was not as a poor refugee under the wing of an old Roman senator, but as a cubicularia with eyes for a splendid young general, and he for her. She glowed.

She knew what her next step must be.

CONSTANTINOPLE - THRACE

.   Back in Constantinople again, Antonina thought nightly of her son. *He's nearly a man now. What to do?* She wanted Belisarius for her own and knew that she should have told him of Photius before. Her concern was not out of shame, or fear that Belisarius would be unwilling to have her - though the thought did cross her mind - but that a bastard boy would be unacceptable in society and that would harm Belisarius' career. It was far from secret that she had never actually been married to Anthemius Antonius. Of course it was different if a man had a son on the wrong side of the bed, but there were limits and she was already straining them. Now it was too late; how could she spring Photius on Belisarius now? *I should have told him, Oh shit, why didn't I tell him when we first met?*

82

When Belisarius returned to the capital he did not think to make a formal proposal of marriage through an intermediary. Antonina was past the age for such things, and the actual details of the wedding could be handled by the manager of one of his estates. But Antonina was busy as any bride-to-be - considering what she would wear on her wedding day, and deciding which cubiculariai she would invite and which she would make excuses not to.

For his part, Belisarius had much to attend to before their wedding day that had nothing to do with that event. For one thing, he wanted to visit the families of bucellarii who had fallen at Dara or Sura. Some lived in Constantinople but others were near his Thracian estates. So for awhile he and Antonina were parted. That was the decorous thing anyway.

Several weeks passed. Now it was early morning and the Thracian countryside was quite still and peaceful. A few birds did squawk loudly to each other about some matter, probably worms, but there was no breeze to stir the autumn foliage. It was damp but a clear sky told Belisarius that the day would be a fine one. A figure was approaching across the field before him. It had exited the tree line some three hundred meters away but was obscured at first by a mist. *Probably off a pond hidden by the woods*, the tactician in the general thought.

What was it to him if someone else was also out enjoying the dawn and the damp and the coolness of the morning? It was nice to be alone here but maybe they would have a nice little chat about something of no importance. That could be nice if the chat wasn't just clichés about the weather. Belisarius spent most of his time concerned with defense and court politics. He was very good at the first, and knew it; but horrid at the second, and knew it. It might be nice to simply speak with someone about the plans for a new cathedral that Justinian was building in Thessaloniki. That he could honestly praise. That would satisfy Justinian if the stranger turned out to be an imperial spy. Or he could start a conversation with reference to poetry. Poetry was not his strong point but that was all the more reason to discuss poets and possibly learn something. Belisarius was not good at just wasting time.

Keeping one eye on the approaching figure, he let his mind roam over other early mornings he had known. Many of them were far from as peaceful as this one; mornings when he had not known the feeling of dew on grass or listened to squawking birds in the trees because he had been devoting his full attention to training infantry or to Persian dispositions in the sands of Mesopotamia. For all the glory that his victory at Dara had brought him, battle was a depressing business. Before the sun had set those desert sands had been covered with Persian and Roman dead and maimed. Once he had slipped and fallen on a bit of grass splattered with blood and unidentifiable human insides. He shook off the memory with a silent prayer to be forgiven for those things he had to do for the empire and the emperor, his emperor. He even offered a prayer for the tyrant, for Antonina had warned him that such a friend was not a friend, and never could be.

The arrival of a household slave brought Belisarius' attention back to the present. He carried a cup filled with hot spiced water which had been drawn from a sweet spring nearby. Like others of his age, Belisarius did not disapprove of a little wine mixed with water in the morning; it was a good start for many men and could be relied upon to improve their mood; but he usually preferred spiced hot water. Some otherwise good soldiers had not the strength to stop awhile after they had tasted their first wine of the day.

He drew himself back to watch the approaching figure. He began to suspect, and then to be sure, that it was a woman, though for many minutes he could not discern anything more. The hot "tea" was good this chill morning. Its vapors refreshed his nostrils. *It is a woman. Not a girl though. Her walk is familiar ... indiscreetly familiar!* The cup lay where he dropped it as he ran down the hillside.

Antonina stopped and stood alone in the field looking even smaller than she was. Her arms were outstretched in greeting. She forced a silly grin to light her face and hid her fear as her soul spoke to her mind: *Do as you must, woman. You must be more than you have ever been before. If you can't say it, it would be better that you had not come. You can still go back to Antioch.* That would not do. There would be no going back to a life of miserable obscurity and without Belisarius. *I may die here, right now.* Though frightened, her mind agreed to the bargain. She dropped her arms and a serious demeanor overtook her whole face and frame.

Belisarius stretched out his arms to embrace his fiancé, who had made the trip from Constantinople to be with him. *Definitely indiscreet.* Antonina stopped him with a hand the way a ball carrier holds off a linebacker. Belisarius was puzzled. Antonina looked at the grass.

She had left Photius in Antioch to be raised as she could not raise him. That had been three years before. She should not have hid him from Belisarius. She had spent long hours trying to fall asleep while thinking of him. Of his welfare, yes, but also of how Belisarius would receive the news of him as someday he must. It would be impossible to keep knowledge of who his mother was from the boy as he approached manhood. Nor had

Antonina intended such when she had left him in Antioch. At that time she'd had no concept of the height to which she would quickly rise. She had only hoped to one day see him again when she was established in some small business after her days of seducing men were over. She had hoped that he might come to join her then and share in the work and profit. All such vague plans were superseded now.

If she did not tell Belisarius, what would happen when one day someone told Photius that his mother was the same Antonina who was a cubicularia in the Great Palace, and the wife of the great general Belisarius? She would be revealed not only as the mother of a bastard but as a particularly cold hearted one who had left her child for a promising new husband. He'd probably kill her as he had the right to do.

"Mi-lord, I have a son ...and a daughter." Her daughter? Antonina had not even kept track of her. As a young teen she had left the baby outside a convent to be raised by the good nuns. Maybe the girl had become one too. No one, not even the nuns, knew who the girl's mother was. She could have kept that hidden but Antonina, in a fit of honesty toward her fianceé, decided to come completely clean.

She waited for his reaction. She felt like hell. Then the hard-heartedness of what she had just said aloud struck her fully and she blanched. She had dreaded this all the months that she and Belisarius had been betrothed. He knew that she had lived with Anthemius Antonius in Constantinople and Alexandria and Antioch; but she'd been unable to tell him of Photius or of the girl for fear of being ostracized and losing him. She did not even know what name the nuns had given her daughter. She had been the child of a simple liaison years before when she was nothing more than a very young street walker. *Our wedding cannot be. I should never have led him on.*

Belisarius was good but he had a position to maintain. It was more than noble that he had been willing to wed, not simply live with, an actress and a prostitute; surely two bastard stepchildren could not fit in too. True, the empress Theodora had been a courtesan and she had a daughter too; but she was the empress and was known to be a vindictive bitch. Whatever others might privately think of her, they would say nothing which could, and surely would, get back to the palace. Besides, her daughter might well have been fathered by Justinian. Antonina's husband was merely a soldier; the finest commander in the Roman army, but still, only a soldier. Belisarius would be damaged and called a fool by the wagging tongues of the city. She waited for his anger and rejection.

"Antonina?"

Belisarius was standing very erect and looking down on her. "Antonina, where are the children?"

Antonina's face was drained of blood. Fear and worry were in her eyes. He had every right to draw his dagger and strike her dead.

Belisarius kept his face impassive for a moment. Then he looked down at Antonina as a father might on a beloved child who he knew to be suffering more disgrace in her heart then he could bear to see. "Antonina, send for them and I will order a feast when they arrive. Your son will be my son, your daughter our daughter. We will not speak any more of this, of the whys of it; but you should not have kept it from me. You must go to a priest and do whatever penance he requires."

Antonina could not look Belisarius in his eyes. She simply slipped slope-shouldered past him. Once again she had far underestimated her fiancée. She had never seen such charity, not even in a priest.

Photius was sent for but finding Antonina's daughter was more difficult. She had left the babe outside a convent-orphanage when only hours old. Antonina had often thought of the child but knew that what she had done was surely the best thing she could have done. Some working girls did raise daughters in whore houses. They would become prostitutes and support their mothers in their old age. At least she hadn't done that. The girl would be brought up in religion.

When she returned to Constantinople accompanied by a troop of Belisarius' bucellarii, Antonina went straight to the convent where she had left the infant nineteen years before. After some vague explanation to a novice she was let into the presence of the abbess. She was unsure how to begin and the nun was not of the sweet variety,

"I left my baby girl here nineteen years ago."

"And I suppose you're wracked with guilt," the abbess said without sympathy. "Now you think to salve your conscience, but that is not what would be best for your child. I cannot help you. Go to a priest and confess how you deserted her."

Antonina could be as hard as the abbess but today tears threatened to break forth. "It is not as you think. It is not for myself that I ask but for my child. I am to be married and my future husband insists that we do what we still can for her."

"That is good of him. Not many men would marry an old whore.... Save for our sacred emperor, of course. But still, I cannot help. I must think of the girl's happiness. She is long past being of age to marry but has not. It

86

is a sad story. What do you expect you could do for her now?"

Antonina found herself on her knees and the abbess softened her tone slightly. She took Antonina's hands in hers but Antonina spoke before the abbess could dismiss her with a prayer. "Her future is assured now. I am to marry General Belisarius."

That changed everything of course. The baby had been christened Callista and she worked in a market near the city's Golden Horn selling pottery. Despite her fear and sorrow a chuckle almost passed Antonina's lips. *She sells pots.*

"She loves a man, a young cataphract named Ildiger. But it is impossible. She has, or at least she has had no family. He doesn't care, but his family does. She is a simple orphan with no dowry, save what little she has saved of her earnings and a bit more from the church's St. Nicholas fund."

An orphan girl without a dowry, in love with a minor nobleman? Surely parents cared as much for their child's happiness in that century as now, but love was something that came after marriage, not before. Most couples wed when they were little more than children, and when the concept of "teens" was unknown. Romance was no more to be trusted in the Christian Roman Empire than it had been in classical times. Parents knew better than twelve and fourteen year olds what sort of a boy or girl their son or daughter would be happy with.

The abbess thought for a moment, than admitted: "Under the circumstances it may actually be best that neither Callista nor Ildiger wed when they were younger."

The good abbess now had reason to help Antonina locate the pot shop where her former charge worked. A generous dowry materialized and the marriage was arranged. When Photius arrived from Antioch there was a feast as Belisarius had promised. For the first time Antonina found herself hosting family and a few good friends. Even her mother was invited. She glowed. Callista called Photius her brother and the following month she and Ildiger had the rare pleasure of marrying entirely for love. Afterward Ildiger spoke alone with his stepfather.

"Father, if I may call you that, I've known Callista longer than you. She is much like her mother. That sounds so strange since they've only just been reunited, but I think the lady Antonina already understands her child better than either of us ever will."

"Oh Lord God, she's a pushy little bitch too? Can you really handle that?" Belisarius stiffed a chuckle. The young lancer sitting before him might be right.

Belisarius and Ildiger were sharing a relaxed hour at the general's home in Constantinople. It wasn't his own house. His only permanent homes were in Rufinianae on the opposite shore of the Bosphorus, and on his estates in Thrace. A family friend had offered him this villa. Soon he would have a fitting place of his own in the city however. Some sketches of his new palace lay on the table, held in place by a simple terra cotta lamp and an empty cup. Justinian had insisted that he have a house near the Great Palace worthy of the victor of Dara, but he had not offered to pay for it.

Belisarius was twenty six but the strain of command had made him feel much older: "Well son, if she chases you out of the house you can always join me in the field. It may be less dangerous." Belisarius was smiling but he was also evaluating the young man in the chair across from him. He rose and stood at a window. From there he could clearly see many fishing boats and a few warships on the Sea of Marmara. The sun was well past the meridian and soon the bells of the nearby new church of Sts. Sergius and Bacchus would be summoning the more religiously inclined to Vespers. Other bells would be summoning others to other churches. That would end the farmers' and field slaves' labor for the day. It would give the monks the opportunity to sing together. Soon, the wives of the poor and the house slaves of merchants and shop keepers would be preparing dinner. Not everyone in Constantinople would eat as well as the general's family but there was no serious hunger either. In the Roman tradition, hearty bread was supplied free by the state. Families grew vegetables for themselves on plots of unoccupied land - vacant lots, we would say. Few were so poor as not to be able to afford a bit of meat, or at least a fish or some sausage on Sundays. Many of the chickens that roamed Constantinople had lost their lives that day, and the fishermen that Belisarius had been observing would soon be heading to markets. Their wives would sell their catch. On the wharves many cats were waiting for them.

"I cannot have a son fighting as a simple cataphract; if for no other reason than that you'd be a magnet to enemy archers. But you've not had tactical training nor been taught to think like a field officer. So I cannot promote you to a staff job at this time. I want you to go to the academy. Photius is going also. After that I'll be better able to judge whether you deserve command responsibility. I can do that much for you since you are blood; but you'll have to prove yourself after you have studied and listened to the officers at the school." Belisarius' voice was no longer that of a father in law but that of a senior officer used to evaluating men. Ildiger actually seemed relieved; that was less fearful. If Belisarius sensed it, he approved.

To the horror of the clucking women of the senator's house, Antonina and Belisarius prepared to be married very soon after their daughter. But it was not that they had to. Belisarius was an impatient virgin, and Antonina was anxious to teach him many things. The wedding of Belisarius to a prostitute would have been more shocking were it not that the emperor had done the same thing eight years before. Such a slippery slope was one that the clucking old maids made much of. Though the clergy were equally horrified they were astute enough about politics to mouth appropriate words about Christ's mercy and his kindness toward prostitutes of his own time.

For Belisarius and Antonina there could be no simple wedding in a parish church of Constantinople as Callista and Ildiger had requested. Belisarius was too important and that would have looked hurried and awkward. So Antonina traveled in a fine coach to a country estate of her husband-to-be with an appropriate entourage and a dowry which included a wagonload of silver and bronze ornaments for their home. No one asked how she had acquired them, but at the wedding feast an old senator and a broadly smiling cousin of the groom would be prominent among her guests and attendants.

Accompanying the procession were several eunuchs and old ladies of the court. Friends of the bride, they were also there to represent the goodwill of their imperial mistress. Theodora herself could not be expected to make the journey, not even to attend the wedding of a victorious general; nor could the emperor; but the message was clear: a new day had dawned in which the daughter of a bear keeper could be empress and that of a charioteer marry an aristocrat. High officials and court attendees would be directed to travel to the boonies to congratulate, certainly the victorious general, but also his lowborn bride. They were also instructed not to feel humiliated.

Antonina's mother could not attend. She now enjoyed a leisurely life on a pleasant estate even farther from the capital. "Regrettably," the trip would be too tiring for her, but a young lady who was a bit awkward in society was there with her cataphract husband who had recently been enrolled in the advanced military academy. There was also a teenage boy from Antioch now in the uniform of a palace cadet. Indeed, Photius was not much younger than Belisarius himself had been when he first met Antonina. Belisarius quickly and joyfully identified both Photius and Callista as his children, as indeed they were by ancient Roman law.

When Antonina arrived, Belisarius introduced her to his household staff and the many officers who had come to honor him. There were Mundus and Sittas, his brothers in arms, and Solomon who Antonina recognized as one of the officers she and Photius had talked with in Antioch. Belisarius also introduced her to his private secretary. She was happy that neither dignitary recognized her from Antioch, for she was far from sure that Belisarius would approve of her having followed him to Asia. After all, a proper Greek girl would never consider such a thing. *But then*, she thought, *I've never been very proper.*

The service was performed by the Bishop of Thessaloniki who had made the arduous trip despite his age. Antonina would have preferred one of the nice priests who had helped her acquire Antonius' Antioch property after his death, but they had Monophysite leanings and, anyway, the bishop was a family friend of Belisarius and would not be denied the privilege. Besides, she had to admit that the less she dwelt on her past the better.

The wedding was a dream she would never have dared to dream. The scene was set in a pretty rural church overflowing with the elite of the empire, there to do her and Belisarius honor. For all their glitter Antonina herself was the center of attention in a silken tunic and gracefully embroidered stola, given her by the emperor and empress of Rome. At her side was the aged Agatha, an aristocrat with a cherished pedigree and a real friend who had nothing to gain from the friendship. There were twenty other palace girls, close friends; and bucellarii lined the road for five miles between the church and her home-to-be. Priests from surrounding villages and estates had flocked there to assist the bishop. There were tables strewn across an acre of sward and on them were great bowls of wine and others of fruit and cold delicacies. Cooks had been busy for days preparing the courses and the smell of roasting lambs, pigs, and freshly caught trout filled the air from dozens of fires laid along one side of the field.

It was all too much for Antonina who had never before been known for a retiring personality. She was actually overwhelmed. She was almost frightened when the groom arrived in full ceremonial armor that shone when the sun glinted off gold filigree work, or where amethyst and emeralds took the light. Belisarius looked taller than ever. His mount was also huge. Beside him, Sittas actually looked dwarf-like though he was a powerful man in his own right. *Or is it my imagination*, Antonina though. *Flavius is so beautiful*.

Before the wedding, the groom changed into court dress more appropriate for a church service, but Sittas and Mundus stood armored by him to represent the military of the empire. The service took several hours but that might be considered short by the traditions of the Greek church. There was much chanting of *Kyrie Elision* and much coming and going by the bishop through the doors of the iconostasis, the decorated screen which separates the altar from the congregants in Greek churches. When finally the Eucharist was complete and the couple had made their vows, the wedding party joined those guests who had not been able to fit into the country church, and had waited patiently listening to the service through the open doors of the building.

When they retired to bed their first night they were accompanied through the halls, in Roman style, by a crowd of well-wishers strewing flower petals and making such ribald remarks as were permitted for that night; the bishop and priests making themselves scarce. But if Antonina was looking forward to a night of sexual delight with a man she really cared deeply for, it was not to be, at least not entirely. Antonina had had too many other nights and Belisarius had not had any. It was not until the third copulation that he could restrain himself more than a full minute, and Antonina had for too long thought of herself simply as a receptacle to be easily aroused. She tried with all her heart and spirit to please Belisarius - and he was pleased - but she could not be spontaneous. She loved him as she had never loved anyone, but what she really wanted was simply to lie with him, chat, and await the dawn. Sex as only to please someone else was something that she never did completely get past.

Feasting and festivities lasted a week. The couple remained on the estate for several more weeks, but then Belisarius had to return to his duties with his troops, and Antonina to hers as a cubicularia.

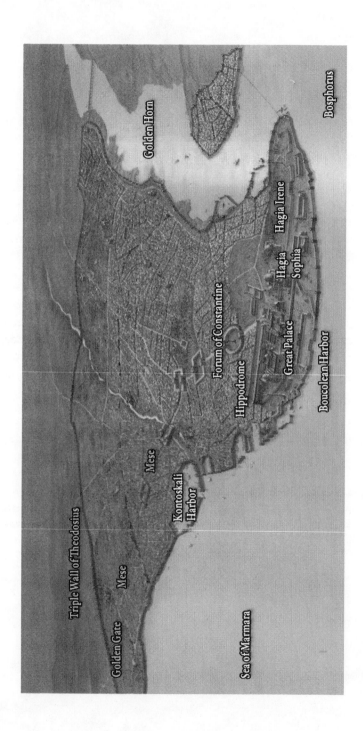

92

CHAPTER 8

532 AD
CONSTANTINOPLE

Antonina's life with her new husband was not to be anything like life with Antonius. In Constantinople Belisarius had servants; many, many excellent servants. At first Antonina could not even properly direct them for there was a hierarchy and the chief men and women among them knew perfectly the proper routine. She didn't. Usually Belisarius was with his troops or at court but she needn't always be in attendance. For a while that left her with nothing but time. She had nothing to do but shop or gossip with other rich women; mainly thin young snobs and fat old beasts. She was uncomfortable and so were they. Though Belisarius was already wealthier than most of them, these aristocratic ladies were not people that she could look down on or dismiss, not even the wastrels and the foolish ones. They were from really ancient families or long married to men of distinction and ability, usually both. It was they who could look down on her. Some did. Others would have done so, were she not the wife of the army's rising young star, the kind of natural leader who might one day take the throne himself. A few, those whom she had invited to her wedding, were just nice people. Yet Antonina was Antonina. She had always been manipulative, and as she came to feel more at home and relaxed, that side of her reemerged. It had to; how else could she protect Belisarius?

Then too, Antonina aspired to more then simple wealth. She wanted that world of culture, grace, and intellect that as a teen she had seen with some of her clients. Before long she would be found chatting up dignitaries like Narses, who were well above her station if not her husband's. That was the game and it was played by everyone in the palace. So far as that was true there was nothing sinister in it, but neither was it particularly elevating. Elevating moments there certainly were however. Antonina was as able as any to help a deserving cubicularia as she herself had been helped. She now had as many worldly pleasures as one could wish for, and knew that she must learn charity even though that was entirely foreign to her nature. Belisarius was charitable, very charitable; but he had never known poverty. Antonina, though she had never actually been poor, certainly knew the world of the poor. The family of a successful charioteer could live well while he lived, but the world they inhabited was not one of culture and grace. It was a rough one of gangsters, hustlers, gamblers; those who by these routes had aspired only to wealth; and like successful mobsters of any time and place had failed to rise from the mentality of the streets.

"Reverend Father. I have sinned many times; you know that. Charity comes naturally to Flavius. It does not to me. So many of the poor are selfish people, who would not themselves help another. It is hard for me to open my purse to them."

"My daughter," the priest held her hands in his. "Remember Antioch where you helped so many after the earth moved. Remember Dara where you stayed with the dying. You are not uncharitable; not all charity is about money. But, Antonina, what did so many righteous and wealthy people actually think of you when you were young and struggling? They must answer for that before Christ; and they will not save their souls with the coins they dropped. You must be strong to be charitable. Your charity should not depend upon the attitude of those you help. Of course, they do not thank you for your coins; they are jealous and feel that God is unfair. As in Antioch and at Dara, you must do what you do because it feels right in your heart, not for the reward of feeling that charity has made you a good person."

———————————

Antonina had not sought out her young general. No, it had just happened. The palace was full of wealthy and well-connected gentlemen. Had she been so inclined, before she had been reunited with Belisarius at Senator Appius' luncheon, she could have seduced one of them. But those days were past. It was Justinian's uncle who had suggested that he ask after a friend of Belisarius' in Antioch. It must have been God's plan. It had been the plan of a good and kind and merciful Deity that she had found herself in love. For once in her life, really in love with someone that she could look up to. Antonina, usually so selfish, would not use the young man; that truly would have been a sin. It was she who could help him. Belisarius was a great strategist and a fearsome soldier, but he was blind to courtly intrigue. Oh, he knew of it in theory, but in practice he did not always see where ambition lay behind a friendly smile; and that was dangerous in the court of Justinian. She would bring savvy to their lives together. He would bring nobility to hers. She determined to share in his exploits and therein find purpose: a thing she had never known before, save only for the weeks that she had treated the injured of Antioch's multiple disasters and the wounded at Dara.

As the months passed, Antonina learned to fit in at court though not without difficulty. At first she was awkward and unfit. She was entirely unfamiliar with ritual or even the right way to address this prelate or that minister, or when to stand and when to gracefully bow in the stiff court dress that she now wore everywhere but in her own chamber. For awhile it was easier for her to take orders than to give them, but Antonius and all those lofty friends of her teenage years had taught her something useful after all: she knew to be silent, and she listened far more than she spoke. This gave her a reputation for discretion. She could also be demure, though from where she got that was a mystery to all who knew her past. Whatever her past, Antonina was reinventing herself as a proper – and shrewd - wife for her aristocratic husband.

Among those dignitaries that Antonina came to know was the emperor's finance minister and lord high tax collector. John the Cappadochian was loyal to the throne but not out of Belisarius' sense of honor. A man like John could be as loyal to another who had taken it as to Justinian. He knew that Justinian was mercurial and feared his moods. Today he was highly regarded but tomorrow he could lose his eyes if the emperor suspected him of treason, as he probably would one day. (At one time or another the emperor suspected everyone.) Alone in his rich villa within the safety of the palace compound, John considered that Belisarius would make a better master; an excellent master. A master who would not put out his servant's eyes on a whim. What John and even Justinian could not understand was that Belisarius would never take the throne while Justinian lived. He had taken an oath. Antonina knew John's kind. She didn't like him but tried not to let that show. She even flirted with him, albeit innocently.

After some training she was ordered to begin waiting upon those who directly advised the Empress. It was a better way to fill her days than gabbing with the girls, but she knew that it was also a promotion of which she was unworthy. Although she was delighted she was also terrified and overwhelmed when after a few months in attendance the Lady Agatha offered her a position in the closest circle of the empress herself. The old lady had been quite forthright in the way that only really old people dare.

"You've already met the empress, Antonina. Her Serenity values a person like you who understands the world outside the palace; someone not raised to be a cubicularia." She said little more but little more needed to be said. After all, Antonina and Theodora did have things in common. Theodora could be unpleasant, but the old lady had understood that was because, like Antonina, she could not speak freely with the aristocrats around her. She could issue orders and they would be obeyed. She could rant like a tyrant and strike fear in the highest dignitaries; but she could not chat, for the ladies of her court felt themselves as much her superior as the sun is superior to the moon. They despised her for her past life. Some of them might even have been jealous that her life had been more exciting than theirs. That would make them doubly resentful. Surely the whole business must have been frustrating for Theodora, the bear keeper's child, and maybe that was why she acted like such a bitch.

"Besides Antonina, you are not so young as many of these ladies. It is understandable that you be helped ahead to make up for lost time. After all, you have the common sense that only comes with age."

Antonina thought of her young husband and knew that what the lady said was not always true. But she had to admit that it usually was. Certainly the younger aristocrats who fluttered around the women's quarters were inexperienced in everything but the niceties of court life; even the nice ones like Kyra, who at least was willing to learn. Most of the others thought that the proper display of dinnerware at state affairs really mattered. That night she confided in Belisarius.

––––––––––––

"Flavius, I've been assigned a new job. Nothing specific; I'm to be available to the empress whenever she may need me." Belisarius was taken aback. Clearly his wife did not understand the full import of what she had been assigned. Other ladies might be charged with filling the Basilia's goblet; a ranking eunuch might have the privilege of emptying her cloisonné potty, but to be always available with no specific duty meant to have the ruler's ear.

They were alone, so Belisarius poured Antonina's wine. "I serve the servant of the empress." They were naked so he knelt on the marble floor before her though it was cold, his head bowed. It was a silliness of course, but Antonina had seen the flush on the cheek of her husband and the general's baton bobbing about. She had seen it in others of rank and responsibility and understood. She made her move, desperately hoping that she had read the signs correctly and that it would please her husband

"Get up!" she ordered and Belisarius obeyed. "If you are to get all excited and subservient when I talk to you, you will indeed serve me when in this room." She pushed him down. A little later in bed the general took charge again but Antonina brooded a bit: *He has so much to learn.*

––––––––––––

While Antonina was adjusting to being the wife of Belisarius and a confidant of Theodora, life outside the palace went on. Ambassadors came and went discussing infractions of the peace with Persia. Merchants ignored the frontiers as they always had both in peace and during periods of warfare, and did their best to evade both Persian and Roman toll collectors. There were rumors of insurrections in the capital and real incursions by barbarian tribes on the frontiers. Men cheated on their wives with impunity. Wives cheated with discretion. In other words: all was normal.

The empire that Justinian inherited from his uncle stretched from the Persian frontier, Palestine, and Egypt on the east and south, as far north as modern Hungary and Romania. But the whole of the western Mediterranean was in the hands of what might generously be called client states: There were Vandal kingdoms in North Africa and Spain, and Ostrogoths in Italy and on the eastern Adriatic shore. Gaul was in the hands of the Franks. All professed a technical allegiance to the emperor as the temporal ruler of Christ's empire on earth; but in practice they acted independently.

In his daydreams Justinian had a vision of a real Roman Empire; one which once again would stretch from the Persian frontier to Spain, and from the African desert north to the Rhine and the Danube. That was unlikely in his lifetime, but taking back the African coast from the Vandals; and, one day, Rome itself from the Goths should be possible for a strong-willed leader. He desired that posterity should remember him for restoring Rome's *Mare Nostrum* of centuries past, together with enormous cultural achievements throughout the empire. In this he was encouraged by his chief minister, the eunuch Narses and by his financier, the enforcer John of Cappadocia who could see personal profit in such dreams. John could even fantasize himself as co-emperor in the west.

Would it be possible? For years while his uncle had reigned, Cappadochian John had stuffed the treasury against the possibility that one day Justinian might seek to fulfill his dreams. He had good generals: Sittas and Mundus, and Constantinus, and John called "bloody John." They were all competent if not particularly imaginative. Belisarius showed unusual potential. Even the new Persian ambassador had spoken highly of him to Justinian: "We would have won at Dara had Belisarius been leading our troops. He defeated our saravan with infantry: half trained boys at that. Unbelievable. Then at Chalcis he sent our Arabs fleeing home. He was supposed to still be holding Dara; instead, there he was coming out of the desert with heavy cavalry. Imagine what he'd have accomplished against the simple barbarians who defy your majesty's rule in the west?" Of course, the ambassador's words had a purpose. He would encourage Justinian to use up his resources in a silly effort to regain the the city of Rome from the Germans, leaving the riches of the east for his master to draw upon.

THE VANDALS

The city of Carthage had, in ancient times, been the home of Hannibal, Rome's most formidable enemy. Now Vandal nobles feasted there on silver and gold tableware. This was plunder brought to the Barbary Coast by Vandal pirates; just as a thousand years later, Arab pirates and slavers would bring loot from their marauding expeditionst to nearby Tripoli. So too, then as later, the local population shared in it but little. The Vandal rulers were Germans of the Arian Christian persuasion who had passed there from Spain after looting Gaul. But most of the native population were either Catholic Arabs or pagan Berbers. (Muhammad would not be born for another century.) For a time after the invasion, Catholic worship had been tolerated; but now under king Gelimer it was not. There were beatings, persecution, torture, and murder of the natives. There were martyrs. Those men and women who were descended from true Roman stock - who had settled there as administrators centuries before - were orthodox Catholic like the Arabs. They also were persecuted. Of the mass of this non-Vandal population only those who adopted the Arian doctrine were admitted to any share of the occupiers' wealth.

Culturally however, the Vandal lords had been entirely absorbed into the ways of their Roman and Romanized subjects, just as Norse raiders in later years would be absorbed into the culture of French Normandy. The Vandals, who had given their tribal name to wanton destruction when they passed through Europe, learned from them the pleasures of the bath and the theater, to admire and imitate classical learning, to wear perfume and silk, and to dine off their stolen dishes on delicately roasted lamb, olive oil, dates, figs, and Bulgur wheat; all of these washed down with wines imported from Italy and Greece. Their fathers and grandfathers had been rough and rugged Germans, and violent; but if their progeny had not entirely given up the sword and ax in favor of commenting over dinner on classical or biblical texts, they now generally restricted their military expeditions to attacks on merchant ships. Which is not to say that they could not fight when necessary; a brother of their king was at war against rebels in Sardinia.

All of this was of interest to Belisarius; war was his occupation, and there was plenty of reason to think that Justinian wanted a war with the Vandals. For very different reasons it was of interest to Antonina too. She did not want that she and her husband of only a few months should so soon be separated. She had not yet become pregnant and she was not young. For the first time in her life the prospect of pregnancy was something to be looked forward to and enjoyed.

Antonina had work to do on Belisarius. He was brave, noble, and loyal - to a fault she felt - but rather stiff. No one would have called him cute. Antonina was thirty three, a little old for playing the cutie, but she'd do it anyway. *What Flavius needs tonight is a tickling. I'll chase him around the bed until he drops giggling. I'll like that and he'd better too. This dominating can really be fun if you like the guy.* Antonina watched her servants going about their duties, dumbly unaware of her plan to entertain her stiff young husband.

Such thoughts were a pleasant rest from her usual preoccupations: Theodora and those others who had power at court. Until her marriage, play had always been a means to an end. Her very survival had always been a fragile thing, always dependent on pleasing some man. Now, thank God, her survival was guaranteed by the most prestigious commander in Justinian's army. Her face darkened as she considered that there were other and very practical reasons to make her husband loosen up a bit. Since Belisarius was so very prestigious, it would be better if Justinian thought that he did not always take himself too seriously. Serious men tended to be either ambitious men or stupid, and the emperor knew that Belisarius was not stupid. That having been noted, Antonina again allowed herself to reflect that her noble husband might be even more to her liking if he were a bit more playful. *No, no, Antonina. What are you thinking? God has given you the finest man alive and riches and dignity you could never have won for yourself. What are you thinking? Love him as he is. He is good. He is kind. Shouldn't that be enough? Of course it should be. ... Yes it is, and I want to be a helpmate to him.*

To say that Antonina became a close friend of the empress would be inexact. Theodora had no true friends, wanted none, and trusted no one. No one would be so trusted that he or she might endanger the royal couple's rule. Certainly Justinian was cautious too but his caution was damnably irregular in her sight. He trusted the most worthless advisers one day and suspected the most innocent the next. He had dreams and was a determined enough administrator to bring them to fruition, but she was his anchor. Theodora, like Antonina, was from the streets where trust was only a word to be used with suckers.

Antonina was a friend to Theodora but it would be as exact to say that she was a useful adjunct, a person who could understand the Theodora of the streets. That was good. Yet Theodora knew that Antonina could also be dangerous to her throne. Antonina understood this also and knew that it was vital to maintaining her place and keeping her husband safe from Justinian's mercurial moods that she not simply ingratiate herself with the empress, but prove by deeds that she and Belisarius totally supported the royal pair and had no higher ambition. That kind of loyalty could not be faked. It would have to be real.

Of course, it should not be blind support. Theodora would never believe that. She herself never blindly trusted anyone, not even Justinian, and would think anyone a fool who did. Justinian liked Belisarius, but envied his wealth and popularity; Theodora hated him, if only because to her a man of honor was an idiot, and clearly the general was not stupid. Surely someday he would turn traitor. Of course, she did not share such thoughts with her "friend" Antonina.

Belisarius' loyalty was of another kind than Antonina's. Few men of intelligence and ability had his commitment. Antonina's loyalty was self serving, but her husband's was one of honor. He had taken an oath to serve the emperor. To him it was as binding as a monk's oath to serve God and be absolutely loyal to his abbot - whatever that man's sins.

Antonina would not try to appear as blindly loyal as her oath-bound husband; Theodora would see through that as a farce. But the empress understood, and Antonina understood, that Antonina's place in society depended entirely upon her goodwill. That goodwill could be bought and Antonina would be required to buy it. More importantly, a street slut could never purchase that place from another empress, one who had not risen from the gutter.

The treason that Theodora feared was that Belisarius might someday decide to take the throne, and that made her hate him. But that he would never do unless ...*unless Antonina pushes him to it.* The empress and servant shared a streetwise view of the world, but Antonina's influence over Belisarius needed to be watched. Antonina paid for her place in society with loyalty.

The sun had risen many hours before behind a villa on Rufinianae, an estate that Belisarius had inherited on the Asiatic shore of the Bosphorus. This estate, or rather suburb, was still within view of the Great Palace. In an emergency the general could be summoned with a mirror signal. On this day Antonina was not expected at court so she turned over and considered going back to sleep. Being married to Belisarius, she did not have to live in the women's quarters, just be available. She could lie abed and consider what had to be done this morning. Although she had not known squat about running an aristocratic household some months before, she had been learning. She had nothing against Rhaskos, the majordomo of the household. He was a pleasant old eunuch, a family friend of her husband's deceased father from his childhood. But she wanted her own stamp on things. Rhaskos had always arranged things to his master's taste and would continue to do so in his private quarters and conference rooms; but Belisarius' taste needed a bit of female tweaking elsewhere, some ornamentation, and that she would supply. She'd just about decided that she'd been in bed too long already when a knock on her chamber door announced Rhaskos.

"A courier from the empress, mi-lady."

Antonina sighed and decided that it would give the best impression if she remained where she was for a few minutes more. When finally the courier was admitted Antonina knew from his beardless face that he was another eunuch, but this one much younger, more handsome, and far more charming than the elderly Rhaskos. His message was simple and straight-forward. "Her serenity wishes to see you early this afternoon. Would that be convenient?"

The order was straightforward, the question a politeness. No one would dare to refuse a summons from Theodora, even if it meant rising from a deathbed. Besides, Antonina was a cubicularia, even if she did not live with the empress' other attendants.

"Of course. I am honored."

The pretty young eunuch bowed gracefully and retreated. Antonina swung from the bed thinking it a shame that such beauty was wasted on a guy – and a gelding, at that. In a moment she was surrounded by her own eunuchs and women who bathed their lady and dressed her hair. They brought a tunic of pale green silk enlivened with a stylized brocade, a flowing stola enhanced with a few semiprecious gemstones, a silk palla to cover her shoulders against the autumn chill, and pretty sandals for her pretty feet. These preparations absorbed what remained of the morning hours and it was frighteningly near to one when Antonina's cutter reached the imperial harbor. Of course the empress had intended that Antonina be rushed. In the months since they had met and the weeks since Antonina's marriage she had become as close to Theodora as anyone save Justinian, but that did not mean that Antonina should take the relationship for granted, and the empress was determined that she would not.

Antonina was surprised when a trusted eunuch ushered her into the empress' private chambers. There were not more than a dozen guards near her bedroom and all of them grandly overpaid and fiercely loyal servants. No high officer was with them. These were all Theodora's own trusted men. Antonina prostrated herself and wondered what deviltry her powerful mistress was plotting that such secrecy was necessary.

Alone together she soon found out.

"Antonina, you and I shared a lot before fate brought us here. I'd pull out the tongue of anyone who spoke of those days but it is so. Tell me, do you ever miss it?"

"Your Serenity?"

"You needn't be coy. You're as much a whore as I am and there was a time not many months ago when you'd have done *anything* for a few coins." She emphasized the word.

"Yes, your Serenity." Antonina played for time to analyze the empress' words. *What is she getting at?*

"And I'll have your tongue out too and fried in oil to go with eggs and bread if you speak of this." For a moment she glared at Antonina, perhaps concerned that she might have misjudged the woman prostrate before her. Then her tone softened. "But we are friends, are we not? I will explain. I love Justinian but sometimes he and I are more like comrades than lovers. He's a bit of a religious stiff. There are fun things that entertainers learn to do; things he cannot fathom, or feels he dare not practice as the elect of God." The empress of the Romans stood and loosed her hair. She let her tunic drop to the floor.

That evening Antonina thought over the incident. It would be best not to tell her husband. *He has such conventional morality. What-the-hell, it's not important.*

NIKE

Justinian protected the Blue hippodrome faction regardless of their crimes. He relied on the Blues as a counter to the Greens, who were often paid henchmen of his political enemies, the patrician families who had ruled before Justin. But if the Blues detested the Greens, it was not out of any affection for their protector.

Both factions sold insurance against the other. Each Blue claimed to protect the city from the scum in the Green faction, and each Green plead his protection of honest businessmen against the murderers among the Blues. Too late Justinian realized the foolishness of his actions in punishing

102

only the Green faction. The city was in turmoil and no citizen dared walk the streets without guards after dark. No woman was safe and the night watch was helpless as well as corrupt. Blues had bought many judges and bureaucrats and when captured were released. Greens were executed. Blues felt unrestrained and Greens felt oppressed. Justinian's favoritism had failed to bring order to Constantinople. At last he tried a more even handed approach. He had several criminal leaders of both parties arrested. Then he saw to it that they were condemned at trial by a judge whom the Blue defendants had considered safe.

"What! Does that fool on his ivory throne think he can get away with this ... and the judge? I bought Tribonian and his lackeys years ago and he has grown fat at my expense. Does he fear the fool more than me? I'll show them both." These were the thoughts and words of one of the Blue gang leaders. "I bought Tribonian and I can buy another chief judge." The Greens were angry too. They were being persecuted by the emperor no matter what they did or did not do.

It was a mild week in January. Winter in Constantinople is usually cold and rainy with an occasional light snowfall. There had been none this season so the angry factions took to the streets. The fair weather was no blessing to Justinian, for many of the Blues and Greens soon gathered in the open air Hippodrome to vent their grievance. It had been in a fit of justice that the emperor had executed leaders of both factions, but the result was that the Blues and Greens could no longer be played off against each other. They formed an alliance and demanded both reparation from the emperor and the head of the judge who had sentenced the men.

Justinian refused.

Without anyone giving an order parts of the city were fired. The old cathedral church of Hagia Sophia and a part of the palace complex were in flames. Many "uncooperative" businesses and the homes of "stuck-up" senators were destroyed. "Nike, Nike (victory)," the mobs of outright gangsters and Constantinople's lowlife yelled as they assaulted the city's prisons to free inmates of whichever party. They swore to toss Justinian into the sea and make a new emperor, one who understood the reality of the world. Was it not the factions who organized entertainments, helped widows, and protected shopkeepers from corrupt guardsmen and the foreigners who came to Constantinople only to line their pockets and avoid the authorities in their homelands? "All Justinian can see is some roughness; that's life.... Would he have us all be monks? The world is a rough place. So we skim a little off rich tradesmen. Don't we keep them safe?"

Justinian panicked. His own guards might be reluctant to defend him. When he appeared at the Hippodrome in an effort to appease the factions with promises, he was nearly mobbed and he retreated. Icons were displayed and attempts to organize a holy procession made. But these too failed. The wealthy of the city as well as many senators from old and distinguished families fled to the Asian shore. The emperor hid in his inner palace which remained untouched by the fires. In the Boucoleon harbor a warship was prepared to evacuate him and the empress, its crew growing more nervous by the hour.

Outside the hippodrome riots went on for a full week hardly checked by the efforts of troops with whips that the city prefect sent into the streets. Constantinople had no real police force; the factions themselves had years before taken over much of that task. It was a bit as though the Mafia or a Chicago mob was policing the city and providing order. The city prefect and his troops were usually wary of interfering with their day-to-day operations and the gang enforcers were generally careful not to invade each others' turf. Businessmen bought protection. It was the emperor's attempt to restore his authority on the street that had resulted in the riot, and now sections of the city were ablaze with no one to put out the fires, another task usually handled by the gangs for a price.

Belisarius and Antonina were at a villa far outside the walls, the guests of a longtime friend of the general, when they heard the news of the riot in the city. At first they thought it a minor disturbance and Belisarius' host simply sent an aide to gather news each day. But on the fourth day the aide brought word that the rioting had become widespread. Clearly the riot was now beyond the strength of the city authorities alone to control. Civil discord was not his responsibility, but Belisarius felt that he must return to the palace in case the life of the emperor himself was jeopardized. Antonina should come too; she might be of some use in council for she knew the factions' leaders well. She had screwed one or two of them when young.

Antonina volunteered that Constantinople would be safer after the affair was put down; if it could be put down: "The hoods are very stupid to gather in the Hippodrome. Crooks should know enough to be secretive but these have gathered publicly in one stadium, with only two exits, where soldiers can get at all of them at once. Justinian should send in troops. Innocents also would die of course, but they'd be lowlifes. They might be innocent of crimes but they're still hangers on. I know their type." For a moment Antonina lost her new-found delicacy. "They're shits who haven't the guts to actually knife someone themselves but who like to hang around those who will. Shits who think only of a little bit of gain and nothing of cheating others, and are a pain in the ass. It's too bad for them but they'd not be missed." *Hell!* she thought, *I've only been in the palace for a few months and already I'm thinking like a noble bitch.*

Even as they prepared to return to the palace an imperial messenger arrived instructing, actually imploring, Belisarius to present himself as soon as possible before Justinian and Theodora. He made it plain that Justinian was frightened although he dared not say as much. No sooner had he left than Belisarius and Antonina followed after him. They just threw on some riding clothes, disdained a carriage, and hopped upon two polo ponies which had been quickly saddled by servants of their worried host. With them was a small bodyguard of their friend's bucellarii; just a few dozen but enough to cut their way through any scattered rabble that they might encounter.

It only took an hour to reach the landward walls. Once inside, Belisarius considered that without passing dangerously near to the hippodrome it would not be possible to approach the palace by land. It was located on the opposite side of the city and near to the race course. Rioting in the streets continued to ebb and flow between different districts, but the orgy of looting and burning had tired the rioters as any orgy eventually must. Many of the rabble were falling back in small groups to the epicenter of the rebellion. Belisarius' borrowed bucellarii could easily have slaughtered the tired criminals and criminal wannabes before them in the streets but would be no match for the thousands inside the stadium if they should sally in force. Besides, Antonina might be taken by the rebels. That could not be risked. At the harbor of Kontoskali within the land walls, Belisarius requisitioned a skiff. He and Antonina skirted the hippodrome and docked without incident at the palace water gate of Boucoleon, their guards following soon after in larger boats.

By then it was evening and they were too late to hear much of the discussion that had split imperial advisers into two camps. The larger of the two advised the emperor to flee by night and rally loyal regiments across the Bosporus. The far smaller understood that whoever held the capital was emperor in the minds of most citizens, civilians and soldiers alike. For Justinian to flee would be near suicidal. The factions would crown their own emperor. Justinian would be tracked down and assassinated wherever he might go within the empire, or be betrayed in a foreign land. Already the rioters had set about forcing Senator Hypatius to assume the imperial dignity. He was aged and he and his brother Pompeius wanted nothing so much as to live out their lives undisturbed. Though it was said that he was truly reluctant, the citizenry respected Hypatius and the factions thought him malleable. The emperor would go to bed that night not knowing whether in the morning he would still be ruler of the civilized world or dead. Neither did Hypatius, who had so far been able to put off assuming the imperial symbols, but was under great pressure to do so. He was being pressured not only by the rabble, but also by men of wealth and position who saw that their riches would be taxed away by the emperor and his finance minister, to pay for the glorious achievements with which Justinian meant to immortalize his reign. It was not clear to Hypatius where duty lay. He only knew that if the rebellion was not successful he and his brother would be held responsible if he assumed the throne; and that if he did not accept it the rioters themselves might kill them for their loyalty to Justinian.

On the morning of the fifth day even the palace guard was becoming restless. They weren't afraid of a mob but they did disdain an indecisive leader, and Justinian, save for prayer, seemed unable to come to any decision to end the rebellion. Yet Belisarius, the hero of Dara, was now with them and he had a large number of his bucellarii available, for they had made their way in groups to the palace barracks. His friend the strategos Mundus, commander of the Illyrian divisions was also there with his retainers. Their bucellarii were few compared to the rebels but they were excellent troops, well armed and armored and, of course, trained and disciplined.

There too were Theodora and Antonina. Antonina was not waiting demurely aside like a proper wife, but instead stood at her husband's side like a shield.

Justinian had another fear. These bucellarii had sworn loyalty to Belisarius and Mundus, not to him. Justinian hated that and feared it. His uncle, Justin, had constantly been concerned that a general who was strong enough to put down a rebellion with his personal troops might also be popular enough to raise one himself. Might his largely ceremonial palace guard find itself fighting tough bucellarii as well as street thugs? What if the rioters raised Belisarius on a shield instead of Hypatius? Escape by sea began to look the more attractive option.

While the men debated, the empress took Antonina aside. "You alone don't seem frightened, Antonina. Have you a pact with those scum?"

"Mi-lady, no! But I am not afraid of them either. If one of them had a brain he'd be terrified. Belisarius is here. He came not because of the emperor's summons; we were leaving for the city when the messenger arrived. If my husband were disloyal he could as easily have gone to the hippodrome and become emperor. In fact, it would have been easier. He would have had his cataphracts and the people behind him. And you? Just Mundus and your guards." Antonina was speaking boldly, but now was certainly not a time for discretion and surely Theodora would value a straightforward defense that made such perfect sense. Going to the hippodrome had obviously occurred to Antonina if not to her husband. Yet they had not. Theodora made a mental note.

Procopius was also in the room and although he could not overhear their discussion it was plain to him that Theodora listened carefully to her cubicularia. It confirmed what he had already concluded: that the flirty Antonina was far more than a mere pretty to decorate a husband's bed. When they had married she had seemed a simple if tarnished woman, one he'd assumed was overwhelmed at what the fates had provided her. Quickly he had realized that she had become much more to both Belisarius and Theodora. She not only understood the world outside the Great Palace, she was strong and ready to give advice; probably good advice. Somewhere in the back of his mind he resented that. Procopius had thought he'd be the general's right hand but with so strong a wife beside him, that position was jeopardized.

Procopius watched as Theodora turned from Antonina to Justinian. Her back was straight and there was anger in her face. The anger was not at Antonina's frank words but at her husband's timidity. Theodora summoned the best Attic phrases she had heard from educated men and put them together in a monologue not unworthy of the ancient authors: "My opinion is that it is inopportune for flight, even though it bring safety. For one who has been an empress it is unendurable to be a fugitive. May I never be separated from this purple, and may I not live that day on which those who meet me shall not address me as Brasilia. If, now, it is your wish to save yourself, emperor, there is no difficulty. For we have much money, and there is the sea, there the boats. However consider whether it will not come about after you have been saved that you would gladly exchange that safety for death. As for myself, I approve a certain ancient saying that the purple is a good burial-shroud."

Procopius made some more mental notes for the book he would one day write.

The decision was made and on the sixth day of the rebellion Belisarius led his bucellarii to one end of the Hippodrome. Mundus led his own bucellarii and the imperial guard through a passage connecting the palace to the race track. Belisarius forced the entrance in person and his men arrayed themselves in battle order within. The one-sided butchery began. Thirty thousand were killed

In truth though, it was not the troops who did most of the slaughter.

107

It was the rebels and criminals themselves. Even while those inside the palace were debating what to do, Narses had been spreading bribes and promises among the Blues. That had added to the rebel's disorder and mutual suspicion. Most died in the panic when they found themselves facing armed and disciplined soldiers. Thousands were trampled or had their heads smashed into brick walls by comrades. Others used the knives which all of them carried in attempts to cut a way out through their friends and enemies. They failed; but before the troops could cut them down they had stabbed and slashed at each other in a brawl such as has never been seen before or since.

The factions had not anticipated their massacre and neither had the troops who carried it out. Somehow the thought of thoroughly excising this cancer had never occurred to any emperor before; or, if it had, none had possessed the courage to try surgery on such a scale. Until that day Justinian hadn't either. The rebels had felt secure in their numbers, especially when word leaked out of the palace that Justinian was considering flight. But Theodora proved herself a tougher fighter than her husband and Belisarius and Mundus did what had to be done. No mercy was shown. These were not enemy soldiers serving their country and king. They were not even honest rebels intent upon replacing a bad emperor with a better. They were murderers and thieves, so the city's criminal element was largely eliminated at one cut. The city prefect could be assured that those who survived would henceforth dwell in the shadows for some years to come. Citizens could walk the streets at night with far less fear than had been possible almost since the founding of the city. Prayers were offered that Christ would have pity and pardon the dead, but in that brutal age, when even the best of men and women and children died of the slightest disease or accident, there was little mourning and no condemnation of the slaughter.

Not even by Antonina, though almost certainly more than a few of her one-time friends and clients had perished. Anyway, it was as likely that they had died from each others' knife thrusts as from her husband's soldiers' swords. She spent an hour in a palace chapel trying to recall any whose death she should regret. Yes, there was one boy, doubtless a man now. But maybe he had escaped, or not been there at all. He might even have turned away from crime sometime in the years since she'd known him.

Hypatius had by now accepted the symbols of office and even begun to act the part of an emperor with verve. He and Pompeius were arrested. Justinian was inclined to spare these old men but Theodora was not. Justinian had to relent. It was his wife's strength which had saved his throne and he was not about to argue. They were executed and their property confiscated. Some time later, however, the emperor was moved by fear that he'd offended God, to restore to their children these reluctant rebels' fortunes and the honor of their ancient families.

It was about this same time that one of the city's many earthquakes finished off the already damaged Hagia Sophia (Holy Wisdom) cathedral. Instead of rebuilding it Justinian ordered a new church built on the same spot. The massive building was completed in only six years and was acknowledged the wonder of the age. Although the dome had to be replaced twenty years later it remains to this day one of the wonders of the world.

Soon afterward, Belisarius and Antonina were able to move into their newly built home on the Sea of Marmara not far from Justinian's palace. The gardens were not finished but that didn't matter. Also about this time, they became fully occupied with a happy affair: the pregnancy which Antonina wished for and had even prayed for. Antonina was getting near the end of her childbearing years and did not at first tell her husband for fear of a miscarriage. She had aborted more than once and feared that God would punish her by killing this little person now in her womb. He did not. If God had issues with Antonina he would not punish Belisarius for her sins. The child was born, a girl, and for a few months mother and father doted on little Joannina. But of course they still had their duties and soon these began to again occupy most of their time. Theodora required her cubicularia at irregular hours and Belisarius knew that his services might at any time be wanted to protect the empire or support Justinian's expansive dreams. They interviewed nursemaids, and Belisarius' mother came from Thrace for what was to be a very extended visit. She would watch over Joannina while she matured. She would also assume much of Antonina's place in the household as Antonina was becoming too much required in the sacred palace to also supervise the household staff. Antonina was almost daily becoming more important to Theodora, but she was more than a close friend and personal servant now. She advised the empress on the rumors and rumbling of the streets which more dignified advisers disdained or ignored. Her advice was not limited to dissecting the scuttlebutt of the rabble outside the palace walls though. Theodora came to appreciate Antonina's political savvy for Antonina had an intuitive understanding that matched her own of the baseness to which men could sink. The most frequent subjects that the two discussed were not fashion, art, or the theater; but Justinian's ambitious schemes, the internecine feuding of his chief advisers; and the strengths and weaknesses of the Vandals.

CHAPTER 9

533 AD
CONSTANTINOPLE

VANDALS & GOTHS

Much as Justinian desired it, the reconquest of Italy would have to wait until after North Africa, though it rankled him that the Roman Empire did not hold Rome. It was well known inside the sprawling palace that after the victory against Persia, Justinian had begun to dream of restoring the frontiers of his state to those of Diocletian, two centuries before. Surely, in time Christ's holy empire would again be coterminous with the civilized world. That would mean restoring the provinces of Gaul and Britain and Hispania. Justinian knew that was beyond his reach, but a start might be made. If he were able to retake North Africa, now in the hands of Arian Vandals, he might afterward be able to reach across Sicily to Italy and wrest old Rome from the grip of the Gothic regime.

Would it be possible? Or worthwhile? There was much argument about it in the counsel chambers and over shared wine. In truth though, whilst they proudly proclaimed themselves to be Roman, by that term the people of Constantinople meant Christian. Even in the empire's pagan heyday the citizens of the Greek speaking parts of the empire had looked down their noses at the true Romans of the west. Not for them was a heritage of crucifixions, gladiators, gluttonous feasts, and ribald comedies. The only Roman things they regarded highly were Roman law and military discipline. They thought of western arts, theology, and philosophy as crude imitations of their own. Christianity itself had been born in the east. Paul had traveled through the eastern cities making converts. The great councils had all been held either in Constantinople or in the Greek speaking cities of Asia Minor.

Constantinople was the New Rome; the greatest city in the empire and from its founding far more important than old Rome. That father of ancient heroes had long since been reluctantly relinquished to the power of one German after another. It had not even been the seat of an emperor since Diocletian. Now that part of the world was firmly in the hands of Gothic kings who, though they might give formal obeisance to the eastern emperor as head of the Christian people, in reality ruled the whole of Italy, the Adriatic coast of Dalmatia, and Sicily. Rome was not their capital; their king Theodoric ruled from Ravenna on the east coast of Italy in easy communication with those of his people across the Adriatic.

Like the Vandals in Africa, the Goths in Italy adhered to the Arian heresy, which is to say that they denied the divinity of Christ, or at least the fullness of his divinity. But like the native population of Africa, the native Italian population were Catholic adherents to the Nicene formula, which defined Jesus Christ as eternally begotten and of one nature with the Father. In this belief they were united with the emperor in Constantinople and his people. It was the Arian heresy that tainted parts of the west, not the Monophysite as in the east.

The native Italians considered themselves to be Roman citizens and the wisdom of Theodoric preserved this fiction. He ruled the Goths as their king, but the Italians nominally as the representative of the Emperor in Constantinople. He even issued a compendium of Roman laws for the native Italians. In practice, of course, he was entirely independent. The relationship worked. The Arian Goths did not insist on "Romans" accepting their theological formulas as the Vandals did in Africa, and the pope ignored the rather mild form of the Arian heresy espoused by the Goths. Roman culture was proclaimed, honored, and encouraged by the Goths who as readily accepted it as the Vandals had adopted North African ways. Moreover, the Arian Goths did not even seize Catholic churches as the Vandals had done but left these to the "Romans," building new structures for their own worship. Furthermore, Theodoric the Great, their king until AD 526, had been reared in Constantinople and had been honored with the Roman titles of Consul and Master Of Soldiers before ascending his throne as king of the Ostrogoths (East Goths). The ways of the "Greeks" were as familiar to him as were German and Italian.

The reconquest of Italy would wait. Justinian did not like it, but for now there was nothing he could do but dream of some day ruling from old Rome. Or, more likely, one day installing a son on that throne, while he actually ran the empire from the more cosmopolitan Constantinople. For now there would be peace in Italy. After all, it had been his own predecessors who had steered the one-time master of soldiers, and his Goths toward Italy just a few decades before. That had been to get him away from Constantinople and at the same time eliminate Odoacer, the previous barbarian ruler of Italy. Justinian would live with that deal for awhile.

But the Vandals in Africa were an immediate opportunity. Their king, though a fully Romanized vassal like Theodoric, was a real enemy who supported piracy and was actively persecuting Catholics. Since the Persian king defeated by Belisarius was dead now and his son and successor wanted peace, Justinian could look to the Vandals. Belisarius' army was the tool that he would use. The Goths would be for another day.

JOHN THE CAPPADOCIAN

Much that Justinian accomplished in his long reign, though of lasting fame did not please the aristocracy of the time. Wars were expensive, so too were his building projects and the funding for these was in the hands of one of the most hated men of that age.

John, known to history as John the Cappadocian and to Procopius as John the drunkard, when not stalking about in his cups, was about as reclusive a person as could be found in Constantinople. He rarely left the palace compound by day and when he did he made no show of it. This was not out of modesty. High officials were expected to travel about the city amid hordes of retainers and hangers-on. It was the Roman tradition. How better could a man distribute largess among the poor, or demonstrate publicly his determination to serve God and the state? John, however, always traveled discreetly in a closed coach or palanquin attended by very few guards, and these not armed and armored warriors to impress the population, but wary assassins who'd bully any crowd away. They were as near a corps of ninja as the Roman Empire could develop.

John was more than unpopular. He was hated; hated even more than the emperor who had at least some popularity on his better days. John was Justinian's tax collector and enforcer. He was certainly a good administrator and a canny adviser to the throne. He knew every means to raise funds for grand projects and when traditional means were insufficient he'd invent new ones. That John was hated was fine with Justinian, for it deflected at least part of the onus from himself.

The hatred for John was an egalitarian hatred. He was hated by rich and poor alike. In Justinian's view the aristocracy had grown fat off great estates and business interests that did not pay their fair share to support the empire. Pressing merchants was another regular source of revenue, while the peasantry could do nothing but pay what they had, and bitch endlessly.

Only the church and the state mattered to Justinian and in that age there was no distinction between church and state. So the emperor ruled the civil affairs of the church and tried to affect a conciliatory voice in its theology. He appointed and deposed troublesome bishops. He wrestled with popes for control of the clergy. He proposed settlements to disputes over matters of faith. Most important, he ruled the nation as the representative of Christ and the equal of the apostles. Those clergy who, like the emperor, affirmed the orthodox decrees of the council of Chalcedon, were reluctant to dispute other matters with him, for they benefited enormously from Justinian's building projects paid for by everyone else. Whether Justinian was truly pious or just fearful for his soul, new churches rose throughout the empire. In Constantinople itself, Justinian was building his new cathedral to replace the old Hagia Sophia, the cathedral church of the Holy Wisdom built by Constantine I. This had been destroyed by earthquake and the fires of the Nike uprising. When completed, the new Hagia Sophia would be a much grander edifice to glorify God and his own rule. John the Cappadocian was just the man to raise the necessary money.

Hagia Sophia was not the only church under construction. During his long reign, in Constantinople alone, Justinian would rebuild or tear down and replace, among others; the church of St. Eirene (Holy Peace), one dedicated to St. Anna, and others dedicated to the Archangel Michael, the military saints Sergius and Bacchus, to Sts. Peter and Paul, St. Acacius, to the holy apostles, and to Sts. Andrew, Luke, and Timothy.

These are only a few of the most notable of the many churches that Justinian built or rebuilt both in Constantinople and throughout the empire. He was also responsible for the final form of the Augusteum, the city's marketplace. He built new palaces and harbors throughout the city and empire; and fortifications all along the Persian frontier including at Dara and Antioch. Even Procopius, who hated Justinian and called him a demon, admits the long hours which the emperor dedicated to refortifying and embellishing the empire. Several of the finest churches: the new Hagia Sophia and the Church of Sts Sergius and Bacchus, as well as the rebuilt Hagia Eirene remain today, having been converted into mosques after the Turkish conquest. Hagia Sophia is now a museum. Hagia Eirene, now bare of decoration, is sometimes used for concerts. The church of Sts. and Sergius and Bacchus, often called the Kucuk, or little, Ayasofia, remains a functioning mosque - bright and very pretty. Yet none of this construction would have been possible without the determination of Justinian and the extortions of John.

If Justinian felt that he needed John, most certainly Theodora did not. Justinian needed Theodora but John was jealous of her power over him. Justinian relied so much upon his wife that most imperial edicts were issued in both their names. Or was that for love? Theodora was intelligent, and was a steadying sea anchor to Justinian's mercurial behavior. John was brilliant, even more ruthless than Theodora, and believed that one day he himself would become emperor. Whatever his competence, Theodora wished him dead before she and Justinian were.

CHAPTER 10

533 AD
CONSTANTINOPLE

Justinian slept but few hours a night, and often arose at odd hours to work on some pet project or troubling business of state. Theodora usually enjoyed sleeping late, but today she'd had an exhausting morning. There had been a meeting with some merchants who had just returned from a minor middle Asian kingdom who had nothing important to say, and there was the usual procession of monks, priests, and bishops - each presenting his own view of the procession of the Holy Spirit, or some such nonsense. There were petitions for clemency, most of which were quickly and emphatically denied. Theodora had long since learned to drive deep within her whatever human feeling she might have felt for the convicted and their families, She did send one petition to Justinian for final decision, but the relieved family knew that to be a formality. Anyway, the culprit was hardly more than a boy and his crime had been simple stupidity; doing the dirty work for a gang leader. (Besides, he was kind of cute.)

"If I ever hear of him again for anything, even picking a pocket, he'll die. Now get him out of my sight." The boy and his parents rose from their prostrate position and fled as quickly as they could while walking backwards out of the empress's frowning presence.

When they were gone Theodora, not generally known either for mercy or humor, broke into a titter. "I liked him." That was her only explanation to the dignitaries who filled the chamber. "Antonina! See that he's kept far away from the hippodrome. I'd rather not have to carry out my threat. Oh, and Antonina, I want to see you alone after we get finished here."

Antonina bowed in acknowledgment. She bowed, but not as low as some other cubiculariai. It might seem a small thing, but by such minutiae are position recognized, and rumors started. The following day it was noted that Antonina now stood several positions nearer the empress. As for the youth? Antonina still had many friends outside the cloistered circle of the court. The author is happy to confirm that a stint under the hand of a tough noncom worked as well then, as now.

With the Nike rioters pacified, Justinian turned his thoughts to reconciling his people to their taxes with images of future greatness. He believed that the populace were just as unhappy as he that the Roman Empire had no real authority in the western provinces. It was a constant refrain in the wine shops, almost as talked about and lamented as a loss at the hippodrome. "We should send an army against the Vandals or the Goths, or both. They're just a bunch of long haired barbarians. Belisarius made even the Persians turn tail and they're tough fighters." It was the old myth: a quick and cheap victory bought by superior troops and superior leadership. Even those few who could remember the humiliating defeat of the emperor Leo's expedition against the Vandals sixty five years earlier, simply attributed it to the knavery of treacherous barbarians and an ill-timed wind. A war would be popular and would restore not only the empire's prestige but its fortune as well. They could imagine wagonloads of captured gold and silver rolling through the city's Golden Gate. Then as now the common wisdom was that: "An expedition will cost us but we'll get it back with interest."

In his chambers Justinian imagined that he could hear the boastful talk. He called a conference of his chief military and civilian advisers. The only thing on the table was his long-held desire to expand the nation's power westward and restore the faded glory of Rome. For once the Persians would not be a problem at his rear; the imperial coffers were adequate, and several of the empire's younger officers had proven their worth in the war with Persia - in particular the Magister Militum Per Orientem.

Most important: at the back of the emperor's mind was the thought that whilst his empire was eternal, the barbarian tribes which had occupied the western parts of the empire for generations were becoming weaker. In this, he agreed with the citizenry. He was convinced that it would not take a massive army to regain North Africa. Belisarius and a few thousand troops could do it; should Belisarius fail, his popularity would fade. It would keep such a popular general in his place. That, in its own way, would also be a victory.

VANDALS

After the death of the Ostrogothic leader Theodoric the Great, Italy was ruled by a female regent. In Africa, Genseric, the greatest of Vandal leaders, was dead and, in his place, northern Africa was ruled by Gelimer, a usurper who had imprisoned the rightful heir. The prospect of victory even over both was enticing to Justinian.

Once Vandals and Goths had been closely linked by bonds of marriage. The Vandal king Thrasimund had wed the Gothic princess

116

Amalafrida, the sister of Great Theodoric. That alliance now worked to the advantage of the Byzantines. Some years past, Thrasimund's successor, Hilderic, had foolishly imprisoned and probably murdered Thrasimund's queen and her six thousand Gothic guards. This rash savagery broke the alliance of the two Arian tribes and Hilderic, fearful of what his folly might have wrought, had hastened to affirm Vandal allegiance to the Empire and seek its protection.

Now Hilderic himself had been overthrown and imprisoned by his kinsman, Gelimer. From prison he called upon Justinian, his suzerain lord, to save him. Dutifully, Justinian wrote to Gelimer requesting that he allow the old man to live out his life reigning over, if not ruling, the Vandals, Soon Gelimer would rightfully inherit the throne anyway.

"You are not acting in a holy manner nor worthily of the will of Genseric, keeping in prison an old man and a kinsman, and the king of the Vandals, and robbing him of his office by violence, though it would be possible for you to receive it after a short time in a lawful manner. Do you therefore no further wrong and do not exchange the name of king for the title of tyrant, which comes but a short time earlier. But as for this man, whose death may be expected at any moment, allow him to bear in appearance the form of royal power, while you do all the things which it is proper that a king should do; and wait until you can receive from time and the law of Genseric, and from them alone, the name which belongs to the position. For if you do this, the attitude of the Almighty will be favorable and at the same time our relations with you will be friendly."

Gelimer refused. Again Justinian wrote asking that Hilderic at least be allowed to travel to Constantinople, there to live out his last days. This too was refused and Justinian had his excuse for war.

Belisarius and Antonina strolled a beach at Rufinianae. They could just make out the palace complex on the opposite shore of the Bosphorus, which rose above massive seaward fortifications. Work had begun on demolishing the old cathedral and boats were carrying the rubble away. Old brick would be used for landfill, broken stonework for a seawall, and the decorative elements be saved for use elsewhere. Justinian was also building a new underground cistern nearby the palace. Maybe some of the old columns would supplement those being shipped from elsewhere to support its roof. The purpose of the cistern was, of course, to hoard water against the possibility of drought or siege, but it would also be a nice cool retreat on a hot summer day. It should be made pretty.

Rufinianae was just far enough from the city for the young marrieds not to be constantly bothered, but near enough if either Belisarius or Antonina was summoned to the palace. They kicked sand just for fun. *Beach sand, not desert sand; much nicer,* Antonina was thinking. They walked toward a wharf where a light imperial barge would soon be finished tying up. No one who did not know Belisarius personally would recognize him as the magister militum, for he was wearing only a simple tunic with a little embroidery, such as any freeman might have. But despite his attempt to look nonmilitary, his bearing gave away at least that he was not a merchant considering how to make a profit at one of the shops in the village, nor a scholar from Belisarius' library out for a walk on a beach, while pondering Homer or Theucidites - or girls. He tried to show only lazy interest as the barge was secured and its few passengers debarked. One appeared to be a man of some importance, for the ship's master was as differential toward him as a slave. The man was used to it too. Like Belisarius he seemed accustomed to command. Also like Belisarius, he showed no haughtiness and was entirely at ease. Without first looking to the captain for approval he jumped nimbly to the pier but then gave a wave of cheerful farewell to master and crew.

The courier was young or relatively so; older than Belisarius but what person of any great rank or position wasn't? He was also intuitive. "Hello! You are an officer, are you not?" After the quickest glance around him the man had headed directly toward Belisarius and Antonina. "Would you kindly tell me where I might find General Belisarius?"

It was Antonina who answered. "Why, he should be nearby for he spent the night with me in that house." Antonina pointed to a mansion which they had left not an hour before. After the briefest moment of confusion the visitor broke into a broad smile and turned to face the general: "Then have I the pleasure?"

Belisarius returned the grin.

"May I speak with you alone? You and Lady Antonina, of course. I fear this wharf has ears and His Serenity has requested your presence tomorrow. I will brief you."

The session behind the walls of the Great Palace was all about work. There was no posturing. Roman emperors had cast off divinity when Constantine the Great made Christianity the state religion, yet they had not fully assumed the aura as Elect of God that they would hold in centuries to come. The dignitaries prostrated upon entering Justinian's presence, but he quickly motioned them to stand. He and Theodora sat but on rather modest thrones; nothing more than ornate chairs. Belisarius was there, of course, as was Antonina though they stood apart, each with their own duties. Belisarius' career was of foremost importance to Antonina and she was happy to know as much about his concerns as possible, but her function was to assist and advise the empress. Theodora would certainly be bouncing thoughts about the expedition off of her.

Narses began the discussion by outlining the emperor's intentions: With the signing of a Persian peace, it was now possible to withdraw the Ephthalite archers and much of the cavalry that protected that frontier; that might not still be possible after Persia had recovered from its defeat by Belisarius. Rome was assured at least a ten year respite, if not the promised eternal one. The victory had motivated farm boys throughout the empire and, wanting to see the world, they were streaming to the imperial standard. The armories were fully occupied with equipping them. New stud farms in Thrace were producing war horses.

As important to Justinian, an African campaign would not be simply a war of conquest upon which God might look with disfavor. The rightful heir to Genseric, who had shown a moderate policy toward the African Catholics, had been imprisoned by his own nephew. This new king faced discord at home and his desert frontier was harassed by Moorish raiding parties. In Vandal occupied Sardinia and even Tripoli there were rumblings of insurrection. The oppressed Catholic population would welcome imperial troops. If there was to be war, it were better to have it now than later.

When he had nearly finished, Narses smiled a thin smile and reminded the strategoi that they were currently without employment. It was not necessary for him to actually verbalize the need of many of these gentlemen of ancient lineage to supplement what modest inherited income they might possess with bounty from a successful campaign. He spoke only of honor, and of duty to Hilderic who was Rome's vassal and whose own mother was the daughter of a Roman emperor. He spoke of the glory of Roman arms.

"Who would not wish to share the honor with our Serene Highness of recovering our lost province?" The honor and profit were enticing but the difficulties that Narses glibly passed over were daunting. Wealth and honor were possibilities, but so were humiliation and bankruptcy if the expedition failed; especially since whoever led the expedition would be expected to enroll many of the new recruits as personal troops to ease the burden on the treasury. As for the call to patriotism: the Persian war had been fought against an ancient enemy. The future of the empire itself, or at least its far eastern provinces, had been at stake. The western provinces had long ago been relinquished and what had the east in common with them anyway? Was it not enough that from time to time the barbarians still acknowledged the suzerainty of Constantinople? Then too, an attack on Africa had been tried before.

One of the older officers spoke up. "Honored Sir. the emperor Leo, of respected memory, attempted to cast the Vandals from Africa, but God did not support the attempt. It cost nearly a hundred thousand Roman lives at Cape Bon and the largest fleet ever assembled."

"Because their commander was a vainglorious fool and a political appointment." Narses' voice rose in anger to hear his monarch's ambition questioned. "I speak of duty, honored gentlemen. Take back Carthage and whoever commands His Serenity's army can then jump to Sicily where other Catholic people live under the barbarian heel. He can finish off the Goths in Sicily and from there sail to Italy and immortal fame."

Narses noticed a frown cross his master's face.

"But let us not get ahead of ourselves. Even if God forbids us Italy, it is a worthy goal to destroy a pirate lair and restore the wealth of Africa to our emperor's throne."

He made a gesture of diffidence toward the emperor and Justinian himself finished the presentation. "Let us not be concerned with the wealth of Africa, though that would certainly be useful to enrich our cities and bring glory to God. No, our mission is holy. My old friend, the rightful king of the Vandals, is being held in a dark prison and may be killed. In his absence the Catholic people are abused by heretics who lack Hilderic's gentle spirit. This is intolerable.

The military elite shuffled. "Our troops have just finished a difficult war with the Persians, Your Serenity." It was Sunica who spoke, not a man who had covered himself with glory. "Of course our Ephthalite mercenaries live to fight and without the spoils of battle are poor, but we cannot win with archers alone. Neither can we win a war with raw recruits. Our more experienced cataphracts are weary. They have homes and families here in the city. They want to rest. They believe they have earned a rest."

John the Cappadocian agreed. He chose his words carefully. Success would make him more wealthy or at least provide funds to cover his previous frauds; failure would reveal the relative inadequacy of the empire's treasury. There was cash enough for a limited expedition but Church buildings were expensive too; so too had been his own palace and his family's villas.

120

"Indeed they have earned a rest, brave soldiers that they are. Besides, Your Serenity, wars are expensive and it is far from certain that we can recover the cost even in total victory; of course, few victories are total. We should further build up our resources before risking what funds we already have. The farmers are taxed heavily now but we could squeeze a bit more from the large landowners of Thrace and Macedonia for the next few years. They have grown unduly rich of late. It would also be wise to make allies of seafarers rather than go to the expense of building a larger navy to transport an army." What John did not say was that an undue amount of tax revenue had been diverted to those who enriched themselves by his friendship. He certainly did not want the emperor looking too closely at that issue; there was money in the treasury, but not so much as there should have been considering the exactions he had made in the name of defending against the Persians.

"If you do decide to help your friend, do it with as modest forces as possible. The empire can disavow a few hundred Ephthalite archers under their own commander. Send arms to support the rebels in Tunis and Sardinia. Undermine Gelimer, but I recommend against attacking Carthage itself, until we are stronger and he is weaker. That way you may win much but if the venture should fail we will be able to absorb the loss."

The emperor seemed lost in thought, reconsidering his dream perhaps. But just then a bishop of Anatolia was escorted into the imperial conference. Why he was admitted and allowed to interrupt the discussion is not known, but Theodora and Antonina were seen to exchange glances.

"My Lord Emperor, Christ has told me that He will march before you in battle and make you sovereign of Africa." The prelate made no mention of restoring the rightful monarch to his throne but that detail seemed to pass unnoticed. Justinian turned his head and met the eyes of Belisarius. They would both have made excellent poker players. Belisarius had not yet shown where his opinion fell and Justinian was not yet ready to show whether John and the generals had diverted him from his grandiose plans.

"Belisarius?"

"Your Serenity, peace is the greatest treasure and I will never advise going to war for vainglory, but what has been said is also true. The Vandals hold our territory in Africa because they took it from our forebears, not out of any right or treaty. Yet they are unsatisfied. Gelimer allows pirates to prey on our merchants and that has caused prices here to increase, which harms our poorest citizens if not the wealthy who have their estates to fall back on. Rumor has it that he himself takes a part of their plunder. That is intolerable in a prince. I take no position as to whether that is sufficient cause for war; let those more experienced in such matters decide. Hilderic is rightful king; an Arian to be sure, but your friend. I and my soldiers will do as ordered. I am not a diplomat but from the strategic view, we know that in Africa we would have the support of the orthodox. The Catholic population is being abused under Gelimer and it seems to me they would support the empire.

"As for Sicily and Italy, I think Your Serenity can decide on the wisdom of fighting the Goths later. Africa is not simply a stepping stone to Sicily. It is valuable in its own right: rich in olive oil, fruit, and wheat. Furthermore, If we can break the power of the Vandal pirates and take their lair from them, trade will be encouraged. Then, we will not need so strong a navy and John will be right in advising against wasting money on one. I do think we have sufficient warships now to protect what transports will be needed if we keep the invasion force small, just so long as Gelimer remains ignorant of an invasion. Building up a greater fleet might give away our plan. We would certainly not want to repeat the horror at Cape Bon."

That settled it so far as the emperor was concerned. As for Theodora? She had reason to humor her husband's whim. In her whoring years she had worked her way across Egypt after being dumped by a minor official, and had fallen under the spell of the charismatic Timothy, a Monophysite patriarch of Alexandria. There she had found religion. Like Antonina, for awhile she'd lived in Alexandria, the heart of Monophysitism. So far as she cared at all, it was good that her husband's attention be diverted against the Arians in the west, leaving the Monophysites of Egypt to go about their lives without persecution. Although she publicly espoused the orthodox creed of Chalcedon, in her heart she was still sympathetic to the Monophysite teaching. Theodora had gone so far as to persuade Justinian of the wisdom of religious toleration in the east. He should attack the Arians in the west but tolerate Monophysites in Egypt where he really had no other choice anyway. The wheat fields of that province were needed to feed Constantinople; a Monophysite insurrection there would be infinitely harder to put down than the Nike insurrection, and the crop might be burned.

All this religious concern may have been smoke and mirrors however; to maintain a fiction that the emperor strongly supported the orthodox while allowing that his wife sympathized with their enemies. It would be just the sort of "Byzantine" subterfuge of which these rulers were entirely capable.

That night, Antonina was jumping with almost girlish delight. "Flavius, Theodora wants me to go with you to Africa. I want to go too. Your Mother and my daughter can watch Joannina for a few months. She'll be so happy."

"Theodora probably wants you to keep an eye on me. That's fine, sweet; our imperial couple doesn't trust anyone. I expected them to send spies; at least I'll know that you're one of them." Belisarius was holding his wife tightly but his face was that of a comrade, not a husband.

"But that's good, Flavius. It means that Theodora trusts me. But, anyway, that's not what she told me to do. She says I'm to help you with civil affairs. You'll be the military governor but we can work together. I think she's afraid that you're too military. You know: honor, discipline, that sort of thing."

"Africa needs a woman's touch?"

Antonina broke into a laugh. "Theodora sending me because I've a woman's touch? Not likely, mi-lord Belisarius. She wants someone who can get dirty."

Belisarius was still holding his wife but more tenderly now. They sat on their bed and Antonina began to undress. Belisarius looked at the floor for a long moment.

"Assuming, of course, that we win the war."

That thought took the joy out of what Antonina had only seen the best side of before. "*No man can serve two masters.*" Antonina considered the words of Jesus. Until now she had never given the saying much thought. "*Either he will hate the first and love the second or treat the first with respect and the second with scorn.*" The words were troubling. She owed Theodora and she loved Belisarius. She would do everything the empress required. She would do anything for Belisarius. He was the most important military leader in the empire, and now she was to be an important personage in her own right. She saw the dark side all too clearly now. Even if she never need oppose Belisarius, still Theodora might want her to do things on her own which her husband would never do. Until today Antonina would have been happy simply being Belisarius' wife. Why did the empress have to complicate it?

And what of little Joannina? Was neither Belisarius nor Antonina thinking of her? Wouldn't they miss her? Belisarius was a soldier who served at the emperor's pleasure. But now Antonina did too, just like a man.

It was the sixth century. Separations were as long and frequent as they were for British naval officers and crewmen in the eighteenth century.

Children of the nobility were raised by nursemaids. Those of ordinary citizens were bred to help with the work of home, farm, or shop, and to care for their parents when they became enfeebled - as they still are today in some parts of the world. Not to be too harsh, children were loved; but the world was different and raw. Most people lived on the edge of starvation which could easily happen when a crop failed. More children died than survived their first few years of life. Injuries left adults and children alike maimed. Joannina was actually blessed to have a grandmother nearby to comfort and spoil her; and, of course, to have Callista and Photius to play silly games with, and admire her toes. Anyway, Antonina expected to be separated for only a few months.

The army of the late Roman Empire traveled with a long tail of supply wagons, spare mounts and arms, religious articles, luxuries for the nobles; and with money changers and hangers-on of every description. The cataphracts brought servants with them and while a few brought their wives, most preferred the uncomplicated life of the single soldier. These employed washer women and errand boys, and at night might be found in the arms of some country wench of poor reputation. The less romantic simply chose a *whore de jure* from among the prostitutes who followed the army.

Justinian didn't like it. At Theodora's instigation he had issued laws restricting prostitution but to little avail. He and his wife had to content themselves with opening large safe houses in Constantinople and throughout the empire for girls who wanted to leave their pimps; reforming the soldiery was out of the question.

Belisarius was different from other officers. He looked forward to having his wife near him, though of course he was concerned how to keep her safely away from combat. Justinian was of a more mixed mind. He had once trusted Belisarius, now, at age fifty one, he trusted no one. It had been Theodora's idea to send Antonina with Belisarius; it would be good to have her loyal associate by his side. On the other hand, Antonina wouldn't be where Theodora could watch her. Justinian began to sweat when he considered that if Belisarius were to be very successful, he and the ambitious Antonina might connive to threaten the throne. They had already allowed it however, and anyway, who was to say to whom Antonina was more loyal: her husband, or her imperial mistress?

Justinian also had another concern. He had ordered each general to strictly obey Belisarius, though he worried about such strict obedience. Divided command weakened an army, but rivalry between commanders made it less likely that any one of them would turn rebel against him.

"Do not be overly concerned, general. So long as you allow me to supervise your investments you shall never suffer poverty. So long as you do your work I'll be able to do mine. Money always follows the successful man and I'm sure that His Serenity expects you to recoup your personal expenses."

Belisarius looked at his secretary with a certain regret. Though common enough even in ancient Rome, even then to admit to such means would have been thought despicable. But it was the way of sixth century Byzantium. There was never enough funding for an expedition but there would be loot from Vandal and Gothic treasuries afterward. Belisarius could barely live as military and court life required on his income alone and at the same time pay and maintain his bucellarii; no dignitary of the empire could or even tried to. The richer a man was the more he was expected to contribute, for public office was a duty of the wealthy; their only pay might be an annual robe of office received from the emperor. Such a theory of duty had been inherited from the empire of the caesars, but it was just that, a theory; and a theory honored in the breach as is clear from Cicero's orations against Verres. Every officer that Belisarius knew, good men and bad, used his position to enrich himself. The general might wish it otherwise but could not make it so. In time he would support seven thousand bucellarii plus the unpaid soldiers sent from Constantinople, plus hundreds of servants on his estates, priests and their churches, mills, workshops, and craftsmen.

"I will not have the common soldier defrauded." His voice was stern. "I will not see peasants impoverished." Then, his expression softened. "But I do not care what must be done to kings and princes or, for that matter, to jackals in Constantinople who enrich themselves at the empire's expense and mine." He paused. "And Procopius, I will expect no less of you."

Belisarius considered the matter closed; Procopius would see to his finances. He knew that he dare not look too closely at Procopius' "investments," but he had lain out the parameters. It would be the secretary's neck in a noose if he caused the general's reputation to be sullied, as was the Cappadocian's. Just the same, he would ask Antonina to keep an eye on Procopius' books. She understood something of the subterfuges that obscured sources of wealth, and her hard life had led her to distrust and suspect even apparently honorable men. She did not consider Procopius particularly honorable.

Maybe that was why that not long after Procopius and Antonina got to know each other they developed an abiding dislike. But there was more. Certainly Procopius could appreciate the grace that the one-time street walker had acquired since her days at the hippodrome, but his aristocratic sensitivity was appalled when, on occasion, she would instead enter a room filled with friends of Belisarius with an unladylike sway of her ass. Nor was such behavior always restricted to when her husband was present. The secretary found it disturbing and odd that when Belisarius was told of her flirting he was simply bemused.

CHAPTER 11

533-534 AD
CONSTANTINOPLE, LIBYA

Belisarius' home in Constantinople was not so much that of a soldier as that of a very wealthy aristocrat. The villa itself was a large rambling affair built of sturdy Roman brick and Greek marble. In the Roman tradition there were gardens that rivaled in splendor, if not in size, those of the Great Palace and these extended down to the sea walls. They were filled with statuary; not so grand as the works of ancient Greece that decorated the palace of the emperor, but nice Roman originals and fine Roman reproductions of ancient Greek originals. Little Joannina could usually be found exploring; crawling along the paths and playing with sticks while her big sister watched over her. There were public rooms for entertaining, a stable, and women's quarters in which Antonina could relax and chat with her servants. These women were a connection with the ordinary citizenry that the well-bred disdained, but a source of the scuttlebutt that Antonina relished

Yet when entering the general's study one knew immediately the life that the owner had chosen. The room was longer than it appeared, for some furniture effectively divided it into two areas of working space. One half held tables that were covered with maps. These and a few flowers were the only decorations in what would today be called a conference room. The other half was even more simple with only a long marble but unornamented desk, before which were a half dozen chairs. Again these were of fine quality, but of simple design. The south wall was entirely windowed. These were unglazed to allow plenty of sun in, but with retractable awnings to keep out the rain. There was a day bed along the north wall where Belisarius could rest while mulling over the details of a future campaign or his present life. He was now twenty eight. Soon enough he would no longer be seen as a bright and daring young commander. His hairline was receding just a bit. That was good. He had trained his mustache to have the fullness of an older man. Soon though, he would not want to appear any older than he was.

In this study Belisarius was looking out over the sea while considering where he could find mules and additional horses on the African coast as spares for his cavalry, when he was interrupted by an old servant and friend. The man was a Christian of sorts but of the Eunomian form which denied entirely the divinity of Christ, as the Monophysites denied his humanity. The man bowed more deeply than was necessary between comrades of many years. He wished a favor of the general and addressed his master in more formal terms than was usual between them in private.

"Illustrious sir." He hesitated and Belisarius became concerned.

"What is it. Are you in trouble? Or your wife? Is she well? Belisarius thought it better to offer help than to wait for his embarrassed friend to ask. Do you need money, my friend?"

"No general. I would never hesitate to ask your help for a good cause. Christlike, I have seen you open your purse even to strangers." He hesitated again. "It is my boy, Theodosius; he wishes to advance himself. He sees a future for himself in the army."

"Not unworthy. He'd like my help? To be honest though, I hardly know your son. I'll do what I can to give him a start, of course, but after that his future must be in his own hands. In the army lives depend on ability and I cannot endanger others even to help an old friend. You understand that?"

"Of course, General, but he's not asking more than your blessing. Would you attend his baptism? Theodosius has decided that it is not so important what one believes as how one acts. He is going to be baptised into your church. I expect he thinks his merits will be more readily appreciated if he shares the faith of his army comrades."

"And of his commanding officer, of course." A knowing grin spread across Belisarius' face.

"Of course. To be honest, I don't that much care myself; but I am too old a man to go changing the faith of my youth. Theodosius is only asking for your presence, but I would ask a further favor. Perhaps after he's baptised you could find him some minor position. It could be considered a baptismal gift. I believe in Theodosius, sir. He is intelligent and knows how to achieve what he sets himself to. If he just had a lift up. ...Well, after that he'll have to prove himself. I would not ask anything more of you."

"Fair enough. Tell me, how does he do in studies, sports, argument?"

"Excellently."

The two men spoke some more. They spoke for nearly an hour till it was time for the midday meal, for which Belisarius invited his servant to join him and Antonina. As they began to eat Belisarius sent a messenger to summon Theodosius. When the young man appeared Belisarius could immediately see that he might have potential. He was handsome but not dandified. He held himself erect and answered questions in a straightforward fashion, neither hesitating while trying to think of a "correct" answer nor trying to cover the ignorance of youth with bluster. "I think a little lift up is well merited," Belisarius whispered to his wife.

Antonina was also impressed. He might be a handsome and intelligent addition to her husband's retinue. It would be a fine thing to show their appreciation for the old attendant's years of service by tying his son to Belisarius with more than the usual simple favors. After dinner she spoke to Belisarius and suggested that he offer to be Theodosius' godfather. when the youth officially converted and was rebaptised into the Catholic faith.

Belisarius thought no more about the matter of Theodosius until the day of his baptism approached. The church required rebaptism for those who had already been baptised, but into heretical sects. The good fathers might disagree upon the necessity of this, but the salvation of souls suggested erring on the side of caution. In the case of Theodosius, moreover, few could accept that the young man could be considered to have been truly Christian when the Eunomians did not accept that Jesus Christ was God. That being so he would surely exit the baptistery an entirely new and sinless man.

Since Theodosius was a person of no social standing the ceremony was held at Rufinianae, away from the fuss and bother of Constantinople, and with only a few friends and witnesses. Still Belisarius and Antonina took seriously their responsibilities as the youth's new parents. Belisarius decided that in so far as Theodosius proved himself capable he would advance his "son."

Antonina particularly took her responsibility seriously, for her godchild had lost his natural mother many years before in an epidemic. Of course Theodosius was not a child but that did not mean that she should ignore him. She happily took the young man into her home and gave him the benefit of her many years of experience in the real world outside of palatial gates. "What the priests teach is all well and good," she said, somewhat echoing her own mother's attitude toward the clergy, "but let me tell you, you won't meet many saints in the army. Your godfather may be one. That's why I have to watch over and worry about him so much. Try to be a bit more practical than Belisarius. He is a good man ... a very good man, and a genius on the battlefield; but good men are the most easily taken advantage of."

On a spring day in 533 by the Gregorian calendar, the fleet which Justinian had gathered prepared to lift sail from just outside the emperor's own harbor in the Boucoleon district of Constantinople. A spectacle had been arranged in sight of the Great Palace. The Patriarch blessed the fleet and the recently baptised Theodosius was put aboard the flagship with some ceremony in trust that his sinless soul would attract Christ's blessing. Justinian himself blessed the brightly painted naval galleys as they passed in orderly rows, then waved with imperial dignity to the transports that passed under sail in a more disorderly, but nonetheless impressive, display. The fifteen thousand soldiers aboard waved at the crowd and raised their arms in formal salute when they passed their emperor.

From the stern castle of the flagship, Antonina waved to her daughter in the arms of her mother-in-law until they could no longer be distinguished. Once again she was leaving a child behind. Almost since Joannina's birth her mother's duties had allowed too little time with her. Theodora needed Antonina. She had come to rely on Antonina as much as anyone and felt that Antonina would be the perfect one to keep an eye on her husband's subordinates, lest any of them have ambitions which did not include the monarchs. Insofar as anyone can become accustomed to separation from family, Antonina had. She had left her first daughter Callista and her boy Photius, and now she was leaving Joannina. The only children that she hadn't left were the twins, whom death had taken from her. She tried not to dwell upon that, and god's hard-heartedness, but failed. At least she'd be with her husband, a real husband, and their baby would be safe in the arms of his mother, a good, wholesome, and anything but stupid woman. In the world of Byzantium, peasant women could raise their own children but court ladies were fortunate if they were able to raise their grandchildren.

While coasting the western Propontis (The Sea of Marmara) the transports were delayed for many days at Heraclea, while some ships which had been especially outfitted to carry horses took aboard several hundred Thracian mounts. This done, Archelaus, the Admiral in command of the sailors, set sail again. Soon he and Belisarius were deep in conversation on the after castle, leaving Antonina with nothing to do. The day was clear and the sea was calm, so she chose to forgo lying in the hot cabin like a proper wife and relax on the fore castle of the flagship, a bireme of one hundred fifty oars, and enjoy the sight of the swarthy, sweating, near naked soldiers pulling at the upper bank of oars. It looked so easy for them; she would hardly have been able to move a dromon's oar, much less do so all day long and with such grace. She looked down on them and they looked up at her. Nothing on their faces betrayed any particular thoughts. Antonina kept hers to herself but did not pretend disinterest. The strength of all those men, their muscles flexing and relaxing, chests heaving in and out… *impressive!* She'd play a little game with herself. *Belisarius is deep in conversation, he won't know. It is just a brain game anyway, no more. Which is the prettiest? Not any of the old guys; every one of them has scars. Not that young boy either.* She smiled to think: *Why he's only working on his first beard. He looks as hard as any of the others though. Slim, strong as any of the others too. Nice strong bronze legs, not too dark yet. No, Antonina. Stop, he's still a boy. Probably not much older than Photius.* Having been reminded of her son, still studying at the palace school, Antonina forced herself to stop daydreaming. But it had been fun. She wasn't sure she'd ever stop looking at the other sex just for the fun of it. But then, why should she? Men didn't.

The first days actually crossing the Propontis were pleasant for all. There was little to be done except to enjoy the fine weather and eat the fresh fruit aboard the ships before it could spoil. Belisarius and Archelaus spent many hours discussing the mission. Belisarius wanted to learn all he could of what he might expect on the African shore. Not a man to waste an opportunity, he also set himself to learning something of seamanship from the admiral while sizing up the man himself. Belisarius thought it of utmost importance that he know exactly how other commanders and subordinates could be expected to act in his absence.

"Have you had enough of ogling handsome sailors, Antonina?" Belisarius had crept up behind his wife.

"No, I'm watching our young man on the second bench."

"Theodosius? He's still in training as a cataphract but for now I want to keep my eye on him. A little rowing will build muscle and give a rest to someone who doesn't need the exercise. Cavalry shouldn't be too proud to share in real work. At Dara I had them digging ditches."

"Um, yes. Do you mind if I talk with him? I don't think the other rowers know that we're related in Christ. This could be fun if he plays along." If a voice could wink hers did.

"I don't think I need worry." Belisarius spoke in an airy way. He meant it. The truth is, he rather liked that Antonina flirted quite a bit more than was considered proper. After all, if she'd been more proper they'd never have met, much less married. He'd be wed to some boring patrician. Their little daughter simply wouldn't be. Of course he'd have kids by someone else and he'd love them just as much; but they wouldn't be his sweet Joannina.

"Hi, your name's Theodosius, isn't it?" Antonina walked just past her godson and stopped. There had always been a slight twitch to her rump when Antonina walked. It wasn't part of a whore walk, just something cute that nature had provided her even as a child. Now she turned back to him.

"Yes, mi-lady Antonina." Clearly, Theodosius had grasped what the lady was about and would play it for the tease intended.

"Do you like the wines of Chios, Theodosius?" Antonina was smiling a curious smile, bright but almost innocent. Almost.

"Indeed yes, mi-lady Antonina."

"Then we must share a cup one day." Antonina slowly turned and continued walking the plank between the sweating oarsmen, twitching. The other rowers, who indeed knew nothing of Theodosius' connection to their commander's family, just stared at him; those who could drag their eyes off Antonina's ass.

Soon enough the other troops learned that Theodosius, Belisarius, and Antonina were related in Christ and that knowledge put an end to whatever ribald speculation Antonina had encouraged. But for days it gave the men something to talk about and that had helped to pass the time. Now they ribbed the young man mercilessly about being related to the boss.

There were other things about Antonina that the crew did not suspect. When ashore Antonina would put on something sheer and sexy at night and lie on the darkened beach till her husband came looking for her. She would be his mistress of the night when his day had been long and dull. She would playfully scold him or spank him under the stars. Belisarius much lamented that there wasn't sufficient privacy for that at sea.

The ships continued south to the Dardanelles, which they passed under sail since regular winds and a tide flowing from the Black Sea always assure swift passage southbound. The sailors were glad of it for they wanted to rest before entering Homer's wine-dark Aegean, which was as regularly troubled by storms then as it had been in the poet's time. Since their ships were not much bigger or more seaworthy than Agamemnon's, rounding the Peloponnese would be a chore.

At Abydos, just before the Dardanelles flows into the Aegean, Belisarius stopped for a few days. Now it is clear from many incidents that Belisarius, though the noblest and kindest of men, was both just and firm when it came to discipline. At Abydos two Ephthalite Huns killed one of their comrades in a drunken fight over some matter of no importance. He ordered the murderers executed despite the general tenor of the time among barbarians to settle such matters by a payment of blood money to the victim's family. All, including his own bucellarii and Antonina too, expected nothing else. There was mumbling and angry threats among the foederati. His junior officers were reluctant to enforce discipline, but Belisarius was determined. If, as he told his wife, this mission was in a good cause and to be blessed by God, then his men must behave in a manner acceptable to Christ, the ruler of all. He addressed the angry foederati in person and without guards. "Those," he said, "who allow a murder to go unpunished are accomplices to it. Those who are intemperate with drink are in breech of discipline and endanger the whole army. I will acknowledge no man my comrade who cannot march beside me with pure and unpolluted hands. We march to restore our emperor's friend and the rightful heir to the Vandal throne. Under Hilderic, God willing, Africa will again take its rightful place as a loyal ally of our holy emperor's realm, but only if we are worthy of it."

Antonina did not entirely share her husband's scruples, nor his faith that the All Mighty would necessarily favor a pure and holy army set upon conquest. But she did recognize the charisma which was his greatest asset after his intellect. Was it not that which had won her to him? *Won me for him? Antonina you are getting far too self important. The greatest general of the empire did not have to "win" you to himself, you tramp.* For a moment she hesitated in her self-admonition. *Though he did reel me in like a fish when he wanted me; not that I put up much of a fight, any fight.* She smiled, put aside recurring thoughts of the young men restocking supplies, and considered fondly her soldier-husband.

When they put to sea again the transports carried fifteen thousand cataphracts, infantry, and archers, plus the cataphracts' war horses. It was Belisarius' concern that they not be separated from the galleys whose purpose it would be to protect them from any Vandal attack when they neared the African coast. Meanwhile they should stay in close order whatever the weather, lest any be lost to storms or just poor seamanship. After all, not all the captains had navigated the western Mediterranean or even out of sight of land. None had ever sailed the pirate infested coast of Africa. At Abydos Belisarius had suggested to the admiral that the lead galley and two others have their sails clearly painted, so that the following captains could see the direction to go. When later they would have to travel at night, the admiral himself suggested that lanterns be raised to all the mastheads for the same reason.

Yet all went well so far as the sea was concerned. The many islands of the Aegean provided frequent harbors for the ships, fodder for the horses, and a chance to relax for the men. The younger ones would play ball games while the older were content to eyeball the local girls.

At last the fleet reached the Peloponnese and rounded Cape Matapan, within easy sight of an ancient temple that had been built to mark the gates of Hades. A few sailors still believed that, but the temple was now a Christian church and that deflected much of the ancient sense of horror. Even so, it was not a beautiful place. The lonely little village around the church was on a good harbor but the naked hills behind could produce little. For all that, it was a pleasant sight in the sun and the sea around them was filled with small boats. Some carried fishermen intent to let their sons view the parade of Byzantine power. Others brought fresh fruit. Each ship captain would buy some oranges for his men to supplement the dried dates they had carried from Constantinople.

Antonina turned away as Matapan finally slipped out of sight behind them. The placid sea reflected the sun, forcing her to squint in a rather unattractive way. The gold accents and brass fittings of imperial warships reflected it also. From here on it was more important than ever that the fleet not be detected; in a few days they would enter the Mediterranean proper.

On the southwest coast of the Peloponnese, they put into Methone for a brief layover before entering the unknown waters of the western Mediterranean. The admiral wisely used the time to gather information from local captains, while Belisarius took the opportunity to exercise the horses and review all his troops together. Like Eisenhower fifteen hundred years later, he held it vital that as many of his men as possible see the person who would order them into battle. Of the imperial cavalry many had been farm laborers until six months before. They had rarely seen him. Even many of his own bucellarii were recruits who barely knew him, save by reputation. Only his Heruli Swedes and the Ephthalite Hun brigades of mounted archers were composed entirely of veterans of the Persian campaign unencumbered by raw recruits.

This was not like Dara. At Dara Belisarius had been able to spend some hours each day with the young men while they trained. At the battle he'd stood with his infantry. They knew him and he knew them. They had gained steadiness from his own. He'd known, and they'd known, that at any moment he might be killed, but there are things that make such knowledge and the fear it engenders tolerable. For Belisarius, duty to the empire was more important than life; the boys of Dara had learned that from him and gained the strength to follow their own duty to their own kinfolk and city.

This was entirely different. Even the cause was not entirely convincing. They were being sent to fight for the oppressed orthodox Catholics of Africa. Fine; but then why were they also to restore an Arian monarch there? They had little sense of purpose to offset their fear.

134

And there was worse. How was Belisarius to motivate his men if Constantinople didn't give a damn about them? Ship's biscuit, insufficiently baked under the supervision of the Cappadocian, had turned moldy in the summer sun. Then dysentery and the humors of the season swept through his troopers killing five hundred; he would fight major battles with fewer casualties. Nothing could be done about disease except to separate the sick from the healthy, but he bought locally baked bread with his own money. He angrily wrote to Justinian demanding that John be held responsible and dispatched a swift cutter to Constantinople.

In the capital the Cappadocian was offhanded about the loss and simply brought plans for another new church in Thessaloniki to Justinian. He laid the blame for the deaths on the heat and suggested that Belisarius had probably taken insufficient measures to prevent the spread of disease. Justinian knew that such advice was self serving and that he should punish John.

"Execute him," Theodora was ranting, as she always did when the subject of the Cappadocian came up. "This is a fine excuse to be rid of the creep."

"And who would replace him," Justinian asked? Theodora had no ready answer. She hated the Cappadocian and feared his ambition. Dare Justinian antagonize all John's minions in the palace and in the provinces, all of whom shared in his embezzlement? If John were to be executed, there would not suddenly be a loyal and dedicated revenue service. There would, however, be fear, and fear is a strong motivating force for rebellion.

The finance minister was merely rebuked. Justinian would not delay his building projects. John was crooked and a creep but he needed the creep.

Everyone in the fleet was glad to put to sea and leave Methone in their wake, but soon there was grumbling. It was hot. They had been unable to purchase many pigs or goats to supply fresh meat aboard ship. There was little breeze to fill the sails of the troop ships as they approached barbarian waters. Belisarius had a problem. The men were angry and bored, and fearful of having to fight a naval battle like that which had decimated the Romans at Cape Bon. He tried to keep them occupied with training but the lady Antonina, who had not forgotten how to please dispirited soldiers, had a better idea:

"Lighten up, Flavius. Wouldn't the men be more relaxed and confident if they were to see me more? After all, if a frail and helpless female is not afraid, why should they be? I can make training a game for them. The best team of archers will win the favor of the general's wife. Your lady will share a cup of soldiers' wine with them... or several cups."

Belisarius understood the wisdom of what she said. His officers could make games of training, on occasion and in a limited way, but it was a coarse matter: an amphora of wine or some coins for the victorious teams. But being cheered by a nice female was more fun. Of course not just any woman could play that part. In one of her better moods, if the empress were inclined to lay aside her imperial dignity, she would have been able to. But she was not there. Nor, had she been there, would she likely have been so inclined. Antonina was.

On the seventh day out of Methone they put her plan to work. The flagship towed an empty keg behind it and archers on paired transports fired at it. The first pair failed to hit the target even once which raised hoots of derision throughout the fleet. The second pair did no better, nor did the third. Even the veterans discovered that hitting a bobbing target from a ship which is itself heaving with the action of the waves is no easy matter. Even the excellent Ephthalite archers mostly failed and they were used to letting arrows fly from the backs of galloping horses. Those few who did hit the keg declined Antonina's offer with effusive Asian grace, lest the Greek soldiers deem it unsuitable for barbarian mercenaries to share wine with a cubicularia of their empress. It was not till they skirted well south of the Italian boot that Antonina would enjoy a cup with a company of Thracian cataphracts.

Before that happy day the drinking water went bad. Spoiled water was a matter for which the Cappadocian was not responsible; the fine weather which accompanied the expedition was the culprit. There was no rain to replace stale insect-infested water. But if Belisarius were to put into a port west of the Peloponnese to replenish, word of it would surely reach Gelimer destroying any chance the Romans might have of surprising him. That a fleet with fifteen thousand fighting men plus their auxiliaries had sailed from the capital could not be kept a secret of course, but its destination could be. After all, Justinian might be intending to finish off the Persians once and for all by a surprise naval expedition via Crete and Cyprus. He might be aiming at the Goths of southern Italy, or attempting to take a piece of property from the north. Belisarius might, of course, be aiming for the Vandal kingdom - but if that were so where would he strike? Carthage was well defended; what could so few men do against it? Tripoli might be his target, for Justinian had already been encouraging dissidents there. Or he might be sailing in support of the rebels in Sardinia. Anyway, it were better for Belisarius not to put into any port and risk word of his actual destination leaking out. To use a slogan from a later war: "Loose lips sink ships." Hopefully rain would come tomorrow, or the next day to refill the water barrels.

Belisarius himself did not seem to suffer. The crew of his flagship only saw him relaxed and tanning himself. Antonina was responsible for that. She had learned the secret of keeping things cool when traversing the Dardanelles with Senator Appius. At Methone she had foreseen the possibility of bad water and had stashed many sealed jugs of fresh water from a clean stream in the cool sand ballast below decks. These she intended for the personal consumption of her husband and his immediate party. There was not enough to share with the fleet but Belisarius knew that he above all could not afford to be taken ill. He did watch for signs of exhaustion or disease among the crews, and every few days consulted with the captains of his other vessels. He made nearly nightly visits to one ship or another to observe the condition of the soldiers. There was another reason for these visits: Hopefully the new men would form as good an impression of their commander as the veterans already had. That would be worth a regiment when battle was joined. In his cabin, the general prayed that their trust would not prove misplaced.

Antonina was relaxing at the rail of the after castle. A light breeze was coming up and the rowers below her knew that soon they would be able to relax and let the wind do all the work.

The greatest military commander of his age never quite understood that women were not just soft men. Certainly Antonina understood her husband better than he did her and could think like a man, whereas Belisarius could never begin to think like a woman. Now it is an old superstition of the sea not to bring women aboard ship. There is reason behind it. Although Antonina's presence had the desired effect of relaxing the men, the very female wittiness which made her popular was a distraction. Worse, no two men saw her in exactly the same light, and that had a potential to cause friction where unity was of utmost importance. Two who watched where Belisarius was blind were his chief of staff, the domesticus Solomon, and his secretary, Procopius. Solomon worried that three months at sea with a rough and lonely crew might compromise Antonina's reputation, if not her actual honor; whereas Procopius encouraged her fraternization. Antonina, herself, did not seem to care if her respectability might be fading with each sunset. Certainly there was no place aboard a fighting galley for her to actually cheat, so why should anyone take it amiss if she flirted a bit with the rowers? It gave morale a boost and she knew that Belisarius trusted her as she did him. Actually, it did not really trouble Antonina whether Belisarius would always be faithful so long as he would always love her. *Men are just rutting bulls*, she had learned in the hippodrome, and it did not bother her.

Her husband and Procopius were in the tiny cabin. "Your lady is much beloved by the troops, Belisarius." Procopius could not directly attack his master's spouse but he could begin to imply that he was a truer friend. A Roman wife enjoyed considerable freedom, but there were limits. A Roman whore could act more freely and Antonina did. She might even flirt with a godson. That there was still much of the whore about Antonina was clear to Belisarius' secretary. He did not think it proper, morally right, or fitting in a commander's wife; neither, he told himself, should the general.

Later that night Belisarius and Antonina were enjoying a fresh-caught pickerel with a bit of spice from the admiral's cupboard and lemon from Methone. "Flavius, you should talk with Theodosius more.He has a quick mind even though his formal education is limited. He knows all the details of the Persian war and something of every Roman campaign of any importance ever. He has read Caesar and Thucydides and Xenophon. Maybe one of his teachers had a taste for history that went beyond the Old Testament and the church fathers."

There was no conniving behind Antonina's words, but she had begun to feel a fondness towards her new son that went beyond the attention one might expect from a godparent. He was intelligent and gentle. He had a high humor which her husband did not. For all his fine qualities, no one would have called Belisarius lighthearted. If she could advance Theodosius in her husband's estimation, she would. That was all. Nonetheless, Procopius had sensed the attraction which the wife of his commander felt for the vivacious young cataphract. That knowledge might be useful one day.

After Belisarius had observed Theodosius in shipboard training with his comrades and had interviewed him in much the way he would have interviewed any young trooper assigned to his command, he decided that Theodosius might have ability and a fine grasp of detail for one so young. He was not so sure of his capability with weapons. Boys like him had a tendency to not survive their first battles and that would be a pity. It was a pity, he reminded himself, when any mother's son died. But that happened in war as it did in many other dangerous occupations, only more often. Still,

138

he could justify removing Theodosius from some of the danger before them, for he could use an intelligent and absolutely loyal staff office; more than a cataphract of uncertain value in battle. Working with his command team would educate Theodosius and make him the more useful. He was assigned to the commissariat with the understanding that he would also closely observe the strategy discussions of the officers. Solomon was uneasy but said nothing - for there was nothing concrete to be concerned about. Theodosius worked well with others and was a fine young man, with a fine future before him if the right people were impressed. Still, there was something Solomon did not like, though not about the young man himself. It was the warm atmosphere in the lead dromon that was disturbing. Friendship between staff members is a good thing in war, even necessary; but duty and determination were what he liked to feel in the general's cabin, not lighthearted humor and chatting about books.

The entire voyage, Constantinople to Carthage, took three months. Desirous of maintaining secrecy, once past the Peloponnese the fleet sailed both day and night out of sight of land across the Mediterranean. Belisarius made only one more stop, but an unavoidable and important one.

When their king had murdered Amalafrida and her Gothic guards, the Vandals had lost the support of their fellow Germans, the Goths of Italy. Unaware that conquering their kingdom was also on Justinian's mind, these Goths had secretly offered the emperor facilities to replenish and resupply Belisarius in Sicily, most of which was also under their control. Belisarius replenished while giving his troops and their frightened horses some rest and relaxation. He also purchased five hundred fresh mounts and sent the civilian looking Procopius to spy out Syracuse in a part of the island held by Vandals.

It was by pure luck or the will of heaven that Procopius met an old friend in Syracuse, the servant of a tradesman who had only just arrived from Carthage. From him Procopius learned that the element of surprise was entirely theirs, for Gelimer was so ignorant of the planned invasion that he had sent his brother Zazo to put down the rebellion in Sardinia. Gelimer, himself, had left Carthage to spend the summer in the more pleasant retreat of Hermione.

The Vandals had lost their best chance to defeat the Romans by failing to intercept Belisarius at sea. The galleys accompanying the Roman expedition would have been sufficient to battle a pirate squadron, but had

Gelimer committed the full Vandal fleet the outnumbered imperial dromons would have been no match for it. Belisarius' greatest concern was not that his army was a third the size of Gelimer's, nor that so many of his troops were untried in battle; it was fear of having to fight a naval engagement. A Vandal fleet had decimated Leo's far larger force when it had attacked them sixty five years before; this time it would be the Romans who were outnumbered. Dread of again meeting the Vandals at sea so paralyzed his soldiers that they made no secret that they would force the transports to retreat before a squadron of enemy warships. Fear is a powerful master. These same troops loudly proclaimed their willingness to face the same enemy ashore, but for a naval action they were intimidated as by a phobia.

Belisarius made no effort to persuade the unpersuadable. He would not fight a fight that was lost before it began. Had they met a Vandal fleet, he would have retreated. He could not say so to the troops himself, but Antonina could hint at that when playing dice with some Thracian or Anatolian cataphracts.

The good intelligence which Procopius procured in Syracuse meant one thing above all else. The Vandals were entirely unprepared. Belisarius must hurry to Africa before the news of his arrival in Sicily reached Gelimer and awoke the vacationing monarch to the danger to his throne. In three days the business of replenishing his ships and loading the Sicilian horses was accomplished, and Archelaus ordered the fleet to sea. The lazy days of resting under the sun were over. Cataphracts honed their spathions, the longer cavalry swords which had long ago replaced the short Roman gladius. That had been a fine weapon for infantry in tight formation on open ground but worthless for a mounted man. Solomon redoubled physical training, Kinks needed to be worked out and tendons stretched. For the few days it took to reach the African shore the wind remained fresh. In the evenings Sicilian beef and pork were a welcome reward. The army almost looked forward to the bloody business before it.

All these things occupied the men aboard the flagship and Antonina was beginning to feel very much like supercargo. One of the men would wave to her occasionally and she would return the wave with a smile, but there was really nothing for her to do. This was certainly not a time for lighthearted teasing. Procopius kept busy confiding in a diary, explaining that if all went well - as surely it must - then one day, when he wrote his book about the exploits of Belisarius, he would be able to enliven it with army tidbits and local color as only an author who had been present could. Persia had been a start. He had confidence that Africa would be taken, and then if God should smile on Justinian's ambition, surely Belisarius was the man who would be entrusted with recovering Italy.

Procopius also was good enough to help the more illiterate soldiers write down their bequests and compose a final letter home, a dreary business, but realistic. Belisarius, himself, stayed mostly to his cabin conversing with each troop commander and often with several at a time to reassure himself of their ability and absolute loyalty to the overall mission. No officer was to trust his own judgment above his or go it alone in any way. That had caused the loss of innumerable battles for the empire. Belisarius would remind them that Justinian had raised him to the long dormant rank of strategos autocrator, the Greek equivalent of imperator. That was the title which Julius Caesar had held and the term from which the title of emperor itself derived. He would then read Justinian's admonition on the subject. Disobedience would mean death. "Talk freely to me of your doubts and suggestions. I need to hear them; but we must have unity in the face of the enemy. No, I am not always right, but above all else we must retain unity and not have each brigade leader free to do whatever he thinks best from where he sees the battle. I alone answer to His Sovereignty."

It was not only ensuring his single command that concerned Belisarius. His orders regarding behavior were stern. "We have come to Africa as liberators; see that the men behave appropriately. I will hang any man found guilty of murder or rape. I will scourge anyone who is found looting. We are far from home. We must retain the loyalty of the Catholics, assure the Berbers of our good will, and show the Vandals by our deeds that we do not mean to dispossess them of any property they have fairly acquired. Every Vandal that we can detach from Gelimer will be one less knife in the night that we must guard against when occupying this land. Do you understand me?" Belisarius did not raise his voice but he would stare at each uncomfortable commander until he accented with a firm "Yes, Sir." Only then would Belisarius smile broadly and turn to making chit chat about wives and children and home. Finally, before dismissing them, the general would order some good wine brought, grin an Eisenhower grin, and often suggest playing the strategy game of latrunculi with a small wager to make it more interesting.

Though Antonina had no part in these manly affairs, both she and her godson did listen and begin to understand the problems of command. Her husband must fight not only the enemy but the ambition and pride of his own lieutenants. It was unavoidable. Justinian had issued strict orders that Belisarius alone commanded. But that had little weight on a far off shore, where each chieftain was either the warlord of some foederati allies or, if a Roman, an aristocrat with cataphracts loyal to him alone. He'd also have friends at court and Justinian was weak and vacillating. Antonina did help in a way her husband could not however. Though Justinian was vacillating and might excuse disobedience to orders regardless of anything he had said before, Theodora was vengeful. Antonina was known to be Theodora's closest friend and confident. She made sure that was not far from any troop commander's thoughts by the simple expedient of chatting about the empress every time she entertained.

She chatted about others at court, of course being careful to aim her darts only at courtiers with a sense of humor or those already sliding out of favor. She detested the Cappadocian and showed it; that didn't matter, everyone hated John. With one hand he paid the soldiers; while with the other he took back their pay as taxes. No one likes landlords either so landlords were a safe subject for vulgar humor. More than a few of the troops under Belisarius' command had enlisted because they could not keep up the rent on a family home. Justinian was taxing the landlords heavily but, bitch as they might, the burden fell on the tenant farmers, not so much on their lords. These spent their days idling about Constantinople in rich dalmatics, pretending to pay attention at church services, and trying to devour each other.

Of all those around the throne the one that Antonina absolutely refused to mock was the eunuch Narses. One could never be sure when he spoke if it were for himself, or if he were publicizing the imperial duo's thoughts and intentions; a very dangerous man and not a man to make an enemy of. *Some day I must prove my usefulness to him,* Antonina thought. *He is surely no one's true friend, but we don't want him for an enemy either.*

Could she make fun of Justinian's religious zeal? He had been trying to find a solution to the myriad disputes. The result was that he was hated by all sides and sneered at behind his imperial back as an amateur theologian who should mind the business of governing and stay away from matters he was untrained to comment on. *No,* Antonina told herself. *Better not to say anything that might get back to him.*

But dare she make fun of the high clergy? Why not? They were rich and the soldiers were poor. One patriarch after another succeeded each other on the patriarchal throne. Some of these were orthodox believers in the formulas of Chalcedon. Some had Monophysite, Arian, Semi-monophysite, Nestorian, Penlagian, and a half dozen variant sympathies. Some were hard nosed while others were compromisers. It was the last who were most bitterly hated both by the orthodox monks of the capital and riotous Monophysite believers in the east. They were all accused of heresy at one time or another by one group or another. It made Antonina's head swim. True, she had Monophysite leanings herself, learned from her former consort Antonius, but she did not hold to them fanatically as it was thought Theodora might. Antonina had been close to the empress in Constantinople yet she did not know Theodora's true beliefs, if she held any. It was suspected that even her husband, the emperor, didn't.

At last the fleet arrived near to the African coast and Belisarius called his last war council at sea. The question at issue was where to land his force. Archelaus, who commanded the whole fleet including the horse transports and supply ships, was therefore in charge of the commissariat. He argued for a direct attack on Carthage. They could hope to surprise the garrison there and quickly occupy the only fortified city on that coast. Belisarius did not overrule him but put before the captains the reasons that he wished to make a slower passage to the capital by land on an old Roman road which paralleled the coastline. Archelaus had argued that if the fleet carrying their provisions and spare arms were to accompany the army on a 160 mile march along the coast, a storm could decimated it entirely or at the least force it to flee to sea. He was in charge of provisioning the army but in such circumstances he would be unable to do so. If attacked by the larger Vandal army the Roman force could not even be evacuated, for its back would be to an empty ocean.

Now Belisarius presented his own plan: "Officers, what indeed is our mission? It is to destroy Gelimer's power. That cannot be done by seizing a city where neither he nor his army are. When his army is destroyed then Carthage will easily fall. Should we choose to attack the city before neutralizing Gelimer, what will we have gained except some walls to hide behind? And if the Vandal fleet should intercept us at sea before we reach the city, our own soldiers have said they will not fight. I do not charge them with cowardice or disobedience to orders, for they have told us that they cannot win. Most of the infantry are inclined to sea sickness in heavy weather; all are afraid of fighting against an enemy far more accustomed than we are to naval warfare, and with warships far outnumbering our galleys. In such a fight our archers would score some hits, of course, but there would be too many targets. Cataphracts and infantry would be useless. In fact our few galleys would be hard pressed to protect them. The Vandals have so many warships that some of them would be able to entangle with ours while others slaughtered the transports. It would be like Cape Bon all over again. Gentlemen, It is not how many days march we are from Carthage which matters, for that is not our goal. To protect it must, however, be Gelimer's. We will march slowly and get our land legs ... give the horses time to recover. We will fortify our camp each night just as the old legions did. Gelimer will have to attack us and then we will have him. His army is larger than ours but all cavalry. The Vandals disdain infantry and I saw in Persia that infantry is not to be disdained. He has few archers and we have the world's best." Belisarius grinned and made a gesture toward the Ephthalite commander.

In the end all agreed with Belisarius. "Persuasion trumps dictating," he would have said, had card games been popular in Byzantium.

The landing began the very morning after sighting land and before any local defenders could gather to repel the Byzantines at the beach. Antonina watched from the flagship as the galleys came close to shore so that the archers and infantry could debark into shallow water. Then the galleys turned away toward the open sea again. Next the transports with their load of cataphracts drew as close as possible. This was the most vulnerable moment. The cataphracts carried only swords, leaving behind their armor and other arms. For once they were the weakest military arm and would have to be protected by those infantry and archers already on the beach. They came ashore in small boats because the transports' draft was too much for shallow water. The cataphracts' beloved horses would be offloaded last and made to swim ashore.

The force had landed near the village of Caput Vada, an unfortified place. Many years before, the Vandals had torn down all the fortresses between Tripoli and Carthage in fear that a Roman army might occupy them. When a Roman attack finally did come in the reign of Leo it had been directed at Carthage itself, one of the only two remaining walled cities, and had failed before even one boot could be put ashore.

The people of Caput Vada were mostly Catholics who welcomed the army as liberators. The few Vandals made haste to leave, in order to save their lives and to warn Gelimer. That was actually good. Belisarius knew that intelligence gathered from civilians usually exaggerated an enemy's strength. He watched as his troops threw up a defensive line essentially the same as Julius Caesar would have: a square trench before an earthen rampart that enclosed the camp. It was hard work but at least the African sun was setting. They would do the same thing after every day's march just as Caesar's legionaries had.

Only when the day's work was completed did the general spare a few minutes for Antonina. They ate their evening meal together. Then Belisarius called Procopius into his quarters and dictated a brief dispatch to be sent by fast galley to the emperor and people of Constantinople. It was simple and forthright.

The first day of September in the 1285th year since the founding of the city of Rome and 533 years after the birth of Our Savior.
An unopposed landing was made this morning on the African coast 160 miles east of Carthage.
Belisarius

Along with Belisarius' brief message, Antonina sent a slightly longer letter to his mother.

Most honored mother:
Yesterday we landed in Africa. I'm so sorry that I did not write to you during our voyage but as you probably know we could not risk some Vandal pirate finding a letter from me on board a ship heading home. I haven't much to write anyway. The trip here was sometimes very bad. We ran out of fresh water while in the Mediterranean. But at other times it was a pleasant, almost dreamy, trip when there was a good breeze and nothing for the men to do but relax. Our godson has learned to row and I've had fun cavorting with the soldiers, all of whom are terrified that Flavius will not like it. They don't know that he thinks a little female banter is good for morale, and it passes the time for me as well as them. Soon enough they will have no time for silly games. In a few days we will begin the march on Carthage and after that I'll be happy to go home to our little Joannina.
I hope she is well. Do not let the old nursemaids around the palace keep the poor thing bundled up in warm weather. My own mother thought that was not good for babies. She believes in fresh air and letting them have plenty of exercise and I grew up strong and healthy. I'm sending a little souvenir for her from the local marketplace. It is a pottery figurine of a Vandal lord on horseback. I'm pretty sure that within a few days they'll be selling images of our cataphracts, just changing the markings a little. Did I ever tell you that I thought of opening a pottery shop before I met Flavius. How lucky I have been. I think the local artists will also be selling charcoal sketches of your son soon, and I'll have one nicely framed and sent to you when they do. I've seen some pretty bad Berber "art" here but I'll see that it isn't some gaudy scene of him riding triumphant over enemy bodies with women and children begging his forbearance.
Please excuse me if I don't write regularly for I cannot know what

will happen day to day. Do not think things are going badly if we do not write as Flavius tells me that we may be pursuing the enemy all day for weeks as he did in Mesopotamia. If so, it will not be easy to get letters onto a ship going to Constantinople.

Please have a copy of this note sent to my Ma. Hug my little girl for me and tell her that momma and daddy will be home soon; and when we come home we'll have a big party with her and uncle Photius.

Give our love and prayers to Ildiger and Callista.

Antonina.

Before sleep that night the exhausted commander thought for a moment of the words of Christ: "Take therefore no thought for the morrow for the morrow shall take care of itself." Obeying his Lord, he lay down and in a moment was asleep. Antonina, on the other hand, was wide awake, once again on a beach and feeling quite useless. It was several hours before she too fell asleep. When she awoke Belisarius was already gone from the comfortable bed which Procopius had obtained for them nearly immediately upon occupying the town. The sun was not yet up but the sky was lightening. Some small boats were landing from the transports, carrying with them items not immediately needed. Those things of most importance: arms, armor, and food, had been dropped off on the beach the first day or under moonlight. *Perhaps*, Antonina thought, *I might be of some use today.* She slipped back inside her tent to retrieve a heavy cloak, for the night air was still cool as nights so near a desert can be. For a moment she thought of how many nights she had spent in or near some gawd-awful desert: at Alexandria and Antioch and now on the Libyan shore.

She strolled between the rows of tents but when she tried to reach the beach through a north facing portal in the earthen rampart a sentry politely refused her exit. She was not to leave, not even to simply watch the unloading. The area had not yet been entirely secured.

Antonina looked around her. *Sand, just sand.* "Do you see a Vandal horde descending on us at full gallop? Who issued the order?" There was a bit of anger in her voice.

"The general," was the reply.

Now Antonina was more than just put out. She was pissed. *I've not been floating around on a big row boat for three months just to be shut up in a tent like some Arab broad.* Of course there was nothing to be done about it. The sentry had orders from the sole commander and he would prevent her exiting, by force if necessary; and Belisarius would approve it if he did. She could see her husband talking with Solomon on the beach that

146

had been forbidden to her. They seemed engaged in watching the unloading, not that it was necessary. Belisarius was a good soldier. He had good subordinates who were all experienced fighting men. Even if they'd never had to make a landing on a potentially hostile shore before, they knew what they were about. Belisarius had approved the logistical details weeks before. All he had to do, or could do, now was watch the preparations play out smoothly. Any minor snafu would quickly be righted by some subordinate.

Antonina climbed atop the earthen parapet and waved. Solomon waved back, as did Theodosius, whose commissariat duties made his presence on the beach necessary. She envied him. Finally she caught her husband's eye and gestured for him to come over. He only waved in reply and quickly returned to discussing with Solomon whatever they had been discussing. He was in his element and no matter how much he loved her, there was no place in it for Antonina. She understood; but still, she was pissed.

The march along the coastal road took fourteen days. Each night the army constructed a camp protected by earthen ramparts and each morning it was torn down to deny it to the enemy. Sometimes they could make only nine miles per day, sometimes twelve, but Belisarius was in no hurry to reach Carthage. He intended to destroy Gelimer's army before reaching the capital. They stopped frequently in seaside villages to assure the locals of their good will. There was only one violation by the soldiers and that a petty one - no more than was to be expected of any passing army, less in fact. On their second day in Africa a few soldiers had slipped away from camp to "liberate" some fresh fruit from a nearby orchard. When Belisarius heard of this he reacted so angrily that the whole army thought him a madman or at least some pious extremist. He had the offending soldiers scourged. He then had the entire force draw up in formation and after making them endure an hour at attention under the African sun, he spoke after the following fashion as recorded by Procopius.

"This using of violence and the eating of that which belongs to others seems at other times only a wicked thing, that injustice is in the deed itself. But in the present instance so great an element of detriment is added to the wrongdoing that - if it is not too harsh to say so - we must consider the question of justice of less account and calculate the magnitude of the danger that may arise from your act. I have disembarked you upon this land basing my confidence on this alone: that the Libyans, being Romans from of old, are unfaithful and hostile to the Vandals. But now your lack of self-control has changed it all and may make the opposite true. For you have doubtless reconciled the Libyans to the Vandals, bringing their hostility round upon your own selves. By nature those who are wronged feel enmity toward those who have done them violence, and it has come round to this that you have exchanged your own safety and a bountiful supply of good things for saving some few pieces of silver, when it was possible for you, by purchasing provisions from willing owners, not to appear unjust and at the same time to enjoy their friendship to the utmost. Now the war will be between you and both Vandals and Libyan, and I, at least, say further that it will be against God himself, whose aid no one who does wrong can invoke. Now cease trespassing wantonly upon the possessions of others, for lawlessness leads to death. If you give heed to these things, you will find God propitious, the Libyan people well-disposed, and the race of the Vandals open to your attack."

Then he dismissed the army which, if not ashamed of the act, at least could appreciate the common sense of Belisarius' words. He also tried to send Antonina to the flagship for her safety, but also because she understood his thinking better than anyone else. She would be an excellent aide to the admiral. Antonina should have felt honored, but instead she was far from pleased. She had not reached the age of thirty five by being a delicate little female to be kept safe on a boat. She was no more afraid than any of the soldiers, which is to say that she was afraid - but as much for her husband, as for herself. Failing to send her to safety, Belisarius detached their godson to protect her against any rowdies who'd had too much wine in the infantry camp. Arms and supplies had all been brought ashore by D-day plus two and repacked for transport by mule, so Theodosius' attention was usually not needed for more than an hour each morning and evening. Belisarius had little need for an assistant lieutenant of the commissariat at the moment.

Belisarius was more fearful of an ambush than a pitched battle on an open field, so he divided the Army into four divisions. The vanguard under a sturdy soldier, his old friend John the Armenian, was comprised of three thousand heavy cavalry. The infantry marched in the middle, and Belisarius with the bulk of the cataphracts took up the rear, where he expected Gelimer would attack. He ordered his eight hundred Ephthalites and Heruli into the desert to flank his advance. The sea protected his right flank and on it his naval squadron floated, ready to evacuate the small army if overwhelmed by the huge cavalry forces that Gelimer could field.

Belisarius had little knowledge of the fertile strip through which he would march except that it was protected by a beach to one side, and the African desert only a few miles inland on the other. Scouts informed him that Gelimer had not returned to Carthage, but was trailing him with a large force of horsemen. Though he feared an ambush, one did not seem possible here. He came to assume that the Vandal king intended to trap him against the walls of Carthage when he reached it.

As he approached to within a day's march of that city there were more Vandal settlers and fewer of the native Catholic population. No local person pointed out to him that at Ad Decimum, ten miles east of the city, the countryside would turn from coastal orchards and olive groves to broken badlands. The old Roman road ran through it well enough but without room for cavalry to maneuver or deploy in line abreast. Belisarius had been right to suspect a trap, but without intelligence about the sudden change of terrain, he marched into it.

When Gelimer heard of the Roman landing, his first act had been to send a rider to his cousin, Ammatas, who commanded the Carthage garrison, requiring him to kill Hilderic, the rightful heir, and also Hilderic's close supporters. Then he was to attack and hold Belisarius at Ad Decimum. This impulsive order was carried out and Gelimer sinfully but legally succeeded to the throne which he had already occupied. With Hilderic dead and Gelimer clearly Rome's enemy, Belisarius was relieved of Justinian's fiction that he was supporting a vassal state of Rome and a suzerain friend of his youth. Belisarius could now openly return the former province to its full and rightful allegiance.

Gelimer also detached two thousand cavalrymen under the command of his nephew Gilbamundus to ride far inland from the coast and hit the Romans from across a salt flat on their left flank when Ammatas bottled them up at Ad Decimum. He himself, with the bulk of his army, would roll up the rear of the Roman column. It was a good plan for at Ad Decimum the broken ground came almost to the roadway. The Roman's in line ahead and under attack from across the salt flat would be unable to maneuver against his cavalry. The plan depended on coordination of three widely spread forces however.

Slowly inexact intelligence trickled in to Belisarius. The way through the Ad Decimum gap to Carthage was uncertain and the exact whereabouts of the Vandal forces unknown. Furthermore, because the city was protected by a large bight of land, the Roman admiral, as unaware as Belisarius had been of the danger at Ad Decimum, sailed out of sight in order to round it. The army was temporally left without any way to evacuate if faced by overwhelming forces. This was about to happen.

Belisarius wanted to engage the main Vandal army along the coast and not have to besiege Carthage. He did not, however, want to fight with his cavalry elbowing each other in the confines of Ad Decimum where the Vandal troops knew every path and obstruction and the Romans didn't. Ad Decimum was not a situation that Belisarius would have wished for. Indeed, it was not one which by any means could be turned to his advantage. All he could do was try to force the gap by brute force and pray that God would protect his fifteen thousand troops from impending annihilation by several times as many Vandal cavalrymen.

The Roman commander ordered his infantry to build the usual nightly camp near to the sea but within sight of the broken ground; but not to dismantle it at daybreak. There they were to stay and dig in. If necessary his cavalry could retreat into this makeshift fort and await evacuation by the fleet when it would return. He might even tempt the Vandals into attacking this fortified position.

Antonina waited in this Roman camp. Theodosius was at her side with orders that she not be taken prisoner whatever the cost. In a bizarre way that frightening order of Belisarius' calmed her. She'd been a whore but those days were gone now; besides whoring had not meant being gang raped by a bunch of Vandals, or far worse, their unwashed Berber friends.

It was good to have the youth with her, but not because of the sword, ax, and bow he carried. Belisarius had assigned him the task of guarding Antonina because he had little faith in his prowess in combat. Antonina valued his companionship because, even now with possible military disaster before them, Theodosius was still able to keep up some lighthearted banter clearly intended to calm both their nerves. Even in Antioch before the Persian war, Belisarius had rarely been lighthearted. Now, with some years of campaigning and the awesome responsibility of recovering Africa for the empire, he'd become more serious still.

"How did you and my godfather meet?" Theodosius asked offhandedly to relieve the tension that was building up despite his efforts. Then suddenly he realized that it was probably not a good question to ask an ex prostitute.

"Not as you might think," Antonina answered. "I was going into Antioch and he was on guard duty at one of the gates." Antonina decided to shock the youth. "I had to pass him every day." She slowly turned her back to him, looked at him over her shoulder, pulled her tunica tight and wiggled her ass. They laughed an innocent laugh, yet Theodosius was not so innocent as not to notice that his godmother of only four months had a very nice high butt. The twitch when she walked was as nice as on a lady half her age.

It was not Belisarius' way to simply flee, or await destruction on ground unsuitable to defense. Before deciding to retreat with tail between his legs he would pray to the Lord of Battles and attack the Vandal host with his heavy cavalry. He ordered John the Armenian to take the vanguard and with his tough veterans charge into and through the Ad Decimum trap whatever the losses. They would be followed by the bulk of the cataphracts. Belisarius, with his own bucellarii, took the rear guard. He expected that he would have to engage the main Vandal army which had been following him for days. He again sent the Heruli and Ephthalites south into the desert to intercept Gilbamundus' anticipated flanking attack, of which he had now been warned by one of the few local Catholics. If John, with the Roman van, could quickly reach the city, which he knew to be only lightly defended, and if Archelaus with his galleys were to reach the city harbor at about the same time, then he just might seize it. If so the main Vandal army would be caught between two fortified Roman camps. It was more a hope than a plan but maybe God would allow it.

God did, but in His own way. Ammatas impulsively rushed out from Carthage with his troops straggling behind him in small groups. With more courage than sense he fell upon John with too few cavalrymen before Gelimer could hit Belisarius in the rear, or Gilbamundus the Roman flank. He killed twelve Roman troopers with his own hand before he himself fell. This opening skirmish was over even before Roman reinforcements from the main body could join in, but they followed retreating Vandals almost to the gates of Carthage, and intercepted other Vandals coming to join the fray. Still, the battle was far from settled. Gelimer was quickly descending on Belisarius' position with his main army.

In the infantry camp, Antonina, more worried than she had ever been for herself, was begging every messenger for information from Ad Decimum. Now the handsome Theodosius by her side was not in her thoughts at all. She could see Vandal cavalrymen riding fast past the camp, no doubt secure that it would easily fall into their hands after they annihilated Belisarius' cavalry. She joined some camp followers from Sicily on the earthen parapet and waited. She looked across some rows of cabbages that separated the Roman infantry from the enemy. Like the other women she had nothing to do but to watch and worry and wait. She told herself that later she would be able to help. She could set a bone as well as a physician or bring a sad smile to a dying man's face. She was not afraid of every movement the enemy made. Like the Persians she'd seen at Dara, the Vandals were fearsome, but so too were her Romans. Belisarius had been busy for months preparing his men; he knew, and had told Antonina, that once a battle was joined there was little that could be done by the commander but fight like a common soldier to set an example. That, and pray; and Belisarius was far from certain that God would aid his troopers to kill other men who were just defending their homes. Prayer might not help but it couldn't hurt. Antonina and Theodosius would do the same.

Gelimer did not hit the rear guard of cataphracts as they struggled in Ad Decimum as Belisarius had expected him to. For unknown reasons he took a rough and circulant path past them in order to join up with Ammatas before the walls of Carthage; just where Belisarius had prayed to engage. At the same time he sent a messenger to the force that he'd sent into the salt flat to flank the Romans. He ordered them to coordinate an attack on the cataphract column as it passed through the narrow defile. He and Ammatas would engage the disordered survivors as they emerged into the flat country between Ad Decimum and Carthage.

He had miscalculated for this time it was Vandal intelligence that failed. Unknown to Gelimer, Ammatas lay dead outside Carthage and the flanking force was intercepted on the salt plain by foederati light cavalry and annihilated by archery. When he came into the open plain west of Ad Decimum he struck John's advancing cataphracts alone as they exited the area of broken ground.

For a time Gelimer had his way with the outnumbered Romans but, by the will of God, the Vandal king stopped and wasted precious time in mourning when he found his cousin dead. It may be he felt certain that with Carthage still in his hands and with his overwhelming numerical superiority he could dispose of the small Roman force at will, separated as its cavalry now was from both the infantry camp and its fleet. He was wrong. While he blubbered uncontrollably over Ammatas, Belisarius led his main body out of the Ad Decimum defile. Now they could deploy properly. Belisarius would not stand on the defensive to be slaughtered when the Vandal usurper should get control of his emotions. Already covered with gore, he took the lead himself. It was a rout and Gelimer fled toward the hills.

It was not until the following day that the Roman fleet sailed unopposed into the harbor of Carthage which had quickly capitulated when the Vandal king fled. Roman troops maintained order on the streets and gave a degree of protection to Vandal civilians who had so quickly seen their world turned upside down. Belisarius had forbidden looting and by now his men knew the penalty for rape. Still, that did not prevent the local Catholics from exacting revenge on their former persecutors and there was a good deal of blood letting. Eventually Antonina arrived with the infantry, Theodosius riding beside her on a great gray stallion left behind at Ad Decimum by some dead or fleeing Vandal lord. They were chatting happily and trying to distract each other from the carnage they had seen as they passed through the battlefield: reeking bloated and mutilated corpses; vultures and jackals; and local Arabs and Berbers looting the field.

The war would drag on for some months in what would today be called a mopping up operation. Gelimer had not been killed or taken prisoner. There would be one more major battle before Gelimer admitted defeat. His brother Zaro arrived from Sardinia to reinforce him. Together they attempted to undermine the loyalty of Belisarius' Ephthalite light cavalry and were sufficiently successful to neutralize this Roman arm if not detach it from Belisarius. The Ephthalite Huns stood back when the two armies met near the village of Tricamaron. On this occasion Antonina was not present. This time it was the Vandal women and children who occupied a camp twenty miles distant from their rich homes in Carthage while she was ordered by her husband to join the other Roman women in prayer at one of the churches of the capital.

Three times John the Armenian led the Roman cavalry in charges against the Vandal center. Twice it held. On the third charge the Vandals and their Moorish allies broke and were pursued all night by the Roman infantry. Zazo died fighting bravely but Gelimer again fled ignominiously.

Under cover of darkness Belisarius' officers were unable to completely prevent looting and rape. Had Gelimer given a thought to regrouping his far larger forces, the undisciplined Foederati mob might have been defeated. It was not until morning that Belisarius was able to restore discipline. The atrocities were stopped. Much Vandal loot was taken, and the Vandal women were given his protection. He also seized the king's vast personal treasure for Justinian. Then for some days he pursued the fleeing monarch.

At this time Belisarius also suffered the loss of his faithful lieutenant, John the Armenian who had forced the path out of Ad Decimum and just broken the enemy line at Tricamaron. To make the loss worse it was not the result of an enemy's weapon but a misstroke by one of John's own men. His friends carried him to a church so that he might die in a peaceful and holy place, rather than on the field of battle with its blood, gore, and the sounds of wounded men and horses. Before dying he forgave the man who'd mortally wounded him, and Belisarius honored John's request that he not be punished. That evening Antonina watched as her husband wrote to his dead comrade's family in Constantinople. This was no place for Procopius' high blown rhetoric. He wrote from the heart. At Antonina's suggestion he omitted reference to John's dying at the hands of a clumsy trooper in his own command. It was not necessary; he had died fighting the enemy and that was all he need say. When Belisarius had finished, Antonina added a postscript of her own for she had known John's wife and children. She suggested that the family spend a few weeks in the Thracian countryside with Callista and Joannina.

Eventually Belisarius was forced to give up the pursuit lest Gelimer's still more numerous troops cut him off far from both his base at Carthage, and from the sea from which he could be resupplied with food in that desolate terrain. He sent lieutenants to occupy a town dominating the Straits of Gibraltar and to take the barely defended cities of Hippo and Tripoli. (The latter already in rebellion against the Vandal king's rule before the arrival of the Roman expedition.)

Gelimer fled to the poverty of a Berber hilltop village and was taken under siege by Herulian foederati. There he stayed through the winter months rather dramatically lamenting his fate on a lute that he'd requested from the besiegers. At last the sight of his hungry son fighting with a Berber boy over a scrap of half baked bread drove him to surrender to the clemency of Justinian. In the meanwhile, Belisarius had set about securing the province. He tried to protect the Vandal population against the vengeance of the Catholics who now seized much of their property. He reluctantly enforced Justinian's edicts against Arian worship, knowing that these laws would only impede pacification. He began the rebuilding of old Roman coastal forts which the Vandals had torn down. Antonina was able to take charge of a few minor matters for him. She arranged food and housing for Vandal women until their families could return from Gelimer's army, and arranged transport for widows to outlying villages where they had family. Even so, as on that first day at Caput Vada, Antonina found herself bored and with time on her hands as her husband worked late into the night reestablishing Roman power throughout North Africa.

In time Carthage was quiet and many of the troops were sent home. The remaining Romans were kept busy with the tedious or unpleasant details of occupation. Belisarius loathed the duties of civil administrator but could not avoid them. Days were long and, of course, hot. It was not the Roman way to siesta during midday as the locals did. Desk work kept Belisarius busy, and it must be admitted, grouchy, late into the night. Antonina did what she could to occupy herself and entertain those junior officers who did not share their commander's dedication to long hours. It was not unusual for her to join a few of them in a wine shop, escorted, as a proper Greek lady must be, by a trusted lieutenant of her husband. She would chat and make off-color jokes with the best of the local entertainers, only stopping just short of compromising her position as the wife of Belisarius. If the drinking went on too long she might dance barefoot alongside the Arab girls until Theodosius would steer her out the door and restore her to her husband.

By day there was very little to do but walk about the town and pretend to admire what remained of a once proudly Roman city: the usual theater, racetrack, and baths. On one of Antonina's walks with Theodosius talk fell to the girls that she saw him eying as they paced the beach.

"It is so hot," Antonina said, "You men can tie your tunic around your waist or go bare chested. We women must stay clothed top and bottom all day in the sun." Theodosius chuckled but added jokingly, "I'd not complain if you did not; were it not that you are my godmother and the commander's lady, of course." Antonina was in her late thirties, but a lifetime of exercise to please men had allowed her to still feel pride in her body. She was not impish young like the girls that Theodosius had been eying, but her build was athletic and her bosom was still high. She looked at Theodosius and smiled. "I've not always been a general's lady. What the hell, I'm as good looking as those tramps you were leering at." She cupped her breasts in her hands to tease him with immodesty and sat upon a rock. Theodosius almost felt required to stare down her bodice. Too much time on a warship under the Mediterranean sun had tanned her. Her skin lacked the alabaster whiteness which for some reason was favored by other cubiculariai, but then, her golden skin had neither their blotches nor their pimples. Theodosius' thoughts began spinning. He changed the subject. But to Antonina it was just another harmless tease. She thought no more of it than of flirting with the troops in a wine shop. In fact it is probable that she thought there would be more happy husbands in Constantinople if Constantinoplean ladies were more playful and less concerned with appearing virtuous to each other.

Antonina soon grew weary of another godforsaken desert post.

Carthage was an occupied city, still unsafe at night and with none of the excitement of Constantinople. Even chariot racing had been suspended to prevent the congregating of large groups. Belisarius did permanently assign his godchild to be her bodyguard and to keep her occupied as much as was possible. Theodosius accompanied her to the theater but she was bored. They examined the Vandal treasury. It contained loot from their sack of Rome a hundred years earlier. This included the Jewish treasures that the emperor Titus had seized in Jerusalem. She was still bored. They spent hours drinking local beverages and discussing politics in cafes along the coastline, and that was better. Antonina knew and understood the baseness of the Constantinople court and Theodosius would toss off witty comments about this courtier or that old eunuch until Belisarius' wife would be wiping tears of laughter from her blue eyes. Rumors began to circulate.

Since Antonina was Theodora's personal representative as well as the commander's wife, when things calmed down Belisarius allowed her to exercise substantial power over some purely civil affairs. It was her husband's pleasure wherever possible to defer to Antonina even in public, rather scandalizing his straight laced biographer. She would take the higher place at the captured Vandal king's palace and dispense justice while Belisarius sat at her feet. No one save she and Belisarius - and certainly not Procopius – grasped that the general's subordination was foreplay. She would proclaim justice against Vandal lords with all the righteousness of a born patrician, knowing full well that few, if any, of the Roman officers standing around the room had anything like an unblemished record so far as corruption was concerned. Nor did she care.

Procopius might have been likened to a new Thucydides, were it not for the venom he poured out on her, as well as on Justinian and Theodora after they and Belisarius were safely in their graves. Yet though Procopius clearly exaggerated when he wrote of Belisarius and Antonina, he did not entirely lie. From him we know that Belisarius grew richer than ever despite the lavish hand he extended to all who needed his help, and the immense expenses that Justinian expected him to shoulder. It is hard to imagine that after the African campaign Justinian did not see Belisarius' growing wealth as his own to make use of instead of increasing taxes to unbearable levels. It is equally impossible not to see that Procopius, who was handling the details of Belisarius' finances, was the one who knew from whom and how to extract money without compromising his master's orders to not harm the innocent. Few but the peasants in North Africa were innocent.

Antonina felt herself a reflection of Theodora, and may have underestimated the power of the patrician officers under her husband's command. As likely, she overestimated her own power to be abrasive toward them. She offended more than one patrician or illustrati and that was a miscalculation. A man might do so at peril to his body, but to be upbraided by a woman was more humiliating.

Certain junior officers who had failed to distinguish themselves were angry at both Antonina and their general. They were prevented by the discipline of Belisarius from enriching themselves beyond their just share of the spoils. They sent a letter, or rather two copies of the same letter, by different routes to Justinian. In it they suggested that the general was behaving in such a high handed way as to seem more the ruler of Libya than the emperor's administrator. They warned that Belisarius might return to Constantinople at the head of his loyal troops and unseat God's chosen. One copy of the letter reached Justinian. The danger to his throne seemed real. Belisarius not only had his own loyal bucellarii at his command but an army of regulars and foederati enriched by his quick conquest of Libya. The history of the empire had been a succession of successful generals seizing power; why should Belisarius be any different?

Justinian, as emperor, had assumed for himself the titles of Pious, Happy and Illustrious, Victorious and Triumphant over the Vandals. He sent a letter to Belisarius complimenting him on the victory won in his name and offering him the choice of remaining in Carthage as governor or returning to the capital along with Gelimer and the other Vandal captives. It was a trap.

Fortunately for Belisarius, (who might have been too politically naive to discern Justinian's intent) the second copy of the letter fell into the hands of Antonina, who represented Theodora, and as such had her own spies and informants. She and Theodosius apprised him of its contents.

"Antonina, this cannot be."

"It can be, and is, Flavius. Do you think because these men obey you they have no plans and ambitions of their own, which do not include being your lieutenant for the rest of their lives?"

"And what is wrong with that?"

Antonina did not answer but Theodosius reminded his godfather that it could not hurt an ambitious officer to show loyalty to Justinian and Theodora above that due to a mere general and servant of the royal couple. What they charged was certainly an obvious possibility and everyone knew that the emperor was naturally suspicious. As he spoke Theodosius seemed unusually nervous but Belisarius hardly noticed.

Treachery in the Roman empire was a constant possibility. Antonina herself at times felt torn between loyalty to her husband and to Theodora who had raised her to the highest ranks of nobility and whose revenge was famously terrible. She thought to remind Belisarius that what the letter suggested might not be so bad an idea, since obviously he had many enemies as surely she had too. He might be in disfavor at court if his achievements were viewed by Justinian as outshining his own. After all, a successful military leader who returned Africa to the empire was more imposing to the man in the street than the codification of laws or the building of churches. Replacing the jealous emperor might be the only way to assure his own safety.

In the end it was unnecessary for Antonina and Theodosius to suggest a course of action. Belisarius reminded them that his loyalty was not merely a promise to Justinian. He had taken a vow of loyalty; an oath before God's altar. That was as serious a commitment as any priest's. He would not disown it just because he could or should according to the practice of other men. "Besides," he said, "Our sacred emperor is restoring the prestige of Rome, securing our borders, raising churches and monasteries, and reforming the law." Whether he was entirely sincere about Justinian's worth or simply giving a pep talk, the others, more cynical, were unable to argue against a man whose mind had been fixed against disloyalty by a sacred oath. They contented themselves with advice on how best to respond to the choices that Justinian had given his general. In the end, Belisarius decided to show his loyalty and disarm his enemies by returning to Constantinople, with only a small honor guard of his bucellarii; leaving the imperial regulars, the foederati, and even many of his bucellarii to police the province.

Before Belisarius left Africa he put his loyal subordinate, the eunuch Solomon, in command; and Justinian sent Solomon reinforcements. These included Antonina's son in law Ildiger.

When Belisarius and Antonina arrived at the capital accompanied by only a tiny fraction of the troops he had commanded, the emperor's suspicions were relieved; as were those young officers who had raised them. Possibly he was ashamed, but for whatever reason, Justinian showered honors on Belisarius, and those bucellarii whom he had left in Africa were recalled to share in his victory celebration. For the first time in hundreds of years, a victorious general instead of the emperor marched through the capital at the head of his troops in something very like the ancient "triumphs" of Julius Caesar and Augustus. Belisarius proceeded afoot from his villa to the hippodrome followed by wagonloads of Vandal treasure, a long parade of disheartened captives, and the Vandal king himself. The instruments of Jewish worship in the temple of Jerusalem were displayed before the crowd before being sent to a church in the Holy City. Surely God had blessed this expedition and a new order was at hand. Could not Rome itself be reconquered now?

Belisarius and Gelimer presented themselves before Justinian in the hippodrome. They prostrated before His Serenity and received gifts from him. Belisarius was entitled to a huge part of the plunder from Africa, second only to that reserved for Justinian, but even Gelimer did not leave empty handed. The emperor raised his former enemy, kissed him, called him brother, and gave him comfortable estates. He would even have offered Gelimer Roman patricianship had he been willing to apostatize his Arian faith.

Throughout all this Antonina stood just behind the empress, proud of her husband who was still more able than her to take ceremony in stride. Perhaps he was mindful of the the old Roman maxim which, in former days, a slave would have whispered in the conquering hero's ear: *sic transit gloria mundi*: all worldly glory is fleeting. Did she think of how far she had risen? Was she reminded that not so many years before she might have been eying the crowd instead of the hero, looking for a perspective client – an elderly merchant perhaps? If so, she gave no sign of it. The day was warm. The sky was blue. Even Theodora was in a happy mood. Did Antonina too spare a moment to remember: *sic transit gloria mundi*?

Justinian had large gold medallions struck with images of himself and the conqueror of Africa as: "Belisarius the Glory of the Romans." He pronounced him a new Africanus and appointed him consul for the following year. This title had long since ceased to carry any real authority; it merely meant serious expenses for the honored recipient, who was expected to show largess to the populace. Still, it had been Rome's highest honor for over a thousand years. Belisarius was nearly the last recipient. After him, the office was allowed to lapse.

At the inauguration of his consulship Belisarius was borne through the streets sitting in his curule chair on the shoulders of Vandal captives. He showered silver and gold coins and much Vandal spoil upon the crowd and issued his first consular decree, dating the document as was Roman custom even at this late time - not in years since the birth of Jesus, but as in the year of his consulship. Antonina beamed and Photius and Callista took turns carrying little Joannina on their shoulders to watch the parade.

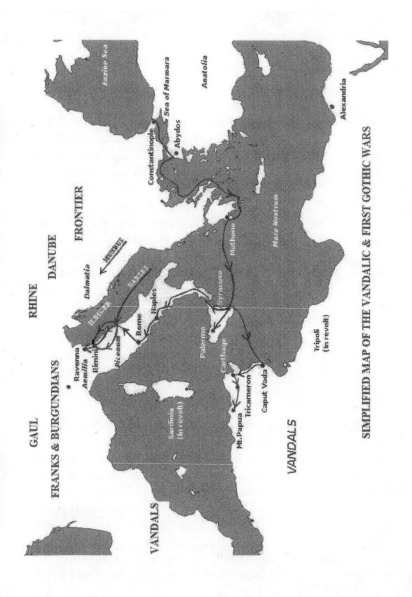

SIMPLIFIED MAP OF THE VANDALIC & FIRST GOTHIC WARS

CHAPTER 12

535-536 AD
CONSTANTINOPLE

Photius, the son of Antonina. had remained in Constantinople, studying and playing big brother to Joannina while their mother was enduring the misery of the African campaign with Belisarius. It had been a huge leap for the young man: one day a carpenter's apprentice, a student, and a very junior member of the Antioch guard; the next, the son of the "New Africanus" and the son of a cubicularia who was confidant to the most important woman in the world. But a few months before, the empire's first general had taken him as his son; taken him into his confidence; and sent him to the palace school to further his education in strategy and statecraft. The young cadet could hardly have been more awed.

It would be pleasing to write that his relationship with Antonina was as good. Mother and son had rarely seen each other as he matured from childhood to manhood. Even now Theodora kept Antonina so close to her that they had little time to share. Antonina had always been a shrewd judge and manipulator of friend and foe alike; now she had also become an urbane woman of the court. That is not so much a criticism as it might seem. She had learned early in life that she must acquire as many skills as possible to survive, and it was an attitude that she shared with the empress.

Photius, on the other hand, was at first more thoughtful than active. He knew theology and philosophy and despised the heresies of Antioch which had infected his mother. If in time, as has been reported, he learned his mother's skills too well, throughout life he still placed the highest value on loyalty. He would be loyal to the emperor, to his new father, and to his new friend, Procopius.

Would Procopius be as loyal to him? Procopius was much like the youth's mother. They were both ambitious and manipulative. Procopius, however, was from an aristocratic if provincial family. He had not Antonina's excuse of having been a struggling slum child. Neither did Photius.

Most of Belisarius' duties as consul were ceremonial. He would appear at the hippodrome and in the senate, which at this time still retained some civic duties, albeit minor ones. He would consult with the emperor's staff and the senate about pending legislation. He would provide entertainments, largely out of his own purse. But all in all, after some months he probably looked forward to laying down the duties which kept him from his troops. His name had been inscribed in the forum along with others in an unbroken succession from five hundred years before the Christ. That was an honor which no turn of fate could ever withdraw from him.

Even before his year as consul was finished Belisarius was ordered by Justinian to war against the Goths of Sicily and Italy. Justinian had determined it was within Roman power to restore these lands to the empire, and was given the opportunity by the internal politics of the Gothic kingdom itself. For thirty three years Italy had been ruled by the wise King Theodoric, still called the Great who, as a young man, had lived the cultured life of a patrician in Constantinople. On his death he was succeeded by Amalasontha, the mother of Theodoric's ten year old grandson. The boy grew to a foolish and dissolute manhood and died young. In order to maintain the power she had exercised as regent, Amalasontha married Theodatus, a nephew of Theodoric. He immediately murdered the woman so as to himself rule without her interference.

However, while living Amalasontha had sought the friendship and favor of Justinian, her nominal suzerain lord. Her murder gave the emperor a legitimate excuse to pursue the reconquest of Italy, a policy he had determined upon anyway. The Romans attacked on two fronts. The general Mundus invaded Dalmatia to hold down the Gothic forces in the eastern Adriatic while Belisarius prepared to launch amphibious attacks on Sicily and Italy itself.

Mundus was a Gepid barbarian but one whose loyalty to Justinian mirrored that of Belisarius'. It was Mundus' troops who had stormed the hippodrome through an entrance connecting it to the palace while Belisarius broke through the main gate to attack the Nike rebels. Such total loyalty to Justinian was uncertain in others and Mundus was rewarded with the Dalmatian command, even though he was a barbarian by birth and less than wholehearted in his efforts to control the ravages of his Heruli mercenaries. Reports of battles in Dalmatia began flowing into the wine shops of Constantinople. Mundus, with his archers. had torn up the Dalmatian coast driving Gothic cavalry before them, and leaving Arian churches desecrated with the blood of Gothic men and the honor of Gothic women.

It was with mixed emotions that mother and father once again entrusted their Joannina to the hands of Grandma Belisarius. Grandma was also troubled about the separation. Joannina was age three now and

162

although she had been with her parents less than a year, she suffered to see them go. Mother and father told themselves that they hated to part from the child and that was true so far as it went. The girl was more like the child of her grandmother than either her mother or father though. Should Antonina have stayed with her instead of once again accompanying Belisarius? Justinian had ordered him to Italy and Theodora had as much as done the same to Antonina. He had his military duty but Antonina's duties were as important to Theodora. She was to do those things that her noble husband might balk at. For one thing, she was to find a way to depose Pope Silvarius, whose support of the throne had not meant that he supported Anthimus, the Monophysite whom Theodora had managed to have appointed patriarch of Constantinople. Less controversial but no less important, Silvarius was beloved of the Gothic enemy, even though their theology differed. He had to go and it would be up to Antonina to find a way.

Theodora had essentially made the choice for her. She must go with Belisarius and let his mother raise Joannina, or stay at home but not at court. If Antonina's choice displeased the empress, Belisarius would also surely suffer her displeasure. *After all,* Antonina could tell herself, *momma did such a good job while we were in Africa that Joannina thinks of her as her mother. Besides,* she thought more ruefully, *I've left children before and they've grown up just fine. I'll write a lot, and maybe the war will be short.*

SICILY

Belisarius led a typically small force of four thousand confederates, three thousand Isaurian mountaineers from Anatolia, some Ephthalite and Moor light cavalry, and several thousand bucellarii in his own pay. His orders from Justinian were to begin the war against the Goths by first attacking Sicily. If he met opposition there he was to simply indicate that he was enroute to Carthage where he would look in on the emperor's newly acquired holdings, and continue to Africa.

In the event, there was but little opposition. Most of Sicily fell to Belisarius without fighting. Only Palermo resisted but the city walls were lower than the masts of the Roman transports. Belisarius placed archers in the ships' small boats and raised them up between the mastheads. A rain of arrows into the city soon inclined the Goths to surrender. As was his way, Belisarius treated the conquered residents with courtesy, and thereby won enough of them to the Byzantine cause that he felt he could leave Palermo with only a small detachment of guards. He proceeded to Syracuse, which opened its gates to him, and scattered largess among the populace on his triumphant entry. So welcome was the victor of Dara and Ad Decimum that the Syracusans would later supply him with grain when he was forced to stand a year long siege in Rome itself. With the loyalty of Syracuse affirmed, the island might be considered pacified but that has never meant being completely peaceful. Belisarius had confirmed Theodosius as the permanent bodyguard for Antonina. Though his other bucellarii were the best of companions in war, they were far from a cultured lot for her to wile away the hours with. As a godson, Theodosius was family as well as a member of the general's staff, for in the sixth century being a godparent was a very serious matter. There was no difference between that and being a natural child. Even marriage to a near relative of a godparent was considered to be as sinful as if the relationship was one of blood.

The pacification of Sicily had been reasonably peaceful but the personal cost to Belisarius had been heavy. Thousands of his guards had to be paid, fed, and housed. He had to provide for their mounts and pack animals. Justinian had failed to provide for these, as it was the policy of the empire that wealthy commanders pay for the personal troops they were required to provide, and the unofficial understanding that the cost would be recouped from looted territory. So it was that Procopius and Antonina quietly hid away a part of the spoils not to be officially reported to Constantinople. It was a culture inherited from centuries of Roman corruption, or such the modern reader would consider it. But though recognized as unsavory at the time, it was seen as simply normal and necessary; hardly a matter for confession any more than consultation fees are considered immoral by a modern American legislator.

Now Belisarius and Antonina prepared for the arrival of Photius, newly graduated from the palace school of strategy and tactics. While he waited, Belisarius was fully occupied with preparations for the invasion of Italy itself. Antonina and her bodyguard had nothing of importance to do however, except to enjoy the sun and warm breeze. Theodosius lay on the beach with Antonina. Her other guards stood in groups not far away and for decency several Sicilian noblewomen sort of joined with them, or at least sat with them from time to time. The day was as fine as any, but hot. At one point Antonina hiked up her tunica and waded into the warm sea but soon returned to sit beside her escort again. The sea had wet her hair and Theodosius watched as she brazenly released it from the confines of a noble Roman lady's coif to fall in scented tresses to her waist. She was his commander's wife, Theodosius reminded himself. ... *Oh fortunate of men.* Then Antonina smiled and laughed a younger girl's bright giggle. It would have been far easier for Theodosius to keep to his duty of simply occupying the general's wife's time with chit chat and parlor games had she frowned. He looked around at her other guards who pretended disinterest, and to the Sicilian noblewomen who seemed unable to decide what was proper behavior around these two people who obviously cared more than a little about each other. Antonina was a tease; everyone knew that. The question was whether or not Theodosius was made of stone? Surely Belisarius should have entrusted Antonina entertainment to some eunuch.

The next day, Theodosius himself went to suggest just that. He got as far as the general's quarters but stopped outside. What would he say? He couldn't just make up some excuse to be replaced in such an easy duty and one safe from death in battle. Belisarius would see through it and he would soon be a dead man. It would be worse and a quicker demise to admit he lusted after Antonina. Neither was an option and so he turned about, worrying for his life and his soul. He returned to his own rooms and for a few minutes considered speaking with one of the priests who accompanied the army. But what would be the use? He could hear in his mind's ear what a priest would say, and he did not need to hear it. Anyway, Theodosius did not really want to lose the sight of Antonina at play or forget the smell of her damp hair.

He and Antonina were more and more to be seen together laughing and happy in each others' company as they went about whatever task Belisarius had assigned to them, or Antonina had assumed on her own as Theodora's agent. One day they were examining the accounts of the Sicilian garrison when Antonina stretched up on her toes to haul a wooden box of records from a high shelf. She should have asked for help, but that was not Antonina's way. She stumbled and fell backwards into the arms of Theodosius. He innocently caught her at the breasts but was slow to release the wife of his general. Antonina looked at him over her shoulder smiling. Theodosius nervously recovered a proper demeanor towards his godmother and the wife of the second most powerful man in the Roman empire, but Antonina trapped his hands on her bosom, and continued smiling naughtily. Their tenderness for each other had been growing in Africa and Constantinople and that had not gone unobserved by Procopius, among others.

"It's OK. I'm not one of the sillies in the Great Palace who think their virtue is more important than friendship."

"Godmother, it would not be right. If we start we will not stop."

"Hush. Don't think so much of what is right. I love my husband more than my life and I always will. But he is very busy and we are very lonely." Antonina's hands were on the sash about Theodosius' waist. Theodosius was almost impotent with fear of Belisarius' wrath, but not quite. He was indeed lonely. As Antonina's constant guard he could hardly visit the whores that satisfied other soldiers' needs and the lady was lovely to behold in the afternoon sun which streamed through the windows. As always there was the slightest scent of thyme about her. She was also strong and possessed of a feminine dominance that broached no refusal. She was not young, nor was she a skinny waif. She was not heavy but definitely full bodied. Nor was Antonina, the Rubenesque lady, accustomed to being refused by anyone in any manner. For her it meant nothing if a man enjoyed her breasts. That she could do for the lonely Theodosius, as she had once done for coins. Belisarius would not need to know. She was not choosing the youth over her husband, she told herself, just passing time in a gawd-awful army post. After all, no one would care if they had been two friends playing a dice game or shooting arrows at a target. To Antonina, it was nearly the same.

It was only the heavy footfalls of Belisarius' guards approaching that ended the awkward moment. Seconds later Antonina was explaining to her husband how she and Theodosius had been stashing a store of Gothic coin among the uninteresting boxes of paper records: purchases of corn and olive oil, of camp wine and of carts, of pigs and goats. It would be sufficient to purchase some mules for the bucellarii and, she added quite innocently, a nice dinner for her and the tired commander at a seaside restaurant.

The explanation was not lost on Theodosius. He had debts and there would be much more loot for Justinian's coffers when they took Italy. His mistress might spare a small part, a thing he would never dare suggest to his commanding officer.

In the weeks following, Theodosius tried to avoid Antonina without alerting Belisarius that anything had changed. He wanted to be a loyal godson and Antonina was his godmother. He dared not ask to be relieved of his duties as her constant guard and companion when away from camp, for that might arouse suspicion in the general, who would recall how cheerful Antonina always was around Theodosius. Instead he asked to be assigned adjunct to a combat command. Belisarius would not hear of it; the youth was not muscular enough. He then requested that he be assigned to duties surveying the recently captured towns for recruits and war material. It would give him the chance to see the wonders of the empire when the caesars had still ruled from Rome, and to visit many holy and beautiful churches and monasteries - for he could rightly claim a more than usual bent for the religious life, if not for a life of holy poverty. This Belisarius

166

reluctantly granted and Antonina as reluctantly yielded to it as necessary. She did love her husband with all her heart - save that little space reserved for the youth. Before long, however, she asked of Belisarius that she accompany Theodosius on these trips except, of course, to the monasteries, where women were not permitted. She freely admitted to her husband that she had come to love the cheerful banter of her godchild which dispelled the sober climate of an army camp at war.

In Africa, Solomon had the thankless task of enforcing the edicts of Justinian, which flowed in a nonstop stream from Constantinople. No use must be made of the Arian churches; there must be no positions in the occupying administration for the heretics. Worst of all for Christians, Arians could not have their children baptised except in the churches of the occupying orthodox.

Were it not enough that the conquered Arians were angry and depressed, many of the occupying "Romans" were themselves mounted Semi-Arians from the northeastern frontiers of the empire. Easter was approaching and even their children could not be baptised unless these imperial Arians converted to orthodoxy.

Herulian children? It seems that when the "Romans" occupied Carthage, Vandal widows claimed the newly enriched Herulian co-religionists for husbands and the soldiers expected to take possession of their new wives' inheritance. When Justinian denied to these veterans the fields, farms, and much of the wealth of the city, their brides chastised them as cowards and Justinian's slaves. They mutinied, and when word of the mutiny spread they were joined by a detachment of Vandal troops who had joined the imperial army after being defeated by Belisarius. They'd been at sea, en route to the eastern frontier, when they learned that it might be possible to recover their homes. Overpowering their imperial officers, they set sail for Carthage with visions of vengeance.

As if Justinian's persecution were not enough, citizens of the orthodox faith retaliated against the Arians for the persecution they had suffered before the Roman invasion. Arian churches were burned. Vandal men were spit upon and Vandal women groped. There were knives in the night. Finally, an army of pagan Moors invaded, either to support their Vandal friends, or just for plunder.

Procopius was in Carthage on a mission for Belisarius when all these foes united against Solomon. The mutineers attempted to slay

Solomon, but with the strategos Martinus and Procopius he fled. They and a mere half dozen guards managed to escape the city in an open boat. They sailed to Sicily, there to report to Belisarius.

As usual, Belisarius did the unexpected. Before the motley array of rebels could form some sort of disciplined army, he landed with but a hundred of his personal guards, whom Procopius had quickly gathered into the only ship available. When they landed in Carthage they were joined by a thousand Byzantine troops who had remained loyal to Solomon. In a famous speech Belisarius exhorted them against the enemy.

"Soldiers, we cannot but bewail the sad necessity which impels us against our comrades. But we possess one great consolation: We have not provoked this war against them and their barbarian allies. Romans have been slaughtered only for loyalty to our emperor. We must be their avengers. Furthermore, these barbarians are contemptible soldiers, united only by a thirst for plunder and crime. They will be frightened and their officers cannot count on their obedience to orders. March against this unworthy foe who puts faith only in his superiority in numbers."

The battle which followed confirmed what Belisarius had said. Of course, being Belisarius, when the fighting was done and the rebels were fleeing, he entreated the same soldiers to be merciful that but a few hours before he had urged to ferocious vengeance.

Carthage was again in imperial possession, as was Sicily. The reconquest of Italy would soon be underway. Belisarius had twice won Africa for Justinian, but when he would leave there for the last time, he knew that Justinian's intemperate edicts would cause endless dissatisfaction in the province for Solomon to deal with. He must have wondered if the reconquest would last, but it did.

Cappadocian John was no doubt an effective aide to Justinian in varied matters, for men of no ability did not long survive in the imperial palace, but Belisarius had little use for the nasty little tax collector from the wilderness of Cappadocia. Not only did he have to pay enormous taxes, he was shortchanged on troops and expected to make up the difference out of his own resources. His resources were many and the general had no quibble with the tradition of supplying large numbers of personal troops. That was expected; that was politics. What he did object to was that John expected him to achieve great victories for Justinian with insufficient support: too few horses and mules and too many federated tribes and mercenaries from border lands instead of reliable imperial soldiers. He knew that if he was to satisfy the emperor's military ambitions in Italy, he'd need a lot more money than his resources alone could provide. Justinian and the Cappadocian were frittering away the empire's wealth on new church buildings to replace even perfectly serviceable ones throughout the realm.

"Glorify God with churches we can't afford?" he said to Procopius one evening before leaving Carthage for the last time. "Glorify God? God *is* glory. It's all just glory for Justinian. ...But don't mention that I said that. His Serenity has the highest motives, I'm sure, but there isn't enough money, and along with their cash John is squeezing whatever support the emperor has out of everyone. I'm a wealthy man and I'll do my part, but how am I to provide all the troops I'll need for his grand projects if I go broke myself?"

———————————

In that age every noble commander dared treason against his nominal superior, without much fear of severe punishment if he failed. If he were a Roman his friends at court would invent excuses to protect him; excuses which the emperor usually found it expedient to accept. If he were the leader of barbarian allies or foederati in the service of the Romans, he had even less to fear. Admittedly foederati were brave when victory and loot were a certainty, but at other times they could be contemptible soldiers, hardly more than pirates united only by a thirst for plunder and crime. Byzantine officers could not count on their obedience to orders when victory was uncertain.

Yet, the empire dared not lose the service of Greek officers or risk barbarian warlords defecting to an enemy. Throughout his service, Belisarius was loved by his troops but often betrayed by his lieutenants. In that age the wonder was that such betrayals always collapsed before they could bring about defeat. Still, the possibility of treachery always circumscribed the possible.

The hour was late at what today would be termed an officers' club, where the officers gossiped among themselves like fishwives. In a private room the wine was still flowing and the half-drunk men were conversing among themselves in a part Greek, and part god-knows-what patois. All the men there were lieutenants of Belisarius. All were loyal to the campaign but also to their ambition. All respected Belisarius but none cared to be forever in his shadow. Some were more rapacious than their commander would have liked. None felt the kind of loyalty that is taken for granted in a modern chain of command. They did not feel duty bound to their commander, who several hoped to surpass. The unacknowledged rule was the same as in office politics: if they could not surpass him by superior ability then they would by tearing him down. Though they also lay petty plots against each other - trying constantly to get some small advantage in the eyes of Justinian - in this they were of a like mind if not actually united. No one of them could take his place beside Justinian in a reviewing stand until the hero of Dara fell a few notches.

None in that room intended actual disloyalty to the empire. It had been good to them, but several of their friends had been demoted by Justinian for implying that Belisarius had been plotting against the throne while in Africa, or for briefly joining the recent Sicilian mutiny. The men in the room missed their old friends, who to their mind had not been treasonous to Justinian, only disloyal to Belisarius. They had feared that his audacity might endanger themselves and their men.

"So, if we win back Italy, what will be in it for the army? My men are tired of fighting. If Italy is anything like the African victory our saintly commander will keep the profits for Justinian and himself." What the youngish commander of a Ephthalite brigade was saying was not wholly true. These officers had all profited by their successes in Africa, just not by enough to please them.

"Oh we'll do all right if we don't try to swallow the whole peninsula." A more experienced comrade was speaking. "We've got to leave something to the Goths, or they'll fight to the last man and boy. I worry about Belisarius being in sole command though."

"This won't be like Africa," another Hun took up the argument. "I and my archers need freedom to act on our own when we're not near him; and Italy is a big piece of land to try communicating back and forth in. We've all got to be able to take advantage of changing circumstances when they occur. I never said this, but Justinian puts too much faith in him. God knows he deserves credit for Africa, and the Persian campaign was just damn brilliant; but no one knows everything. Frankly, I think it would have been wiser to attack Carthage directly before Gelimer even knew our army was off his shore. Gelimer wasn't even in Carthage. He'd have had to take the city back from us."

"Then we'd have had to stand a siege by an army several times the size of ours;" rejoined the voice of experience, "and Gelimer would have brought up a far larger fleet than ours and destroyed our ships right there in the harbor."

"Maybe; but we were nearly nailed at Ad Decimum. And that was our glorious imperator's fault. He had poor intelligence." Everyone at the table was in agreement now.

"Exactly. Poor intelligence. He should have known. We have spies. Frankly I think he just didn't trust the intelligence he got. I never heard of him sharing it. He damn near got us annihilated at Ad Decimum. It was Armenian John who bulled his way through to Carthage. The point is: Yes, Belisarius is smart but he's not the only smart one here. Don't misunderstand. He's smart and I hope we do well in Italy. I just wish he'd listen more. He could get us all killed if we're here and there all over the countryside waiting for orders from him. It won't be easy. We've got to take Naples, Rome, the Gothic capital at Ravenna, and those are only the big cities. Its a long way between them and we can't afford to bypass garrisons between them, which I'm afraid he'll do. The guy thinks he's invincible but we've not enough troops to hold every town that has a wall or castle."

"Oh, I don't think he thinks he invincible. He's not forgotten that he nearly lost it at Ad Decimum," a wizened graybeard from Macedonia was speaking. "But the Goths aren't the Vandals and you're right; Italy is big and will be harder to hold. And look how few men we've got; twelve thousand. Frankly, I don't like a split command, but you're right. In such a big place he's got to let his officers follow the battle wherever it leads. He can't be everywhere. Besides, what if something happens to him? We'd have to work together without a sole commander anyway. And what of the troops? Do your Huns answer to you or him?

"Yeah," someone interjected, "We must work together. God knows Belisarius is in command, and I'm glad of it. He's good. But we must all work together. Sometimes he's kind of rash. That could get him killed and us too, and the whole army with us."

"I hope he leaves some of the loot for his subordinates this time." Constantinus, who was the only senior commander present, added this with a grim half smile as the meeting broke up without having exactly breached discipline. The following day there was loose talk in the ranks and not all the officers hurried to enforce discipline. Some of the more junior ones were particularly indiscreet.

Word of the incipient mutiny was quickly brought across the sea to Belisarius in Carthage. For experience, he entrusted the newly arrived Ildiger with temporary command there, and with Solomon and Procopius and his hundred absolutely loyal guards he boarded a galley. The hundred sweating oarsmen quickly returned their commander to Sicily and the mutiny faded away at his approach. He succeeded in ending it simply by a few words to the soldiers, rather than his officers and with the power of his name. His words and reputation disarmed the rebels and renewed loyalty more effectively than confronting them with force, even if he'd had any at hand. Excuses were made; oaths of loyalty were given and received, and a few ring leaders found themselves transferred to duties where they could do no harm.

"Soldiers of Rome, whether you are Ephthalites or Heruli, or Macedonian, or from Anatolia, or Thrace, you joined the greatest army of the world and were proud that you would be restoring the empire of the caesars. You have been betrayed by some of your own officers; few, it is true, but on these distant shores the most important thing is unity, and some endangered that. When you joined the army you knew that there was great danger; that is the life of a soldier. But you have not deserved to be placed in danger unnecessarily. Yet that is always the result of disunity. You are the finest soldiers in the world; you proved that in Africa, but we have many enemies on these shores and we are far from home. There must be no dissent from our purpose, and it is I, not insubordinate lieutenants, who must answer to our holy emperor."

Belisarius contented himself with lecturing Constantinus about watching his tongue among junior officers. Belisarius did not much like the man, nor he his commander; but he had an excellent reputation for effectiveness in battle. "Tell me, if you think I'm wrong, not a bunch of foederati. They are unfamiliar with Roman discipline and loyalty. They must never suspect a hint of hostility between those of us who are near Justinian."

CHAPTER 13

536
S ICILY

While Belisarius was in Carthage Antonina had been browsing the local bazaar. She was in a foul mood, made more foul by the fact that her husband was risking his life in Africa while she was standing in safety and boredom in front of a pottery shop. *Damn!* For a moment she recalled how owning such a stall had once been her highest ambition. The memory did nothing to improve her mood. That had been six years before, and here she was on a lousy beach again; same as in Alexandria, same as in Asia. Everyone envied her. Was she not married to a fine man? Such a fine man to marry a whore. But at least as a whore she'd had some fun: parties and occasional quiet dinners with some Greek aristocrat or barbarian lord. She was rich and respectable now, but where was she? On a damn beach again, with Belisarius off to Carthage, and not even Theodosius near by on this hot, stinky afternoon. At least Theodosius might bring some bright talk to her, not just the idle chatter of the Sicilian women or the stiff "Yes Mam" of the stalwart guard who took his place this day. Unlike this guy, Theodosius, though the son of a servant, was one of those who were at home with the aristocracy of Constantinople. He could talk about other things than war. Unfortunately, today he had some other business which needed attending to.

She had received a typically brief note from Belisarius that Carthage was pacified again, so she need have no more fear for him today. That was good. With a hundred men, he had reconquered Africa; only Belisarius could have done it. She should have been proud. but Instead on this beautiful day, she was simply pissed.

Of course, Procopius and a few others besides Theodosius were knowledgeable about matters outside an army camp, but their restraint in her presence was a poor disguise for their patrician disdain for a "lady" that they might have once seen perform lewdly on the stage. *Well, Theodosius will be back tomorrow from whatever silly mission Belisarius has sent him on.* That thought was unfair and she knew it. Belisarius was not inclined to create silly missions just to keep his officers busy. Probably, it was something routine and boring though. But maybe he'd bring some news. At least that was something to look forward to and Theodosius was so much fun.

It's just a fling, she told herself. *We'll get over it, he and I; after all*

I'm no kitten anymore. He'll find some nice girl and Flavius need never know.

Belisarius' work kept him distant from Antonina. Meanwhile Theodosius was close. Belisarius carried the weight of responsibility. Theodosius was fun. Antonina never was known for discretion and all too soon the rumor mill informed Belisarius of her fling. Procopius claims that a disgruntled slave brought two youths to Belisarius who waited upon Antonina in her bedchamber, and they swore that they had observed her and Theodosius sinning against him; though to this author that seems an improbably sloppy infidelity.

Belisarius' reaction to the revelation was not so much anger at his wife but sadness. None in that straight-laced group could understand why Belisarius sent assassins to drag Theodosius to a husband's justice but did nothing to punish his wife. Surely she deserved death not alone for betraying her marriage vows, but also for humiliating a revered consul of Rome and general of the empire. According to Procopius, Antonina overheard Constantinus say that he would have killed her had he been Belisarius, and that later she took vengeance on him. However, Belisarius was mindful of the woman caught in adultery and spared by Jesus from being stoned. Like those accusers who faded away from Jesus in the Gospel, he himself felt guilty. He had ignored Antonina these past months. He'd been busy, of course, but Antonina was still Antonina and he had left her alone and lonely in an army camp. Antonina had no false piety nor pretended modesty. He knew that men still found her desirable. Though her beauty was slightly fading with the passing years, she retained a bubbly flirtatious manner that still seduced even him when she wanted something. Why should it not similarly effect other men so far from home? She was weak, but it was natural for a woman with a past like hers to be less than horrified by infidelity. Not for her the pretense of more genteel women who act stiff necked and dull while their husbands do whatever they want far from home and surrounded by poor and hungry native girls. Not that male fidelity mattered to anyone but the priests anyway. It was a double standard, and one that Antonina ignored. The surprise was that Belisarius blamed himself that his wife was as unfaithful as his friends liked to boast of being. Antonina would not have been horrified had her husband been unfaithful, or even much cared. It is probable that the former prostitute excused the whole thing to herself as no more than the "handshake" of *The Graduate;* but to Procopius it was inexcusable and unforgivable: exactly what might be expected of a low-born woman.

Belisarius was saddened but it bewildered Procopius that he blamed himself and Theodosius and forgave his unfaithful mate. Procopius

174

attributed it to sorcery by Antonina or to her caresses and did not much distinguish one from the other. Certainly the caresses were real; that's how loving couples make up.

But as for Theodosius, he was the son of an old retainer. Belisarius had taken the young man into his own home and given him army promotions beyond what he had earned. Lust and loneliness he could understand in Antonina, and forgive. The same behavior in an officer and godson who had never needed to scratch a living from the grubby streets of Constantinople was simply mean and dishonorable behavior. Theodosius fled to a monastery in Ephesus. Procopius does not even consider the possibility that the young man possessed a true vocation to religion.

After a long talk with Antonina, who plead Theodosius' and her innocence, Belisarius recalled the assassins that he had sent and wrote a kind letter to Theodosius asking him to return. If it is true that he now believed that Theodosius was innocent, possibly at that time he was; for Procopius admits that Theodosius lived in fear of his godfather discovering his infatuation. Still, the attraction between Antonina and Theodosius cannot be denied. If they had not yet slept together, they did enjoy each others company and in time that would lead to infidelity. Whether there was infidelity in Sicily or just something close to it; there must also have been more than boredom and sexual attraction. How else can it be that later, when living in Constantinople after the first Italian war, Belisarius would forget his earlier suspicions and seek the return of the younger man, at that time once more a monk in Ephesus? It had to be because of Theodosius' wit which enlivened the lives of himself and the by then visibly aging Antonina.

As for the slaves? Apparently they had been irate at some behavior of Antonina toward them. At any rate, a commander's slaves who know inside information and are prepared to gossip about it cannot be trusted. Antonina spoke to her servant Eugenius, and certainly they disappeared. Whether Procopius tells the truth about them being mutilated and murdered cannot be known. Though Procopius hated Antonina, he admits it was a rumor. Even if the atrocity was invented, it was still a time of war. Men and women died daily. Personal servants had to be trustworthy. These were potential traitors. Their possible deaths, if not the rumor of mutilation, might have been both punishment and to make an example for others who were privy to confidential information; for Eugenius' mistress was not only the general's wife but also the delegate of Theodora.

———————

While awaiting Theodosius' return Belisarius kept closer to Antonina and she to him. It is possible that she was more bothered by her husband's understanding than by her sin. It shamed her that she had betrayed him and he had not sent her away to some convent-prison, or simply taken her life as Constantinus had suggested as a proper course for a cuckolded husband. She'd thought she understood him, now she knew that she did not. He was as strict a disciplinarian as any officer, and could order death sentences upon deserters, thieves, rapists, and cowards; but also a Christian in practice as well as in name. To him this was not a public affair which needed to be quickly punished as a matter of military discipline, but a private matter between husband and wife. Antonina was certainly skilled in manipulation but nothing in her upbringing had prepared her for unsolicited forgiveness.

Theodosius returned, trembling, and for the next several months Antonina tried as best she could to distance herself from him, as he did to keep from her. Belisarius kept Theodosius in his household for he enjoyed the young man's company and was now convinced that his cheeriness was all that Antonina looked for in him; certainly understandable and in itself innocent. When they were together, however, guilt was lost in infatuation. Antonina would say: "Shut up," when Theodosius beguiled her with descriptions of ancient ruins. "Go away," he would say moodily when they'd had too much wine and cheese. Neither meant it and both knew that; yet they tried.

It troubled Procopius no end that Antonina had the sort of power over her husband that he could not. After all, he was Belisarius' faithful servant. Not only was he the general's loyal secretary and trusted financial adviser - and of course in time his biographer - but he had even on occasion taken on dangerous missions for Belisarius. He had scouted Syracuse for him while that city was still held by the Vandals. He had been with Solomon when they'd escaped with their lives in a fishing boat from their own mutinous troops in Africa. What he never understood was that Belisarius assumed this sort of behavior. To him danger was as much a part of Procopius' job as an officer of the realm as was his own loyalty and personal bravery due to the emperor, whether the emperor was a good man, a caring man, a man worthy of respect, or just a jerk.

Time passed. Procopius does not know whether to attribute Antonina's power over her husband to magic potions or caresses. Maybe because he was a eunuch himself he did not even consider true love a possibility. To him potions, caresses, and teasing were the same; simply Antonina's way to an end. How much he must have wished that he could observe them in their private chambers. Publicly, Belisarius might attribute a sore ass to riding his warhorse, but it was not unknown for him to discover a burr of unknown origin in the loin cloth which in that age served him for underwear.

Antonina lay reclining on a high couch, her husband on the floor by her feet. *She has so many enemies;* he thought, *but they won't dare do anything while I am here.* Thus the greatest general that Rome had ever produced was protecting an aging ex-whore. She in her turn lovingly provided him with sour looks, flirtations with his embarrassed subordinates, and sometimes a small crop judiciously applied when alone in their bed chamber.

WHACK!

"Mistress, do you think we're sinning?

"Why?"

WHACK!

"Because we're enjoying ourselves too much and we're getting too old to have children by it."

"The monks must be having a ball then, what with thrashing themselves and each other with nettles every night."

WHACK!

"That's different. They do it for the good of their souls, not for fun."

"You think so. Hah!"

"Why yes."

"Sometimes I think my husband is as innocent as people say."

"What people?

"Your secretary, for one."

WHACK!

"Oh, who cares what he thinks. He's good with money and I value that. But I don't care what he, or anyone else, thinks about us. If I did, I'd be doing nothing all day but worrying about what people think. That's probably what he does. The guy's a gossip but he brings me information that I'd never get through other channels."

"Are you worried for your soul?"

"A little."

"Then offer your suffering for sinners."

WHACK!

WHACK!

WHACK!

It was evident to all that Photius and Theodosius hated each other, and both Photius and Theodosius were ambitious for wealth. Skulking around and noting every rumor was Belisarius' secretary. He was loyal to Belisarius, but out of self interest. He cared for Photius because the lad's growing cynicism mirrored his own. He hated Theodosius because he hated Antonina. The bitter eunuch did not actually show support for either Photius or Theodosius until he wrote his *Secret History* in later declining years; he just enjoyed the gossip.

He hated Antonina whose place near to the general he envied. If anyone could have nipped the growing fondness of Antonina for Theodosius it was he, either by counseling Antonina, or by himself betraying her to Belisarius, and thus perhaps saving the lives of the slaves who would accuse her. His hatred for Antonina was too great for him to council her, and his fear of Belisarius too great for him to warn his master. Instead the little man had hovered about, enjoying it all and waiting for her affair to self-destruct. Without her, he thought, Belisarius would need him more than ever to protect him from the plots of his enemies.

Procopius would have us believe that Belisarius was blind to Antonina's amours. The author prefers to believe that he was understanding and forgiving if Antonina also loved another man, at least so long as there was no outright infidelity. As much as Belisarius loved his wife he knew that there was a hole in her life which he could not fill. He tolerated and even approved her flirtatious manner, firmly believing that at day's end she would return to him. Antonina's flirtations went far further than she had intended, however, and that gave the little secretary delight - a delight which he shared with Antonina's son who, regrettably, was on far worse terms with his mother than with his stepfather.

"Dad, doesn't my mother embarrass you sometimes."

"No."

"But she runs around the camp like some teenager at her first banquet."

"You think she should act her age?"

"Yes."

"Photius, if Antonina acted her age, I'd never have married her."

"But Procopius says...."

"Screw Procopius. He's got his head stuck in a latrine. He's a prude who'd be perfectly happy listening to a theology lecture from the patriarch. Your mother would be bored, and so would I."

Photius' admiration and loyalty to his stepfather were unbounded

178

but they never really understood each other. He tried to love the mother he had not seen for years, but her actions were enough to turn around an idealistic young man who had been raised a devout Christian. His mother had left him to learn carpentry whilst she rose to the highest positions in Byzantium. It was his stepfather who had determined to love and treat him as his own son from the very day he learned of the boy. It was Belisarius, not Antonina, who had brought the youth out of obscurity to the emperor's court. Photius was somewhat weak in body and it was Belisarius who always took care that he not be exposed in combat as Ildiger, the husband of Antonina's first daughter, was. He had not been raised in poverty but neither had he been raised to the riches that he thought himself entitled to as Antonina's son. This nettled him and he was determined to become rich. He saw Antonina opening opportunities for Theodosius which she rarely did for him. Of course he would inherit from Belisarius and Theodosius wouldn't, but he loved Belisarius and would not allow himself to look forward to such a sad day.

He could not know the agonies Antonina had endured for him or why she had provided for him by sending him to a kind master when she could not stay in Antioch. He could only see that she had deserted him when he'd been a teen and gone to live life in a palace while he struggled with carpentry. It was his stepfather who had summoned him and adopted him as his own. He loved Belisarius and was loyal to him, but to no-one else.

As for Antonina's feelings for her son: Procopius would have us believe that she was constantly seeking his ruin because he interfered with her liaison with Theodosius. Procopius was blinded by his own hatred. He, himself, acknowledges Photius' growing corruption and his depredations to which Belisarius was blind. These sins mattered not at all to Procopius. To him they were the way of the world.

What we do know for certain about Antonina is that after her probable affair in Sicily, and for the five years of the first Gothic war, there is no further suggestion by the jealous Procopius of anything improper between her and Theodosius.

CHAPTER 14

536 AD
ITALY

In a peaceful age Theodatus, the Gothic king, might have been regarded as a far-seeing monarch, genuinely more interested in the arts than in war. Among the learned at his court in Ravenna was Cassiodorus, a civil servant and adviser to the king, and the last Roman worthy to be called an intellectual. But this was not the time for intellectuals to be leading the Goths. The mild ruler was so fearful of losing both his throne and his life that he negotiated a surrender to Justinian before Belisarius even invaded the mainland. However, a Gothic victory in some small skirmish against Mundus in Dalmatia in which the Goths were victorious and Mundus was killed, caused Theodatus to gain heart and reverse this cowardly course.

Theodatus was no worthy adversary for Belisarius in strategy or tactics; nor was he the equal of Justinian in chicanery and deception in diplomacy. He was a coward who had murdered his wife to secure the throne in his own name. He was a weakling and soon the Goths realized it. Now Belisarius received orders to invade Italy and he landed without opposition at Reggio where the local commander, as cowardly as Theodatus, fled the mainland even before Belisarius arrived, and then surrendered himself to Byzantine troops in Sicily. Like Benedict Arnold twelve centuries later, he was rewarded for his treason and lived out his life in Constantinople loaded with honors and contempt.

However, the cowardice of these two should not impute the bravery of the Goths generally or of their other commanders. The Vandals, though individually brave, had grown soft amid the pleasures of Carthage. The Gothic cavalry were equally brave but better soldiers. They were to be treated with the utmost respect.

From Reggio, Belisarius marched on Naples keeping to the coast so that his fleet could support him. At first it seemed that Naples might fall without a siege or a battle, but its walls were strong and it was heavily garrisoned. Its native Italian occupants were divided as to whether to stand a siege or turn against the Gothic garrison. Belisarius offered them clemency, and to the Goths he offered a choice of either the freedom to march away or honorable employment in the Emperor's armies of the east. The Goths were not tempted, but the Italians were - until some citizens reminded the rest that if they did not assist the Goths, and the city should fall, Belisarius would be free to proceed against Rome. If he failed to take Rome, Theodatus would take bloody vengeance against the Neapolitans for not supporting the garrison;. Whereas should Belisarius succeed in taking both Naples and Rome and destroying the Gothic power in Italy, the Roman commander was well known for his clemency even against those who had fought the hardest against him. For once the virtue of Belisarius may be said to have worked against him militarily. Naples decided to stand a siege and rely upon the Byzantine commander's humanity, should he take the city anyway.

At first Naples withstood Belisarius. It was protected by the sea on one side and on the other its walls were built upon a steep embankment. Though Belisarius cut its aqueducts, the city was well supplied with wells of fresh water. It withstood several assaults. It was already late autumn and if Naples would not surrender soon, Belisarius would be faced with two equally hard alternatives. He could raise the siege and turn on Rome, but that would leave an enemy garrison at his back; or he could continue the siege. To do the latter, even if Naples succumbed fairly soon, would mean dealing with Rome in the winter. Worse, if Naples held out till spring, Theodatus would be able to gather troops from all over Italy and even from Dalmatia where Mundus had been defeated and killed. Then the Goths would have a numerical superiority several timed what they already had.

However, fortune in the form of an intelligent and innovative Isaurian trooper saved Belisarius from having to make the choice. The man had been exploring an aqueduct which Belisarius had cut. When crawling along its channel he discovered that where it pierced the city wall, the ancient builders had cut the channel through a natural rock. The opening had originally been just large enough to permit the passage of water but not of an enemy. After several centuries, fissures had developed in the boulder and now it would be possible to enlarge the passage without making so much noise as to alert the garrison. Belisarius ordered this done and then summoning one of the leading citizens warned him honestly that the city would fall the following day and he would not be able to forestall pillage and rape by his barbarian foederati if it resisted. The Neapolitans did not believe him, so in the night Belisarius sent a team of sappers into the city through the aqueduct, while other troops outside raised a clamor to hide the noise of their passage. Those excavating muted the sound of their chisels by covering the walls with bags of sand. Antonina's son, Photius, asked the honor of leading the six hundred soldiers assigned to the aqueduct but Belisarius decided on a more experienced officer. Yet he resolved to rely more on his only son, and told Antonina so. Antonina had heard of how Photius had taken the initiative and even assumed command before her husband relieved him. She knew that she should be proud of him, so like herself in audacity if nothing else, but she was not. She felt nothing and knew that was wrong. Had they spent too many years apart? It was as thorough he were someone else's child, a nephew perhaps; a small part of her life but far from the whole of it. When her gentler thoughts strayed to her children, they were to little Joannina in Constantinople.

The six hundred infantry who passed through the aqueduct quickly captured a part of the walls, allowing others to scale them from the other side. Naples fell. The siege had lasted three weeks. Huns stripped the churches of their gold and silver chalices. As Belisarius had warned, in the night vengeful soldiers slaughtered Goths and Italians alike. As quickly as possible Belisarius restored order, himself going about the city and restraining violence.

"Let the Neapolitans know by your forbearance the shame of their refusal to accept your friendship," he would say. When that was not sufficient to restore discipline his Thracian guards did so. By morning he had put an end to the slaughter and released to their families the women his Ephthalite Huns had seized as slaves. Then he went to the Gothic garrison and offered them employment in the emperor's armies. This time the warrior race accepted, the alternative being servitude on some imperial farm without even the camaraderie of camp life.

When word that Naples had fallen reached a Gothic army near Rome they declared Theodatus deposed. When he attempted flight, a personal enemy cut him down on the road to Ravenna.

He was quickly replaced. Witiges, an officer of humble birth, but one who had distinguished himself, was raised on Gothic shields in the field. He wisely determined to put off attacking Belisarius since his forces were widely scattered throughout the kingdom. He left Rome garrisoned with but a few hundred men and retired to Ravenna, there to organize and equip a mighty force with which to deal with the Byzantine invaders in the spring.

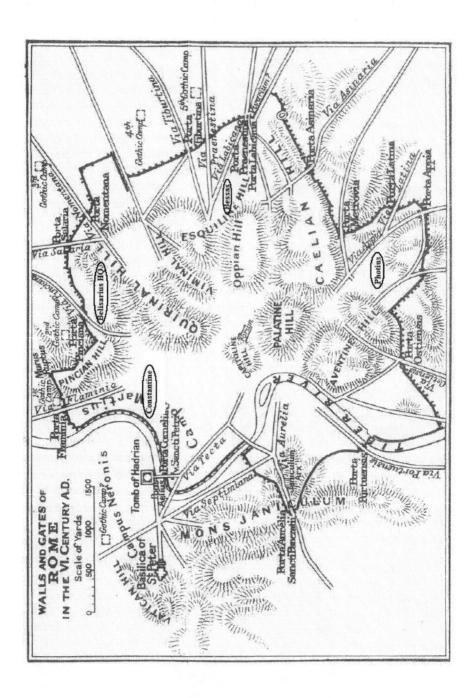

WALLS AND GATES OF
ROME
IN THE VI. CENTURY A.D.

Scale of Yards

0   500   1000   1500

ROME

With Naples secured it was time to march on Rome itself. The Catholic citizenry were so firmly in support of the attacking Byzantine army that they formed a fifth column. The Gothic commander knew he could not defend twelve miles of walls with his tiny force while there were so many dissidents within. He allowed the Byzantines to march in through the southeast-facing Asinarian gate on December 10, as the Goths marched out through the Flaminian directly opposite; from there to begin the march to Ravenna.

Inside, Belisarius could take but little time to admire the remnants of antiquity. He left it to Antonina and Theodosius to visit the famed temples which were falling into ruin or being used for some mundane purpose. While at it they were to make a survey of private wells, and also report any Roman official seen to be hoarding what would be needed by all. For many days the tall Theodosius could be seen leading the general's wife along the broad boulevards, she sitting side saddle as if on a Grecian urn. The citizens could easily imagine that one day the little lady would be queen of Italy.

Rome was still a large city, though no longer the capital even of Italy, and with a much smaller population than at its prime. Belisarius could see that even with local levies it would be difficult to man the extensive and broken walls against the siege which Witiges was certainly preparing. He did manage to do what could be quickly accomplished. Crumbing brick was reinforced with masonry from dilapidated buildings. Some new bastions were constructed by conscript labor. The dry moat was cleared and widened. But the populace were no more pleased with the prospect of a Gothic siege than they had been by a Byzantine one. They tried without success to persuade Belisarius of the untenability of the defenses. His only answer was to remind them that they were Romans, not a rabble. He directed that Syracusan grain from his ships in the Tyrrhenian Sea be carried overland to Rome's granaries. He sent parties of local citizens into the surrounding countryside to glean all that might be saved before the advancing winter or Witiges put an end to gathering provisions.

Inside the old and badly deteriorating walls only remnants of the ancient city remained in anything like the elegance that they had once presented. Some few pagan temples had been converted to churches: the

Pantheon had been successfully transformed, but not many others were architecturally suited to that use. The Senate House still served a Roman aristocracy that the wisdom of Theodoric had permitted to remain functioning as leaders of the native Italians in matters of little importance.

Cattle and sheep were now driven down what in pagan days had been the Sacred Road, under the arches of the fori where once legions had marched in victory parades. It was a strange mixture that Theodosius, Antonina, and the learned Procopius saw and reported on: in part a sad reminder of glory past; in part still a major city of Italy if not the world; in part just rustic, with a population that knew its history more by stories told and embellished by old men, than by familiarity with Roman literature. For better and for worse Christianity and Christian literature had replaced the classics for all but a minority of the learned, and these were becoming fewer and more poorly educated with each passing decade. It was in Rome in the time of Theodoric that Boethius, the last Roman philosopher to deserve that name had lived. With his death the lamp of Classical learning had nearly gone out. Now what light there was emanated from Flavius Cassiodorus who in his lifetime ranged from classical scholar to religious writer, but who served not the city of Rome but the Gothic court in Ravenna. Regrettably, his writings make no mention of Belisarius' campaign in Italy, though certainly as Witiges' first minister he would have been involved in the diplomacy, if not war plans.

In Constantinople, Theodora had "suggested" to Belisarius that Antonina be installed as an arbiter of civil disputes, thus freeing him for concerns about defense. It was done. Few of his officers could have done as well: Bessas, himself a Thracian Goth, both capable and cruel, was too avaricious to be trusted to mete out justice; Constantinus had proven himself a brave and competent commander, but he was too vain not to annoy the locals. Nothing need be said about Bloody John, who would join Belisarius later, other than the name given him by Procopius. Besides being of questionable value in administration, such men were too valuable in the field to be released for civil duties. Anyway, Theodora wanted honest reports from her cubicularia about affairs in Rome, not reports from mutually jealous officers. Procopius was directed to assist Antonina. Though he felt that their positions should have been reversed he understood that Antonina had the empress' ear and Theodora had quite probably indicated to Belisarius that Antonina should be the one in charge.

As soon as it was possible, Belisarius dispatched Bessas and Constantinus to seize several towns of Tuscany, and set up a network of scouts to watch for Gothic movements. He would put into practice the lessons of the school of strategy and tactics, for Italy would not be subdued

186

by a few dramatic victories as had been the case in Africa. It would be a long slog, attacking or defending every major city and many a fortified town along the way to Ravenna.

When Witiges and his Goths reached Rome in March they nearly took the city in one day and Belisarius nearly lost his life. They approached Rome from the northwest, but the Tiber blocked their advance against the city. Belisarius had foreseen the Gothic need to cross by the Milvian bridge which was the single span near to the city. Here was where Constantine the Great had defeated Maxentius in the first case of a Christian army defeating a pagan one. Now Belisarius fortified the historic structure and installed a garrison there.

The approach of the Gothic horde so frightened this garrison that it fled - not into Rome, as might just possibly have been pardonable - but into the countryside. At daybreak the Goths discovered the bridge to be undefended and, like the allies at Remagen in WW II, quickly threw a force across to keep the defenders from destroying it.

Belisarius knew nothing about this until he, with a troop of guards, was observing enemy movements across the Tiber. Suddenly they were charged by mounted enemy on their own south bank and forced to fight their way back into the city.

From the city wall Antonina could see it all but she could do nothing. She could see her husband as she had never seen him before. The general was superior to any trooper with sword or ax. Like a whirlwind he decapitated or unhanded every Goth who came near him, at least twenty who were able to breach the line of Thracian bucellarii who fought like demons from hell to protect their patron. One by one many Thracians died or dropped to the ground severely wounded, but Belisarius continued to kill their killers. The situation was worsened by certain Roman citizens who, preferring Gothic rule, had joined the enemy and now encouraged the Goths to fire at his horse, a bay with a white mark on its face. The Thracians arrayed themselves more tightly around their leader and a brave trooper named Valentine detached himself from Photius, whom he had been guarding, and charged suicidally into the Gothic cavalry. He died but in death bought Belisarius and the others enough seconds to disengage and charge for the Flaminian Gate. Procopius and Antonina watched the man die and Procopius memorialized him in his history. The Roman force had been one thousand men. They lost many, but left a thousand Goths dead on the field.

Antonina could not stay still, but it would be like treason to turn from the sight. With heart in mouth she watched her husband and the few hundred remaining guards race for the gate pursued by all the Gothic reinforcements able to cross the bridge. Had she been a weaker woman she might have fallen in place and cried when they reached the city gate, which somehow remained closed to them.

"Open it, damn it! Open the gate! It's Belisarius, you cowards - not the Gothic army. He'll have you flayed if he lives through this and so will I if he doesn't. Run, Theodosius. Go get some men with guts and help him."

Theodosius hurried to obey his mistress and had Antonina's attention not been totally fixed on the battle outside the wall, she might have been proud of how he took command of a troop of cataphracts and prepared to sortie and attempt to take the Goths in the rear. It wasn't necessary. Realizing that the garrison at the gate was too frightened to open to him, Belisarius wheeled his mount, and with his remaining bucellarii close behind him, charged his pursuers. Confounded, the Goths briefly retreated to regroup. Now Belisarius wheeled again and this time the garrison opened the gate.

"He should flay the whole lot of those cowards.."

"No mi-lady." Theodosius was again with his mistress. "It is enough that they will not dare show themselves in any wine shop where other troops are drinking

That evening Antonina found Belisarius at prayer. "For Valentine," she asked?

"Yes. I owe him my life."

Antonina knelt beside her husband and took his hand. She spoke softly: "'Greater love than this no man hath, then he lay down his life for his friend.' If Valentine has not been a saint till now, today he became one."

The next morning Belisarius called his senior strategoi together just inside the Pincian gate. From this point a rider could reach the Flaminian, Salarian, and Nomentana gates in minutes, for the wisdom of the builders had provided a clear covered way just inside the walls.

"We haven't much time. Witiges will attack as soon as he has siege weapons ready. His troops are Germans who will not tolerate a strategic delay. That is our edge on the barbarians. They have never besieged a city, in Witiges' lifetime anyway, and will be impatient. But we will have to stop siege towers. Brace the gates against rams. Check the city's arsenals. I want ballistae, onagri … and, Photius, see if the jaws of the lupi are still working at the gates.

"Theodosius, see if there is still any money in the city treasury. Cash is always an incentive to a tiring enemy. Antonina, go with him. I don't want you wandering around alone."

Belisarius was carrying the weight of command at a time of near panic among the citizens and anxiety, if not fear, among his troops. Even so, that last remark was sharp and unkind. Antonina was not some brainless bimbo who needed to be hidden away from the action. She bristled.

Belisarius was occupied with the gates and similar defensive matters long into the night. It was not till well into the third watch that Antonina at last convinced her husband to take some food and rest. He had done what could be done before morning and fell asleep immediately, but Antonina laying beside him watched his face for long minutes in the little light an oil lamp emitted. How could he look so calm, she wondered? *He has done everything he could do. He leaves the rest to God.* She had long since forgotten the slight of that afternoon. She was very proud of her hero.

———————————

Belisarius was possibly the only one in Rome to sleep soundly that first night of the siege. There were rumors of Gothic attacks that did more to confound both his army and the civilians than any real action would be likely to have. With every breeze which stirred the trees the citizens imagined the sound of Gothic ladders attacking the walls, while the army feared the size of the enemy force. With the dawn Antonina found her husband awake and giving order after order to a long line of subordinates, impressing on them the need to hold whatever position was assigned to them, and not to rush off to defend some other part of the wall only because of rumors.

"It is impossible for the enemy to win," Belisarius told his officers. At that time none could understand the commander's calm. They thought it but a tactic to relieve tension. Belisarius did not explain lest dissidents take his words to Witiges. He would simply repeat: "It is impossible for the enemy to win," and silently thank the generals he'd chatted up in Constantinople and the experts on siege warfare in the school.

In those first weeks of occupying the eternal city, Antonina began the task of civil administration in a city under siege, and to hold herself ready to assist her husband in any way he might use her. Watching him at a desk, she began to realize why he had spent so many hours in Constantinople preparing all that he could before sailing. There were enough details that could only be dealt with now without his having to delegate who would do what: who would hold what position, bring food, prepare detachments of guards, assist the surgeons, and all the other details that he had arranged weeks before. She also began to appreciate the value of a staff, but only one that would always follow orders; or better yet, anticipate them. That was a rather rare quality in sixth century Byzantium. It seemed to her that the younger the staff officer and the less impatient of obeying orders, the better he performed. She took a bit of pride in the faith her husband put in her son, though for his own sake Belisarius continued to deny him opportunities for martial glory - he had nearly lost the lad at the Flaminian gate that first morning of the siege.

For the next three weeks both sides prepared for a decisive battle. Belisarius reinforced the old Aurelian walls as best he could, and himself took command of the section between the Flaminian and Pincian gates. He walled up the Flaminian but at the urging of the populace left a section of wall near the Pincian gate to totter on a ruined foundation. Clearly this was where Witiges should attack; the wall was weak and his principal camp was nearby. Yet both the Goths and the citizens firmly believed that the wall at that point was protected by St. Peter himself. One morning Antonina and Theodosius were walking past the gate when the lady stumbled on a brick which had come loose.

"Damn! Why don't these Romans fix that wall? Look at it. It's falling down. If the damn Goths come in here my husband will probably get himself licked right here. History will forget all he has done and damn him for an idiot for leaving the city so vulnerable."

"The Goths will not attack here, dilapidated as it is. They believe that St. Peter will never allow this section of wall to fall."

"It's almost falling of its own accord."

"Yes. I know and so do the Goths; but if we reinforce it we will show a lack of faith. That could worry the citizens more than a weak wall for they too believe the legend."

"I haven't that kind of faith."

"Nor I, mi-lady. I'm inclined to think old Pete will help us if we do our part, but not otherwise."

"Uuumm." That was all that Antonina said.

The Pincian wall was never attacked, though each time she passed Antonina eyed it with the disapproving look that wives have. It amused Belisarius once he was certain that the legend had the same strength in both Gothic and Roman minds.

"I hope that belief, even if unfounded, will keep the Goths out. Witiges knows the legend and even if he doesn't believe it many of his men

190

will. It is futile to order your troops into a battle they believe they cannot win. Even so, this is where I'll keep my headquarters."

From the windows of a once proud palace which Belisarius had commandeered as a regimental headquarters, the army leaders could clearly see several of the nearest Gothic camps to the north and west. Most of the west was protected by the Tiber and the southern walls were as yet unthreatened, though surely Witiges would soon add garrisons there. Belisarius would need to place a reliable lieutenant to watch the southern approach, one who could be trusted to take action on his own if necessary without undermining his authority. The south was far more important to defense of the city than Witiges seemed to realize. Although it was unlikely that Witiges would choose to fight his way up from the south and engage in man to man fighting within the city itself, to leave that part of the defenses unthreatened made it easy for Belisarius to be resupplied from the port of Ostia or receive food from the Campania up the Latin Way.

"Photius, I need a reliable officer to protect our supply lines."

"Yes father," Photius answered; then aware that they were discussing military affairs, rephrased himself. "Yes General."

Belisarius looked him in the eye. He did not smile, but at least he did not frown. "I want you to scout the roads to the south. Procopius has an eye for detail; bring him with you, and some lancers; and for God's sake, if you spot an enemy, get back inside the walls."

Photius would be trusted to watch for Gothic movements that might threaten the two roads from the south, the Latin and Appian. It was of sufficient importance to please his son and the danger would not be too great.

CHAPTER 15

537 AD
ROME

The attack came early on March 30. It took Belisarius only a moment to realize what it was that had disturbed his sleep. He quickly rose and threw on a tunic. He took no time to more than wave a kiss to Antonina before running into the street. To the amazement of a few guards that he was passing, he suddenly dropped to the ground and put his ear against it, but only for a moment. Even before he stood up he was calling out orders to rouse the garrison and have the bells of the nearest church ring an alarm to warn the other posts. When an orderly appeared at his headquarters' door he yelled at him to carry word to Constantinus, Bessas, Peranius the Iberian and the other commanders that a major attack was imminent.

Indeed Belisarius was not the first in Rome to be disturbed from sleep by the little earthquake outside the walls. Before the bells nearest the Pincian gate rang out their warning, those of a church near the Nomentana gate peeled. Within two minutes the city was alive with ringing bells and shouting noncoms.

A mere spoiling attack hoping to find the guards at one of the city's gates asleep would not have been of great concern; the guards were awake and in the course of the siege there would be sixty nine battles large and small. But the ground had spoken to Belisarius of the movement of thousands of men and horses. Witiges had launched his spring offensive. If he could take Rome quickly he would be able to remove his troops from what would become a pestilential bog with the spring rains, made worse by the flow from the aqueducts that he himself would soon cut.

Belisarius' subordinates at the Flaminian section rushed to where their commander was. His orderly brought the general's armor. Those civilians still in the city stood around looking worried and asking every passing soldier what they should do. Some were anxious to help protect the city; most their own hides. When Theodosius came rushing up still fastening a bit of armor at his shoulder, he hardly needed to hear his orders to know what his duty would be this day. "Go! Protect Antonina; she's in your charge. And don't let her do anything brave and stupid. I've enough to keep me occupied."

All morning the enemy host assembled before several gates so that the defenders could not know where their main attack would come. But finally that became obvious when several large wooden towers pulled by oxen and covered in wet hides to protect them from fire arrows were seen to be approaching the wall near the Salarian gate. Belisarius hurried to the spot as did those few officers who did not have a specific duty. Mostly these were young infantry lieutenants who would lead squads charged with removing the dead and wounded, and with pouring fresh sand on the battlements when they would become slippery with blood. The surgeons were at their stations and the cooks were preparing something hot and filling for the soldiers who would likely not eat again until night, and for those who would never eat again.

Belisarius watched the approaching towers with an equanimity which baffled his subordinates. Such towers usually sheltered a great battering ram with which to break a gate and fifty or more men whose bows would overreach the city wall. It was good to be calm in danger. It stiffened the frightened if their commander calmly paced before them, his hands behind him, and a stoic look upon his face which revealed nothing of his thoughts. But Belisarius was more than stoic he actually seemed unconcerned. Finally, when the towers were within a hundred yards, with several Gothic nobles in gilded armor directing them, he asked a nearby infantryman for an arrow and the loan of his bow. Not many archers could have brought down a man at that range, much less been able to pick out a single man within a group. Belisarius did.

"Another arrow, guardsman."

Another Gothic noble fell, his chest transfixed despite the scale armor that both he and his horse wore. Then a third fell before the remaining flower of Gothic aristocracy retired out of range leaving a few hundred infantry to protect the towers from a Roman sally. The towers advanced, but Belisarius was not finished.

"Captain! Have your archers fire at the oxen." Having given what should have been the most obvious - but also the most important - order of the day, Belisarius turned away and descended a ladder. "That will delay them a bit."

On the wall several hundred Roman infantry and Ephthalite archers watched their commander dumbfounded. Why had no one but Belisarius thought to shoot the oxen? It was a simple thing, but no one else had thought of it. "That's why he's in charge and I'm not," one of the more modest officers admitted. "He'd also make one hell of an archer" a Ephthalite Hun opined in a thick accent and street Greek. No one disputed either remark. Antonina watching from the window of a villa knew without hearing what the troops were saying. She had seen it all and had known what would happen. She had known what Belisarius would do when she

194

saw oxen pulling the Gothic towers. *Dumb. Dumb as a paving stone.* Most of the people at court in Constantinople were more or less smart. These Goths were like the touts she had known at the Hippodrome. It wasn't education either. The Gothic lords were well educated by the standards of the day. Dumb is more basic than that.

At her side Theodosius was also watching the events on the wall. He admired his commander but he had not envisioned what would happen. Now Theodosius was not dumb but neither was he a tactician. Belisarius would have destroyed him in a game of latrunculi and he knew it.

"Theodosius, don't be so protective. You've got me a quarter mile from the action," said Antonina.

"Orders are orders," Theodosius replied with a smile.

"Orders can be stretched. Find us some work to do. Belisarius didn't say that I had to be shut up like some teenage cubicularia with a powerful father not to be offended. I can treat a wound as well as most battle surgeons; not every injured man needs to be crippled by some medic in a hurry."

"Unladylike, mi-lady."

"OK, I'll only treat the Greeks, not the Huns."

Theodosius smiled again, not sure whose wrath he would prefer: Belisarius' or Antonina's. But he did lead the way through safe alleys to a dressing station where together they made themselves useful. Antonina could indeed clean and bandage a wound with skill while her protector ran errands, also keeping one eye on his mistress that she not leave the safety of the villa cum hospital. They assisted the surgeons throughout the day, till dusk when the battle at the wall finally ebbed. By then both were filthy, but they continued to comfort the wounded until late in the evening. A few of the great Roman baths were still functioning so before heading to the General's quarters they were able to be rinsed off by a slave, take a very quick dip to finish off, and dress in some clean tunics that another slave had found. For modesty the slave had brought the biggest to be found for Antonina, as though she gave a hoot. Heck, she felt more alive than she had in weeks. She and Theodosius had been useful and now they were clean and smelled nice as well. Not bad for a day of battle.

As for Belisarius, the Goths withdrew from the Salarian gate after the initial attack, pursued by a cloud of Ephthalite arrows and ballistae darts that could, and did, pin an armored man to a tree. But reports of battle elsewhere reached him. These came from two other positions at once. The Goths were attacking at both the Praenestine gate to his south east and at the

195

tomb of the emperor Hadrian to his southwest. Belisarius had little concern for the latter. The massive structure - more a fort than a tomb and today known as the Castillo Sant' Angelo - was under the command of the aggressive (if arrogant) Constantinus. But at the Praenestine, Bessas, although another worthy commander, was being hard pressed by Witiges himself.

At that point the city wall was rather low and another even lower wall, originally intended to enclose wild animals in the days of human slaughter at the Coliseum, had been built between two angles of the main one. Both walls had fallen into disrepair over the centuries and Gothic war machines were smashing the rotten brickwork. Not withstanding this, a disheartened group of infantry were yet attempting to hold the outer wall and being mauled.

As soon as Belisarius felt he could safely leave the defense of the Salarian gate to subordinates, he ordered some of his best infantry to follow him and raced under the protection of the covered way to aid Bessas. Quickly summing up the situation, he ordered that the defenders retreat to the inner defense and lay aside all their weapons except swords. Now the Goths joyfully breached the lower outer wall, only to find themselves confined between the two defense works and too densely packed to form a battle line when Belisarius and Bessas led the Romans against them. The slaughter was not unlike that of the ruffian factions in the Hippodrome five years before except that the Goths did not kill each other, but in confusion to escape fell to Roman swords. Those who tried to rescale the outer wall and escape mostly fell to arrows directed at them from atop the inner defense. When at last the Gothic survivors succeeded in retreating, it was possible to draw the wounded of both sides within the protection of the walls. They were given over to the surgeons and the priests each doing his task in the safety of a nearby church.

While this was happening on the eastern side of the city, Hadrian's tomb was being attacked by a Gothic infantry force, which was able to closely approach by using the arcades and porticoes of the original church of St. Peter's, the predecessor of the present basilica. The tomb was held by a mere handful of Roman infantry who were without their leader. Constantinus, rather than keeping his assigned place, had led the bulk of the defenders against a minor but unexpected attack elsewhere. A small group of Goths, had perceived that very few troops manned the defenses at a spot near the Porta Aurelia and began to ford the Tiber (which it had been assumed by Belisarius would form an adequate defense). Constantinus led a squad of cavalry against them and the Goths quickly retreated. However, while he was about this business his station at Hadrian's tomb had come under attack. The defenders were reduced to breaking off parts of the statues that decorated the mausoleum and casting them against the Goths who were scaling the building's walls with ladders. Fortunately for Constantinus these troops held the fort until he returned to his assigned duty and led a charge which broke the Gothic attack and preserved the integrity of Rome's defenses.

But the day's work was not over. Having met defeat at three points the Goths were disheartened and in no mood to resist when to their dismay they saw Belisarius, who should have been killed many times that day, alive and leading his finest cavalry from the Salarian gate directly at them. Bessas led another force from an adjoining sally port, and together they mashed the Goths between them with a double envelopment. They fled and the Byzantines burned the towers and rams, ladders and ballistae with which Witiges had tried to intimidate them.

Procopius confided to his diary that thirty thousand Goths died that day and an equal number were wounded. Belisarius was as exhausted as any man but spent hours supervising the reestablishment of order. The Gothic dead needed to be quickly buried, many between the double walls where he and Bessas had slaughtered them. The rubble at Hadrian's tomb was cleared. Frightened citizens were herded into churches where mid level officers reassured them of their safety. Spent arrows were collected for reuse, and swords and axes sharpened.

Finally, Antonina, now bathed and scented, herself washed the grime from his body. He nearly fell asleep but rose to perform one more duty. He could have put it off until morning, but who could know what morning would bring - Another attack, perhaps? He called for Procopius and dictated a letter to Justinian. Procopius has preserved the text. A modern might excuse Justinian if he found Belisarius to be lecturing him in much the same voice as he'd used when writing to the Persian commander Perozes at Dara. In his defense, many lives were at stake; it was no time for circumspection. Then too, Procopius may have added some thoughts that Belisarius intended to be delivered verbally and more diplomatically by his courier.

Now all that has been achieved by us hitherto, whether it has been due to some kind fortune or to valor, is for the best; but as to our prospects from now on, I could wish better things for your cause. However, I shall never hide from you anything that it is my duty to say and yours to do, knowing that while human affairs follow whatever course may be in accordance with God's will, yet those who are in charge of any enterprise always win praise or blame according to their own deeds. Therefore let both arms and soldiers be sent to us in such numbers that from now on we may engage with the enemy in this war with an equality of strength. For one ought not to trust everything to fortune, since fortune, on its part, is not given to following the same course forever. But do thou, O Emperor, take this thought to heart, that if at this time the barbarians win the victory over us, we shall be cast out of Italy which is thine and shall lose the army in addition. Besides all this we shall have to bear the shame, however great it may be, that attaches to our conduct. For I refrain from saying that we should also be regarded as having ruined Rome's citizenry, men who have held their safety more lightly than their loyalty to your kingdom. Consequently, if this should happen, the result for us will be that the successes we have won thus far will in the end prove to have been but a prelude to calamities. For if it had so happened that we had been repulsed from Rome and Campania and, at a much earlier time, from Sicily, we should only be feeling the sting of the lightest of all misfortunes, that of having found ourselves unable to grow wealthy on the possessions of others. And again, this too is worthy of consideration by you, that it has never been possible even for many times ten thousand men to guard Rome for any considerable length of time, since the city embraces a large territory, and, because it is not on the sea, is shut off from all supplies. Although at the present time the Romans are well disposed toward us, yet when their troubles are prolonged, they will probably not hesitate to choose the course which is better for their own interests. For when men have entered into friendship with others on the spur of the moment, it is not while they are in evil fortune, but while they prosper, that they are accustomed to keep faith with them. Furthermore, the Romans will be compelled by hunger to do many things they would prefer not to do. Now as for me, I know I am bound even to die for your kingdom, and for this reason no man will ever be able to remove me from this city while I live; but I beg you to consider what kind of a fame such an end of Belisarius would bring you.

"Thank you, Procopius." Belisarius patted the bed. "Antonina, let's go to sleep." By the time Antonina slipped under the covers. he already was asleep.

Since his attack on the walls had failed miserably, Witiges settled down to besieging the city. Belisarius hated standing a siege. Not only was hunger and pestilence a given, boredom and indiscipline would threaten his authority. Every commander under him would have his own ideas. Some would want to treat with the enemy; others would prefer to die in a hopeless attack. Mutiny by the first group could be put down by swift action. Belisarius would assuage the blood lust of the others by frequent sallies to disrupt and inconvenience the Goths, whilst Rome's civilians stole some bags of grain.

Justinian did send reinforcements but they were few in number, and Belisarius was unable to spare men to hold the river route from Porto on the coast. Communications with the sea were not entirely broken, however, as it was still possible to bring supplies up a more difficult and circuitous route from Ostia, the original port of Rome, although by this date its docks and warehouses had fallen into disrepair. This route was rough along a deteriorating road and up the shallow and winding Tiber. To stretch what resources of food he had and for their own safety Belisarius ordered most of the city's women and children, as well as the aged, and slaves who might be disloyal, to leave the city. These removed themselves without molestation by the Goths, down the Appian Way to comfortable exile in the Campania, or by boat along the Tiber, to Porta from whence they sailed to refuge in Sicily.

Witiges cut the aqueducts feeding the fountains and baths of Rome. They had also powered water mills that ground the city's grain. The senate met and spent many hours considering whose nephew should be charged with engineering a way for the remaining slaves to do this work. While they were making speeches and deals Antonina arrived and suggested that the august body retire to a park alongside the Tiber. When they arrived they were amazed to see that a pair of wheels had been unfixed from their mountings in a mill and remounted between boats below a bridge on the river. Constricted as the water was when passing through the arches supporting the span, it exited with enough force to turn the wheels.

"Brilliant," a senator said. "Let's move the other wheels onto the river. Whose idea was it?

"Belisarius'," Antonina said as she walked away, as though it were no big thing for her husband. She just loved showing up the old jerks for the idiots they were. *Probably inbreeding*, she though. It was not a Christian thought, or a charitable thought. It was mean spirited, which was why it was so satisfying. *Mill wheels or not, they'll soon be hungry enough.* Antonina understood hunger.

Belisarius had won himself a minor place among inventors, and his technique of allowing rivers to grind flour was imitated into the nineteenth century.

As Theodora's representative, Antonina had authority in many civil matters. She could and did give orders to officers of the Byzantine commissariat and medical staff, and to any native Roman whose help she required. Nor would it help any of them to appeal to Belisarius who was happy to entrust non military matters to someone whom he trusted. Wells of clean water were "found" in cellars, white linens were "donated" by Roman aristocrats for bandages, and even a few church vestments were "liberated" to make litters for the wounded. Monks buried the dead and the priests were delighted that the only work assigned to them was comforting the dying and saying masses for the deceased. Pope Silvarius remained out of sight. He was a loyal Catholic who had offended Theodora by refusing to enter into communion with her Monophysite choice for patriarch of Constantinople. Doubtless he was in prayer, though whether for victory, or for the dead and wounded, or for himself is not known.

Though the aqueducts were down there was an adequate supply of water from wells, and from cisterns which caught the rainfall. But the citizens missed their luxuries. How little they realized that it would get far worse than having to haul buckets and settle for occasional sponge baths. Witiges sent logs and bodies down the river to smash and foul Belisarius' water mills, but Belisarius ordered a chain run between the arches of the bridges where the wheels were. This caught the refuse and the dead. Before the Goths might completely encircle the great city he again sent teams into the southern countryside to gather as much of the early spring foliage as might be edible.

Antonina, Theodosius, and Photius stood the siege of Rome with Belisarius. The military details are a study in siege defense. While the Goths made many fruitless assaults upon the city from the seven camps with which they partially ringed it, they neglected for months to stop supplies coming from the south. Even after they finally cut the water route up the Tiber, Belisarius was able, by distracting the Goths with sudden sallies, to send foraging parties to harvest fields at night. His enemy should have either controlled these fields or destroyed them. Worse for the Goths, by cutting the aqueducts Witiges turned his own camps into a marsh where malaria bred and infected his army.

At last Witiges realized how much relief Rome was obtaining from the Campania. Employing the existing masonry where the arches of two aqueducts crossed he constructed a strong-point to control the countryside between the Latin and Appian Ways. But by then it was June, fully six months into the siege. It was hot and the pestilence was getting worse.

Pets and strays were eaten of course, but Belisarius was able to partially stock the granaries and occasionally even raid Gothic supplies with quick cavalry sorties that masked foraging expeditions. His Arab light cavalry would cross between the Gothic camps at night to gather edible plants while their mounts grazed. Sometimes they were even able to "liberate" a few sheep or a dog, and return before the Goths could organize an attack. He would also send parties by night just to harry the Goths, on occasion leading one himself. If Witiges and his men had thought that besieging a city inconvenienced only the besieged they had just learned otherwise.

When Belisarius lead such a sortie, Antonina would stand the night through on the battlements, awaiting her husband's return. Theodosius would join her, and if no one was near, sometime put an arm around her waist to reassure her. She made no objection. Antonina had never been one for false modesty. Her husband understood this and loved her for it. Theodosius did too. He knew that Antonina had seen more of the world and its falsities and pretensions than many of the soldiers or any philosopher. A little innocent closeness between them helped them through the nights and through the siege. When Belisarius would return toward dawn he just wanted to sleep. That was OK, Antonina was just happy that he had survived. She would spend the time till he awoke looking at him, trying to understand just what sort of man it was that she had married: a great general, a fearsome soldier, a saint, and a lover. Antonina had known many men and been fond of a few. One marries one of them; that doesn't mean one does not love the others. Theodosius was fun and he was there when Belisarius wasn't, but Belisarius was the finest man that Antonina had ever known.

Witiges had alienated the Roman populace by executing a group of their senators, whom he had confined in Ravenna at the beginning of hostilities. When Justinian's promised reinforcements arrived - sixteen hundred Ephthalite cavalry under Martinus and Valerian - the Romans were happy to see Belisarius take the war to the enemy, at least in a limited manner. To quote from the delightful English historian, Thomas Hodgkin:

"Meanwhile the Gothic blockade, into which the siege was resolving itself, was of the feeblest and most inefficient kind. Leaving all the praise of dash and daring to the scanty bands of their enemies, the Goths clung timidly to their unwieldy camps, in which no doubt already pestilence was lurking. They never ventured forth by night, seldom except in large companies by day. The light Moorish horsemen were their especial terror. If a Goth wandered forth into the Campania alone, to cut fodder for his horse or to bring one of the oxen in from pasture, he was almost sure to see one of these children of the desert bearing down upon him. With one cast of the Moor's lance the Goth was slain, his arms and his barbaric adornments were stripped from him, and the Moor was off again full speed towards home before the avenger could be upon his track.

"Belisarius, on the other hand, organized his defense of the city so thoroughly as to leave as little as possible to the caprice of Fortune. To prevent his own little band of soldiers from being worn out by continual sentinel duty, especially at night, and at the same time to keep from starvation the Roman proletariat, all of whose ordinary work was stopped by the siege, he instituted a kind of National Guard, He mixed a certain number of these citizen soldiers with his regular troops, paying each of them a small sum for his daily maintenance, and dividing the whole amalgamated force into companies, to each of whom was assigned the duty of guarding a particular portion of the walls by day or by night. To obviate the danger of treachery, these companies were shifted every fortnight to some part of the circuit at a considerable distance from that which they last guarded. After the same interval the keys of every gate of the city were brought to him, melted down and cast afresh with different wards, the locks of course being altered to suit them. The names of the sentinels were entered upon a list which was called over each day. The place of any absent soldier or citizen was at once filled up, and he was summoned to the general's quarters to be punished, likely capitally punished, for his delinquency. All the night, bands of music played at intervals along the walls, to keep the defenders awake and to cheer their drooping courage. All night too, the Moors, the terrible Moors, were instructed to prowl round the base of the walls, accompanied by bloodhounds, in order to detect any attempt by the Goths at a nocturnal escalade."

From atop the city wall, Belisarius and Antonina were observing some movements of Gothic cavalry when Theodosius came up to them carrying cups and a jug of water. This he'd mixed with a bit of honey and the juice of a lemon – lemon trees still being available from what had once been the decorative gardens of Roman villas. While they sipped at this Belisarius' attention was drawn to a group of Gothic officers.

"I've seen them before but at the Praenestine gate. Witiges must be moving his troops from camp to camp, or at least the officers."

"Oh, I've seen them all, Theodosius said while pointing. That one is 'Pinky.'" Belisarius and Antonina almost laughed. Indeed the Goth was dressed in an absurdly pink shirt and trousers. "And the guy next to him, he's 'Four Fingers.'" He lost a thumb to an Herulian ax some months ago." This was Theodosius at his best; disdaining the very men who might one day kill all of them. "That man riding up is 'Cloisonne.' His armor sparkles like the sun, but he never gets too near the fighting."

Now Antonina was grinning and even her more serious husband allowed himself a smile. "Careful that they don't hear you. You make them sound more a mob of robbers than a noble enemy. They mightn't like that." Now they all tittered and began hurling unkind comments in the direction of the enemy officers who stupidly came nearer to hear what the Byzantine officers were saying. At this the levity ceased and Belisarius asked a nearby archer for the loan of his bow. Cloisonne took a shot in his sword arm.

Finally, in three major sallies Belisarius cost the Goths four thousand men. Elated by these victories, though vastly outnumbered, the citizens of Rome and many of his own troops clamored for a decisive battle.

Belisarius knew that to refuse this request while hunger stalked the city would be to court disaffection and desertion. He therefore planned a battle which he thought would cost him little, rediscipline the army and citizenry, and even discourage his enemy. He enlisted those civilians who clamored for a battle; these generally being the same type of street toughs that he had engaged at the hippodrome in Constantinople five years before. These recruits he stationed at Hadrian's tomb to intimidate the enemy with their warlike clamor but ordered them not to advance beyond the security of the fortification.

With his cavalry he broke from the Salarian gate. For a time the battle swayed one way and the other. As often as the Byzantines broke a Gothic force a fresh one would assault them. But while this battle flowed one way and the other, disaster met the Roman recruits at Hadrian's tomb. Disobeying their orders, the undisciplined civilians charged a Gothic unit. For a brief time they were successful until, undisciplined as they were, they began to loot the dead. Minutes later they were taken under fire when the Goths turned to the attack.

Belisarius managed to lead all his chastened forces back within the safety of the city walls without undue losses, but that was the last pitched battle fought. The war settled back into one of siege. Antonina stood the siege like a trooper. *But I'm not a trooper,* she thought. *Why did he take me to this awful place? To see the sights?*

That evening Antonina felt she should invite Photius to share dinner. A slave had located a small amount of salted meat – just enough for a single sparse meal, so there was no need to share it outside her household. (She did, however, see to it that the slave received a share.) As one might expect, dinner started off rather seriously with Belisarius leading an analysis of the day's battle.

"Well, that's done. I don't think the local Romans will want to face Gothic lances again for awhile. Photius, you did well today; but you must remember not to get ahead of your bucellarii. You are a prime target, being my son. If you were to be taken alive I would not be able to save you. Do you understand?

"Yes, sir." Photius used the formal form of address of a subordinate officer to his commander. "I would neither expect nor desire any more help than what you might do to assist someone else."

"Antonina, I hope that you understand too. Photius insists on proving himself in battle. I'll have better uses for him after he's proven his manliness to himself."

"I understand." Antonia spoke without emotion. One might think that she showed less concern for Photius' survival in battle than did her husband; but, in fact, she was concerned, if no more so than for Belisarius or Theodosius.

As dinner progressed and wine flowed, conversation became livelier. It became clear that Belisarius worried over Photius as a true father might. Photius was brave but not as strong as many in the army, and a bit too headstrong to stand back from a fight. Belisarius wanted to keep him safe but without disgrace.

"Photius, you are no longer just a leader of a few squadrons, but a senior officer. Your men depend upon your ability to make quick incisive decisions, not upon your prowess with a sword or an ax. Oh, I know that I fight too much myself. I'm inclined to let myself get into trouble. But I'm always with the finest bucellarii in the world. I suggest that you do as your father says, and not as he does."

Antonina tittered and nodded in agreement. She would have broken into a laugh if the subject under discussion were not one of life and death. As the conversation continued it took more of a turn to tactics. Not feeling qualified to participate, Antonina jumped up from her seat and with an aristocratic laugh announced that she intended to behave more like a

Roman. She took her plate and goblet to a nearby couch on which she sprawled Roman-style to listen. *How like myself Photius is in many things,* she thought. She also acknowledged that to not be an unmixed blessing. *If I had stayed at the table we would be butting heads before the evening was out.*

Belisarius brought Antonina along with him as he toured the defenses. They rode together, or, more exactly, Antonina rode on her husband's quarter, as he was engaged in conversation with Theodosius. She couldn't hear what they were saying, but suddenly Belisarius' voice was raised, a thing that was unusual if not rare, and Theodosius hurried off. Now Antonina rode up beside Belisarius who remained silent, even sullen.

"The guards on the Praenestine gate were drunk last night and I hear about it the next afternoon. If the Goths had known, we'd all be dead. For all we know, the Goths could even have been behind it, but your friend Theodosius was just defending the guards."

Antonina said nothing. To defend Theodosius would be unwise. Besides, Belisarius was right. She knew that she had grown too fond of Theodosius, but the thought of being on the end of a Gothic pike was more than unpleasant. Anyway, Belisarius had far too much to attend to now without having to enforce discipline. That should have been done by others. Then Theodosius would only have had to report a flogging to his commander instead of an unpunished breach of discipline. Belisarius would have simply nodded an approval and that would have been the end of it. As it was, he'd have to take needed time to harangue his lieutenants for their slovenliness.

"Where did they get that much strong wine anyway?" Belisarius was still fuming. "As likely as not it was from the Goths. For all I know it may have been spiked with opium. Witiges must be getting unpopular by now. He is getting desperate for a victory, and our guards nearly hand it to him for a few flagons of wine."

Belisarius was so angry that he might have ordered some executions were it not that he was unsure that the Goths were behind the affair. It might just as well have been that some soldier found a stash in someone's cellar. Even so, the officer in charge would be reduced to the ranks and the whole army informed of how he and his men had endangered them. Belisarius also considered a few whippings, but finally concluded that he did not want a reputation for harshness; humiliation would probably be more effective.

That evening Antonina had the pleasure of watching the offending garrison paraded before the entire army, or at least those not needed to man the defenses. They were hooted and jeered and Belisarius gave one of his famous harangues. He blamed not only the drunken guards but the noncoms and lieutenants for laxity. That would end now; the troops would in fact feel let down if their officers did not begin to inflict penalties for the slightest indiscipline. They understood that, besieged in a distant land, their lives depended upon being an army, and not a rabble in arms.

Belisarius had his hands full. He readily left to his wife the details of civil life. Antonina had long since shown her aptitude. Whereas Belisarius was inclined to trust in the honesty of suppliants, even when he despised their cowardice or avarice, Antonina was calculating and assumed the same of everyone who came before her. Whereas Belisarius was known for his Christian mercy, Antonina was not. Belisarius could slit a nose or mete out capital punishment, but that was for discipline, not out of spite.

Antonina saw herself as simply the cold instrument of Theodora and Roman law. Mercy was weakness, Theodora had told her, and Antonina knew full well the danger of showing weakness in a city filled with hungry riffraff. If they were to successfully stand the siege, control would be vital. Day by day she would sit as though enthroned and mete out harsh justice to petty criminals like those who had treated her like a piece of meat at the hippodrome. She had more sympathy for the wife who had killed an abusive husband than with thieves and muggers. The wife had only offended against one man and probably a deserving one. The hoods made their living off the the whole of the society in which they claimed membership; a logical absurdity.

Though Belisarius was restrained when that served discipline better than severe punishment, he had instructed Antonina to be strict with those who defrauded the poor. She had known that kind herself and hardly needed instruction. Such men did not even have enough conscience to be ashamed. She had no authority to order executions but many had their backs ripped. Of course Antonina knew that some small crimes were simply the acts of desperate people. These cases were the saddest, but the hardship of the siege must be evenly felt. It was wrong that one family should starve so that another be adequately fed.

She reserved her gentler side to acts outside of her official duties. She had acquired a small supply of honey, and would have her servants distribute it on bits of bread, a little at a time, to the city's remaining children; those who had not been able to flee because of sickness or

206

crippling injuries. She remembered how much a bit of honey bread from some baker had once meant to her in the world of the hippodrome, where few people gave away anything without expecting something in return. She also thought of Joannina, back home in Constantinople, where every courtier would be offering her sweets. *These kids have nothing. Some have lost their parents.* It was done anomalously, of course; she had a reputation to uphold; but she hoped that Christ Jesus would weigh such small acts and a Divine thumb against her many sins: "As you show mercy, so shall mercy be shown to you."

Treason was properly the business of Belisarius, so it was that both he and Antonina interviewed any civilian suspected of aiding the Goths. Belisarius would be troubled for their souls if they were executed, so he was inclined toward mercy when he felt remorse was heartfelt, and the treason was the result of starvation. Antonina's view of people was less charitable. More often she would be content with justice. Fortunately for many, only Belisarius could order an execution.

After nine months, when the besieged had lost the excess weight of comfortable bergers, and the troops were themselves in danger of losing their fighting edge from hunger and disease, a messenger was caught trying to exit a sally port in the night. Hidden in his garments was a letter from Pope Silvarius, offering to open a gate to Witiges. It was brought to Belisarius and Antonina that same night.

"Damn, he's the pope. I can't just arrest him."

"Certainly you can, Flavius. He's a traitor."

"He's the pope."

"The pope, more than anyone else, must uphold the empire. If Silvarius supports the Arian Goths, he betrays his duty both to Christ and to the empire. We must set an example. ... Dammit; I sound like some priest. Anyway, you're in military command, but Theodora made it clear that I have to represent the throne; her throne, which Silvarius has betrayed. I will try to judge him like I have every other traitor, but you must be present. Not everyone recognizes my authority. As you say: 'He is the pope,' and I am still a woman."

Belisarius did not sleep well that night. Had Silvarius actually betrayed the empire, or merely the empress? He knew that Theodora had intended that the archdeacon Vigilius be made pope instead of Silvarius, for Silvarius had loudly attacked the deposed Monophysite Anthimus, and had refused to accept him as patriarch in Constantinople. Theodora had even sent letters to Belisarius with instructions that Silvarius be arrested on whatever pretext could be found. He had pretended not to be able to deal with Silvarius at the time, but now he must. Did he also suspect that Silvarius' letter was forged as historians have claimed? If so, it was at the instigation of his empress who wanted Silvarius dead. So long as Belisarius did not know that for a fact he could accept the letter as the plaint of a shepherd trying to save the lives of his flock. Maybe he could save the pontiff's life. The next effort against him might be less subtle, perhaps a knife while he slept, to be blamed on some disgruntled priest or an Arian assassin.

In the morning Belisarius ordered Photius to carry a private message to Silvarius urging him to assent to the empress' wishes regarding Anthimus, for his own survival and for peace in the church.

"Your Holiness, for your own good, listen to what my father asks."

"Captain, I cannot accept having a heretic on a patriarchal throne just for my own good."

"Holiness, I know little of theology; but I do know that confrontation can be avoided, and it should be for the sake of Christ's empire. It is usually possible to be vague, at least until troublemakers die or the world changes. I'm sure that Anthimus can write a confession of faith that does not insult your beliefs."

At first Silvarius seemed willing, but in the end he refused. The issue was joined and Belisarius felt he had no choice. What had to be done, had to be done. Besides, Silvarius might quite well be guilty of treason after all. That afternoon Belisarius again sent Photius to Silvarius, this time to arrest the pope. However he refused to take direct part in the charade; were he to do so and find Silvarius guilty, he might have to punish the old priest with death. Instead Antonina took the high dais, resting on a couch as Theodora's representative, and Belisarius sat at her feet.

"Tell us, Lord Pope Silvarius, what have we done to thee and to the Romans that you should wish to betray us into the hands of the Goths?"

Silvarius made no reply of innocence or excuse, for the verdict was already settled. Even before Antonina finished speaking, Silvarius was stripped of his papal insignia, given a monk's robe, and sent into exile. It is said that Justinian later reversed Theodora's demand and ordered that Silvarius be returned to Rome to face a fair trial. If so it was too late for him. Silvarius died in exile before this could be arranged against the machinations of his successor as pope, Theodora's favorite, the archdeacon Vigilius.

Again, Belisarius slept little that night, but Antonina rested well, comfortably in the knowledge that she had further ingratiated herself with Theodora. *Who cares who's pope,* was her last thought before falling into a

208

sound sleep.

Belisarius decided to send a small and innocent looking group of civilians to Naples. Among them would be Procopius who would try to organize a relief force composed of reinforcements expected from Constantinople and some cataphracts who had earlier been scattered among several small cities to assure their continued allegiance. With these troops, Procopius was to bring supplies to Rome via the lightly besieged route from Ostia.

At the same time, Belisarius was concerned for Antonina. She had angered the Roman clergy and citizens in the Silvarius affair. Silvarius had been guilty either of treason, or at the very least of disregard for the dignity of Her Serenity, the empress, whose earlier summons to Constantinople for consultation he had ignored. But still, he had been their pope. Vigilius, his successor, appeared a spineless fraud, who'd acquired the papacy by the support of Antonina; and possibly a large bribe to some of the clergy. The overall result was that the populace was inclining ever more toward surrendering Rome to Witiges. It seemed to the pious that a woman outranked the general. There were even rumors that she was a sorceress. It were best for morale and for her own safety that Antonina also leave the city. A few nights after dispatching Procopius who had easily slipped through the Gothic lines, he determined to send out another force, part of which was to seize Tivoli and another part to take Terracina, thus flanking the besiegers and cutting their supply lines. With the troops sent to Terracina he included Antonina. She and a few guards were to proceed into the Campania, thence to continue to the safety of Naples.

As Antonina had always underestimated Belisarius, he now under-estimated his wife. Instead of proceeding to Naples, for once, she and Procopius worked in tandem. Both rallied troops whom they found wandering about singly or in small groups.

They rallied hundreds. Antonina was no longer the tease who had drank wine with troops on the way to Africa. As in the Silvarius affair, she was the emissary of Theodora and was to be obeyed. Still, when it pleased her mood there was a lilt in her voice to match the firmness, and she would join the soldiers surrounding her in some of the less bawdy verses of tunes that armies have marched to for centuries.

At last two thousand cataphracts arrived at Otranto from Constantinople and proceeded by rapid marches to the Campania, where they met up with the troopers of Procopius and Antonina. An additional three thousand Isaurian cavalry commanded by Narses' friend, Bloody John, later landed at Naples and from there proceeded toward Ostia.

To occupy Witiges and prevent him from attacking these two relief columns, Belisarius effected a distraction: one might think that having been besieged and starved, the Byzantine defenders would be cowering behind the city walls. Such was not their general's way. A wall, as any commander can tell you, will only hold off a determined attacker for so long. Eventually even the mightiest defenses must fall, if not from attack by the besiegers or from starvation, than from cholera or the typhoid that always spreads in a besieged city. Yet walls are a fine place behind which to mass cavalry and to loose them on the besiegers whenever any weakness or weariness is perceived.

While Antonina and Procopius were moving toward Rome, with wagonloads of supplies and with the two thousand cataphracts who had joined them in the Campania; and while Bloody John was disembarking his Isaurians and moving on Ostia, Belisarius directed a distraction at the walls. He ordered some of the Romans to unblock the Flaminian gate, which he had blocked up early in the siege; there being far too many gates to defend them all. The distraction was made. A thousand of the weakest cavalry sallied from the Pincian gate to harry the Goths. They then retreated, pursued by most of the enemy host. As they did so, Belisarius with his main force, rode out the Flaminian gate. There was a slaughter. It wasn't actually an envelopment of the Goths, for the Gothic host completely overlapped the two Roman forces. Rather, it was that Belisarius drove confusion into their lines. Those who were pressing the thousand weak cavalry back against the Pincian gates were now attacked by Belisarius and his cataphracts. Instead of joining up with his men outside the Pincian gate, however, Belisarius continued to drive like a ballista dart directly into the midst of the main Gothic force, which was hurrying to the scene without thought of forming any sort of coordinated force.

Soon after this, Witiges sent ambassadors to Belisarius to negotiate the city's surrender, suggesting that the Goths would in turn allow the empire to retain Sicily. Belisarius, who was in a humorous mood, countered that he would never surrender Rome, but that he was willing that the Goths should seize the former imperial territory of Britain from the Anglos and Saxons. Finally both sides agreed to a truce of three months to begin, not immediately, but with the Christmas holiday and continue to Easter. During this time, the Goths would send ambassadors to Justinian to arrange peace.

210

Were his failure to take Rome not enough to humiliate the Gothic king, Belisarius himself with but a mere hundred men passed through the enemy encirclement by night, in order to visit the forces which Procopius and Antonina had gathered. He urged them to hurry to the city and, in an expansive mood, assured them that the starving garrison of Rome would march out and protect them if necessary. He and his hundred then calmly returned to Rome before dawn. The meeting must have been a sight: Belisarius in battle armor, and Antonina in charge of the relief column, probably not in armor but surely not in court dress either; as sturdy a leader as anyone at that meeting.

The next day, Procopius and Antonina and whatever officers were with them decided among themselves that the road to Rome was too broken for the tired oxen and the carts which had just brought the desperately needed provisions from the Campania. Antonina, who was presiding over the conference of all these menfolk, suggested that Bloody John's recently arrived troops set to fixing thick boards to boats as a shield against enemy arrows. Then they all sailed up the Tiber from Ostia to Rome, employing oars where necessary. The Goths, by now weary of the siege - and aware that it would soon end by treaty - made no move to attack. On an early December day, relief finally reached the ancient capital

As noted, Belisarius had already improved the food situation by sending a force of cataphracts to outflank the Gothic besiegers at Tivoli and Terracina. Now the besiegers were the besieged: Farmers who had sought refuge in Rome were sent to harvest the crops which Witiges had planted to feed his army, and it was the Goths who were with reduced rations. Were that not enough, disease, which had bred in the swamp created by smashing the aqueducts, began to ravish their camps.

Antonina arrived safely and was warmly greeted by Belisarius and Photius. She was a person very much in charge of the troops she headed, and of her own life as well. The Byzantine army was resupplied and it was the Goths who were hungry. Yet Antonina was still a lusty woman. In her quarters she dropped her tunic and with it the cuirass that Belisarius always insisted she wear underneath for protection from stray missiles. She ordered a bath, a real bath, and her servant, Eugenius, sent some slaves to gather wood outside the city walls to heat a tub of water. Eugenius also found some oil and a sponge, and from somewhere a silk stola which had been hidden away.

"It was too pretty to use for bandages, mi-lady. I knew that some day you would need it. Besides, silk doesn't make good bandages. I've sent some slaves to scrounge through a deserted Gothic camp for anything special they can find. We have food enough now, but nothing celebratory. Will Theodosius be joining you for dinner?"

That was the wrong thing to say and Antonina's face showed it, though all she said was "No. Not tonight."

Nor did Antonina miss Theodosius that night.

With the dawn Belisarius was up and about again. He called a meeting of his chief lieutenants. At last he could take the offensive if the truce failed; at last, he revealed to his troop commanders why he had been so confident of final victory.

"The only Gothic archers are their infantry, which horsemen can easily avoid. In open battle your cataphracts by using their bows will decimate the Gothic cavalry without letting them close enough to do our men any harm. We have stood the siege of Rome. Were we to fail in Italy it would have been here. Fortunately, the enemy has a particularly poor idea of how to besiege a city, especially one the size of Rome."

Bessas spoke. He was himself a Goth, but like Belisarius from Thrace within the empire: "Damn, for a year we've been tied down, and I never thought of that. I'm sure, it never crossed Witiges' mind either. But why have a truce now? We can take them on in an open field now. We're winning. "

It was time for Belisarius to elaborate: `"Witiges knew that the only way for him to win was by tying us down in this city. Fortunately we were able to outlast him. Plague in his camps helped decide Witiges to give up the siege early, but he was losing anyway. Soon one of his lieutenants would have assassinated him and sued for peace. Yes, peace is surely at hand, and I will not see either our own men or Goths killed unnecessarily. Justinian will win Italy at the table, but we will keep the pressure on Witiges to come to an early agreement."

CHAPTER 16

538 - 539 AD
ROME

Not long after Antonina had again settled into her civil duties, there was an incident: one which gave her some decidedly unchristian satisfaction. In the Tuscan town of Spolitium, the strategos Constantinus had taken - as plunder for himself - two heirloom daggers belonging to a senator of Rome, and the senator had begged Belisarius that he be made to return them. The appropriation of the daggers had been in clear contravention of Belisarius' orders against plundering a city which had opened its gates to him. It was theft, pure and simple: if theft in the tradition of armies in all times and places, Belisarius ordered that the daggers be returned. Constantinus refused to obey but could offer no reason not to. He had brought himself into a humiliating situation from which he could not extricate himself without loss of face. He had refused a direct order of his commander and now assumed his commander would have him executed, though Belisarius assured him otherwise. He was distraught and angry. *How dare this general side with a civilian who has never so much as lifted a sword in defense of the city or empire?* Antonina waited for the affair to play out. She wanted justice done. What happened must have pleased her, for it was Constantinus who had suggested that Belisarius should have killed her for her alleged infidelity with Theodosius in Sicily. When called into the presence of Belisarius who demanded he surrender the daggers, Constantinus was in fear of his life, and determined to sell it dearly. He attacked the unarmored Belisarius and would have killed him had not Bessas intervened whilst a guard in armor took the thrust. Constantinus was summarily executed. Should Belisarius have pardoned his subordinate? Procopius believed that, had Antonina not intervened with her husband, in that Christian age he would have, even though discipline certainly called for the death penalty. On other occasions Justinian had done as much. If calm had prevailed Constantinus' impetuous anger might only have meant reassignment to another theater. However that may be, Antonina was not dissatisfied. *He was a jerk. He lived like a jerk and died like a jerk. But OK, I will not gloat, Lord; I shall pray for his soul instead.* In a curious way that gave her as much satisfaction as gloating would have.

Even before the truce was finalized, Witiges lifted his siege of Rome, one year and three days from its commencement and without any gain, but only in humiliation. In Persia, Belisarius had refused to attack a fleeing enemy. But this was different. The Gothic army was still larger than his and retiring, not retreating, to safety within the fortress city of Ravenna; there to regroup and resupply if peace talks should fail. Besides, they had brought starvation and disease to Rome. Children had died of hunger. Perhaps Belisarius could not resist getting some payback.

He did not delay. Despite the weakened condition of his troops, he attacked one half of the retreating Gothic army after the other half had crossed the Milvian bridge and were unable to assist their comrades. Many were forced into the Tiber and drowned. Many more were slaughtered by the Romans. When Witiges could at last disengage he retreated, or fled, towards his capital. Antonina watched it all from a high tower that her husband had ordered to be constructed, and from which observers had watched the movement of the Goths at several of their camps.

"Look at them go, Theodosius. See how they try not to look in a hurry, yet no one seems anxious to be in the rear guard."

Between Thracian cavalry charges, Ephthalite archers continually fired into the Goths at the bridge. The Goths covered themselves with their shields but had no means to reply in kind, their archers being already out of range on the far side of the Tiber.

"I know it is unchristian, mi-lady, but it is good to watch them fall."

"Christian, smitchen. Tell it to the priests." For a few seconds Antonina actually did a little dance, holding Theodosius' hands in hers like a child would. When she recovered a demeanor befitting a Roman lady she gave his hands a last squeeze.

"It is Christmas eve. I must go and bathe and put on something pretty for my victorious husband. Hell, no one else could have held the whole Gothic nation off for a full year. I think there has never been a siege like this in all history." She paused, looking down on the outsized tunic that had often served her for dress during the siege. "There has never been a soldier like him. Alexander be damned; he had his dad's phalanx. My lord only has his own Thracians and a bunch of smelly foreigners. OK, that's not fair; we all smell now." She paused again and laughed. "*I called him my lord. Well he is.*" Then she collected herself and gave Theodosius a parting smile. "Well, he is my lord. He's my husband. No one has a husband like my lord Belisarius.... But no one calls him cute, sweetie."

The next day Antonina wrote a letter to Joannina:

I have told you, my little one, of the wonderful things that there are

214

in Rome. Now that this city is in our sacred emperor's possession, you will one day be able to visit also. There are beautiful churches and arches and a race track and statues and fountains everywhere. Do you know that this city was the center of the world before Constantinople was? Ask Grandma. She will tell you all about it. An artist here has drawn some pictures for you of me and daddy at these wonderful places.

What I could not tell you before was that we have had to fight another king here. I can tell you now that we have Rome and he will never return there. Daddy and his brave soldiers are chasing the enemy army.

We went to Christmas services today in a beautiful old church and the priest gave a long long talk about the birth of Our Savior. Then we had a feast. While we were fighting the enemy there wasn't much food, but there is plenty now. We had wild duck with buns, and nuts with honey. I wish you had been here to enjoy the feast, but we will have another one when we come home. Meanwhile, do whatever grandma says and try to learn your letters so that you can write to us and read what we write to you. Daddy is very busy but I'll ask him to add just a few words to this note.

Momma

I'm sorry that I cannot write more but there isn't much that I can add to what momma has written, except to tell you that we both miss you very much. Soon we will be leaving Rome to chase the Gothic army out of Italy. Do not worry. Their king has almost given up already.

Daddy

Photius added a postscript of his own. Joannina might remember him better than her parents, for he had remained with her in Constantinople during the year of the Vandal war.

The author can only imagine what other things Antonina and Belisarius might have written home at other times during the five years of the first Gothic war. Surely, there would have been letters back and forth; and surely, there would have been midnight musings between husband and wife about their daughter. They would have queried every messenger from the capital. As all parents, they would have worried about every bout of the sniffles that they heard of, and of every sickness that was "going around" in Constantinople. Antonina would have praised every drawing that came from the child; and Belisarius would have worried whether she was learning many studies in which a child her age had little interest. Do what they might, however, it still would have been difficult to stay abreast of

Joannina's growth physically and mentally. Maybe they watched other children of her age. Maybe they knew in their hearts that when they did return home they would be strangers to her. Antonina, at least, must have known how much a stranger Joannina would also be to them. They did what they could. I will not extend this narrative with further letters, but letters there surely were. There were also little gifts that they knew Joannina waited for and valued; and visits from couriers returning to Constantinople who were ordered to visit the child, but not to worry her with talk of the war.

Christmas services had been held in Constantine the Great's Basilica of Sts. John and Paul. At the same moment Justinian was inaugurating Hagia Sophia in Constantinople. It had taken less than six years to build the largest and most elaborate building in the world. To quote from the dedication:

"This sacred church of Christ evidently outstrips in glory even the firmament above, for it does not offer a lamp of merely sensible light, but the shine of it bears aloft the Divine illumination of the Sun of Truth and it is splendidly illumined throughout by day and by night by the rays of the Word of the Spirit, through which the eyes of the mind are enlightened by Him who said 'Let there be light!'"

Procopius also wrote of it in *The Buildings*: "Who could recount the beauty of the columns and the marbles with which the church is adorned? One might imagine that one has chanced upon a meadow in full bloom, for one would marvel at the purple hue of some, the green of others, at those on which the crimson blooms, at those that flash with white, at those, too, which Nature, like a painter, has varied with the most contrasting colors. Whenever one goes to the church to pray, one realizes at once that it is not by human power or skill, but by Divine influence that this church has been so wonderfully built. The visitor's mind is lifted up on high to God, feeling that He cannot be far away, but must love to dwell in this place He himself has chosen. All this does not happen only when one sees the church for the first time, but the same thing occurs to the visitor on each successive occasion, as if the sight were ever a new one. No one has ever had a surfeit of this spectacle."

Belisarius decided to tweak the Gothic nose. Gothic troops in several towns deserted their posts, and Belisarius garrisoned them with his own troops. Witiges demanded the towns be returned, but since the towns had not been captured but had been deserted by the Goths, Belisarius refused. Yet aware of the fragility of the coming truce, he sent Bloody John with two thousand cavalry to Alba on Lake Celano. John was to avoid inciting combat but, should the Goths attack him, he was to occupy the entire of province of Picenum. Knowing John's predilection for violence, Belisarius specifically warned him not to injure the native Italians. He was to leave no Gothic strong point in his rear and to hold any treasure that he might seize to be evenly distributed with those who had stood the year-long siege in Rome. He also ordered Martinus and Ildiger. who had recently arrived in Italy, to harass the retreating enemy army, which was slowly making its way across the Apennines toward Ravenna, until such time as a peace was signed by Justinian and came into effect. Meanwhile, he himself would maneuver to keep a Gothic garrison at Osimo behind their walls.

One of the towns that John seized was Rimini on the Adriatic coast. Belisarius intended to gamble that the Goths would not bother to seize a minor post if it were held only by a skeleton garrison. Therefore he sent Martinus and Ildiger accompanied by Procopius, to give John instructions to quit the town with his heavy cavalry and join them in harassing Witiges. John did not agree and would not obey. He insisted on staying put with his two thousand horsemen to plunder the city he felt was his to loot since he had occupied it. For some unknown reason Procopius chose to remain with John, possibly expecting to see some great martial effort that he could describe in his narrative of the war. Surely events at Rimini would be more memorable than simply observing Belisarius' besiege Osimo. John's obstinacy backfired. When Witiges found two thousand Byzantine cataphracts in Rimini instead of a deserted town, he thought them to be a target worth his effort and one which might reestablish support for him among the vacillating Gothic nobles. With all his faults, John was an effective warrior but his stubbornness cost him dearly. He and his men repulsed attack after Gothic attack, but provisions in Rimini were running out.

Fortunately for him (but not the mission), at this point Justinian's Grand chamberlain, Narses, arrived in Italy with seven thousand fresh cavalry. Either Justinian had awakened to the possibility of total victory in that land and decided to send formidable reinforcements to Belisarius, or else Narses, a brilliant and surprisingly warlike eunuch, had persuaded the emperor to allow him military glory in his old age, for he was already in the sixth decade of his life. The latter makes sense since by this date Justinian was becoming increasingly paranoid and fearful of Belisarius' popularity with the populace. The general had even dared lecture his emperor. It were best that Belisarius be made to share the glory of conquering Italy.

Belisarius did not like Narses and the feeling was mutual; but Narses had been of assistance to the emperor in the days of the Nike insurrection. If Mundus and Belisarius had done the slaughter, it was made easier by Narses who had moved discreetly among the leaders of the Blues. With bribes in hand he had reminded these thugs how, until recently, the Blues had been the favorites of Justinian and could be again. Were Justinian to lose the throne, how long would the alliance of the factions last: a year, a month, a day? Justinian may have felt that he owed Narses an opportunity for military fame; as likely, he did not want Belisarius to glean all the glory for himself. For Narses, it was a happy confluence of motivations.

When word arrived that the Rimini garrison had only a week's supply of provisions, some officers felt that Bloody John should be left to suffer for his disobedience to orders, but Narses spoke in favor of relieving Rimini. Though a friend of John, Narses made no direct effort to defend the disobedient commander. He deflected Belisarius' anger by suggesting in jest that he could throw the insubordinate subordinate from the walls of Rimini, but not until after the garrison had been relieved. More seriously, he pointed out that John's troops would be of use to Belisarius. Furthermore were Rimini to fall, the reputation for invincibility that the Roman army had acquired would be lost. Ruefully, Belisarius had to admit that Narses' arguments made strategic sense, and that such was the way he himself should be thinking. Anyway, two thousand loyal and hard fighting cataphracts should not be made Gothic slaves because their commander had been seeking to loot a town.

The generals laid aside their anger and huddled together to form a plan for the relief of Rimini. The city was on the coast and with the arrival of Narses' force the small Roman naval force was substantially enlarged. Belisarius left off besieging Osimo which was held by a strong Gothic garrison. He hated leaving it at his back but had no choice. He ordered that the siege be maintained but only by a small guard. With Narses beside him to gain combat experience, together they would lead a flying column of Roman cavalry along the ridge of the Apennines. Martinus, with a mixed force of cavalry and infantry, would take the faster route along the paved Flaminian way. Gothic scouts could be trusted to exaggerate the size of both. Especially, Belisarius instructed Martinus to stretch his troops as thinly as possible by day, while lighting more numerous camp fires than necessary at night so as to deceive Gothic scouts as to his strength.

The attacking forces formed a trident. Besides the two units driving north by land, Ildiger with the largest force took ship and arrived off Rimini at the same time as Martinus. It was June, and were it not for the

218

seriousness of the mission and urgency of their march, it would have been a delightful trip for Belisarius and Antonina after the horror of the Roman siege and the desolation of the Roman countryside. The Tuscan hills would have been as lovely as now, crossing the Apennines in the mist as beautiful. Perhaps Theodosius would have commented poetically to Antonina. Even Belisarius might have spared a grunt and lamented the mischief which has always haunted this so beautiful country. But there was not time for such romanticism.

The Goths besieging John in Rimini took flight when they saw Martinus' army approaching accompanied by a large flotilla of troop ships. This they were totally unprepared for; it had been worrisome enough that Belisarius was approaching from the hills. They left most expeditiously.

"Brave souls, aren't they Procopius?" Antonina was speaking with Theodosius and with Belisarius' secretary who had stood the Gothic siege with John and was some pounds lighter and much relieved to be with friends again.

"Look at that man's armor. Isn't it nice though?" Theodosius spoke. "He must be a leader of some sort. See how he is leading a whole cavalcade north with the utmost speed."

"It's just armor. A bit shiny but just armor."

"Oh no, dear godmother. See how his cuirass gleams with silver and gold like that of some vain emperor of old."

"So he's a vain man."

"Probably stolen from a tomb." interjected the ever observant Procopius. "Notice that the rest of his arms are that of an ordinary trooper."

The chit chat ceased when they observed Belisarius riding up on his famous bay. "Another bloodless victory to your credit, godfather. We will have no need of the priests' services tonight."

"Oh no. Let them offer prayers of thanksgiving. I am not one to take any joy in killing." For a moment Belisarius spoke more as godfather than commander. "We do our duty for Christ's empire but must one day answer before Christ himself, 'Thou shalt not murder.' If we can win a town without loss on either side that is far better than that we butcher an enemy." The others crossed themselves in shame, even Antonina.

Later, inside the walls, the victorious generals were anxious to remind John of his folly. This he could not deny but when Belisarius teased him with the comment that he would not find it easy to repay his debt of gratitude to Ildiger of whom Belisarius had grown immensely proud to have as a son in law, John would not be cowed. He replied that he owed nothing at all to Ildiger but everything to his friend Narses, a comment that was overheard by several lieutenants of lesser rank. Antonina thought it wisest to send a personal message to Theodora, so as to warn their imperial majesties of the dissent which had been brewing since Narses' arrival. This, she warned them, threatened at some future time to break out into open conflict between the Praepositus of the Sacred Bed Chamber and her husband.

Some junior officers were unhappy with being assigned less important duties than a relative of Belisarius, and his faithful subordinates: Martinus, Valerian, and Bessas. It did not occur to them that, had they been more trustworthy and less ambitious for themselves, their loyalty would have been rewarded. Soon, they would suggest to Narses' receptive ears their belief that he was at least as fine a strategist as Belisarius. With his newly arrived force and those loyal to themselves they actually outnumbered those troops who would always be loyal to Belisarius.

"Let Belisarius subdue the interior of Italy town by town if he likes, but you should assume a separate command and retake the rich Aemilian towns for the emperor. That is where the greater riches are and there is plenty to satisfy our soldiers and Justinian too."

Of course Narses was not so naive as to think that these were their only motives. It could not hurt any of them to have helped Narses fulfill his dream of glory. Even at his advanced age he was in extraordinary good health, and far more fit than one might expect of a spoiled court eunuch. He might remain at his post for some years yet, and he would owe them.

To all this they added pure sugar: "It is not fitting, Narses, that Justinian's right hand should be subordinate to a mere general. It might be different if you were Belisarius' clear inferior in matters of strategy, but it was you, not Belisarius, who insisted on the successful relief of our brother John. Certainly the emperor must have intended that you hold independent command; why else would he have sent so high an official?"

"Flavius, you must put this little eunuch in his place." Antonina was laying beside her husband. He had not said anything but Antonina knew his moods, and he was troubled. She had never seen him so disheartened before. Concerned about the outcome of some pending battle? Yes, of course. Exhausted? Yes. But never so disheartened.

"Why has Justinian saddled me with this man? Doesn't he trust me?"

"No, husband; Justinian trusts no one but Theodora. Surely you must know that."

"Justinian could have sent any number of others. I cannot simply order around his Grand Chamberlain. Tomorrow I will call a meeting and explain fully why we must take our time and pacify this country town by town if we are to hold it. Witiges still has larger forces than ours in Ravenna, Milan, Liguria, Osimo, and Orvieto. From Orvieto the Goths might retake Rome if our forces are split. I have already had to weaken them in order to garrison the towns we've already taken. Not only that but Witiges has friends among the Franks. He may make common cause with them. Some have already crossed the Alps."

At the meeting, Belisarius laid out his concerns before Narses and the other generals. He explained that he thought it best to split the army into two, but only two, units; one to relieve Milan where the Romans were besieged by a Frankish army which was taking advantage of the turmoil in Italy; the other to drive through Umbria and Picenum and take Osimo. He himself would lead either division and another general, probably Narses together with an experienced subordinate, the other.

This was not enough to assuage the ambition of Narses. He rose and offered an opinion, or rather a statement of what he would do. In another age it would have been considered insubordinate. Even in sixth century Byzantium it would have been considered just short of that. "What you have laid before us is doubtless true as far as it goes. But I hold that it is quite absurd to say that this great army is equal only to the accomplishment of these two objects, the relief of Milan and the reduction of Osimo. While you are leading such of the Romans as you think fit to those cities, I and my friends will proceed to recover for the emperor the province of Aemilia. (In other words, the southern bank of the Po from Piacenza to the Adriatic.) This is a province which the Goths are said to especially prize. We shall thus so terrify them that they will not dare to issue forth from Ravenna and cut off your supplies, an operation which they are sure to undertake if we march off to besiege Osimo."

Narses' insolence forced Belisarius to give up his usual conciliatory style. Narses had overstepped and that must be made clear to the eunuch's friends. Belisarius withdrew a letter recently received from Justinian:

We have not sent our chamberlain Narses to Italy to take the command of the army, for we wish Belisarius alone to lead the whole army to wherever it may seem best to him. It behooves all to follow him in whatsoever makes for the good of our empire.

That should have been clear enough. It should have put to rest Narses' outsize ambition which had so concerned Antonina and cost Belisarius much needed rest. It did not, for Narses picked out the last words and gave them a twisted turn claiming that Belisarius' plans were "not for the good of the empire." He could claim some authority here as he was as near to being Justinian's prime minister, as was possible in that age of absolute rule. He thought himself qualified to make that decision and be at least the command equal of Belisarius; much in the way that the military of the Soviet Union had been constrained by political commissars who shadowed them in all their actions.

The two men retired out of hearing and returned to the conference smiling. Clearly a compromise had been reached, one which left Narses with his head still on his shoulders; aware, however, that he had dangerously overstepped in a country under military rule by his opponent and far distant from his Imperial protector. Peranius, a Georgian supporter of Narses, was ordered to take Orvieto; which as Belisarius had noted could have been used by the Goths as a staging point to regain Rome. Belisarius and the remainder of the army together with Narses and Bloody John would move against Urbino, only a day's march from Ravenna.

Whatever agreement Narses had made with Belisarius broke down under the Walls of Urbino. Bloody John did not want to join with his commander in a long siege of this strongly guarded fortress town while easier victories could be won in Aemilia with its wealth of gold, silver, and slaves. With Narses at his side he lost any fear of Belisarius. He and Narses simply slipped away with their part of the army, leaving the business of strategic victory to Belisarius. Put another way: Belisarius, who was rich already, could have the glory of taming Italy; John would be content to rape her; and Narses would enrich Justinian's treasury. Thus off they went.

They should have stood with Belisarius. With his reduced forces Belisarius prepared to batter the fortress walls. His men would attack under the cover of branches cut from a thickly wooded hillside. Arranged over and around them, the branches would deflect stones from overhead, and arrows would be caught by the branches at their sides. To everyone's shock, as this forest approached the walls of Urbino the garrison pleaded for Belisarius' famed compassion. For countless years a single spring had been sufficient to water the town but in the previous days it had failed. They opened the gates.

Antonina climbed the walls and played Pallas Athena with shield and lance to the delight of Theodosius and the troops - and certainly Belisarius also, though he affected a husband's scowl.

Meanwhile though Aemilia was of little strategic value in the pacification of Italy, John bypassed Gothic strong points to secure its rich towns for the empire and loot them for himself.

It was now January 539 AD. Belisarius sent the bulk of his army into winter quarters with only the light duty of watching that the Gothic garrison at Osimo stayed put. He with a smaller detachment proceeded against Orvieto. This strategic city had been besieged by Peranius who though unable to take it had succeeded in so blockading the city that the garrison was reduced to eating rats, a delicacy which replaced the city's cats already sacrificed to the soup pot. With the approach of Belisarius, the garrison gave up any hope of being relieved by a friendly army and surrendered.

It was now a year since the raising of the siege of Rome. Rimini had been relieved and Urbino taken. Aemilia was securely under Bloody John's bloody boot, and Orvieto had fallen without the loss of a single trooper. All was not well though. At this point the author must briefly detail a Gothic atrocity to which the factious cabals of Narses and Bloody John contributed however unintentionally. After Witiges had retreated from Rome, Belisarius at the entreaty of the archbishop of Milan, had sent a small force to occupy Milan and some outlying towns whose citizenry were favorable toward the empire. Three hundred Thracian and Isaurian troops took up garrison duty in Milan but Witiges sent a strong army to regain what was to him a treasonous city. Were that not enough, a force of Burgundians were sent by the Frankish king Theudibert to join in the siege. The citizens and the tiny Roman garrison were soon eating mice themselves. When Belisarius ordered an army under what should have been the competent command of Martinus and Uliaris to go to their relief, inexplicably they dallied week after week on the banks of the river Po and at last sent a message to Belisarius asking that Bloody John in Aemilia, and Justin, a subordinate officer of Narses, be sent to reinforce them. The order was given but John refused obedience saying that he obeyed Narses alone. In fury Belisarius sent a blunt letter to Narses who was encamped at Rimini, detailing how his insubordination was endangering the entire mission. Narses was ambitious and insubordinate, but not disloyal to his emperor; he ordered John to relieve Milan. Though late in the game that would have worked had John not suddenly become ill. By the time he could march the city was lost. All this would not matter to our narrative which passes over innumerable other battles and sieges were it not that I cannot pass over the last days of Milan under Roman rule. The Goths offered to allow the garrison to retreat from the city unmolested but refused the same to its citizens, swearing that all would die for their treason. Horrified, Mundilas, the Roman commander, spoke bravely to his starving soldiers urging that they.... Well, let me simply quote his words which are more noble than any this author could write:

"Every man has an appointed day of death, which he can neither hasten nor delay. The only difference between men is that some meet this inevitable doom gloriously, while others, struggling to escape from it, die just as soon, but by a coward's death. Let us show that we are worthy of the teaching of Belisarius, which we have all shared, and which makes it an impiety for us to be anything else but brave and glorious in our dying. We may achieve some undreamed of victory over the enemy, and if not we are nobly freed from our present miseries."

The little garrison was too exhausted to rise to noble martyrdom. Mundilas' exhortation failed and the city fell. The Goths did allow the Byzantine soldiers to pass through their lines but then began an orgy of blood that disgraced the name of a noble race. The brave praetorian prefect of the city, seen by the Goths as a simple traitor, was hacked into small pieces of meat and fed to their dogs. After this, all three hundred thousand Milanese men were rounded up, bound, and slaughtered in a blood orgy which surpasses any single such horror in the worst of modern warfare, either in the so-called civilized or the less "developed" parts of the world. With their axes and swords still bloody and their own clothing reeking with brains and guts, the Goths raped every wife, daughter, and mother of the dead men. Then these were given as slaves to the Burgundians in payment for their aid. The city was razed to the ground.

When Martinus and Uliaris returned to where Belisarius was encamped, he refused even to see them. Justinian relieved Narses but welcomed him back to the palace without punishment or any public reprimand. This was not to be the end of the eunuch's military career.

Belisarius was now formally installed as sole commander over a land that bled from Rome to Rimini, and hemorrhaged blood where John had dealt out death without any of Belisarius' concern for life. In the spring, Belisarius marched. The fortress of Fiesole fell to Justin. This officer had been one of Narses' lackeys, but in the absence of the grand chamberlain he turned his loyalty to Belisarius. Belisarius himself undertook to attack Osimo.

During these weeks of intermittent conflict, Gothic envoys had traveled to Constantinople to arrange peace with Justinian. Since it was the emperor's intent to retake the whole of Italy, and since Belisarius was on the verge of accomplishing that, such a negotiated peace should only have been one that gave nothing more to Witiges than was needed for him to save face.

Belisarius could put an end to any hopes that Witiges might still

224

harbor by holding the Gothic capital of Ravenna, though to take it would not be an easy task. The city was located deep in marshland which made cavalry operations difficult, and was linked to the seaport of Classe from which hunger could be relieved or the Gothic garrison reinforced by sea.

Famine was on the land. Most of the farmers had fled Northern Italy and what few remained could produce only a poor harvest. If the horror was to end for the citizenry it could only be after a decisive victory by one side or the other, and that could only be at Ravenna. This was delayed by an unexpected attack by Franks from trans-alpine Gaul against both a Gothic army inside the walls of Pavia, and two Roman armies which were besieging it. It was a brief interruption. Belisarius sent a letter reminding the Frankish king of the danger to his own throne that he courted by angering Justinian. Even more persuasive was the scarcity of food and a summer plague. The Franks soon retreated, delaying, without effecting, the outcome of the war.

In March, Belisarius began the siege of Ravenna itself. This city was well protected by strong walls and the impervious marshes between it and the sea. It did not matter. The Goths within were dejected at so many losses to Belisarius, and now their own queen was suspected of assisting their national enemy to set their granaries and weapons stores afire. When he heard of this, Belisarius was delighted. Yet, Justinian himself nearly lost the war from his throne room in Constantinople.

In Persia, Chosroes, a young and warlike prince, had come to power over the corpses of several relatives. When his domestic feuding was done he looked at gaining for his country and his fame parts of the eastern Mediterranean held by Byzantium. Ambassadors from Witiges had approached him, and suggested that now was the time for battle, since Rome's best general was engaged against their sovereign. Byzantium was strong but not so strong as to successfully fight a two front war. Belisarius was a brilliant strategist and tactician and personally brave, but he could not be on both fronts at the same time.

When intimations of Chosroes' plans reached Constantinople, the emperor feared for his vital eastern frontier. Without Belisarius at hand to strengthen his determination, Justinian's resolve momentarily collapsed. When Gothic ambassadors arrived, Narses recommended that he quickly end the war by negotiation, without allowing Belisarius a total victory. He agreed to allow Witiges to keep his throne and with it all the territory north of the Po and most of his treasure. When word of the treaty reached Ravenna, the Gothic king could hardly believe it and quickly signed. Belisarius, beginning the siege, was dumbfounded and could only assume that his emperor was misinformed as to the situation in Italy where the whole Gothic kingdom was teetering on the edge of defeat within weeks. He called together his generals, and required that each of them, for his own good, put his opinion in writing. None supported him, either out of fear of Justinian or because they dreaded maintaining a siege in Italy, especially one in violation of an agreement signed by their emperor. In some cases they no doubt refused out of envy of Belisarius and remembrance of their happy days looting and raping under Bloody John

What followed was the only known instance of Belisarius disobeying orders. He was determined to end the Gothic presence in Italy and drag Witiges and his treasures before the emperor. To his advantage the Goths themselves, fearful of some Byzantine trap, refused to lay down their arms unless Belisarius ratified the treaty in the field. He refused, and that dashed the new found hopes of the Goths. Here the author must beg to delay the narrative of Antonina for a few pages to concentrate more on the biography of her husband. I will quote from Philip Stanhope, Lord Mahon, as to what now ensued:

"The Goths resolved to depose a sovereign whom they had always found unfortunate, and to elect as his successor, an enemy whose valor was attested by their overthrow, and whose virtues had extorted their esteem. Under the auspicious command of Belisarius, they trusted to obtain a higher pitch of power than that to which even the great Theodoric had raised them, and it was not the title of Gothic King, but of western emperor which they urged him to assume. It is probable that their views of conquest passed the bounds of Italy, and extended to France, Africa, and Spain. Witiges himself was forced to acquiesce in this extraordinary scheme, and to add his entreaties to those of his subjects, and to place his abdication at the feet of the Roman general. A wider field has rarely been opened to ambition, and it might not have been difficult to obtain the approbation and support of the Roman army. Though Belisarius had many enemies among the officers, every soldier was his devoted partisan; since the same qualities and exploits, which provoked the envy of the one, secured the attachment of the other. For the distant authority of a feeble and unwarlike sovereign, they would have preferred the exaltation of their victorious general, well acquainted with their merit, and by his new dignity enabled to reward it. On the other part, Belisarius could not be ignorant of the dangers which must attend his continued loyalty, of the secret cabals against him in the palace, where his late disobedience might be magnified into mutiny and treason. Narses also was present with Justinian; Narses who had inflicted too many injuries on Belisarius, to be capable of forgiveness, and who added the merit of a general to the familiar intercourse of a domestic, and the practiced cunning of a courtier."

It was a common kindness of the general, when possible not to stay in the camp of his guards on a Saturday night or to show up on Sunday mornings before the noncoms had put the place in order for the day. The horses needed to be watered, Divine Services held, and new recruits hustled into something resembling formation. Besides, it was nicer in some village church away from the sound of several thousand men taking their daily crap. Antonina found her husband in a chapel a few miles from Ravenna itself. He was alone without even a bodyguard. Was he thinking or praying?

"Flavius, you must consider the Gothic offer." Belisarius made no reply.

"You must think of yourself and the good of so many people. The Gothic armies are still more powerful than the empire's. All they lack is good leadership and some mounted archers. Those we have. It is not as though you would be trying to unseat Justinian; he would remain emperor in the east, and the west - which you have won despite his poor assistance - would again be part of the empire. How could he refuse you the title of augustus in the west; when he was never ruler here? And I'm quite sure the locals, Italians and Goths both, would prefer your rule to his tax collectors. It would not be treason."

Antonina had made the best case possible. Belisarius rose from where he had been kneeling in the Italian tradition, turned to his wife, kissed her and simply said: "I took an oath." Then with a thin smile he added: "Anyway, it is safer to be a loyal subordinate than an emperor." More seriously, he knew that a divided nation would only lead to endless conflict between the two sides as it had in centuries past. He had seen enough of needless bloodshed.

It was what Antonina had expected. To continue with Lord Mahon's narrative:

"Belisarius was deeply impressed with his oath of allegiance, from which no personal considerations could absolve him, and knew how to despise an usurped and precarious throne. He resolved, however, by a seeming compliance to hasten the surrender of Ravenna and the captivity of

Witiges. ... It had been required that Belisarius should solemnly swear to protect from injury the inhabitants of Ravenna, but with regard to his stipulated assumption of the imperial dignity, no promise was exacted by the Goths who thought his own ambition a sufficient security. A fleet laden with provisions was then permitted to steer into the harbor of Classe (the port of Ravenna), the gates of the Adriatic capital were thrown open to the Romans, and Belisarius triumphantly entered an impregnable fortress, which for more than two hundred years from this time, proved the firmest bulwark of the eastern empire in Italy. The Goths, who still surpassed their victorious enemy in numbers, viewed his scanty battalions with shame and surprise, and the indignant females spitting in the faces of their husbands and brothers, pointed with bitter upbraidings to the pigmy stature of the southern soldiers. In compliance with his oath, and his own maxims of discipline, Belisarius prevented any outrage on the part of his forces, and carefully preserved inviolate the property and persons of the Goths. On the other hand, Witiges was detained, though with great respect, a close captive in the palace ... but his treasures, the accumulated wealth of the great Theodoric, became the spoil of the conqueror. ... Pavia alone shut her gates, until the reign of Belisarius should be publicly made known. Such hopes were quickly disappointed. As soon as the ramparts of Ravenna were secured, and a share of the barbarian garrison dismissed to the tillage of the neighboring districts, Belisarius proclaimed his unshaken loyalty, and declared that he would remain, and that the Goths must become the faithful subjects of Justinian.

"The reduction of Ravenna, by Belisarius, inflamed still further the jealous animosity of his enemies at Constantinople. In spite of his recent declaration of fidelity and refusal of empire, Belisarius was secretly accused of aspiring to independent power."

Narses persuaded Justinian that Belisarius was needed in Persia for he had no wish that his rival secure for his prince the whole of the land which he and bloody John had only ravished for the exchequer and themselves. Justinian was easily persuaded. In Italy Belisarius had been offered a crown, he might not refuse a second time. Besides, the Persian threat was real and more important. Italy was an adventure, a loss on the eastern front could destroy the empire. But Justinian went further than to just replace Belisarius in Italy. Narses had shown strategic sense in insisting on the relief of Rimini; he now suggested that the mopping up operation could best be done by multiple generals rather than another sole commander. Unity of command was less necessary now and surely the emperor did not want to place such power in the hands of another man;

especially one who might not have Belisarius' sense of duty to his sovereign. Of course, Narses might also have felt that with Belisarius occupied on the vital eastern front, if it should turn out that a sole commander was again needed in Italy.... Well; he knew better than anyone how to finish the job. He was old and without immediate family. He would be the best and most politically safe person for Justinian to send.

Whatever such self-serving advice, as the Persian threat grew Justinian knew that he needed Belisarius, truly loyal or not, as much as he needed John the Cappadocian, Narses, and a notorious tax collector called Alexander "The Snips," whatever their flaws. He surely worried that Belisarius might not choose to resist another petition from the Goths, and recalled him to Constantinople before the mopping up operation in Italy was completed. To continue quoting from Lord Mahon:

"Belisarius "without hesitation had determined on obedience. To the Goths his continued loyalty seemed altogether unaccountable, and the squadron at Pavia vainly implored him in another embassy to raise the standard of rebellion, and no longer to prefer the situation of a slave to that of a sovereign. Lamenting his refusal, but encouraged by his absence, the feeble garrison of Pavia resolved to make one further effort for the maintenance of the Gothic monarchy, and it will hereafter be seen how, by the recall of Belisarius, and the imbecility of his successors, this slight spark of revolt was blown into a formidable flame, which pervaded once more the whole of Italy, which was again repressed by the hero of this history, and finally extinguished by Narses."

CHAPTER 17

541 AD
ASIA, ITALY, CONSTANTINOPLE

Justinian's ambition was to revive the Roman Empire in the west, not to engage in endless frontier squabbles with King Chosroes of Persia. It seemed that Chosroes could not see, as Justinian did, that neither side would for very long allow its frontier to be moved far from Dara and the Euphrates. The Euphrates was a natural barrier protecting Persia. Dara and the other cities along the frontier constituted Byzantium's in-depth defense, and must not be lost.

Chosroes likewise had ambitions that went beyond frontier squabbles, Persian history lauds him for beautifying its cities, irrigating more land, reforming the bureaucracy and the law, and giving refuge to Jews, heretics, and the pagan philosophers who were fleeing Justinian's persecutions. But most important for this story, he raised a class of minor landowners to the nobility. These country squires were less troubled by aristocratic ideals of chivalry than were the saravan nobility who had formed the backbone of Kobad's army. They were as competent as the saravan, and there were more of them. They were known as dehgans.

Chosroes dreamed of conquest. He engaged in war with the nation of the Ephthalites to his east, some of whom served as Byzantine mercenaries. To his west, if he could take and hold Antioch in Syria, he would have access to the Mediterranean. He was also tempted by a rebellion against corrupt Roman rule in the land of the Lazi to his north. If he could obtain a Black Sea port there he would not have to first occupy the whole Anatolian mainland to threaten Constantinople. The riches of Syria and Palestine tempted him, and those of Constantinople even more. He would strike eastward toward Syria and Palestine and north to the Euxine (Black) Sea. Constantinople itself would be endangered, Of course, he would not be able to hold so much territory, but raids would be a realistic threat leading to favorable negotiations..

No Roman emperor could permit Chosroes to obtain his ambitions regardless of the cost. For now we will leave Italy and Belisarius and return to the east, only noting that the Gothic throne itself passed through several persons and was eventually given to Totila, a man who could be cruel, but who never broke his word to friend or foe, and who - like Belisarius - had too keen an understanding of warfare to expect victory through numbers alone.

Unlike Justinian's expansive schemes in the west, his second war with Persia was not desired. True, Justinian had attempted to detach the allegiance of certain Persian allies but that was nothing unusual, pawns in the power game but not enough in itself to cause a breach in the peace. It worked both ways. While Belisarius and so many other of Justinian's best commanders were occupied with Witiges, Chosroes' Saracen ally Alamoundara, had continued to raid Roman territory, unrestrained by his overlord.

When Chosroes, himself, decided that the empire was vulnerable in Cilicia and Syria he attacked westward. He first attacked the frontier town of Sura and by deceit took it from a Roman garrison even while the city's surrender was being negotiated. He demanded gold or silver from every town he came near between the Euphrates and the sea. Some he took by storm, others by subterfuge, others he permitted to stand unmolested on payment of all their wealth. A city would always be spared if it paid enough. This first invasion by the young Persian monarch was as much a mission in search of cash with which to fund the defense of his Ephthalite frontier as it was the beginning of his war of conquest against Byzantium.

As reports of Chosroes' spoliation in Asia were received in Constantinople, Justinian promised relief. In expectation of this, the Roman commanders there sought refuge with their armies in the cities of Hierapolis and Antioch. It is a sad commentary on the quality of Byzantine generalship that the strategos Bouzes, with the best of his troops, deserted the citizens of Hierapolis on the approach of Chosroes' army and simply disappeared, leaving the citizens with no choice but to surrender to Chosroes and pay a ransom.

Then Chosroes marched on Antioch. Its citizen militia fought bravely but the city fell to the Persians when, after a brief defense, the imperial garrison fled. Then he enslaved the survivors and burned the town. Beautiful Antioch, which had survived earthquakes and fire, he burned to the ground.

Yet if the Roman armies did not cover themselves with glory and their commanders were either incompetent or cowardly, the people of those cities which escaped being attacked behaved nobly, freely giving of their wealth to ransom the Antioch prisoners. Chosroes wanted the prisoners, not for any reason of statecraft, but only to sell as slaves and enrich himself. It is reported by Procopius that farmers gave their mules, and whores from Edessa their fine silks and jewelry to ransom the prisoners. Instead, all this treasure was confiscated by Bouzes, the same Roman commander who had

232

hidden behind the walls of Hierapolis. Bouzes, like the generals who succeeded Belisarius in Italy, was inclined to think more of his need for personal gain than of the strategic situation. Though he was a thief and had a reputation for not honoring his commitments, it must be noted that he was not an out-and-out coward. He was just second rate as a man, and incapable of independent command.

Ambassadors arranged a temporary peace, little more than a truce. Chosroes returned to his capitol of Ctesiphon, near Babylon, relying on a pledge made by Roman ambassadors that Justinian would pay tribute. (This was disguised as the Roman share for the maintenance of a Persian garrison against Asian hordes at the Caspian Gates.) But he did so like a hoodlum, still burning and looting any town en route which refused to pay him ransom.

ITALY

The recall of Belisarius in 540 to command in a new war with Persia was not the end of affairs in Italy. The author would happily end the Italian narrative here, were it not that Belisarius had to return to Italy in 544 to do it all again.

The reasons are clearly put by lord Mahon:

"At the departure of Belisarius from Ravenna, in obedience to the commands of his sovereign, the conquest of Italy might be considered as entirely achieved. The Gothic monarchy lay powerless and prostrate, and the faint opposition of a handful of soldiers in Liguria, appeared only, as it were, the last convulsion of its expiring agonies. The single city of Pavia, which still delayed its submission, would doubtless soon have followed the example of the rest, when the hopes of its garrison were raised by the recall of Belisarius, and still more by the faults of his successors. Justinian had rashly appointed to the vacant command eleven generals of equal rank, neither respected by the soldiers, nor united amongst themselves and who seemed only to value their high office as affording superior facilities for spoliation. The administration of the revenue had been entrusted to a crafty scribe, who, from a slender patrimony, had risen by the most nefarious means, to a possession of enormous wealth. ... Deeply skilled in every refinement of chicane, no pity or remorse ever checked his rapine; and from his skill in diminishing the size without altering the appearance of gold coin, he was commonly known at Constantinople by the bye-word of

Alexander Psallidion, or the snips. On his arrival at Ravenna, he found Italy exhausted by the calamities of war; but this consideration was far from restraining his active ingenuity. Heavy taxes were imposed on all classes, and confiscation levied from the estates of the wealthy on the plea of pretended debts to Theodoric and the other Gothic kings. Under this oppressive yoke, they might derive some consolation from the perfect impartiality of Alexander, who defrauded the Byzantine soldiers no less than the Italian subjects. Instead of fixed and regular payments, the money for their subsistence was partly withheld and partly doled out in scanty and uncertain remittances; and the veterans found no other reward for the perils they had encountered and the wounds they might display, than neglect and destitution. According to the strong expression of Procopius, the troops were reduced to beggars; all sense of honor was relaxed, all subordination destroyed; some forsook their encampments for the pillage of the neighboring country, while others (barbarian foederati) in disgust deserted to the enemy. The Italians, groaning beneath the tyranny of those whom they had hailed as friends and deliverers, turned an eye of regret to the happy reign of Theodoric, and looked with hope and favor to the reviving strength of the Goths at Pavia."

Before this spoliation and while Belisarius was still in Ravenna he received personally sad news. The Armenians had risen in revolt against an unworthy and avaricious Roman governor. Justinian sent Belisarius' old friend, Sittas, to put down the rebellion. Sittas and Belisarius had been friends since their first campaign, when they had been comrades in arms against the Persians at Persarmenia. He tried to end the dispute peacefully. He promised the Armenians that he would appeal to Justinian to relieve their distress; and probably of more use, to write to Theodora whose sister was his beloved wife. Unfortunately, not all the Armenian force knew of the agreement and Sittas fell in battle against some rebels.

"I know all too well the fortunes of war. But he was my friend." This was all that Belisarius would say to Antonina. She wished he were not so taciturn. Even she could not always read her husband's moods, any more than he could hers.

With Sittas' peace mission a failure, the Armenians proceeded to stir up further enmity between Chosroes and Justinian, reminding the Persian monarch that Belisarius, far and away Justinian's best general, was still engaged in pacifying Italy. Ambassadors from the Goths also reminded Chosroes of the advantage to him of waring against Justinian while they themselves were in arms. The empire would have to fight a two front war.

Justinian reached out for allies to defend his eastern frontier and discourage these Persian ambitions. Not only did he make contact with the far off Christian kingdom of Ethiopia, then called Axiom, which at that time had an Arabian frontier with Persia, but also with the Huns of central Asia. His attempt to enlist the Huns failed miserably; instead of assisting they recognized Byzantium's weakness. These mounted bowmen raided Dalmatia on the Adriatic, and penetrated even to the suburbs of Constantinople before turning back from its defensive walls loaded with loot. Before retreating they slew many farmers and carried others with them into slavery.

CONSTANTINOPLE

The return of Belisarius to the Asian front was a military necessity, but Justinian also had other reasons to replace him in Italy. He needed the funds that hated tax collectors raised to beautify the slowly aging capital and complete his empire-wide building program. Belisarius had seized the treasure of Witiges but he was not the man to drain the citizens too. Besides, the war in Italy seemed nearly done with, while in the east Chosroes was breaking the peace whenever he felt the whim.

Justinian worried about Belisarius' loyalty. The Goths had offered a crown to him. He'd refused but not before hinting that he might take it. True, he'd only done that as a stratagem to bring his army unopposed into the Gothic capital, but still:

"It was best we ordered Belisarius home." Justinian was speaking with Theodora. "Even better to get him to the frontier as soon as possible. No parade this time. The crowd loves Flavius more than us, and my Uncle Justin always warned me against men like him."

"Yes, dear. We'll have a nice greeting prepared, but private: We'll say: 'Sorry, Flavius, there's no time for a triumphal parade, you're needed in Asia again. I've heard that the Persians would rather not face you. We can arrange appropriate rewards after that is dealt with.' Besides, I expect that the general has already squirreled away some cash in Italy and is looking for new opportunities."

"Theodora: I'm not so sure of that. There are honest men in this world. He's entitled to a part of the Vandal and Gothic hordes, and if I know Belisarius, he'll not go beyond that and what he may need to pay his troops.

Alexander, our friend the Snips, will not be so soft hearted."

"There may be honest men, but I know there were few honest women in the hippodrome. I'm sure that our beloved Antonina has stashed something extra away, just in case her husband ever finds out that her Theodosius is more than a godson to her."

"Let us not talk of that. It depresses me."

Justinian was nearing sixty and becoming more paranoid with each passing year. The victories of Belisarius were a fine feature of his reign that history would always remember him for: the resurrection of the glory of the empire, and the ancient capital again in imperial hands. But Narses would remind him that Belisarius might turn against him. He must insure the first and prevent the second. His glory must shine despite an appropriate humility. In public, the emperor was kind and calm and understanding; in private he was a frightened man, imagining assassins everywhere and intriguing constantly to protect his throne and life.

In the palace complex, Justinian ordered the building of a new reception hall. It would be decorated with a large mosaic depicting his most successful general presenting the captive Vandal and Gothic kings to him. The senate would meet under the mosaic. The populace would be invited to pass before it while a choir sang hymns glorifying his reign and associating himself in everyone's mind with the rebuilding of Christ's empire. That would be a pleasant enough homecoming for Belisarius as there would be no triumphal procession this time. Then the general must make haste to Dara.

From Ravenna, Belisarius and Antonina, together with Theodosius, took ship for Constantinople. Despite that it was winter, the voyage was a pleasure and a rare opportunity for the general to relax and laugh at the jibes of his godson, directed at the various blowhards and fops that surrounded the throne of Justinian. Theodosius knew better than to mock the emperor and empress themselves, for neither was known for a sense of humor, and the ship no doubt had ears.

Theodosius could do a very convincing imitation of Narses' rural accent, of which Narses, himself, seemed unaware. He strutted about the cabin – but never within sight of crew members - in a clear imitation of the patriarch's self-important walk. As Cappadocian John he bowed and scraped, and picked purses.

Neither Antonina nor Theodosius showed undue affection for the other. If Theodosius poured Antonina's wine, that seemed just familial affection to most observers – but not all. Procopius did not accompany them, but arrived in Constantinople soon after they did. He was happy to listen in the wine shops to the suspicions of some of the ship's crew who were more inclined than Belisarius to suspect the worst of womankind. He was less happy to hear of Theodosius' fine imitation of him – scribble, scribble – or of how much Belisarius and Antonina had enjoyed the show.

When the trio debarked, Belisarius was in high spirits. He and Antonina would finally have a bit of time with their daughter. It had been five years since they had seen the little girl who was six now, and had not seen either mother or father since infancy. Six years was literally a lifetime to little Joannina. To her, Antonina and Belisarius were just names that her grandmother spoke of every day. It was not easy for the little one to suddenly love them as parents, and it must be admitted that it was not the joyous reunion that mother and father had dreamed of. It took a few days for the child to warm to these new people in her life. She would hug her grandmother and follow the old lady around. But time and patience finally won out. If momma was a bit scary and daddy showed his love by stern attempts to teach her history, at least grand-mama wasn't put off by them. Mama and papa also had some unexpected difficulty relating to the child, but this too soon passed. After all, one's child usually resembles one's self or one's mate as much in attitude as in appearance, so even though they had not seen Joannina since infancy, after a few uncomfortable days she was not a stranger.

Very soon, she was to be found swinging between mother and grand mother as they walked; often toward the palace. There Antonina would leave the child with her grandmother while she spoke to the empress. On only one occasion did Theodora ask Joannina to come into a marble room where she sat on a cushioned chair instead of a throne. She picked up the child and tried to be pleasant, but Joannina squirmed away. There would be no repeat of that rejection.

After one of Antonina's typically long audiences with Theodora, she, Joannina, and Belisarius' mother would usually return to their own palace, not far away; or sail across the Bosphorus to their estate at Rufinianae. But Antonina was determined that her daughter see how life was lived outside the palaces of the rich and powerful. She and Joannina would dress simply and with only a few disguised guards roam the city. She would not expose the child to the slums or the hippodrome but they spent many hours shopping in the marketplaces where ordinary people bought and sold. They walked along the Golden Horn and talked with fishermen, ate mackerel on bread, and petted the half-feral cats that sat patiently waiting for fish heads.

However, there was no disguising the importance of her father who would arrive home surrounded by guards or, on a Sunday afternoon, take Joannina with him as he went about the city distributing alms, proceeded and followed by hundreds of Thracian and Isaurian horsemen in dress armor and with lances that reflected the sun.

Certainly Joannina more easily warmed to the more light hearted Theodosius, and Belisarius was happy to have a godson who could supply mirth for the child which he knew himself to lack. His mother, who was far more observant than her son, was more reserved. Theodosius was a fine young officer, a happy face around the big house, always ready to offer help instead of summoning some servant. Still, she was uneasy, and in subtle little ways tried to insinuate to her son that it were best that Theodosius not be quite so close, godson or not.

Photius, also being of a more suspicious bent than Belisarius, was at least as concerned. Though not a bad person, Photius was never the saint that Belisarius was. He was very much like his mother, and although he had never wanted for the necessities of life, he shared with her a cynical view of the world and their friends. In time this would lead him to play the game of court politics too well for his reputation. In Italy he had often been in the company of Procopius and between them had amassed a much richer profit for Belisarius than the general had expected as a large but fair share. Later in life he would be condemned for behaving with even more avarice for the emperor when he was made military governor of Palestine. John of Ephesus, the source of what information we have on Photius outside of his participation under Belisarius, shows a distinct prejudice against him because of Photius' efforts to raise funds for the emperor's grand projects. One must not forget though that John was a high clergyman, disgruntled because Photius extracted money from the church. It was an age when tax collectors skimmed a part of the collected revenues as salary for themselves, but did Photius personally profit unduly? Certainly John would have said so had that been the case. Whatever the truth of his actual accusations, Photius was entirely of a practical mind like his mother. He filled the imperial coffers, and the equally worldly Procopius always spoke highly of him.

In Constantinople, one evil report upon another arrived at the desk of Belisarius. There were stories of atrocities, of senseless killing, of the usual rape and pillage. Belisarius had seen his thirty sixth birthday. He had also seen all the horrors of war, but these reports troubled him. He had fought against Persia ten years before, but the war with Kobad had been war

238

waged between armies. The reports he received now were of a criminal in a crown, raiding defenseless cities and all too willing to compromise his lofty statements of intent for gold and silver. Belisarius would have liked to simply arrest the man and turn him over to his wife for a thrashing. Whatever his merits at home, in Syria Chosroes was but a thief who had destroyed Antonina's and Photius' home town of Antioch. *Beautiful Antioch.* It was in Antioch that Belisarius had met Antonina, and lost her for a time. *How pretty she had been, and tough too.* Belisarius dragged his mind back to the papers on his desk. There was no time for reminiscing.

Justinian had recalled Belisarius from Italy to confront Chosroes but it were better that his general not be too successful. Belisarius was the darling of the crowds who thronged the hippodrome, no doubt recalling his part in destroying the power of the thugs there. Justinian determined to send his general with insufficient troops for a great victory, simply to take command of the forces already on the border. If necessary, he could reinforce him later, after Belisarius was forced to entreat his succor.

The hippodrome: Justinian might have smiled to remember that Belisarius' wife had started life there, just as Theodora had. Theodora had been born the child of a bear keeper at the hippodrome, but with the crown of empire she had become dignified and distant. The people resented the haughtiness that she had assumed together with the purple. Antonina was as tough but she still retained a degree of commonality with the crowd. Unlike Theodora, she would smile and wave, move freely among them, and was even known to tell a dirty joke. Indeed, Justinian thought (no longer smiling,) she might be more of a threat than her husband. Antonina was ambitious for herself and for Belisarius. Belisarius was loyal, but if anyone could move him to seize the throne it would be her, and the crowd would love them for it. But Theodora and Antonina were friends. He would speak with Theodora. Antonina must be controlled even more than her husband.

Antonina was entirely capable of punishing a slave or firing anyone who did not deserve to serve her husband or herself; but she was not unkind to her household staff without good reason. She would remember Agatha, the old cubicularia who had made her welcome at the palace thirteen long years before – it seemed even longer - and be consciously polite to those in positions inferior to hers. God help anyone who crossed her though. The memory of her former life had been pushed far to the back of her mind by her very real part in preserving Byzantine sovereignty during the siege of

Rome. Her recent memories were of dancing like a child on the walls of Urbino and of slipping through the Gothic lines to raise an army in the Campania for her husband, then watching as *her* troops entered the great city. As Theodora's right hand she had sat in judgment of others. She had even condemned and exiled a pope.

This woman who had endured warfare like a man was less than ever concerned with the rich and gossipy females of the women's quarters. She expected the best in her home but that was for the majordomo to handle and he did it well; she no longer wanted to have anything to do with household affairs. Her place was at Theodora's side not fussing over a vase of roses. She was no longer impressed by fine clothing. Only if a dalmatic did not perfectly fit her maturing figure did she seem to notice. Of course most of the cubiculariai were much younger than she, and though she was always clothed more richly, in the manner of matrons everywhere, she felt no need to compete. The once beautiful Theodora was aging too and not nearly so gracefully as Antonina. The empress had lost any shading in the ivory skin which had first attracted Justinian to her, though one would not yet call her complexion sallow. However, unlike Antonina, she was losing weight and her physicians seemed worried.

Yet, the empress had always been strong. If she retired earlier now and more often took a mid-day nap ... well after all, even if no one would say it, she was a mere woman.

Antonina would accompany the empress to a couch in the women's quarters that overlooked the Bosphorus. The two would chat while the empress rested. Antonina would tell her of Rome but she hadn't an historian's eye for the broken old stuff that lay about that city. That didn't much interest Theodora anyway. Of more interest to her was what wealth might be retrieved. Mightn't some of the things there be brought to Constantinople for sale to foolish aristocrats and undereducated social climbing merchants?

Sometimes the conversation drifted to even less serious matters. Antonina would describe and imitate the dances of African girls, or expound on the sight of some young cataphract rowing on Homer's wine dark sea.

"Screw the wine dark sea."

"Screw the cataphract."

"How is your godson, Antonina? He was with you throughout the recent campaigns. Was he brave?"

"It was not necessary for him to be. Flavius would not let him see action."

"Oh, that's right. He was your personal guard."

"Yes."

"Don't play the innocent with me, Antonina. There was something going on between you."

"Mi-lady!"

"Coy. OK for now. I understand that Belisarius loves the boy too... the young man I mean. He was growing his first mustache when I last saw him."

"He continues to live with us and I'm glad of it. I shouldn't say...."

"Go on. I probably know what you were about to confide anyway."

"Theodosius is a delight to both Flavius and me. My husband needs someone to brighten his day. I do what I can to please him but I'm not really the chipper type either. I think I lost that during the siege. The things Theodosius says would come off as just dumb gossip if I said them, but from him they make us both laugh. I would hate to lose him so I find things for him to do."

"Of course you do, Antonina. By the way, soon Justinian will be sending your husband to Syria again. The Persians seem to have forgotten what happened the last time they fought him. I have need of you here. I am surrounded by people that I cannot trust. I can trust you. Don't go with him this time. Besides, you need a rest."

"As you wish, Mistress." Without Theodora, Antonina was nothing but the wife of Belisarius. With Theodora, she was a power. The empress' wish was a command.

"Besides, I really would like you to remain here and get to know your little girl better. I think Belisarius can quickly pin back the Persians' ears, even without your help. Meanwhile, stay here with Joannina ...and Uncle Theodosius, too," Theodora added, seemingly as an afterthought. It would do her and Justinian no harm to place a little distance, both physical and emotional, between the greatest potential threat to their thrones and her husband."

Antonina was by Belisarius' side when he presented Witiges and the Gothic treasure to Justinian and Theodora. The formal meeting had been choreographed for the benefit of the senators in attendance. They all prostrated but Justinian raised his most successful general to his feet with one hand and gave his other to the general's wife. Theodora remained on her throne but managed to affect a pleasant smile. After Justinian greeted Belisarius, Witiges surrendered his kingdom, though Pavia was still in arms. At the time it seemed a small matter. When Witiges abjured the Arian doctrine Justinian embraced him. He bestowed lands and a fine villa adjourning that of Gelimer's on the former monarch. He read a decree of the senate making Witiges a senator and patrician. Then Witiges withdrew to his honorable exile, never to be heard of again, but presumably living and swapping stories of the good old days with the former Vandal king.

The formalities over and Witiges and the senators dismissed, Justinian became even more relaxed. He brought his guests to see the yet unfinished new mosaic. He had ordered that Antonina be depicted, as well as her victorious husband - much as they can still be seen in the extant mosaics in Ravenna. "My dear Flavius, we are most grateful to you. And Antonina, it has come to our attention that you've become a warrior yourself. That was quite something that you managed in the Campania. I mean, a woman raising an army and fighting through to Rome. I thought only Theodora would have it in her to do such deeds." Then the emperor paused while Theodora glowered. "I have some news, however, which may sadden you. Your godson has asked me to tell you that he was leaving on a ship heading for Ephesus this morning. He feared that if he delayed to tell you himself, he might not be able to drag himself away. You see, he intends to join the monks at the St. Cyprian monastery. "

Antonina blanched while Belisarius looked bewildered. "Theodosius? Why? He likes to visit churches and monasteries but not, I think, to live in one. He's always been more inclined to the high life than to prayer, St. Cyprian will be too hard for him. In fact, he'd been looking forward to getting back to the city here. We all have friends that we've not seen in years. There is so much for all of us to get caught up on. You know how he loves gossip. If I want to know what's going on beyond the battle front I've always been able to ask him. Theodosius is a cosmopolitan; I've never thought of him as monk material."

"Nor have we," Theodora interjected while Antonina continued to look stunned. "Antonina, if you'd like, I could write to him ... ask him to put off taking vows. I'm sorry that Flavius can't stay at home for awhile more - hopefully he'll scare the Persians off quickly - but while he's away.... You've all been so close in Italy. It would indeed be nice if you and Theodosius could enjoy the city for awhile, at least until your husband gets back. Then if he still wants to go monking you'll have your great general at your beck and call." Theodora looked at Belisarius and smiled an unusually sweet smile.

"Not that you're much of a party goer, Flavius." Justinian took the opportunity to support Theodora, though he wasn't at all sure that bringing Theodosius back was a good idea. "Face it Flavius; you're dour."

There was a bit of laughter at the general's expense but he took it in

242

good humor, happily seconding the empress' offer to try persuading Theodosius to return.

For the remainder of the winter, Belisarius prepared himself and his bucellarii for the coming mission. There would be none of Italy's green hills and sweet streams, but only hot sand. Now, he was gone all day and late into the night as he prepared the myriad details. He sent Procopius and Photius on frequent missions to provide from his own resources for the seven thousand cavalry who owed him personal loyalty. Though he had lost many of his original Thracian and Macedonian bucellarii to attrition in Africa and Italy, these had been more than replaced by Vandals and Goths who had joined the imperial standard after being defeated. As commander, he had chosen the best of these and those who seemed most willing to serve the empire to be his personal troops. Of course it was not quite the same. His new bucellarii were good but they were not from villages on his own estates. He had known some of the dead troopers since his first clash with the Persians at Persarmenia. These had been men proud of their personal loyalty to Belisarius which death itself could not breach. Not that Belisarius had ever required personal loyalty to death; such was for tyrants. Yet Like Valentine on that first day of the Gothic siege, they had willingly given it, which made it all the harder when he had to send a message to their homes that Paulus or Georgio, or Theogard had lost his life for the Christian empire.

With age and responsibility, Belisarius had developed a great mustache and - one might agree with Justinian - a dour attitude. Many lives were in his keeping and he'd never been a lighthearted person. He loved Antonina dearly but rarely showed it. The bloom of first infatuation had faded. It was a long time since they had taken moonlit walks together as in the Sicilian countryside. By day he was busy with the details of command, and when night came he was too tired to want anything more than dinner and sleep. There was sex but midnight spankings were fewer. Antonina had been with him through hardship and victory and she told herself she still loved him, but she was lonely. So, though it may be insisted that Belisarius and Antonina still loved each other in the mature way of couples everywhere - even Procopius could not deny that - Antonina no longer felt "in love." They had been married for ten years and the romance had flown.

In Ephesus, Theodosius had refused to take vows, asserting that he was as yet uncertain of his vocation. When sure that Belisarius and Photius had left Constantinople, he was more than happy to answer Theodora's plea to put off taking vows a little while longer and return to Constantinople. He had to. He was broke and his creditors were not to be taken in by his supposed religious vocation. Had he not been a gambler he would have already been rich. He was suspected of taking large sums in coin when he had been charged by Belisarius with the safe duty of managing the treasuries of Genseric in Carthage and Witiges in Ravenna; probably the very money that Belisarius would later be accused of misappropriating. But then, who hadn't enriched himself in Carthage and Italy; and who hadn't lost it again? Now, he needed money again. There were prisons for those who could not pay.

Antonina really had no desire to visit the desert. She wanted to remain with Joannina. Moreover, Justinian had been right: five years in Italy had left her very out of touch with what was happening in the imperial court and the city. There was much catching up to do and she had assured Belisarius that if their godson would escort her she would be happy until he returned. After all, she was no longer a mere cubicularia. At age forty three, after five years of playing warrior, she wanted to act as a momma again, and enjoy some night life too. Also, she wanted to remind Theodora of who her best friend was. Belisarius was seven years younger and a guy; he still had time to go adventuring against the Persians, but she didn't.

By late May Belisarius was away on campaign, and Theodosius was coming to her at her own husband's request. Antonina sat by a pool in her magnificent villa and considered the life Belisarius had given her:

I should be worried for him but I'm not;
Flavius is always in the front line but he's always OK.
He has his bucellarii.
He's no kid anymore; he could get himself killed.
He won't.
He's off to war, and I am a bitch.

CHAPTER 18

542 AD
ASIA

On this expedition Belisarius did not go by sea. He and his seven thousand bucellarii rode the Roman road through Anatolia, arriving at Dara in early June. The frontier land was as uninviting as ever.

His thinned Thracians were reinforced by former enemies whom he did not know, or entirely trust to stand and fight a losing battle. However, during the winter and spring Belisarius had trained these Gothic lancers to use the bow; certainly not as well as the enemy, but the enemy would not know that. The new corps of Persian dehgans would not have the advantage over them that he'd had in Italy.

My Antonina:
I've found some reinforcements at Dara, but they are a mixed lot. There are the usual unreliable Arab light cavalry, refugee troopers from the battles of last year, and the youth of the city. These last few are infantry. They are disinclined to go on campaign leaving their own city unprotected. To force them would only encourage desertion when disciplined and durable troopers will be needed.
Sorry, but I have no time to write more now.
Flavius

Beloved Antonina:
I wish you were here with me today.
Tonight we are camped outside Dara of fond memory. Our old comrade Martinus was in command when I got here. He had to pay off the Persians last year; now, he has blood in his eye. But his troops are a poor lot; I'm afraid they are worn down from the defeat at Antioch. Poor Antioch; I have such memories of it and you. Now it is mostly gone. Apamea also fell before I arrived, and Edessa had to pay off Chosroes to prevent capture. I've heard really disturbing news of Bouzes who was holding it. They say that he confiscated some money that the people of that city raised to ransom Chosroes' prisoners taken at Antioch. Some of the ransom seems to have come from old friends of yours. I'll try to recover it but for now the military situation must come first. Bouzes is a competent troop commander, if unimaginative.

Tell Joannina I'll be home soon.
Flavius

Antonina re-read the letters. *Short. Military. Not a word about anything interesting.* Except for the few lines about Antioch and Bouzes (whom she'd never liked anyway), there was little that was personal. Old friends? Unlikely that any of them were still in the business. Most of them would be washer women now, or dead. Antonina had waited weeks for a letter and when it came it said little. She had been with Belisarius throughout the Italian campaign and knew the strain behind her husband's brief words, but she was in Constantinople now. She lay the letter on a table and went looking for Theodosius.

Antonina:
We've just learned that Chosroes has been busier than I thought. He's taken Petra on the Euxine while I was training troops here. Tomorrow I plan to head for Nisibis, but some of my officers don't think it is a good plan - Bouzes especially. You remember Bouzes. The man is brave, but a bit of an idiot.
Kiss Joannina for me.
Flavius

Antonina received the brief note. How different it was from the words Belisarius had for her when she was younger. It had never been Belisarius' way to write long letters but this was ridiculous; one little scrap of paper with not a word of love.

She was being unfair and she knew it. Belisarius loved her and had proven it many times in their lives together. He just had trouble writing words that he felt looked silly on paper. He was a man of action, not romance. *But couldn't he at least write how much he wanted to hurry back to me? Ah, shit, he's in his element now, not at a desk reading reports or trying to be polite with courtiers. He's marshaling troopers. He's among swords and lances, bows and smelly horses.* Antonina suspected, and she was probably right, that he was happy and in no hurry to get home to her and the drawing rooms of Constantinople.

But the drawing rooms were now Antonina's comfort zone. These days she was the *grand dame* of a coterie of the more intelligent cubiculariai. Most of them were much younger than she, better versed in all the niceties of sixth century court life, and more immoral than they wanted to appear. They also exaggerated every bit of gossip that came across the palace wall. When not waiting upon the empress or lecturing her young

246

friends about life outside the palace, Antonina would look for the only person she could trust: Theodosius. Together they would read the letters her husband sent and make comments. Most of the letters, like the ones quoted above, were not what Antonina wanted to hear. Antonina's comments were not always kind, and Theodosius would have to reassure her that she really was the most important thing in her husband's life. Then one of them would touch the others' hand and they would walk into some garden or to the stables for a ride away from the stultifying atmosphere of the palace with its Homer-quoting intelligentsia, twittering young cubiculariai, dull priests, and prissy courtiers; especially the damn prissy courtiers who hadn't even the honesty to admit that they hated each other.

> *Beloved Antonina:*
> *Tonight we are encamped about seven miles from Nisibis. The enemy is commanded by a very capable fellow named Nabedes. I've tried to learn what I can about him. I'm told he's smart and not the kind of man who scares easily. I've just explained my plan to my subordinates. Bouzes is becoming more of a pain every day. He didn't fight at Edessa when he had a good defensive position, but now he wants to attack Nabedes in Nisibis itself. Some of the others supported him. Of course I could have just given orders but that would risk reluctance at the worst possible time, especially by our Arab allies. What I want to do is draw the Persians nearer to our camp where they can't just retreat behind Nisibis' walls if they're losing. I'd like them to have a long run to get home and with their backs to our spears. If the city opens its gates to them we'll try to get in too, if not they'll have an even longer walk back to Persia. Or maybe, if they surrender to us and if they're willing to take the emperor's pay, we can send them as reinforcements to Italy.*
> *Flavius*

There was a long postscript:

> *One more word. The battle was fought and everything went wrong. Nothing would hold young Nicetas and Peter back. They had some bucellarii under their personal command and while I was occupied with Bouzes they moved against orders almost to the city. All I could do was to send them a message warning them to wait for the main body. I also warned them that the Persians know that our troops usually eat their rations at noon. Sure enough, come noontime everyone relaxes right under the*

enemy's eyes. Nabedes attacks them. I saw the dust of the Persian advance and I took our cataphracts ahead to help. We only had a small detachment of heavy cavalry available to move quickly. Our infantry joined in but had a lot of ground to cover. Nicetas' and Peter's force was decimated before I could get to the battle but, thank the Savior, the rest of my bucellarii came up and hit the enemy with a wall of lances while they were stripping corpses. Those Goths we brought back from Italy fought like demons for their pay; I'll never doubt them again. We won the day but most of the enemy escaped back behind their walls. I doubt they'll want to meet those Goths again. I don't have time to besiege them but if I bypass the garrison, I'll have an enemy at my rear when we move on Persia proper.
    Flavius

    By the way, could you join me?

    Not a lot better, Antonina thought. But at least he misses me, I think. He'll be alright though. He always is. Theodosius can do without me for awhile.

––––––––––––

    It is not the author's intention to relate the details of the year's campaign in detail. Belisarius won battles despite barely loyal subordinate officers, and many of his Persian prisoners were enlisted to fight for the empire in Italy. Yet because the Arab allies that he detached as a scouting force turned instead to looting, Belisarius was unable to bring Chosroes to decisive combat before it was time for the army to retire into winter quarters.

––––––––––––

    When Justinian entered his wife's sleeping quarters she interrupted him before he could raise the subject of Belisarius.
    "Husband, finally I can prove that your Cappadocian friend, John, is not only a sleaze but disloyal to you."
    "Not again, Theodora. I'm tired. It has been a long day and I'm not so young as you. We'll talk tomorrow."
    "No! We'll talk now. Antonina has told me of a plot to murder us and put her husband on the throne. No, Belisarius is not disloyal. Stiff necked, self-important, and righteous yes: but loyal, too. It seems that Antonina was chatting with John's daughter, Euphemia. She's a sweet thing but she's still a bit naive. In this case that's just as well. The child let it out that that rat would prefer Belisarius to you, and Antonina to me. He thinks

248

you're too mercurial, which you are. He's afraid that if you knew the extent of his tampering with the tax revenue you might one day decide that his eyes are not needed."

Theodora made a motion with her hand like a blade slicing across someone's eyes. "Belisarius would not do that to someone who'd helped him to the throne, but you should if he tries and fails, *sweetheart.*" She drew out the last word. Anyway, I've told Antonina to feel out the girl and if John so much as hints at a coup, we'll know."

"I need John," was all that Justinian could say to defend the agent of his avarice. Theodora looked at him in disbelief. "Go to sleep, dear. *Try* to sleep well."

It was not long before Theodora was satisfied. According to Procopius, Antonina let on to the child how jealous Justinian was of Belisarius; how he had sent him to Persia when some other competent commander might have sufficed; not out of necessity, but so that Belisarius would not have the glory of the final triumph of Roman arms in Italy. She spoke of how unfair it was of Justinian to deny her husband a larger part of the spoils from his African and Italian campaigns, and for Justinian to send him off to Asia for fear that her husband might seize the throne.

At this point the author will simply quote from the history later written by Procopius. Speaking of these concerns which Antonina had voiced, he wrote:

"Euphemia was overjoyed by these words, for she too was hostile to the present administration by reason of her fear of the empress, and she said: "And yet, dearest friend, it is you and Belisarius who are to blame for this, seeing that, though you have opportunity, you are not willing to use your power." And Antonina replied quickly: "It is because we are not able to undertake revolutions in camp unless some of those here at home join with us in the task. Now if your father were willing, we should most easily organize this project and accomplish whatever God wills." When Euphemia heard this, she promised eagerly that the suggestion would be carried out, and departing from there she immediately brought the matter before her father. He was pleased by the message (for he inferred that this undertaking offered him, himself, a way to the royal power), and straightway without any hesitation he assented, and bade his child arrange that on the following day he himself should come to confer with Antonina and give pledges.

"When Antonina learned the mind of John, she wished to lead him as far as possible astray from the understanding of the truth, so she said that for the present it was inadvisable that he should meet her, for fear lest some suspicion should arise strong enough to prevent proceeding; but she was intending straightway to depart for the East to join Belisarius. When, therefore, she had quit Byzantium and had reached the suburb (the one called Rufinianae which was the private possession of Belisarius), there John should come as if to salute her and to escort her forth on the journey, and they should confer regarding matters of state and give and receive their pledges. In saying this she seemed to John to speak well, and a certain day was appointed to carry out the plan. The empress, hearing the whole account from Antonina, expressed approval of what she had planned, and by her exhortations raised her enthusiasm to a much higher pitch still.

"When the appointed day was at hand, Antonina bade the empress farewell and departed from the city, and went to Rufinianae, as if to begin on the following day her journey to the East; hither too came John at night in order to carry out the plan which had been agreed upon. Meanwhile the empress denounced to her husband the things which were being done by John to secure the tyranny, and she sent Narses, the eunuch, and Marcellus, the commander of the palace guards to Rufinianae with numerous soldiers, in order that they investigate what was going on, and if they found John setting about a revolution, that they might kill the man forthwith and return. So these departed for this task. But they say that the emperor got information of what was being done and sent one of John's friends to him forbidding, him on any condition to meet Antonina secretly. But John, disregarding the emperor's warning, about midnight met Antonina, close by a certain wall behind which she had stationed Narses and Marcellus with their men that they might hear what was said. There, while John with unguarded tongue was assenting to the plans for the attack and binding himself with the most dread oaths, Narses and Marcellus suddenly set upon him. But in the natural confusion which resulted the body-guards of John came immediately to his side. One of them smote Marcellus with his sword, not knowing who he was, and thus John was enabled to escape with them, and reached the city with all speed. If he had had the courage to go straightway before the emperor, I believe that he would have suffered no harm at his hand; but as it was, he fled for refuge to the sanctuary, and gave the empress opportunity to work her will against him at her pleasure.

"Thus, from being prefect he became a private citizen, and rising from that sanctuary he was conveyed to another, which is situated in the suburb of the city of Cyzicus called by the Cyzicenes 'Artace.' There he donned the garb of a priest, much against his will, not a bishop's gown, but that of a presbyter, as they are called for he was quite unwilling to perform the office of a priest, lest at some time it should be a hindrance to his entering again into office."

Eventually Justinian did recall him but by then he was too infirm to serve.

When word of how Antonina had brought John low arrived in Dara, Belisarius was far from proud of his wife. He wrote in anger:

"This business besmirches my honor, Antonina. It was done without my knowledge or agreement. You should not have agreed to put even a suggestion of disloyalty before John. I took an oath in Justinian's presence to support and defend him always. I will keep that oath and it should not be suggested otherwise even if it was done as a subterfuge. John is a thief and a scoundrel, but this whole affair was base and the person hurt by it is his innocent child. I would never have agreed to be a part of it."

Antonina, who had been expecting praise from her husband, was stung. It was bad enough that he was in goddamn Asia again, and expecting her to join him. It would be worse when she got there: a damn desert outpost with a husband too busy to pay her any attention. She'd not even have an assignment from Theodora as she'd had in Italy; just be a soldier's wife and chat with whoever could spare her the time. Yes, Photius was with Belisarius, but he'd be busy too. Besides, they never seemed to agree on anything. Antonina worried. Belisarius had Photius at his side, a young man with ambition; ambition which must be curbed lest he use his position to enrich himself while his naive godfather stood aside, occupying himself with the Persian enemy. That could embarrass both Belisarius and her. She wrote letters to friends at court and in Asia urging that Photius be transferred to some other post far from both her and Belisarius. Vicious rumors of a falling out between her and Photius began to circulate and be exaggerated.

Gawd; I'm jealous of my own son. Damn! Damn! What's wrong with me anyway. Damn! Damn. Where is Theodosius? At least he knows about something besides what it takes to push some dehgans back to Babylon. He can take me to a concert and afterward we'll laugh about the queer musicians over some wine. Honor be damned.

Antonina did little to allay the rumors that she and Theodosius were lovers; and the charismatic novice-sans-monastery now had enough money to purchase the regard of older men, and charm the twittering old ladies of the city. But it was not his. Theodosius was wasting Belisarius' money and

Antonina thought him charming for it; or, more likely, convinced herself of it. Theodosius was a drain on her husband's resources. Belisarius owned large estates and plantations, mills, scriptoria, and other business interests. These were beyond her reach, but not the cash she had hidden away to keep some of his wealth from Justinian's grasp. The emperor suspected it and had sent Belisarius to the east with the grand title of Master of Soldiers for the East but practically no imperial resources. Belisarius would have to pay his bucellarii and provide horses and supplies out of his own pocket. Theodosius added to the drain.

For all that, both Antonina and Theodosius knew that their affair could not last much longer, and try as they might to keep the flame alive, both saw the end coming. It had been oh so pleasant for Antonina to be treated like a teen romance by Theodosius and to feel young in his presence; but dumb. How could a woman so skilled in every other worldly matter be so blind? She wasn't blind but she had deluded herself with the same skill that she had used to delude John. She knew what Theodosius had become; she also could remember the fear he had shown that first day when they'd been inventorying the riches of Genseric. That had been eight years before. Theodosius had been young and innocent. She had never meant more than to allow him a fling. Now he was as experienced in the ways of the world as she, and not nearly as cute as he had been then. He had certainly never loved her in the way Belisarius had. He'd been far more fun to be sure, but she was not proud of what he had become. It was time for Antonina to act her age; no one is perfect and Theodosius was no Belisarius.

Theodosius was wasting her husband's money. They had soiled his bed. She had loved him more than her own son.

Damn, I am a bitch.

Their affair was winding down to its belated conclusion, but first Antonina would provide for his safety in some far off city. She decided to entrust a large sum of her husband's remaining cash for him to invest somewhere in the Asian silk trade. It would be safe with him while her husband and his finance chief were away, and if her boyfriend should skim some off the top to pay his gambling debts, well, she could consider it payment for services rendered.

It was not necessary for Antonina to break up with him, for Theodosius did it. The gigolo accepted a portion of Belisarius' more liquid assets, then considered it best to take his leave from Antonina. Surely the rumor mill would advise her husband of their renewed affair. He took ship to Ephesus as though to return to St. Cyprian, but with Belisarius' gold well hidden.

When a courier from Constantinople passed on rumors to Photius that his mother was playing the slut while her husband was risking his life, he was not understanding. He knew the importance of money and understood better than his love-blinded mother the game that Theodosius was playing. The young Photius lost his last feeling of duty toward her. He informed Belisarius.

"Father. I don't know how to say this. If I thought it possible to spare you pain, you know that I would do so. But it is better that you hear it from me, than from anyone else. At least, from me, you will believe it."

Belisarius braced himself for what he knew was coming. It had been only a matter of time until he'd have to face what he had suspected for many months but had hidden from himself under a mantle of work."

"Father." Photius was on his knees. Proud as he was with others, he would kneel before Belisarius, and receive whatever angry outburst he must, even a dagger thrust. "Father, my mother, your wife, probably did betray you with Theodosius in Sicily. I cannot know for sure about that; but certainly she is doing so now. I'm not telling you this because I hate the man, although I admit that I do. But if I don't tell you someone else will. Not only is my mother sleeping with the bastard, she has enriched him with your wealth."

There was probably a long pause, and likely some pacing; then according to Procopius, Belisarius responded:

"Be assured that I love my wife with all my heart. Should it be granted to me to punish the dishonor of my house, I will do her no harm. But so long as Theodosius lives I cannot condone her misconduct." It might disturb the feminist reader – as it did Procopius - that Belisarius wanted vengeance on Theodosius, but looked upon his wife as just possessing the weak nature of women generally, and with her lover's death would be forgiven. The author prefers to believe that he understood the weakness of all humankind and would not condemn "the woman caught in adultery" while ignoring the sins of those righteous men, and women who were joyfully damning her for it. Simply put: Antonina was his wife. He had vowed to love her till death.

After Theodosius fled to Ephesus, Antonina set out for Asia, feeling guilty but unaware of the greeting she would receive. Belisarius had just captured the Persian fortress of Sisauranum, but had decided it would be best not to overextend his lines of communication by continuing deeper into enemy territory. He returned to Roman soil in time to welcome his cheating wife. The campaign was ended, for Belisarius had forced the Persians to return to their own country. Procopius indicates that he might have pursued the fleeing enemy, who had been stricken with plague. He might have acquired some loot that way, but any territorial gains that he'd make would certainly have been lost again in the peace talks which were already underway. The Syrian frontier as it had existed was well fortified and neither country would endanger its future security by surrendering its forts. Belisarius had chased Chosroes' army around the desert and frustrated that monarch's designs, but in the end, peace would be negotiated between ambassadors. Belisarius knew that the result would again be the *status quo ante bellum*. He had done his job. He had frustrated Chosroes' designs, though Roman and Persian troops would continue to clash near the Black sea for many years. Now he wanted to turn his attention to Antonina and the godson who had betrayed him.

Antonina took the same old Roman road as her husband had to Dara and arrived not to his usual smiles and faulty attempts at chit chat but to be greeted by a mere lieutenant and put under close guard - house arrest, actually. She remained incarcerated for three days without even servants to inform her of why she was being so treated.

That wasn't really necessary though. Antonina knew what she had done and could easily imagine how word of it had reached Belisarius. She loved him. Despite her sins and despite his preoccupation with troops and horses and supply lines, she loved him. She had just loved Theodosius too. Theodosius was cheerful; Belisarius tended to the moody. Theodosius was chatty; Belisarius was often preoccupied. Theodosius took her to the theater and concerts; Belisarius didn't. Theodosius shared with her a worldly cynicism; Belisarius read Marcus Aurelius for consolation.

But Theodosius was a bit vain; Belisarius was modest, though not with the false modesty of Justinian. Theodosius was avaricious; Belisarius earned every centenaria laid aside as his portion of the spoils of war. Theodosius was often blind to those who were not members of the court; Belisarius was known for rewarding bravery out of his own purse and providing homes and sustenance for wounded veterans in their own towns or on his estates. Theodosius was civil to slaves; Belisarius was kind. Belisarius was rich. Theodosius wanted to be, but wasted his own money and that of friends.

What was Antonina like by this stage of her life? Of course she was nothing at all like the clumsy whore of the hippodrome, hiding self loathing behind a tough exterior. Nor had she anything in common with the nervous out-of-her-depths young bride and cubicularia of Constantinople. At forty three she was enduring a mid life crisis and she was becoming matronly.

For three days Antonina saw no one but her guard. Her servants weren't allowed near her and Belisarius stayed away. He knew that he'd melt

254

like butter in the Syrian sun if he spoke with his wife.

What a life I've had. A bit of everything: I've been a whore, the empress' friend, a soldier, and now a prisoner of my husband. Antonina might have smiled were it not that she was angry as hell. *Humiliated! How dare he treat me like some criminal, locked up with a guard at the door. Belisarius may not owe me, but Theodora does and she'll hear about this.*

Belisarius felt lousy, as he always did on occasions when he'd suspected Antonina's behavior. He too felt humiliated. *Doesn't she ever think of the consequences of anything she does? Enough, I've a reputation to consider. Troops won't respect me. I should send her back to her mother.* But Belisarius knew he was only kidding himself. Antonina was Antonina and he could no more imagine living without her than disobeying his army oath of loyalty. In the end he'd give in. He knew it. In a strange way that actually gave him satisfaction. Theodosius was another matter however. Already Photius had left for Ephesus. *He'll drag the thief to justice. Damn; Antonina's no spring chicken. It must have been the money; my money. He plays the gigolo while I'm risking my neck. I can't always be with her. I have a duty. Duty must come first. Antonina should know that. She should find someone trustworthy to keep her occupied when I'm away; not a damn gigolo and thief. Did she really sleep with the bastard, a guy that I trusted her with? Why? Oh, Antonina, what have I done that you sleep with our godson ... and what am I to tell his father? Damn, I have to kill the bastard and tell his old man that I did it.*

Then a courier brought a message from Constantinople:

To the Illustrious Belisarius, Greetings:

Congratulations on your recent victories against the Persians, though, as you must see, the final issue remains in doubt, perhaps to be settled in the spring.

As soon as affairs can be put in order in your camp, you are required to turn temporary command over to our strategos Martinus, and then return with utmost speed to our presence, together with your wife, the Lady Antonina.

Justinian

From its simplicity and relative informality it was obvious that the letter was composed by the emperor himself. Justinian had signed it with his name and without any of the usual titles; but then Justinian knew Belisarius too well to put on airs if the note were not to be seen by others.

Privately the courier warned Belisarius to be on guard, and he told Belisarius that the monarchs were troubled about the disclosure of Antonina's infidelity. He said that Theodora had insisted that he should bring his wife back beside him when he returned to Constantinople in triumph.

When Belisarius received the letter he went to Antonina's room where she sat glowering at him. His words were colder than he felt: "Justinian has summoned us to return to Constantinople." That was all he said before turning and leaving with his guard.

CHAPTER 19

542 AD
CONSTANTINOPLE
ASIA

Although Theodora sat stone faced on a high throne-like chair, the emperor had descended and had perched on some broad steps, hardly above the discordant couple prostrate on the marble floor of an antechamber to the throne room proper. He wore no imperial raiment and seemed intent on playing the old friend to the general and his wife which, of course, he had once been.

It was Theodora who spoke first, and hers was a regal voice. "Belisarius, we do not deny that you have served the empire well. We have not even until this day interfered with your enrichment of yourself beyond all right and justice. We have, however, now had enough of your haughtiness. You go about our city as though it were yours and your friends have been found advising high and low that you would be a better emperor than Justinian. They have been punished, but because of your past services to us and the love we bear for Antonina we have abstained from punishing you. We shall continue to abstain if you and she are reconciled. Know, Belisarius, that she has been of the greatest value to me and I expect that you will treat her with the greatest dignity and respect. Were it not for her you would be commanding some small fortress on the Hunnish frontier."

"In all things public I have obeyed your majesties, and always will. But do as you will with me; our private lives are ours alone, and no power can command them." Belisarius' voice was strong, even harsh; strange for someone prostrate on the floor below the meanest woman in the world. Still, both church and civil law were on the general's side, according to the compendium of laws which Justinian himself had ordered to be made.

Clearly that was so. Clearly, too, Belisarius was not to be intimidated. Justinian first threw a glance at his wife than spoke in a far milder tone than she and gestured for the couple to rise.

"Belisarius, have you never loved another woman than your wife?"

Belisarius did not dissemble. "Yes, of course I have."

"And what did you do about it?"

"Why nothing, Your Serenity. We were friends. Many times I have had female friends. Antonina knew them too."

"And did she not mind?"

"I don't think she cared. They were just friends." Belisarius looked at his wife trying his best to look accusing.

"Antonina, what did you think of Belisarius' 'friends.'"

"They were always my friends too. Truly I think I'd have understood though if they'd been more than friends to him. There was Aileen. Aileen was intelligent and cheerful. With Aileen he had no responsibilities. She made him laugh. ...And she had a nice butt. Admit it, Flavius, she has a nice butt."

"But I never slept with her," Belisarius interrupted coldly.

"And I'd not have cared … well not too much, if you had. You're a man and believe me, I know men. I never required that you be a saint and I'm hardly one. You knew that when we married." Anger showed in Lady Antonina's eyes but whether it was true anger at her husband or to cover her own embarrassment and shame no one could say.

"Now that's it. That's the problem, isn't it?" The emperor spoke softly. He was known to have a way of disarming his critics with his understanding manner, even if sometimes it was only a ruse. This time, however, he had nothing to gain. Theodora's imperious approach had failed; now, Justinian was simply trying to mediate between two old friends.

"I took an oath," Belisarius began. "Just as I did to you. And I've kept them both and always will."

"'And always will.' Exactly Flavius." The emperor was doing his best. "But not everyone keeps their oaths; nor is an oath a substitute for love. You've kept your oath; Antonina hasn't. But do you still love each other?"

Belisarius looked at his wife who now sat on one of the steps below Justinian where he'd indicated that she should relax.

"I do."

"And you, Antonina? I know that you love Theodosius, and I can see why. He's quite the jolly one and now you've made him rich with Flavius' money. But he does not have to bear the responsibilities of your husband. It is easy enough to play the cheerful friend - just like this Aileen - when your job isn't to send others to be killed. He can be off to some party with you or riding through the countryside on a pretty day. Don't you think that Flavius would like to do that too? He could be enjoying life - would like to - but must instead be providing for his men so that as few as possible will die. Yes, he can be too much like a monk but he's actually got much more to worry about than some cleric. He's got real responsibilities. Believe me, Theodora and I know the problem. But let me put it to you directly … and tell the truth: Do you still love Belisarius, prig that he is?"

"Yes."

"As much as when you married him?"

Antonina, who had been looking at the marble floor, raised her head and looked Belisarius in the eyes. "Yes."

"Well that's it then. I'll make it easy for the both of you. As your emperor I order you to be reconciled. You are to make every effort to please each other, not yourselves. That is what marriage is. It is about pleasing someone else. Yes, romance is about being pleased and marriage is about pleasing another person. I do not say you should stop loving Theodosius; but Antonina, you must follow your husband's example. Loving Theodosius needn't mean sleeping with him."

From her throne, Theodora had been watching and listening. What her husband had said and required was good, unrealistic but good. Now she added a few important words of her own, trying to moderate her haughty style. "Belisarius, I doubt that Antonina could ever forgive you if you harmed Theodosius. Not that he doesn't deserve your anger but anger will not help the situation. I have given orders that he and Photius be found and Theodosius be returned to his monastery alive after I've had a little talk with him. I'll also see to it that his abbot keeps him focused on the good of his soul. I've also learned that Theodosius has become quite wealthy. That money will serve us well to outfit your next expedition." Theodora knew that those funds had been stolen from Belisarius with his wife's connivance and recovered for his godfather by Photius, but it were best for everyone that not be mentioned. The empire did indeed need money, and Belisarius had become very rich as a result of his campaigns.

Belisarius and Antonina left the Imperial presence together, though they did not look like sweethearts. An imperial edict is not enough to undo hurt or restore trust. The author would like to report that all was well thereafter but Justinian could not make that happen, and Theodora for her own reasons preferred that the couple not be too comfortable together. Justinian feared Belisarius' popularity and Theodora feared Antonina's ambition if not her husband's. She contemplated how to sow just a little enmity between them again while at the same time drawing Antonina closer to herself. As for the couple themselves? Between bouts of glowering over breakfast there were flashes of kindness. They tried not to forget their hurt but eventually the night came when Antonina could not resist spanking the great man as of old. Things were not perfect in the Belisarius bedroom but they were better.

An imperial dispatch brought Photius to Constantinople, but not before he sent Theodosius under guard to Cilicia, where he was to be kept in a hidden prison. Photius brought Theodosius' stolen treasure with him but that was not sufficient to satisfy the angry empress. That Photius should dare to hide Theodosius from her so angered Theodora that she threw him into a hidden cell from which Procopius claims that he did not escape for three years.

"What of my son, Photius?"

"Have no fear, Flavius." Justinian's words helped to sooth his general's fear. "He is safe and I will not let any harm come to him. For a time it is in his own best interest that he remain quietly where he is. Theodora can be a bitch."

Whatever the length and truth about his incarceration, Photius afterward became a monk, an Abbott, and finally a tax collector for the throne. Allegedly, he was so villainous in this work that even the emperor upbraided him.

Belisarius was depressed - clinically depressed, a depression not diagnosed by Procopius, nor at first understood by Antonina, the one person who needed to. She realized now, more than she had in years, how much she loved Belisarius; yet she still mooned over her lost Theodosius. In his despondency even Belisarius missed the cheerfulness of the man which had brightened many a dull journey or relieved a night of sorrow after a day of meaningless and fruitless skirmishing. Indeed, sometimes Theodosius had relieved Belisarius of the duty of writing to the relatives of old friends with sad news of their deaths or wounding. He had helped Antonina in the business of sequestering some of his wealth where Justinian could not steal it. For some reason which the general could not quite place, he had not entirely trusted Procopius who dealt quite well with his day to day finances. He had trusted Theodosius and now he missed, if not Theodosius himself, at least having what he had thought to be a cheerful right arm.

It wasn't just Antonina's affair with Theodosius which had soured Belisarius. He had changed. If Antonina was no longer the victim of a cruel world but now a part of the establishment itself, Belisarius was no longer above it, but its victim. When he had defeated Kobad he had been lauded by emperor and citizens alike. When he had defeated the Vandals he'd been rewarded with riches and an imperial triumph. Now Justinian seemed to fear him; Theodora hated him; and Antonina didn't seem to care what he did:

Have I been wrong in not taking the throne when I could have? There is so much I could have done for Christ's empire. Have I been stupid for not screwing some slave when I could have? I've been horny and lonely, and Antonina wouldn't have given a damn. The monks think it's easy. Oaths! Why keep them? All they do is help those who don't keep them. I spend five years recovering Italy and what does Justinian do? Tax the life out of that country until it asks for the Goths to come back. Then what does he do? He sends eleven idiots who are losing the whole thing again. What did I do it for? For the empire, of course. Then Justinian neither appreciates my work nor is able to keep it. A waste. A waste of my time and worse: a waste of so many lives. I may just as well have stayed home and grown grapes. Maybe then Antonina would have been a nice country wife and we'd be raising Joannina together instead of bringing slaughter and ruin on so many places; and for what?

The Persian war will start again and I'll be expected to do some miracle. With what? Justinian spends every cent he raises on buildings and paying off barbarians. The priests love him. Meanwhile the farmers suffer. I rebuilt the empire for him; now it's going to ruin. I've wasted my life. What have we got to show for all the horror that I've done? Just some African desert.

On a bright morning Antonina answered a summons from Theodora, intent on further cementing the bond that Antonina had forged between them with the affair of John the Cappadocian.

"Dearest lady," the empress spoke as to a friend. Yesterday a pearl was brought to me so beautiful that I think no one has seen such as it before. I'll show it to you." Then taking Antonina by the hand she brought her to Theodosius, whom her agents had located where Photius had imprisoned him in Cilicia. Theodosius was dressed in the robe of a monk. It was awkward. They hugged for a moment but without passion.

This was a conundrum for Antonina. Last month's imperial audience had reminded her that she did love her husband. *Funny how I could forget that. We've drawn apart. There were too many other things. Now Theodosius is back and hiding in the palace itself. If I see him again and Belisarius finds out, I'm dead. And if Belisarius doesn't find out I'm a lousy cheating wife again.* Right and wrong did not enter Antonina's calculations any more than they had Theodora's, for as Belisarius would have said: "Antonina is Antonina."

261

Thereafter, Theodora kept Theodosius hidden in the women's quarters, promising him high office. She even promised him direction of the army when any ambition of Belisarius could be shamed and he brought low. Of course that was a ploy more than a promise for Theodosius was more a courtier than a warrior. Just as Antonina was Antonina, to her last days Theodora was the calculating Theodora.

Antonina was too smart not to see the trap. Theodora and Justinian had reconciled her and Belisarius. Why then had Theodora brought Theodosius to tempt her? Answer: *Because she could.* Were she and Belisarius to be really close again, she might lead him to take the throne. *Divide and conquer. Gawd, Theodosius was fun, but what would I do without Flavius.* That thought had never occurred to Antonina before. To cheat on him was one thing, but to live without him was something she could not bear.

The next day, Antonina lay prostrate in a church; not because she was particularly religious but because she was trying to settle in her mind whether to rely on prayers, or on the spells she had learned from Egyptian girls in darkened rooms beneath the hippodrome. She had already fashioned a lead statuette in the image of Belisarius, which she had prudently left outside in an alley. It might help; she had known amulets and prayers to dubious deities to bring lovers together. No, that wasn't exactly right. They had brought a lecher his heart's desire. Incantations with offerings could sometimes work: *"I adjure you that by eating this precious fruit, he may have the desire for me that I have for him; that he may desire me always; that he may desire me now, right now."*

She'd never learned the name of the demon or jinn or power that "prayer" was to be directed to. It didn't matter. She had at last decided not to betray her husband's trust with spells learned in a life long left behind. They might work but they would certainly be a cheap and terrible trick to play on her too saintly husband. One that he would never forgive, were he to find out. He'd forgive her almost anything else, even Theodosius she was sure, but not that. She wasn't sure if her prayers to God and the saints would be heard either. The priests frowned upon praying for love and her motives weren't the cleanest, but she'd try anyway. Maybe God would grant them because she'd rejected help from demons.

That decision made, Antonina felt clean, though unsure of the gamble. She left the church, where it was dark, to offer her prayers in the sun at one of the roadside shrines that festooned the city; but first she retrieved the little statuette of Belisarius. Should she save it just in case prayers failed, or would they fail because she saved it?

I am the wife of a saint. My job is to protect him from the unholy.

262

Antonina threw the statuette with all the might she could muster and watched it arc into the Bosporus near to where the Chrysopolis ferry docked. If she was expecting something dramatic she was disappointed, or maybe she was happy that nothing awful occurred. It sank like the dead thing it was. With long, clean, and happy strides Antonina went home to her husband, praying as she went, not to the saints whose pictures decorated churches, but to any prostitute who had ever loved a good man and found peace and salvation in that love. She had no name to address but surely in the heavenly vault some girl would listen to her plea and lay a petition at Christ's foot.

ASIA

Byzantine spies discovered that Chosroes was gathering an army to raid into Palestine and take the holy city of Jerusalem. Justinian shelved his wife's vendetta against Belisarius and sent him by remounts of post horses alone to the frontier.

Though monotheists themselves, the Persians worshiped God under the appearance of fire and had no regard for either the Jewish or Christian heritage. That Christian heritage had enriched Jerusalem with innumerable churches graced with gold and silver and jewels. The empire would no doubt also pay well to ransom captive priests and bishops, and even more for the return of the many relics that Chosroes might seize with ease.

The two Roman commanders who might have challenger Chosroes in the field, not unreasonably hid behind the walls of convenient fortresses. There, they prepared to hold out until Justinian would send thousands of reinforcements to save them; or the Persians complete their pillaging and withdraw. Maybe they believed that Christ Jesus would not permit Jerusalem to fall and would send angels to defend it. Neither Justinian nor Jesus complied.

What might have been Belisarius' thoughts? He had fought the Persians before. He had defeated them but it had not been an easy victory. Persian cavalry were tough; tougher, he may have thought, than the Roman armies cowering behind fortress walls while a pagan enemy was threatening the Holy City itself.

What can I do anyway? Justinian won't release another army and the troops in Asia are dejected and in no shape to fight.

Antonina? There's no time to think of Antonina now; nor Photius. She must still moon over that bastard Theodosius anyway. Theodora says to leave him to his abbot, but I think she loves him herself. The guy's a con man. He turns female heads for a living. ... And I liked him too. Damn! With every thought Belisarius became more depressed and sullen. What kept him from giving way to an unmanly sulk was duty. Jerusalem, where the Lord had been crucified, was threatened. But what could one man do?

When the lone rider arrived in Syria he lodged in the town of Europum, where he found a few low ranking officers of a like mind with his: to confront the enemy with whatever force they had and trust in Christ Jesus. That was a bit of cheer and together they began to gather stragglers and form a tiny army. The generals Bouzes and Justus - the latter a nephew of Justinian - had united their forces in the town of Hierapolis to await reinforcement. From there they sent a message explaining the situation as they saw it, and advising Belisarius to take charge of their city and await reinforcements. Belisarius' reply to the generals behind the walls of Hierapolis has been recorded by Procopius as has been his successful defense of the Holy Land with nearly no troops. Though depressed at the paucity of soldiers with which to stop a major Persian advance, as well as by the personal troubles which continued to haunt his mind when alone in bed each night, there is no hint of anything weak from the victor of Dara as the situation is described by Procopius:

"'If, now, Chosroes were proceeding against any other peoples, and not against subjects of the Romans, this plan of yours is well considered and insures the greatest possible degree of safety; for it is great folly for those who have the opportunity of remaining quiet and being rid of trouble to enter into any unnecessary danger; but if, immediately after departing from here, this barbarian is going to fall upon some other territory of the Emperor Justinian, and that an exceptionally good one, but without any guard of soldiers, be assured that to perish valorously is better in every way than to be saved without a fight. For this would justly be called not salvation but treason. But come as quickly as possible to Europum, where, after collecting the whole army, I hope to deal with the enemy as God permits.'

"When the officers saw this message, they took courage, and leaving Justus with some few men to guard Hierapolis, all the others with the rest of the army came to Europum. Chosroes, upon learning that Belisarius with his whole Roman army had encamped at Europum, decided not to continue his advance, but sent Abandanes, one of the royal secretaries to Belisarius, in order to find out what sort of a general he might be, but ostensibly to make a protest because Justinian had not sent ambassadors that they might settle the arrangements for peace as had been agreed. When Belisarius learned this, he picked out six thousand men of goodly stature and especially fine physique, and set out as for a hunt at a considerable distance from the camp. Then he commanded two guardsman to cross the river with a thousand horsemen and move about the bank there, always making it appear to the enemy that if they wished to cross the Euphrates and proceed to their own land, the Romans would not permit them to do so....

"Now when Belisarius had ascertained that the envoy was close at hand, he set up a pavilion of some heavy cloth, and seated himself there as one might in a desolate place, seeking thus to indicate that he had come without any equipment. And he arranged the soldiers as follows. On either side of the tent were Thracians and Illyrians, with Goths beyond them, and next to these Heruli, and finally Vandals and Moors. Their lines extended for a great distance over the plain for they did not remain standing always in the same place, but stood apart from one another and kept walking about, looking careless and without the least interest in the envoy of Chosroes. Not one of them had a cloak or any other outer garment to cover the shoulders, but they were sauntering about clad in linen tunics and trousers, and outside these their girdles. Each one had his horse-whip, but for weapons one had a sword, another an ax, another an uncovered bow. And all gave the impression that they were eager to be off on the hunt with never a thought of anything else. So Abandanes came into the presence of Belisarius and said that king Chosroes was indignant because the agreement previously made had not been kept: that envoys be sent to him by Caesar (for thus the Persians call the emperor of the Romans), and as a result of this Chosroes had been compelled to come into the land of the Romans in arms.

"But Belisarius was not terrified by the thought that a multitude of foreigners were encamped close by, nor did he experience any confusion because of the words of the man; but with a laughing, care-free countenance he made answer, saying: 'This course which Chosroes has followed is not in keeping with the way men usually act. For other men, when a dispute arises between themselves and any of their neighbors, first carry on negotiations with them. Only if they do not receive reasonable satisfaction, then finally they go against them in war. But Chosroes first comes into the midst of the Romans, and then offers suggestions concerning peace.'

"With such words as these he dismissed the ambassador.

"Now when Abandanes came to Chosroes, he advised him to take his departure with all possible speed. For he said he had met a general who in manliness and sagacity surpassed all other men, and soldiers such as he at least had never seen, whose orderly conduct had roused in him the greatest admiration. He added that the contest was not even. For if Belisarius be conquered, Chosroes would only have conquered the slave of Caesar; but if by any chance he were defeated, he would bring great disgrace upon his kingdom and upon the race of the Persians. Also, even if the Romans were defeated they could easily save themselves in strongholds and in their own land, while if the Persians should meet with any reverse, not even a messenger would escape home. ....

"Then Belisarius with the whole Roman army crossed the River Euphrates and immediately sent messengers to Chosroes. When the messengers came into his presence they commended him highly for his withdrawal and promised that envoys would come to him promptly from the emperor, who would arrange with him that the terms which had previously been agreed upon concerning the peace should be put into effect. Then they asked of him that he treat the Romans as his friends in his journey through their land. ....

"The Romans were loud in their praises of Belisarius and he seemed to have achieved greater glory in their eyes by this affair than when he brought Gelimer or Witiges captive to Constantinople. In reality it was an achievement of great importance and one deserving great praise. At a time when all the Romans were panic-stricken with fear and were hiding themselves in their defenses, and Chosroes with a mighty army had come into the midst of the Roman domain, a general with only a few men, coming in hot haste from Byzantium, had set his camp against that of the Persian king. Then Chosroes, either through fear of fortune, or of the valor of the man, or even because deceived by some tricks, cut short his advance, and took to flight, though pretending to be seeking peace."

Chosroes was happy to regain his own capital with his army intact. He did not entirely keep his word to forgo hostilities en route, but raided a Roman city on his retreat. Yet substantially the peace held and Belisarius expected to be sent to Italy again to undue the damage done in his absence.

CONSTANTINOPLE

Before that could happen disaster struck Constantinople, much of the Roman empire, and the whole of the Persian empire. Procopius describes the pestilence that hit Europe, recurrences of which were for centuries afterward known as the Justinian plague:

266

"During these times there was a pestilence, by which the whole human race came near to being annihilated. It started from the Egyptians who dwell in Pelusium. Then it divided and moved in one direction towards Alexandria and the rest of Egypt, and in the other direction it came to Palestine on the borders of Egypt. From there it spread over the whole world, always moving forward and traveling at times favorable to it. For it seemed to move by fixed arrangement, and to tarry for a specified time in each country, casting its blight slightingly upon none, but spreading in either direction right out to the ends of the world, as if fearing lest some corner of the earth might escape it. ... This disease always took its start from the coast, and from there went up to the interior. And in the second year it reached Constantinople in the middle of spring. Apparitions of supernatural beings in human guise of every description were seen by many persons, and immediately upon seeing this apparition they were seized by the disease. Now at first those who met these creatures tried to turn them aside by uttering the holiest of names and exorcising them in other ways as well as each one could, but they accomplished absolutely nothing, for even in the sanctuaries to which most of them fled for refuge they were dying constantly.

"Later on they were unwilling even to give heed to their friends when they called to them, and they shut themselves up in their rooms and pretended that they did not hear although their doors were being beaten down, fearing, obviously, that he who was calling was one of those demons. But in the case of some the pestilence did not come on in this way, but they saw a vision in a dream and seemed to suffer the very same thing at the hands of the creature who stood over them, or else to hear a voice foretelling to them that they were written down in the number of those who were to die. But with the majority it came about that they were seized by the disease without becoming aware of what was coming either through a waking vision or a dream. And they were taken in the following manner. They had a sudden fever, some when just roused from sleep, others while walking about, and others while otherwise engaged, without any regard to what they were doing. And the body showed no change from its previous color, nor was it hot as might be expected when attacked by a fever, nor indeed did any inflammation set in, but the fever was of such a languid sort from its commencement and up till evening that neither to the sick themselves nor to a physician who touched them would it afford any suspicion of danger. It was natural, therefore, that not one of those who had contracted the disease expected to die from it. But on the same day in some cases, in others on the following day, and in the rest not many days later, a bubonic swelling developed; and this took place not only in the particular part of the body which is called "boubon," that is, below the abdomen, but also inside the armpit, and in some cases also beside the ears, and at different points on the thighs. ….

"There ensued with some a deep coma, with others a violent delirium. …. Those who were under the spell of the coma forgot all those who were familiar to them and seemed to be sleeping constantly; and if anyone cared for them, they would eat without waking. But some also were neglected, and these would die directly through lack of sustenance. But those who were seized with delirium suffered from insomnia and were victims of a distorted imagination; for they suspected that men were coming upon them to destroy them, and they would become excited and rush off in flight, crying out at the top of their voices. And those who were attending them were in a state of constant exhaustion and had a most difficult time of it throughout. For this reason everybody pitied them no less than the sufferers, but not because they were threatened by the pestilence in going near it's victims. (Neither physicians nor other persons were found to contract this malady through contact with the sick or with the dead, and many others who were constantly engaged either in burying or in attending the ill held out in the performance of this service beyond all expectation, while with many others the disease came on without warning and they died straightway.) The dying were pitied because of the great hardships which they were undergoing. When patients fell from their beds and lay rolling upon the floor, they were put back in place, and when they struggled to rush headlong out of their houses, they would be forced back. And when water chanced to be near, they wished to fall into it, but not because of a desire for drink. (For most of them rushed into the sea.) The cause was to be found in the diseased state of their minds. They also had great difficulty in eating, for they could not easily take food. Many perished through lack of any man to care for them and they were either overcome by hunger, or threw themselves down from a height. In those cases where neither coma nor delirium came on, the bubonic swelling became mortified and the sufferer, no longer able to endure the pain, died. … Now some of the physicians who were at a loss because the symptoms were not understood, supposing that the disease centered in the bubonic swellings, decided to investigate the bodies of the dead. And upon opening some of the swellings, they found a strange sort of carbuncle that had grown inside them. Death came in some cases immediately, in others after many days. With some the body broke out with black pustules about as large as a lentil and these did not survive even one day, but succumbed immediately. With many also a vomiting of blood

268

ensued without visible cause and straightway brought death. Moreover I am able to declare this: that the most illustrious physicians predicted that many would die, who unexpectedly escaped entirely from suffering shortly afterward. Others, that they expected to be saved, were destined to be carried off almost immediately. Of those who received no care many died, but others, contrary to reason, were saved. And again, methods of treatment shewed different results with different patients. Indeed the whole matter may be stated thus, that no device was discovered by man to save himself, so that either by taking precautions he should not suffer, or that when the malady had assailed him he should get the better of it; but suffering came without warning and recovery was due to no external cause. ....

"Now the disease in Constantinople ran a course of four months, and its greatest virulence lasted about three. At first the deaths were but a little more than the normal, then the mortality rose still higher, and afterward the tale of dead reached five thousand each day, and again it even came to ten thousand and still more than that.

"And it fell to the lot of the emperor, as was natural, to make provision for the trouble. He therefore detailed soldiers from the palace and distributed money. When it came about that all the tombs which had existed previously were filled with the dead, then they dug up all the places about the city and one after the other, laid the dead there. But later on when those who were making these trenches, were no longer able to keep up with the number of the dying, they mounted the towers of the fortifications and tearing off the roofs threw the bodies into them in complete disorder. They piled them up just as each one happened to fall, and filled practically all the towers with corpses, and then covered them again with their roofs. As a result of this an evil stench pervaded the city and distressed the inhabitants still more, and especially whenever the wind blew fresh from that quarter.

"Then the emperor himself became ill with a swelling of the groin. And the pestilence fell also upon the land of the Persians and visited all the other barbarians besides. For a time the plague ravished Persia worse even than in Europe."

CHAPTER 20

542 AD
CONSTANTINOPLE

Justinian recovered and with peace he could demote and disgrace his top general. He no longer need pretend that they were still friends. As he saw it, Belisarius was his rival, possibly for the throne itself, but of a certainty for popularity.

A courier was dispatched to inform Belisarius of the monarchs' delight in his having defeated Chosroes without loss of life. He indicated that Justinian and Theodora had in mind a special reward for him when he returned to the city. It was a charade. As soon as Belisarius entered the imperial presence he was attacked by one minister after another who charged him with disloyalty and fraud. Was it true that he had said that should Justinian die from the plague he could not guarantee obedience to Theodora unless the senate proclaimed her authority to rule in her own right, not merely as the deceased emperor's wife? At least one cousin of Justinian was known to have ambition to rule; did he support him or "her gracious majesty?"

"Would you have supported this man against the rights of our mistress?"

"I would obey my oath."

"And what did you swear?"

"To obey my lawful sovereign."

"Who is?"

"Justinian, and, of course, Theodora to whom he entrusts many matters."

"Were Justinian to be taken up by Our Lord and Savior, what then? Would Theodora still reign?"

"I have not considered that question in any great detail. It is a political matter and for the senate to resolve. I am not an expert on the law."

In the end there was no evidence against Belisarius. He did not deny the scuttlebutt, but so what? It had clearly been a simple discussion of where a soldier's duty lay; hardly treason. Besides, he was more popular than either Justinian or Theodora. They were reluctant to risk the anger of the crowd should they proceed against so popular a hero.

"God knows, Justinian, even if Belisarius does not seek the throne, how could he resist a crown if the crowd were to force him to the hippodrome, as they did old Hypatius during the revolt?"

"Yes, my dear; you are, no doubt, right. He does not want to violate his oath, but he must hate us after all that has happened. If he were raised on a shield by the army and approved by the crowd and the senate, he would be their emperor, whether he had sought it or not."

"It is not necessary to charge Belisarius at all, your sovereignty," a cloying aide advised Theodora. "We can imprison his underling, Bouzes, on the same charge of sedition. He has not covered himself in glory and has no support either with the crowd or in the senate. It would be a signal to Belisarius. With Bouzes under confinement I doubt that he would even dare to confront the emperor about any money you might need. Besides, his stepson remains under your power. Belisarius would not wish to see him tortured."

No charges were filed against Belisarius. However, Justinian took it into his head to still obtain his remaining wealth by claiming that Belisarius had amassed too great a fortune; that he had not sent to the imperial treasury the lion's share of the booty from Africa and Italy.

He was quietly advised that such a charge was unfounded. Yet despite that no formal charge could be brought against Belisarius, a commission was sent to the cities of Asia to look into his actions there and find excuses to seize his wealth. He was stripped of command and Justinian seized his retinue of seven thousand bucellarii. The scarred were immediately reassigned throughout the empire lest they mutiny in support of the lord for whom they had sacrificed themselves in a hundred battles, feints, and skirmishes. Theodora, herself, encouraged some favored imperial eunuchs to toss dice for the tallest and better looking.

Thus Justinian treated his one time friend and the man who had turned the Nike revolutionaries against each other; the man who had three times turned back the mighty armies of Persia. Thus he treated the man who had regained Libya from the Vandals. Thus he treated the general who had won back Sicily and Rome, Naples, and the whole of Italy from the Goths; he who had brought two powerful kings prisoner before him - perhaps the one man in Constantinople who had determined never to betray the throne whether its occupant was worthy or not. Justinian was a great emperor but his paranoid fear of Belisarius' ambition has permanently stained his memory.

Photius' loyalty to Belisarius seemed to threaten Theodora. She had arrested him without charge simply for confounding her relationship with Antonina by removing Theodosius. Procopius complains that Belisarius, now in disfavor, made no effort to rescue Photius from the dungeon (or more likely, secure quarters) in which Theodora had imprisoned him.

Photius loved his stepfather and had always shown him the kind of loyalty which Belisarius himself had for the emperor. In his childhood Antonina had certainly loved Photius. He had been nearly the only bright thing in her life in Antioch. Yet to his eyes she'd deserted him. All his filial affection was directed at his stepfather. Yet Belisarius made no move.

As a teenager his mother had not even known Photius. The young man that Belisarius had summoned to their marriage was nearly a stranger to her; a stranger whom she admired as an officer and had tried for ten years to love; but one who was too close to her husband when she was straying like a cat. Any love she still retained had been severely strained. Had he not pushed from his mind any remaining loyalty toward her when he determined to reveal her affair?

That Belisarius was a broken man is obvious from what Procopius next tells us. Many officers who had also failed to support Theodora in Justinian's illness were punished and Bouzes was imprisoned in a lightless prison for nearly two and a half years. Belisarius spent many an evening pacing the floor, indecisive as he had never been against an armed enemy. His remaining friends at court were few and his jealous enemies many. He was in no position to help Photius.

Belisarius did not offer to counter another attack by Chosroes and fell under further suspicion of treachery or cowardice. This was the imperial couple's excuse to strip him of the remainder of his wealth. He was officially scorned and left without dignity. For Belisarius under these conditions to have made any move to defend Photius, even had he still the psychological strength to do so, might only have brought about his admirer's death. The best service he could do the young man was to distance himself and pray that Antonina would appeal to the empress. *Surely she can't want him in a cell.* But Antonina could not help. Her love for her grown son had been weakened by years apart and as she saw it, she could not help him without harming her husband:

Who I have harmed enough. But soon, dear sainted whore in heaven; soon.

For a time we know nothing of Belisarius except that because he would not bend, he remained under the displeasure of Justinian and particularly Theodora. Was he haughty? Yes. Was he obstinate? If so, he had the right. His stepson, who had revealed his own mother's infidelity, had been arrested by Theodora for this service of which, just as likely, Belisarius would have preferred to remain ignorant. According to Procopius, Belisarius was at least as angered by Theodosius' theft of his fortune as by Antonina's infidelity with him; though it difficult to see how Theodosius could possibly have threatened the financial "ruin of his house" as Procopius testifies, nor for that matter why he should have. But whatever.

Who would not have been depressed, disturbed to the extreme by the ingratitude of his monarchs, the worsening Italian situation in his absence, and the betrayal by his wife? Theodora thought him arrogant. The last thing that Belisarius was feeling at that moment was arrogance. He was feeling hurt. Why would a man who had so often faced death for his emperor or even for some troopers feel hurt like a little child? His emperor had betrayed him, probably to please Theodora. Oh, Belisarius knew that Justinian was a jerk, but he was still emperor of Rome and until now he had thought Justinian a damaged friend of sorts. In the past, Justinian had rewarded loyalty. Belisarius held honors that only a member of the imperial family would normally hold. He had been consul in Constantinople, his stepson a senator and consul in Rome. There had been talk of having Justinian's nephew and heir, Anastasius, marry little Joannina when they were older. Now Justinian was acting like a spoiled child. For no reason that made any sense he had disgraced and robbed his most loyal subject of his estates. Belisarius' bucellarii were scattered to God knows where, and his stepson was in some dark hole of Theodora's. Why? Because Justinian had needed Belisarius' treasure to buy off barbarian princes, to buy more toys to impress the priests, or to buy his way to paradise? However, if Belisarius had ever thought of raising the standard of rebellion now was not that time.

After the humiliation and disgrace he had received at the hands of Theodora and her eunuchs, Belisarius did not know what to do. He had no desire to do anything. His life had been a waste; honorable behavior, "a chasing after wind" as the biblical preacher had said. The world was in the hands of the mean spirited, and always would be. He had no desire now to do anything. He would not complain, nor remind their majesties of his years of outstanding service. He would not give those who had used his naivete any sense of triumph. They were below disdain. All Belisarius wanted to do was to go to bed; alone. Antonina would never understand; or so he thought.

Yet, for once the general was wrong. He had never understood the source of Antonina's strength. Though her own feelings of worthlessness had been years before, she understood his helplessness as those who have never been victimized cannot. She had frequently had to ignore the smug superiority of the worldly, but had repaid them whenever she found one under her power. Belisarius was the great constant in her life. It was Belisarius who had always protected her. Theodora was a protector, too, but only out of self interest. A pope had been deposed and humiliated to please her and people had died because of their vengeance. Now Theodora had repaid her by humiliating her husband. Belisarius alone had protected her out of nothing more than fondness.

Enough! Antonina sat herself down on her expanding butt and made some calculations: for a moment she was able to recall in all their detail the months she had spent with a young guards lieutenant in Antioch. She remembered how frightened she had been at their wedding when the flower of Roman nobility had first spoken to her as though she were a lady. She remembered how Belisarius had always allowed her to be her flirtatious self. What was to be an occasional excursion to war fronts to keep an eye out for treasonous officers, had turned into being an agent for Theodora, to do whatever dirty business the empress dared not ask of Belisarius. She thought of how Belisarius had taken her with him to eternal Rome instead of shutting her up at home like a proper Greek wife. If Antonina had been less than overwhelmed by the majestic remains of the old empire in Rome, that was her failure, not Belisarius'. *Thank God for his mother who raised our daughter. Poor Joannina without her mother.*

She thought of Theodosius too. Who had benefited by that relationship? He'd been fun, a digression on the boring road of life. But what had he been to Belisarius? A traitor in his own home and bed. *And I encouraged him, even giving of my husband's wealth to him as though it were my own.*

Was she Theodora's friend? No, she was the empress's pander to do what a more noble person would not. Belisarius could not disgrace the pope to please Theodora. She had. She had followed Theodora's example in too many ways. In the hippodrome, even as children they had seen murder and petty vengeance. In Asia and Africa and Italy she had seen how cheap life could be. Life had meant little when someone had gotten in Theodora's way, or hers. Belisarius might have spared Constantinus. She had persuaded him to carry out the fullness of the law. With Theodora she had shared a hatred of the stiff and prissy and that had led her to success and power. She had served her mistress instead of her master and her mistress was a cheap slut too. For the first time since her days of whoring Antonina felt cheap. Cheap, despite her rich dalmatics and jewelry.

She was forty four years old and Belisarius still loved her. *My master? Belisarius has never thought of me that way, even when I was just a street girl. Flavius is not himself. Some demon wants to bring him down. No, it doesn't take a demon, only Theodora and me. He must be cured of this deep sadness. He is the finest man in the world and Theodora mocks him because she fears him. Flavius wants to die. He mustn't die. I will not let him die.* Antonina decided that it was time for Theodora to pay her back for her many services.

The next day she made some excuse to be gone but admonished the household staff to remain on their guard lest Belisarius do something rash. He was depressed and Antonina knew he had no fear of death. Even the priests' teachings against suicide might not dissuade him. Justinian had turned against him and allowed Theodora to humiliate her husband, falsely accusing him of enriching himself at the emperor's expense. Her eunuchs had stolen his beloved bucellarii. Their best friend, Theodosius, had soiled his bed and stolen his wealth. She herself had betrayed him, not once but almost from the day that Theodosius had been baptised. Belisarius might be capable of anything. Belisarius had fears, but they were not the fears of a coward. Procopius errs when he says that Belisarius feared assassins. Almost alone and surrounded by the enemy he had slain twenty tough Gothic soldiers. In the first Persian campaign he had led a rescue party against a far stronger enemy just to save the lives of some troopers. Belisarius did fear but not for his life. His was a fear without target, worse even than what an acrophobe feels on a rooftop, or a claustrophobe in an elevator; for there is no escape from nothing. He could have easily dealt with an assassin or even several but an extended and undirected panic attack was paralyzing. All that he could do was to lie down and hope that the end would come soon and that Christ Jesus might forgive him for all those he had sent to their graves in a futile life.

Little Joannina was away enjoying a country estate with her grandmother; away from the unhealthy smells and heat of a Constantinople summer. Free from the constraints of city life, she was probably learning to swim and jump horses, and was old enough to have a crush on some little boy. For a moment the thought relieved Antonina of her own depression and she smiled at the thought of her little girl. *She has everything that I couldn't give Callista and Photius.*

Callista and Photius? Callista the pot merchant. Antonina smiled again despite the seriousness of her mission. *She has a good husband now, thanks to Belisarius, not me. Photius? Where is he now? I'll have to answer to Christ Jesus. Did he get away from Theodora?* There had been rumors that Photius was in prison, or worse, hidden away in some dank hole where

276

Theodora was thought to keep her personal enemies. *I've sinned against my own son for a paramour, but it's like I never knew him. But I must try to help him. Belisarius would but can't. If he tried to, Theodora would make it worse for Photius. Certainly she would. Besides Belisarius has just given up. He must blame himself for Photius' situation; but what can he do? Nothing. He feels that they're both already dead.*

The empress was not expecting what happened when Antonina entered her private chambers. Antonina had not even asked permission, or been announced.

"Your Serenity." They were in private so Antonina did not prostate. She did bow. "Your Serenity, I must ask that you and Justinian desist." It was the bravest thing that Antonina had ever said. She was confronting the meanest woman in the world without any cards to play.

"All right."

Antonina could not believe that Theodora had relented without bargaining. Theodora never gave anything without payment of some kind. *What is she up to,* Antonina asked herself?

"Who are you pleading for, Antonina? Your husband or your son?"

"Both."

"All right. Go to your husband and wait. As for Photius, he would have killed your sweetheart, dear."

"He's my son."

"He hated Theodosius, and he would have even had Theodosius not been your darling little sex-doll. He can be vicious and I want to teach him a lesson. There are consequences if you cross me and when he crossed you he crossed me."

Antonina blanched. What Theodora said had been brutally honest, but true. It hurt. "He's my son."

"Which is why I'm going to let him escape, but not yet. Now that's enough. I owe you a lot, Antonina, and I like you. You may be the only friend I have except for Justinian. So I'll do this for you: I'll speak to Justinian. I expect he'll be more than happy to have his best general restored to him, now that he has his treasure. We are still at war in Italy and Chosroes has broken the peace in the east."

"Justinian was once our friend."

"Justinian was very sick. He nearly died. We both worried because your husband was both rich and popular. He could have taken the throne. But you must not speak ill of the emperor, Lady Antonina."

The empress was speaking in an unusually soft, nearly

conspiratorial voice now, but the stiff form of address that she had just used left no doubt that Antonina had overstepped. Then she moderated her reproach with a little humor. "Were it not for Justinian, I'd still be blowing cocks somewhere, Antonina, and I'm too old for that sort of life."

The empress paused. It was not her way to show a gentle side, so she continued to speak in a low voice as though reluctant to speak at all. "By now you should know that Justinian is no one's friend. He'd like to be, but he dare not. Today's friend is often tomorrow's enemy. Your husband has always been loyal but circumstances can change people. Belisarius was rich. We needed money. He's arrogant. We wanted to break him, but we never intended that he sicken and die."

Flavius is not arrogant, Antonina told herself. *He just expects more in people than there is in them.* But she had pressed Theodora enough. She said nothing. She bowed out thinking: *Theodora is no one's friend either. We understood each other. We're both manipulative, cynical bitches.* She considered her own situation, as Theodora had probably intended. *Theodora has the emperor, poor bitch. I have Belisarius.*

Then Antonina went home to lie close by her husband. For weeks she lay holding him throughout both days and nights until one evening a servant announced a messenger from Theodora. Antonina quickly dressed, expecting a summons to the palace. In the corner of her eye she could see that Belisarius had stretched himself upon the bed as though to be unresisting of whatever new misfortune was at their door; a dagger, or poison in a cup of wine, or under the guise of medicine?

Even allowing for Procopius taking delight in exaggeration, it is impossible to believe what next transpired without reference to clinical depression. When the messenger approached his sleeping room, according to Procopius, Belisarius just lay quietly awaiting a dagger thrust. However, instead of death, the messenger brought so haughty a letter from Theodora that at any other time Belisarius would have rejected its effrontery. Lacking any other source one must with some reserve assume that Procopius gives at least the correct gist of it.

You are not ignorant, my good sir, of all your offenses against me; but I owe so much to your wife that I have determined to pardon all your offenses for her sake, and I make her a present of your life. For the future you may be of good cheer as regards your life and fortune. We shall know by your future conduct what sort of husband you will be to your wife!

What transpired thereafter would have been in their privacy and Procopius' yarn can be safely discounted as the imaginative narrative of things about which he could not know, so often to be found in ancient writers. What we can trust from Procopius was that although Justinian had seized Belisarius' wealth, he now returned a large sum. Belisarius would need it. He would again use it in the empire's service. He could no longer bring himself to serve Justinian the man, but he would serve his country.

In the meantime, Theodosius died of dysentery. Belisarius probably did not know that Theodora had been keeping him safe inside the women's quarters of the Great Palace; but Procopius does not claim that Antonina's infidelity had continued under her depressed husband's eyes. It seems that his death caused the last remaining scales to fall from Antonina's eyes, for we hear no more of discord between her and Belisarius. Theodosius had been one of those persons - men and women both - who, no matter how much you may see through them in their absence, yet are entirely convincing in person.

Belisarius was restored to his dignities and placed in command of all the imperial cavalry. Still fearful of him however, the royal couple gave back only a part of his estates and did not restore his many faithful bucellarii.

He was once again offered command in the east.

This was not to be. Antonina was determined to be with her husband wherever he campaigned, but also determined not to return to the place of her disgrace. Instead he accepted command in Italy which eleven generals and innumerable tax collectors had practically lost to Justinian. If Belisarius' honor had been completely restored, Justinian had also insisted on a crippling condition. His many wars, and the need to rebuild and reinforce forts on the Persian border, had left the empire's coffers depleted. His massive building campaign had bled the nation, as had his many bribes to retain the loyalty of foreign princes. Belisarius was to outfit the troops out of his own purse.

CHAPTER 21

544-548 AD
ITALY

Belisarius and Antonina, now forty six, set out together for Italy just as a letter arrived from Photius. He was resting in a monastery in Ephesus and might like to remain there. They left behind Joannina, now eleven and showing an interest in all things that young girls think important as they are about to blossom into young ladies. Clearly, she took every opportunity to leave the shelter of her father's country estates and indulge herself with the livelier pleasures of the city.

The empress indulged her greatly, having long since suggested a marriage between the girl and her nephew Anastasius. What could be stronger than the union of the two most powerful families in the realm? The future of the dynasty would be assured. Surely Belisarius would support his only daughter's husband. The year was 544 AD and Justinian was sixty one. Belisarius was twenty-two years his junior and in the prime of life. Justinian needed an heir and no general would dare raise the standard of rebellion against a new emperor who had Belisarius as family. Let bygones be bygones.

Belisarius and Antonina were not so sure that they wanted the alliance. There was much of greatness in the imperial couple but they had also done much evil. Belisarius was unwilling to break his oath of allegiance, but he had long since ceased to like them. A marriage alliance would strengthen the ruling family. Was that a good thing? Antonina hated the idea. Had they not humiliated Belisarius and inprisoned her son?

Why was Justinian sending Belisarius to Italy but without support? To Justinian and Theodora he was too popular to have in the capital and Theodora could not be sure of her handmaiden's loyalty anymore. *Damn*, she must have thought, *Antonina had to choose between Theodosius and Belisarius, and between me and Belisarius; and both times she chose him. If she stays here it will gall her until she goads him into taking the throne.*

Theodora may have been right. When she revealed her thoughts to Justinian the emperor concurred. Furthermore, he had his own more strategic views: *Italy is lost. I sent eleven generals and all they did was try to undermine each other.* That too was true. The two most worthy, Bessas and Bloody John, feuded. With the loss of a single battle the entire Roman army fell apart. Only some Persian mercenaries acquitted themselves with honor. These were former prisoners of war whom Belisarius had sent to Italy in the emperor's employ. The other Roman troops proved worthless. These were mostly barbarian allies who had been too long deprived of their pay by Alexander the snips. Eleven generals led eleven armies into eleven forts. When at last Justinian sent a relief force its worthless commander lost it. To once more quote Lord Mahon:

"The Byzantine armada had been annihilated by the forces of the Goths or the storms of the Mediterranean. All the open country was possessed by Totila. The public revenues were intercepted, and the troops still maintaining some separate cities became every day more turbulent and ungovernable from their increasing arrears. Under the dominion of an insolent soldiery the Italian citizens endured rapacity and outrage in every form, their household effects were plundered, their daily food was snatched from them, and their complaints were answered with blows. Accordingly their disaffection to the Romans, and wishes for restoration of the Gothic monarchy, grew more and more ardent and decided, especially when they observed the generous conduct and fair promises of Totila. In their letters to the emperor the Roman generals did not dissemble their despondency, they gave up everything as lost, and unanimously declared their utter inability to carry on the war.

"Embarrassed and dismayed by these reports, Justinian once more summoned Belisarius to the post of danger, but neglected to supply any sufficient forces, and even withheld the domestic guards of which the general had recently been bereaved. Attended by only a handful of his veterans, Belisarius traversed Thrace where, by lavish donations, he succeeded in mustering four thousand youthful volunteers. ... He made camp at Dyrrachium, seized some towns but failed to take others. After grasping the full extent of the revived Gothic power he could only send a sad and pleading letter to Justinian:

"'Great prince, I am arrived in Italy, unprovided with men or money, with horses or with arms, nor can any spirit bear up against such disadvantages as these. In my progress through Thrace and Illyria, I collected by great exertions, a handful of raw and undisciplined recruits, whom I can hardly furnish with weapons, and whom I find unfit for almost every purpose of war. The troops already stationed in Italy are deficient both in numbers and in courage. Their minds have been debased and enslaved by their frequent defeats; and no sooner do the barbarians approach, then they relinquish their horses, and cast their arms on the ground. To raise any taxes is impracticable, since the provisions are in the possession of the enemy; and the long arrears of pay which our soldiers

282

vainly claim loosens every tie of discipline and duty. A debtor is but ill able to command. Be assured, my sovereign, that the best part of your army has already gone over to the Goths. Were it sufficient for success that Belisarius should appear in Italy, your aim would be accomplished: I am now in the midst of the Italians. But if you desire to conquer, far greater preparations must be made; and the title of general dwindles to a shadow, where there is no army to uphold it. My own personal guards and veteran soldiers should, in the first place, be permitted to rejoin me; and it is only by full and ready payments, that you can secure the useful service of the Ephthalite Huns and other barbarian mercenaries.'"

A friendly postscript asked after the welfare of Joannina. But he made no mention of Theodora's suggestion of a marriage between their houses. The letter was dispatched overland in the hands of Bloody John who had said that he had some personal business to attend to in the capitol. Indeed he did. He delayed in Constantinople, securing his position near the throne by marrying a niece of Justinian. By the time he returned to Italy, any initiative that prompt reinforcement might have given Belisarius was lost.

Rome itself, which had until then remained in Byzantine hands, fell to the Goths before Belisarius could reach it. In that city there was both unselfish nobility and depraved avarice. The Romans delegated the archdeacon Pelagius, a future pope, to negotiate with Totila, but when Totila offered to treat the Romans kindly, but not the Sicilian population who had attempted to supply the besieged with grain, Pelagius refused the offer and returned to the city to share in the misery of its citizens. On the other hand, the Byzantine commander Bessas horded the small supply of grain within the city and, according to the unreliable Procopius, only released small portions to those who could pay an extravagant price.

Belisarius began his march to relieve the ancient capital. He left Antonina with a young officer named Isaac to organize the commissariat at Porto, and dispatched Bloody John to scatter a few Goths in Apulia who might otherwise interfere. He told John to then join with him at Porto, the harbor which normally supplied Rome. Instead John, being John, raided up and down Lucania. It was thus left to Belisarius to seize Rome alone. Armoring some boats with animal hides, he advanced his force by sails and oars up the Tiber. He constructed a tower on two of his largest craft, which he had lashed together, and when the fleet of relief ships came under Gothic attack from a bridge, his dismounted cataphracts fired arrows and hurled firebombs from these. Where Totila had blocked the river with an iron chain and wooden towers, they burned the towers with fire grenades and, under cover of the Gothic confusion, loosed the chain. Again, to quote from Lord Mahon:

"At this moment of triumph the fruits of victory were snatched from Belisarius by the double disobedience of his officers. The opposite vices of youth and age appeared to have conspired against him. Bessas had found in the famine of Rome such ample gratification for his avarice that he rejoiced in the continuation of the siege, and was unwilling to see its close until the last remains of wealth had been wrung from the wretched inhabitants. On the other hand the martial spirit of Isaac was roused by the success; he forgot his orders (to remain at Porto.) He advanced with all his troops against a Gothic encampment, and after a first advantage from surprise, was defeated and taken prisoner with his followers."

Belisarius had landed on the eastern Adriatic coast. Porto was the sole fortress that Belisarius held on the western coast. Fearful of losing the only place from which his tiny army could evacuate he ordered a retreat to save that town even while the relief of Rome was nearly in his grasp. It was one of the few tactical mistakes that Belisarius is ever reported to have made. Porto was actually still in Roman hands. Then he fell ill with fever and nearly died. The British historian Thomas Hodgkin describes his brilliant but ill-fated attempt to take Rome. It failed but Hodgkin emphasizes the love of Belisarius for his wife which, possibly together with the illness that must already have been upon him, explains his mistaken decision:

"The town of Porto was nineteen Roman miles from Rome. About four miles above it, where the river was narrowest, Totila had caused a boom to be placed to block the passage of ships bearing provisions to the starving City. This boom consisted of long beams of timber lashed together and forming a kind of floating bridge. It was protected by a wooden tower at either end, and was yet further strengthened by an iron chain stretched across from shore to shore a little below it, in order to prevent the boom from being broken by the mere impact of a hostile vessel.

"The counter-preparations of Belisarius were very complete. Having lashed together two broad barges, he erected a wooden tower upon them sufficiently high to overtop the bridge. Trusting nothing to chance, he had the measurements of the bridge taken by two of his soldiers who feigned themselves deserters. To the top of the tower a boat was hoisted filled with a combustible mixture, pitch, sulfur, rosin, an anticipation of the dreaded "Greek fire" of later ages. Surrounding the barges, and partly

284

towing them, was a fleet of two hundred swift cutters laden with corn and other necessaries for the starving Romans, but also bearing some of the bravest of his soldiers, and turned into ships of war by high wooden ramparts on the decks, pierced with loop-holes for the archers. Detachments of infantry and cavalry were also stationed at all the points of vantage on the bank to support the operations of the ships, and especially to prevent any advance of the enemy upon Porto.

"Having made these preparations, Belisarius entrusted the defense of the sea-port, containing as it did all his stores, his reserve troops, and above all his wife, to Isaac of Armenia, with a solemn charge that come what might, and even should he hear that Belisarius himself had fallen before the foe, under no conceivable circumstances was he to leave the post thus committed to him. At the same time he sent word to Bessas to support his movements by a vigorous sortie from the city against the Gothic camps. This message like so many others of the same kind, failed to shake the 'masterly inactivity' of the governor of Rome. The Goths had full leisure that day to concentrate their whole attention on the operations of Belisarius.

"With some labor the rowers urged the laden cutters up the river. The Goths, confiding in the strength of their bridge and chain, remained quiet in their camps. Soon they found out their error. The archers from the cutters dealt such havoc among the Gothic guards on either shore that resistance was quelled and they were able to sever the chain and sail on in triumph up to the bridge. Now the Goths perceived the danger and swarmed down upon the bridge. The fighting here became terrific. Belisarius, watching his opportunity, steered the floating tower close up to the Gothic fort commanding the north end of the bridge, which stood close to the water's edge. The boat laden with Greek fire was set alight and skilfully thrown into the very middle of the fort, which was at once wrapped in flames. In the conflagration two hundred of the Gothic garrison, headed by Osdas, the bravest of the brave, all perished. Encouraged by this success, the archers on board the dromons sent a yet thicker shower of arrows at the Goths on the shore. Terror seized the barbarian ranks; they turned to flee; the Romans began to hew the timbers of the bridge to pieces; the revictualizing of the hungry city seemed already accomplished.

"Seemed only. By one of those tricks of Fate upon which our historian (Procopius) delights to moralize, in the very moment when he seemed to have won her, Victory flitted away out of the grasp of Belisarius. A rumor, perhaps a premature rumor, of the success of the morning's operations, especially of the severing of the chain, reached the ears of Isaac at Porto. Forgetful of his general's solemn charge, and only envious at having no share in the glory of the triumph, he sallied forth with a hundred horsemen, crossed the Insula Sacra, and suddenly attacked the Gothic garrison of Ostia, who were commanded by the gallant Roderic. In the first skirmish Roderic was wounded, and his soldiers, whether from fear or guile, turned and fled. The Imperialists entered the camp, and found a store of money and other valuables therein, which they began to plunder. While they were thus engaged the Goths returned in greater numbers, easily overpowered the hundred Romans, slew the greater number of them, and took the rest among whom was Isaac himself, prisoners.

"The mere failure of this foolish attack would have been in itself no great disaster. But as adverse Fortune would have it, a messenger escaped from the field and bore the tidings to Belisarius at the bridge, 'Isaac is taken.' 'Isaac taken,' thought the General: 'then Porto and Antonina are taken too.' At this thought, says the historian, 'he was bewildered with fear, a thing which had never happened to him in any previous peril.' Yet even this bewilderment is for us the most convincing proof that they were chains of love, not of fear (of her connection to Theodora), which yet bound him to Antonina. He at once gave the signal for retreat, in the hope that by a speedy return he might surprise the victorious barbarians and rescue Porto from their grasp. When he reached the seaport (which it is to be remembered was only four miles from the scene of action), he found all safe there, and recognized by what folly of his subordinate and what misreading of the game by himself he had been cheated out of an already assured victory, he was seized with such deep chagrin, that his bodily strength, perhaps already weakened by the unwholesome air of the Campania, quite broke down. He sickened with fever, which at one time caused his life to be despaired of, and for some months he was unable to take any active share in the conduct of the campaign."

Now Antonina could repay a long overdue debt of love. Belisarius had not taken her life either in Sicily or in Asia when he'd had every right to. With God's help she might be able to save his. She did not leave it entirely to the physicians to treat her husband for she had seen too many die under the care of the best of them. All were students of Galen, and none were inclined to listen to the old women who routinely treated peasants. Antonina did however. Physicians had a terrible record of success. Did the women's herbs and advice help Belisarius to recover? Did her prayers to Sts. Cosmas and Damian? Who knows? Antonina would not use the dark spells of pagan deities that she had long ago learned; Belisarius would have preferred to die. She did plead for the mumbling of holy hermits. Religious cynicism flies away when death is near.

Were that not enough to keep her busy, Antonia also had to keep Belisarius' subordinates from tearing each other apart, as the eleven generals had done, or each going off to follow his own ideas of how the war should be fought. Fortunately, Belisarius, though bedridden, was not always of unclear mind. He might recover. No one, not even John, wanted to have tried to take his place during the sole commander's illness.

Eventually Belisarius did recover but he had lost the initiative. Totila had effectively garrisoned the most important cities and linked them with an effective web of couriers and flying columns.

Worse, Belisarius had only failed to relieve a siege of Rome, but in his illness the city was betrayed by some guards on the Asinarian gate. The Goths entered by night and before dawn the garrison had entirely fled and some citizens were butchered. It must be admitted to Totila's credit that like Belisarius at other sieges, he quickly put an end to the slaughter though he allowed his soldiers to loot the homes of the rich. That was the way of the world in the sixth century. In a fitting retribution, Bessas was forced to retreat across the Tiber with none of his ill-gotten treasure. Totila also decreed the destruction of the city. That he did not carry this out may be laid to the credit of his enemy. To quote the letter of Belisarius to Totila:

The most mighty heroes and the wisest statesmen have always considered it their pride to adorn a city with new and stately buildings, while, on the other hand, to destroy those that already exist has been reserved for the dull ferocity of savages, careless of the sentence which posterity will pass upon them. Of all the cities which the sun beholds in his course, none can vie with Rome in size, splendor, or renown. It has not been reared by the genius of one man, or by the labor of a single age. The august assembly of the republican senate, and a long train of munificent emperors have, by the progressive and accumulated toil of centuries, and by the most lavish expenditure of wealth, brought this capital to its present high and acknowledged preeminence. Every foreign country has furnished architects for its construction, artists for its ornament, and the slow result of their joint exertions has bequeathed to us the noblest monument of ancient glory. A blow aimed at these venerable fabrics will resound equally through past and future ages. It will rob the illustrious dead of the trophies of their fame, it will rob unborn generations of the proud and cheering prospect which these trophies would Afford them. Consider also, that one of two events must occur. You will in this war either obtain a final victory over the imperial forces, or yourself be subdued. Should your cause prevail, you would by the havoc which you meditate, overthrow not a hostile city but your own, while your present forbearance would preserve for you the first and fairest possession of your crown. If, on the contrary, fortune should declare against you, your mercy to Rome will be rewarded by the mercy of the conqueror to you; but none could be expected from Justinian, after the desolation of his ancient capital. What benefit can, therefore, in any case accrue to you from so barbarous an outrage? All mankind have now their eyes turned towards you: your fame is in the balance, and will incline to one scale or to the other, according to your conduct on this decisive occasion; for such as are the deeds of princes, "such will be their character in history."

Totila thought long about what Belisarius had written and then dismissed his envoys with a promise of forbearance, which he kept. While transcribing Belisarius' letter the author could not but be put in mind that in his own youth the city of Paris was likewise spared by the forbearance of the German General Dietrich Von Choltitz, who disobeyed the order of Hitler to destroy that city, thus at the risk of his life avoiding the damnation of his memory.

Totila left Rome intending to recover Ravenna on the opposite coast. But Belisarius decided that to prevent this he would reoccupy the eternal city, now deserted by both combatant armies, and force Totila to return and besiege him there. Leaving some guards at Porto he took his main body, small though it was, to Rome. Grain and other supplies were brought up the Tiber from Porto and in the few weeks available before Totila could bring his own army back, the city walls were rebuilt and reinforced as well as could be quickly done by filling gaps with rubble. The dry moat was cleared and planted with pointed stakes and Belisarius and Antonina settled into his old headquarters to await once again a Gothic attack; this one to be led by a far more competent commander than Witiges.

Twenty five days later Totila arrived. The very next morning, he attacked. Lord Mahon relates with pride how the Roman soldiery, who had so often fled or betrayed their cause, fought all day, pouring missiles into the Gothic ranks. Before leaving the city, Totila had destroyed the gates, yet the open portals, which might have been easy routes of passage for the Goths, were defended by the flower of a few remaining bucellarii. They were held. When the next day, Totila renewed the attack, Belisarius, as he had so often done during the first siege of Rome, instead of lurking behind the walls, ordered a counterattack and the Goths retired in disorder.

Totila gave up the fight to take Rome but posted strong forces in the vicinity to watch over his enemy. Belisarius was now able to emplace new gates and for a second time sent the keys of the city to Justinian.

In time a letter arrived from Joannina, describing in great detail the joy their imperial majesties had shown. She also spoke of how Theodora's nephew, Anastasius, had joined her in celebrating her father's victory. Obviously, the two were getting on quite well. Antonina wondered if that was a good thing.

"Look at this, Flavius! Joannina says that Theodora 'lets' Justinian play with the keys, as though Rome was his toy."

Belisarius was not amused. "Men died to send him that toy. Has he forgotten how he lost it?"

Antonina knew better than to argue with her husband about combat losses. She knew that Belisarius was depressed by talk of the human cost even when he was victorious,. Once he had heard Constantinus refer to the "butcher's bill." That indifference to the lives of others may have weighed against him after he'd tried to kill her husband. She changed the subject.

"Our little girl asks permission to rouge her cheeks."

"No. She is too young. She'll have need enough of such junk when she is older. I don't believe in rushing such things."

"Oh, husband, you are a prude. Besides, she isn't such a little girl any more. She is noticing boys."

"Anastasius?"

"It certainly seems so. She describes him in great detail: tall, blue eyed, handsome."

"Blue eyed? If she's noticed the color of his eyes, she's in love."

"Puppy love, dear. Do you think we should encourage Theodora's wish that they marry some day?"

"That depends upon why they want the marriage. But if Joannina continues to like the boy, and if he's not like Justinian ...well, that matters too."

Antonina knew better than to continue the discussion about Joannina's future. Nothing could be settled now and her husband had work to do. She just kissed his expanding forehead and brought a goblet of wine and some Italian pressed meats to his desk.

Unable to move freely throughout the countryside, now made hostile by the deprecations of the eleven generals and the snips, Byzantine forces moved from place to place by ship along the Adriatic shore. Their movements did not always succeed. Storms decimated the fleets and at times the defenders were too numerous for the Byzantine soldiers to successfully make a beach landing. For five years Belisarius and those generals who obeyed his orders fought and captured some cities but, for lack of sufficient troops to hold them, could not seize the countryside. It is not the author's intent to write a military biography of the general so I will pass over the details and recommend to the interested reader the immensely pleasant fourth volume of Thomas Hodgkin's *Barbarian Invasions of Italy.*

Meanwhile, Antonina was daily growing more distressed. Her letters to Theodora imploring assistance for her husband went unanswered. Had she displeased the empress by putting off their acceptance of a marriage between their daughter and Anastasius? Had she used up all the good will she had spent years amassing in the empress' service simply by choosing her husband over her? How could even Theodora be so hard hearted as to let the little expedition be destroyed? And why if Italy no longer mattered to the imperial couple had they sent Belisarius there? Had they sent him nearly alone to fail or be killed and thus remove him as a threat?

The answer to the last question was obvious. Unwilling to chance their thrones by killing Belisarius themselves, and unable to find any fault in him, they had put him on ice in Italy to accomplish nothing, but either die an honorable death or be available if ever really needed. Cold. If Antonina had ever in her life thought that she had chosen wrongly in loving Belisarius, she no longer did. She ordered her servant, Eugenius, to prepare her old cuirass, polish it like silver and have the thing decorated with cloisonne. If Belisarius was to be wasted on a hopeless quest then she would ride beside him, with pride in him for all the army to see.

The indecisive years slowly passed. Both Belisarius and Antonina received word that their aged mothers had died. Justinian sent some weak reinforcements but these were commanded by drunken, incompetent, and cowardly generals. Belisarius could achieve nothing of substance. Despite always having his wife with him, he again began to reflect upon a life which seemed wasted. He dismissed from his mind how, three time, he had sent the powerful kings of Persia back home when they had threatened the Roman frontier and even the holy city of Jerusalem. He didn't care that the fertile fields along the Libyan coast had been restored to the empire. Instead he was overwhelmed that after winning back Italy, the birthplace of the empire, Justinian had lost it again by the deprecations of his tax collectors, and that he had been starved of the few thousand good troops who could have retrieved it. Italy seemed lost. He had to find gold to pay his few troops by extorting it, not from the peasants it is true, but from landowners who had welcomed the Byzantines when they had first landed from Sicily so many years before.

He missed Joannina. She was fifteen now and they had never spent more than a few months together. She had been less than a year old when he and her mother had sailed off to the African war. On returning, they'd had but a few months with the now three year old before heading off for the first Gothic war. After that he again had but a few months with the girl, then eight, before leaving for the second and third Persian campaigns, divided by only a few months. Then when he should have been enjoying two years of happy family life, he had been depressed, cuckolded, mocked, and for a time impoverished until ordered into a frustrating Italian campaign that could not be won with the scant forces that he had. In all, he had known Joannina for less than four years total and two of them had been the worst in his life. Now, Theodora was intent on marrying his daughter to her nephew. If Procopius speaks the truth (he was not there either) she had forced them to shack up together, and they had fallen in love. Or was it the other way round? Procopius is unclear and cannot be trusted.

Finally, in frustration, Belisarius sent Antonina herself to Constantinople to place a petition - or should we say an ultimatum - before Justinian and Theodora: give him the resources to retake Italy, or recall him. But Justinian had just been devastated by the death of Theodora, and was more involved than ever with the theological disputes of the east. He was also aware that he had drained Italy of any good will he might have once had there. He chose the latter course. This book is only written to recount the life of Belisarius through the eyes of Antonina so the author will complete the sad story of Italy in two paragraphs of his own and with and a quote from Maj. Anthony Brogna's *The Generalship of Belisarius*:

Justinian replaced Belisarius with the aging court chamberlain Narses and gave him the thousands of troops which he had denied to Belisarius whose ambition he had always feared. It is likely that Narses himself persuaded Justinian to make a last full blown attempt to regain Italy. Ever gracious, he no doubt gave Belisarius full credit for his accomplishments but he may have conveniently omitted reference to himself having suggested that the conqueror be replaced by eleven rivals. He was certain that he could bring an end to the war which Belisarius had only seemed to win with the capture of Witiges. "The return of Rome to the empire will by the crown of your reign, Majesty."

Narses was a man of ability and with these troops he did win the war in Italy and Totila himself was killed. Totila was briefly succeeded, but the Gothic monarchy soon collapsed. It was all for nothing. Within twenty years Byzantine rule was ended by a Lombard invasion. Save for Sicily, allied states in parts of the south, and what would for the next two centuries be the Byzantine exarchate of Ravenna, the peninsula was lost. Ravenna would be an important outpost but not the whole of Italy. Justinian's dream of renewing the western empire, which with more commitment and less rapacity he could have achieved, had failed.

Although it was Narses who won the Second Gothic War, Anthony Brogna in a thesis presented to the faculty of the U.S. Army Command and General Staff College credits Belisarius with making the victory possible.

"Although Belisarius would never lose a battle over those four years, he would never come close to securing the peninsula. ... Belisarius would as (Michael H) Hart explains: '(conduct) a 'hit and run' campaign among the fortresses, and from port to port.' Belisarius basically conducted a raiding strategy that bordered on guerrilla warfare. His objective was to insure that Totila could not consolidate the peninsula. With so few troops available to him, and without his elite Household cavalry, he was never able to face Totila on the field in a major battle.

"Yet, this unconventional campaign was appropriate and a success. To quote (John Julius) Norwich: 'Early in 549 Belisarius returned to the capital. After the glory of his first campaign, his second had brought him only five years of frustration and disappointment. But he had saved Italy, at least temporally, for the empire. Had it not been for his energy and resolve, in the face of the most discouraging conditions imaginable, there is little doubt that the Byzantines would have been expelled in 544; thanks to him the foundations for reconquest were laid for the second time, making it relatively easy when the moment came for his old rival (Narses) - possessed of all the resources for which he, Belisarius, had appealed in vain - to win the victories and the acclaim that should rightfully have been his own.'"

CONSTANTINOPLE

When Antonina arrived in Constantinople, she had found the city in mourning. Theodora had died of cancer, the ravishes of which could already be seen in the Ravenna mosaic of the once beautiful empress. In that mosaic, Antonina and her daughter stand beside her, both stately and beautiful, for Theodora had intended that Belisarius' wealth, prestige, and power be joined to hers in a marriage between a favored nephew and

292

Joannina. Antonina, however, rejected the estate of her noble husband supporting the family of Theodora and had postponed the marriage while the empress lived.

Theodora, even more than Justinian, had wasted Belisarius' life and talent with a mean spirit that Antonina could not forgive when she looked at the broken man who now sat dejected beside her in their villa. If the marriage did eventually happen, it was after Theodora's death and did not effect the succession or the fortunes of her nephew. They may have been lovers, They certainly were friends. We hope they became husband and wife. When Justinian himself died another nephew was awarded the crown.

Without Theodora beside him, Justinian - through weakness or kindness, depending upon the temperament of the historian - tempered the vindictiveness of his reign. He not only pardoned the leader of an assassination plot, but restored him to an army command in the continuing Gothic war. Without Theodora's constant suspicion, he reconsidered his treatment of Belisarius. Belisarius had always been loyal, one of the few around the throne of whom that could be said. Why had Theodora always hated him? Besides, Belisarius was more useful as a bulwark of his throne than as a disappointed minion.

Justinian commanded the appearance of Belisarius and Antonina, who were escorted by some of the general's old guards and friends. Justinian restored much of the general's estate and reappointed him to his old command as Magister Militum Per Orientem. He also named him chief of the Imperial Guards over the senators and patricians who would normally have had that high honor. None objected.

Then the emperor, now seventy seven and feeling very alone without Theodora beside him, withdrew more and more into the details of theology which had always intrigued him as a man, and occupied him as a monarch and the temporal head of the church. In fear of death he devoted more of the nation's wealth to building and endowing churches and monasteries. He allowed the army to rot. He paid off tribes that threatened the imperial frontiers instead of fighting them until, at last, the Bulgar khan Zabergan crossed the frozen Danube, pillaged the Peloponnese, and moved through Thrace to threaten Constantinople itself. Almost as an omen of his reign, the last in a series of minor earthquakes brought the great dome of Hagia Sophia crashing down. To again quote Lord Mahon:

"As heathens, they (the Bulgars) were ignorant or careless of the sanctity of churches and of convents, and freely despoiled the first of wealth

293

and the second of beauty. Crowds of captives were hurried along in their train, without regard to sickness, pregnancy, or age, and the newborn infants were left like corpses on a field of battle to the dogs and birds of prey. The Long Wall of Anastasius might have arrested the progress of Zabergan, but its solidity had already yielded to time and decay, and it is compared by Agathias, in his usual rhetorical style, to an unprotected sheepfold, where the preying wolf, far from encountering a bite, is not even threatened by a bark. There were no troops to man it; no military machines to play upon the enemy, nor any engineers to direct their use. Several breeches were open and accessible, and other parts were demolished by the assailants with as little hindrance, says the historian, as any private dwelling. Continuing his march from hence, the savage chief pitched his camp at the village of Melantias, on the banks of the river Athyras, and no more than twenty miles from the capital. ... The emperor himself sat trembling in his palace. By his orders all the churches in the European confines of the capital, from Propontis to the Euxine, were hastily stripped of their precious ornaments, and the sea was covered with barges, and each road with chariots, conveying these and other treasures to the shelter of the walls. Near the Golden Gate, where the attack of the enemy was expected to take place, a useless crowd of officers issued their contradictory and unheeded orders. ....

"In this general confusion and fright, Justinian and his subjects turned with hope to the illustrious conqueror of Africa and Italy, whose strength was broken by old age and military labors, but whose heart was still alive to the call of loyalty and honor. The struggle was no longer for increase of territory or dominion over foreign nations, but for the very existence of the Roman empire, and Belisarius prepared to crown his glorious life by a last and decisive battle. He resumed his rusty armor, he collected a handful of his scattered veterans, and his contemporaries were astonished at observing, amidst the weakness of decrepitude, all the martial spirit and buoyancy of youth."

It must have pleased Antonina to see the love of her youth armed and giving orders, as though he were again fighting at Dara. He showed not the slightest fear or depression but only justified confidence as he always had. She recalled that he had been thus confident that the Goths would be defeated in Italy. All others thought only of the smallness of their force and the weakness of their defenses. He alone had realized that without mounted archers Witiges could not win.

Antonina told an aide to bring out her old cuirass and polish the cloisonne. It was a tight fit but she managed it. Belisarius simply nodded a proud approval when he went to encourage the citizenry with their spears and pikes and found Antonina there before him, issuing orders which none seemed inclined to question.

"Flavius, you are needed where our old friends can see you. I can take care of matters here."

"I'm sure of that, wife. If any Bulgar gets through, give him a thrust for me. You men, listen to her. Antonina was at Dara and Ad Decimum. She stood the siege of Rome. She led an army in the Campania. She knows more about war than most of the so-called generals at the palace. Obey her, as you would Justinian."

Belisarius could muster but three hundred old friends and a multitude of raw recruits. There were also a few squads of imperial scholari, but these sons of patricians were nearly useless for anything but posing outside a palace in dress uniforms. He led this unlikely mob to the village of Chettos. There, as in Italy, he had numerous camp fires set to deceive the enemy as to his numbers whilst he fortified the town's small ramparts. By day, he put the scholari to work drawing branches so as to disturb the dust and further deceive Zabergan as to his strength. He sent scouts to determine the Bulgar strength, and put peasants to work preparing a ditch and earthworks. If the recruits were frightened, his aging veterans were cocky. Belisarius addressed them:

"In remembering your ancient achievements, do not forget the calm and cautious demeanor which secured them. Judgment, and not headlong courage, is the true arbiter of war. How else durst I, with my hair already whitened by old age, and my failing limbs grown unfitted for fatigue, plunge into the toil and tumult of another campaign, unless I relied on those faculties which continue unimpaired amidst bodily decay? ... These barbarians are accustomed to predatory inroads, like robbers they know how to rush forth unexpectedly on their prey, but are little practiced in the art of disposing a battle with skill or awaiting it with firmness...."

As usual a fort was but a post to Belisarius. He dispatched two groups of one hundred mounted veterans on either side of a defile in a woods through which Zabergan would pass. He had provided his recruits with whatever stakes and pikes were available and told them to raise a great clamor so as to attract the enemy into his ambush. Belisarius himself led an attack against the van of the approaching Bulgars while his cataphracts in the woods attacked from either side.

Zabergan had led two thousand of his men into the trap to face three hundred aging Romans. Those who survived, together with Zabergen's five thousand other troops, wisely retreated in fear and fled in terror when they learned that their opponent had been Belisarius himself.

Belisarius intended a pursuit but Justinian rejected it, maybe out of fear that the Bulgars would realize the true numbers that opposed them. At any rate, if the prejudiced Procopius is to be believed, his paranoid emperor was more fearful of the fresh popularity of Belisarius than of the Bulgars, who were now running away. Belisarius was received coldly, but by now he probably didn't care. Justinian was Justinian, as Antonina was Antonina. The leopard doesn't change its spots. The Bulgars retreated into Thrace but from there were sent home with gifts from the emperor. This outraged the citizenry. They sang the hero's praises and told their children how they had bravely supported the three hundred under the command of their legendary leader. Antonina and Belisarius simply retired to live out their days in quiet; loved and respected, and Belisarius, carrying his titles.

Thus ends what is known of the lives of Belisarius and Antonina or can be reasonably conjectured by a novelist. It is believed that Belisarius and Justinian died within months of each other. All else is legend. In the end we pray that Justinian accepted that Belisarius had always been his most loyal supporter, not because he was Justinian but because he was the emperor, albeit a jerk.

As for his daughter; the historical record is unclear, but it is thought by some that with Theodora's death, Antonina relented and the lovers were able to marry with her blessing.

The many doctrinal disputes within the empire had ebbed and flowed throughout Justinian's reign. Curiously, Justinian, himself, long the champion of orthodoxy, turned to the Monophysite position in his last years. Theodora would have been pleased. Or would she have? There are those who believe that the whole business of Justinian supporting orthodoxy while Theodora favored the Monophysites was a carefully nurtured fiction. That, indeed, would explain Justinian's swing to the Monophysite position after he no longer had Theodora by his side to favor them. A cynic might suspect the whole thing a charade to divide and conquer and thereby secure the couple's position on the throne were it not that Justinian was involved all the years of his reign in trying to make peace between the opponents. Did the empress actually provide long-term asylum for Monophysite prelates within a building connected to the Great palace itself, and without the supposedly orthodox Justinian caring to interfere? Following the lead of Procopius historians consider theirs to have been a duel reign with each often not aware of the others' doings. Is that really likely? Theodora had no legal position of her own. Had she survived Justinian, would the senate, army, and people have allowed her to rule alone? Such is material for alternative history. Certainly Justinian allowed her great power and they are often presented as co-rulers, but it must be remembered that Justinian could overrule Theodora at any time he wished, as he is alleged to have done in requiring that Silvarius be returned to Rome to face a fair trial.

The great dome of Hagia Sophia was rebuilt even higher, and in time for Justinian to reconsecrate it before he died. It was and is the most lasting physical achievement of his rule and the symbol of his deep religious feeling. It remains in Istanbul today and is still one of the most beautiful buildings on earth.

Justinian and Theodora had done much to restore the empire. How that would play out in the future Justinian could not know, but he had done his part. For a certainty, they had ruled long, and often with wisdom if sometimes in an arbitrary way. No revolution had succeeded. The imperial system which had so often been disturbed by ambitious generals was secure for now because Belisarius had been unwilling to follow that well-beaten path. That had meant lives of prosperity and security for the Roman people. Wars are expensive and taxes were high. Procopius charged Justinian with avarice, and he was hated by the wealthy landowners, Procopius included; but there is no evidence that he brought poverty to his people outside Italy.

When Justinian lay on his deathbed he could no doubt recall many failures, but he could take comfort in the successes of his reign. Between wars he had rebuilt and extended the Syrian and Black Sea fortifications. From his window he could see the dome of the great cathedral. Feuding between religious factions continued but it gave pleasure to the disputants without at the same time stimulating revolution against the state. The mishmash of Roman legal opinions had been codified and remains with us today. Thanks to Belisarius the always ambitious Persians had been kept within the natural frontiers of that state. Africa was restored to the empire and was supplying the people of Constantinople with agricultural products. In Italy, Narses seemed to have finished what he had forced Belisarius to leave incomplete. When Belisarius died Justinian likely ordered that the hero receive a state funeral. He owed him that.

That Justinian had mistreated Belisarius and denied him the victory in Italy was one of those things that he had need to share in his final confession, along with far worse things. However, Belisarius had just died and Antonina had retired to one of their estates in Thrace or Rufinianae, where she was surrounded by admiring neighbors and visited by aging generals with their wives. Many of her husband's old bucellarii would have been on the estate too with children and grandchildren who would listen to their parents' too often told tales of martial glories past and the antiquities of Rome, regrettably once again under the heel of the snips.

The last few years of Antonina's life she probably sought to make some amends before God for her sins. After Belisarius' funeral Justinian took much of his wealth as taxes for the insatiable maw of the exchequer; but Antonina was still rich by most standards of then or now. (It is pleasant to believe that before she died Theodora had made Justinian promise that Antonina would never be impoverished.) She may have sent relief money to the poor of Antioch and Rome and to wherever needed. Sometimes she'd have prayed, and sometimes her old cheeks were stained with tears, as they had not been since she was a little girl. With what remained of her fortune she reluctantly donated to the church, being careful to require that it be used only for the poor. She would not purchase prayers to be said by some fat priest distracted by thoughts of dinner. Theodora had long since commissioned retirement homes for retired hussies of the theater and hippodrome. Some might consider them prisons but at least the aging ladies were assured of food, lodging, and some comforts, so there was no need of Antonina's charity there. Instead, she'd offer help to the monastic orphanages though she had reservations that the holy monks too aggressively steered their charges into the religious life.

"Dear whore in heaven, I dare not pray to our Lord, so will you do me this last favor? When I die I want to be with Flavius. If I go to hell, I will never see him again. Please tell our Lord that I am not asking for a palace, just to be with him."

It is said that Antonina eventually entered a convent – probably to die, as was common in that age. Before she would fearfully present herself before the heavenly throne, however, she had one last thing to do. Belisarius had requested that she use part of his estate to endow a small church in Rome. He had been far less certain than Antonina that they had not sinned in dethroning Pope Silvarius. This was done. Santa Maria in Trivio was built and though unrecognizable today, the Renaissance remodelers retained the original dedication stone, citing Belisarius as its founder. The priests would forever pray for his soul. *As though his soul needs their mumbling*, Antonina would have thought, but she carried out her husband's wishes anyway.

Resquiescat in Pace, Antonina.

298

AFTERWORD

"All this can be properly attributed to folly, for it is she who sees that a wife is attractive to her husband and a husband to his wife, that peace reigns in the home and their relationship continues. A husband is laughed at, cuckolded, called a worm and who knows what else when he kisses away the tears of his unfaithful wife, but how much happier it is for him to be thus deceived than to wear himself out with unremitting jealousy, strike a tragic attitude, and ruin everything!"

... Erasmus of Rotterdam

Within two hundred years of the founding of Constantinople old Rome itself was in the hands of barbarian invaders and western Europe was politically divided. Yet the empire did not die. The term Roman remained and came to signify both a single Christian unity of all the European and Mediterranean kingdoms vaguely centered politically in Constantinople and spiritually in Rome; and also the Eastern Empire itself: "the Land of the Romans." For centuries this empire was the largest and most powerful state west of China.

I have effectively ended this novel with Belisarius' defeat of a raid by a Bulgar force on Constantinople in the year 559 AD when he was 54 years of age and Antonina 61. Justinian was 77 and Theodora had recently died, probably of cancer, at age 62. The exact ages of all these people are unknown which raises a problem with Antonina. She was certainly older than her husband; but by how much? Procopius wrote that Antonina was age sixty at the beginning of the second Gothic war in 544. Assuming that their daughter, Joannina, was born the year after her marriage to Belisarius in 531, that would have meant that Antonina was 48 when she was born; something so unlikely that it would certainly have elicited mention. But Procopius was probably being snippy. There is no certainty of the birth dates of any of our participants, and the death dates only of Justinian and Theodora, though it is thought that Belisarius died just a few months before his emperor's demise. It seems to me that an age difference of seven years is plausible between Antonina and her husband, so I have used 498 for the birth of Antonina and 505 for Belisarius. That would make Antonina thirty three when she married Belisarius, and he twenty six. As to the exact ages at various events that I give from time to time, all I can plead is that, assuming the birth dates I have given, they are within twelve months one way or the other.

I have not mentioned many things. For example, troops under Belisarius' command were often sent to take or fortify some Italian town, but that would add nothing to the story of Antonina, so I've kept such references to a minimum. There was a conspiracy at the time of Belisarius' return from the second Gothic war to assassinate both him and Justinian. It was discovered while the general was still at sea and would have added nothing to the story, except to confirm that the rebels believed Belisarius' loyalty to be absolute. I do give a bit of detail in the notes at the end of this volume. I should mention here Justinian's extreme clemency toward these conspirators who like others before them received little or no punishment and sometimes retained or regained the imperial favor. This particular rebel had been poorly treated by Theodora while she lived and that may be why Justinian treated him kindly. Since sedition and treason were so common in the world of Roman politics, Justinian may have thought that a policy of divide and conquer was his best way of remaining on the throne. He may have thought it better to spare an adversary and regain his support than to execute him and lose his services.

In the last years of Justinian's reign Belisarius himself was alleged to be involved in an assassination plot against the monarch. He was investigated but no charge could be made. Supposedly his fortune was confiscated but a large portion was returned to Antonina after his death. None of this is certain or likely. There is also a legend that because of the conspiracy Justinian had Belisarius' eyes put out, but there is no mention of that until hundreds of years later and most historians put it together with George Washington chopping down his dad's cherry tree. More likely, the general's public history ends with the Bulgar attack.

I have not bored the reader with every detail of the first Gothic war and especially the second. There were dozens of battles and sieges (sixty nine during the siege of Rome alone in the first Gothic war), but the title of this novel is *Antonina,* not *Belisarius* and it has been my intention to show the general through her eyes, not to write a military history. Of course I cannot entirely avoid events of importance which so far as we know did not involve Antonina.

We would wish to know more about Antonina. Unfortunately nearly our only source is the prejudiced Procopius, who hated both her and Theodora. He also hated Justinian, John the Cappadocian, Bloody John, Narses, and nearly everyone else he writes about, except Photius. He liked Photius, but his good opinion of Antonina's son may be balanced by that of John of Ephesus. That churchman writes of Photius' later life so it is probable that there is truth and opinion in both narratives; as well as a lot of self and class interest. (For more on John's opinion see Photus in the names appendix.)

Likewise, some historians have suggested strategic reasons for the disobedience of Belisarius' subordinates where Procopius only reports small mindedness, greed, and jealousy. There is no doubt truth in both views just as there is truth in what he writes of Antonina. Having made that excuse, insubordination must finally be more deleterious than occasional losses in a campaign. If Belisarius was loved by his troops as legend has it, his officers may have seen him as overbearing, ambitious, self important, and a bit of a prig. Even Procopius who wrote so adoringly in his *Wars* turned against Belisarius and wrote the *Secret History* because his hero refused the crown from the Goths - or so it has been suggested. It seems strange that Procopius accuses Belisarius of thievery in Italy. In fact Belisarius used his wealth in the empire's service. It was the way that the spoils of war were distributed at that time, and no worse than what, according to Procopius himself, all the other participants were doing. I've suggested that it was normal – even necessary - behavior. I suspect that our historian was unhappy that more of the wealth was not distributed between himself and the subordinate generals. Otherwise, why did Justinian permit it while Belisarius was winning, and only condemn it when it looked a convenient charge to dismiss him? I also want to point out that the charges brought against Belisarius were that he took an unfair share of the treasuries of enemy kings, not that he stole from the people as Procopius charges with other generals. It has also been put forward that though Procopius turned against Belisarius in the *Secret History* he later returned his allegiance to the hero.

I quote below Procopius' abridged judgment on Justinian and Theodora so that the reader can judge how unlikely are many things that Procopius says:

"Many in my position never believed that they were really two human beings, but evil demons, and what the poets call scourges of mankind, who laid their heads together to see how they could fastest and most easily destroy the race and the works of man, but who had assumed human forms, and become something between men and demons, and thus convulsed the whole world. One can find proofs of this theory more particularly in the superhuman power with which they acted.

"There is a wide distinction between the human and the supernatural. Many men have been born in every age who, either by circumstances or their own character, have shown themselves terrible beings, who became the ruin of cities, countries, and whatever else fell into their hands; but to destroy all men and to ruin the whole earth has been granted to none save these two, who have been helped by Fortune in their schemes to destroy the whole human race....

"It is said that Justinian's mother told some of her intimates that Justinian was not the son of Sabbatius, her husband, or of any human being; but that, at the time when she became pregnant, an unseen demon companied with her, whom she only felt as when a man has connection with a woman, and who then vanished away as in a dream.

"Some who have been in Justinian's company in the palace very late at night, men with a clear conscience, have thought that in his place they have beheld a strange and devilish form. One of them said that Justinian suddenly arose from his royal throne and walked about and that at that moment his head disappeared, while the rest of his body still seemed to move to and fro. Afterward the head joined the body again, and united itself to the parts from which it had so strangely been severed.

"Another declared that he stood beside Justinian as he sat, and of a sudden his face turned into a shapeless mass of flesh, without either eyebrows or eyes in their proper places, or anything else which makes a man recognizable; but after a while he saw the form of his face come back again. What I write here I did not see myself, but I heard it told by men who were positive that they had seen it.

"They say, too, that a certain monk, highly in favor with God, was sent to Byzantium by those who dwelt with him in the desert, to beg that favor might be shown to their neighbors, who had been wronged and outraged beyond endurance. When he arrived at Byzantium, he straightway obtained an audience of the Emperor; but just as he was about to enter his apartment, he started back, and, turning round, suddenly withdrew. The eunuch, who was escorting him, and also the bystanders, besought him earnestly to go forward, but he made no answer, but like one who has had a stroke of the palsy, made his way back to his lodging. When those who had come with him asked why he acted thus, they say that he distinctly stated that he saw the chief of the devils sitting on his throne in the midst of the palace, and he would not meet him or ask anything of him. How can one believe this man to have been anything but an evil demon, who never took his fill of drink, food, or sleep, but snatched at the meals which were set before him anyhow, and roamed about the palace at untimely hours of the night, and yet was so passionately addicted to venery."

If Procopius saw Justinian as a devil, he saw Theodora as the most depraved of humans. He accuses both her and Antonina of many abortions before their marriages. (Though how he'd know such things is hard to imagine. More likely it is a scandelous assumption.) He also accuses Theodora of giving birth to a son whom she made to disappear when he visited her after she became empress. He does not say that she had him killed but does say that he was never heard of again. Some historians have suggested that the visitor was a fraud, but if so his appearance would hardly have merited notice in the *Secret History* unless he was killed. It is as possible that Theodora sent him away with a substantial stipend and a warning to stay away.

Of Theodora's life before marrying Justinian, Procopius wrote:

"She often went to a supper at which each one paid his share, with ten or more young men, in the full vigor of their age and practiced in debauchery, and would pass the whole night with all of them. When they were all exhausted, she would go to their servants, thirty in number, it may be, and fornicate with each one of them; and yet not even so did she quench her lust. Once she went to the house of some great man, and while the guests were drinking pulled up her clothes on the edge of the couch and did not blush to exhibit her wantonness without reserve. Though she received the male in three orifices she nevertheless complained of Nature for not having made the passage of her breasts wider, that she might contrive a new form of coition in that part of her person also."

Phew! None of this vindictive invalidates his history however, particularly since Procopius was himself a participant in much of it. The bare facts are assumed by historians to be correct, however prejudiced and mean minded his interpretation of them. More curious is his report of Justinian's preoccupation with religion. He built churches throughout the empire and was deeply involved in the theological disputes of the age which he tried to mediate, hardly what one would expect of a demon.

As to his attitude toward his boss, Procopius is more approving of Belisarius than of others, except that he feels that Belisarius was a weakling and love blind when it came to Antonina. Yeah, yeah, yeah! I think he was jealous. In the *Secret History*, Procopius attributes the death penalty imposed on Constantinus to Antonina, indicating that Belisarius might have been inclined to spare him. Maybe so, but if so, his mercy would have gone far beyond clemency. Belisarius would have had to consider what was best for the good of the army. One can't simply let would-be assassins escape punishment, at least when caught in the act.

Procopius wrote three books, the longest being *The Wars*, largely a biography of Belisarius with the addition of much relevant information about the politics that led up to the wars and the activities of other commanders.. He also wrote a much shorter and more boring book (*The Buildings*) about the building projects of Justinian, both his churches and fortifications, probably to please the monarch who may have been jealous that Procopius had given so much credit to Belisarius in *The Wars*, rather than to him. What most interests people today, however, is his slanderous *Secret History* or *Anecdota.* Since it is basically an attack on Antonina and the royal couple one has to try to look under the invective to find the truth about these people. Certainly Justinian was one of the great rulers of history and one who took Christian ethics and the sticky web of sixth century theology seriously. He was supported by Theodora who also did much good, particularly looking after girls from the theater who had not had her good fortune. Procopius hated Theodora. Certainly she appears the stronger of the monarchs in his narrative, and that much may indeed be true, though according to Procopius, Theodora rather spoiled herself, sleeping late most days. Justinian was very austere and, unlike his wife, he was, or at least gave an impression of being, sympathetic and understanding.

Of others too, one certainly must read between the lines. He attacks Bloody John unmercifully but could not have charged him with frequent disobedience to orders unless that were true. Why then did Belisarius not simply execute him? Well, he was a political general close to Narses. Eventually, he even married into the imperial family. Still, he could have been given another honorable assignment. One must suspect that there is more to John than Procopius tells us. Having said that, John did disobey orders - Procopius did not simply make up facts. So did others when they thought they knew better than a distant "Single commander" what the situation around them was. That would, for example, explain Bessas' refusal to support Belisarius during the siege of Rome during the Second Gothic war, at least as well or better than Procopius' charge that he wanted more time to plunder the citizenry.

Now the author must confess to a totally unfounded supposition. There is nothing in his narrative to indicate that Procopius was a eunuch as I have made him out to be; but then, there is nothing to say otherwise and certainly eunuchs were common at the time. Clearly he was jealous of Antonina's influence with Belisarius and I think it is not unreasonable to suggest (but only in a novel) that he could not comprehend either the relationship between Belisarius and Antonina, or Antonina's infatuation with the young Theodosius. What can be affirmed with more certainty is that he was decidedly anti-feminist, and a social prig; traits which were then, and remain now, entirely acceptable; whereas Antonina's sins were not then, and are not now, acceptable behavior in the female of our species.

As to his actual biography: Procopius himself tells us that he was born at Caesarea in Palestine towards the beginning of the sixth century. After practicing law in his native land, he migrated to Constantinople. There he gave lessons in elocution, and acted as counsel in several law cases. He was promoted to official duties in the service of the State and was commissioned to accompany Belisarius during his command of the army in the East. He also served with him in Africa and during the first Gothic war but not in the later Persian and Italian campaigns. How he actually first met Belisarius is unknown and I have supplied a fictional meeting. There is no reason to believe that he acted as an imperial courier.

Did Belisarius' companions also bring their wives to war? Probably not, since much is made of Antonina and her family but no mention at all of anyone else's relatives save those of Justinian and Theodora. I suppose they were left at home and I presume that is what Procopius expected of officers. One may wonder how many legitimate children these other generals had the opportunity to father. Certainly there was a good deal of going about by officers but it would have been dangerous to travel all the way from Italy to Constantinople and back just for some rest and relaxation.

Procopius does insist that both Belisarius and Theodosius defrauded the crown but clearly that was the way that the military was paid at the time. Today the west might call it corruption but it would still not be seen as such in many parts of the world where that is the way wealth is distributed by tribal chiefs to those who are loyal to their warlord and clan. Besides, I've suggested that he may himself have handled Belisarius' finances. Certainly, if Justinian expected his commander to pay for an expedition he must have expected to blink at how the money was raised. After all, he did not care how tax revenues were acquired so long as they were brought in by tax farmers who enriched themselves with whatever they could acquire above what the exchequer demanded of them. In the second Gothic war Belisarius had to pay for his troops out of his own pocket and was unable to recover it because he had already seized the royal treasure for Justinian in the first

Gothic war and because Italy had been wasted in the intervening years that he was not there.

Along the same lines, Procopius writes of Theodosius: "Photius was naturally disposed to show his spite against anyone who supplanted him in another's good graces; but he was quite right in feeling jealous of Theodosius, because he himself, although Antonina's son, was quite neglected, whereas the other was exceedingly powerful and had amassed great riches. They say that he had taken treasure amounting to a hundred centenaria of gold from the treasure-houses of the two cities of Carthage and Ravenna, since he had obtained sole and absolute control of the management of them." That is probably an exaggeration since he was needing Belisarius' cash soon afterward when he fled Constantinople for Ephesus. Notice that the author only has an unidentified "they" making the charge.

I submit that it is impossible for Procopius to have known the exact details of the private lives of Belisarius and Antonina as he claims to. Certainly it was not unusual for ancient historians to invent details just as it was normal for them to put great speeches in the mouths of their subjects. Procopius was an aristocrat. To me, he neither understood nor wished to understand women like Antonina and Theodora. They were simply below him, even below peasants; hardly a Christian attitude.

Which brings us to the question of whether he was a Christian. Sometimes he writes as though he were, sometimes as though he was a pagan or agnostic. Certainly there were still some pagans at the time but they probably did not have many positions of importance. (Some attempted to open the old temple of Janus during the siege of Rome.) However it was also normal throughout the time of the Byzantines to imitate the style of ancient authors. He may have felt that his narrative would seem more objective if he distanced himself from the whole theological mess of those days.

Military historians rank Belisarius as one of history's ten best generals; some rank him as one of the three best. It is difficult for a modern person in the developed world to understand the greatness of Belisarius' achievements. Caesar conquered Gaul, Alexander most of the then known world, and Napoleon much of Europe. Expansive as Belisarius' conquests were they comprehended less territory. But he was almost always outnumbered, often times by well equipped and well led forces, and that was the least of it. Subordinate officers in that day were of wealthy, ancient, and powerful families, well connected at court, who would not necessarily obey orders. Consensus was necessary but command by committee is always doomed. He had to tread a fine line and lead by persuasion.

Did he suffer defeats. Yes, of course. Callinicum was at best a draw, though one can argue as Procopius does that the battle was forced upon him. After all, he had not yet achieved the aura of invincibility among his subordinates that history has since allotted him. Ad Decimum is another matter, however. It is hard to excuse his falling into a trap because of poor intelligence. He should have arranged for better. Were it not for his archers and John the Armenian's heroic dash through Ad Decimum to the open ground beyond, Belisarius' life and career might have ended there. At best it would have been another Dunkirk with his fine cataphracts leaving their horses and armor for the enemy and swimming to sea under cover from despised foederati archers.

There is another reason to respect Belisarius however. Great conquerors have often been vainglorious and with little empathy with those whose deaths and misfortune they were responsible for. To this author, the two great exceptions were Flavius Belisarius and Ike Eisenhower. To both these men, only the righteousness of their cause justified the horror. One who criticizes all war may recall that to men like Justinian and Belisarius an orthodox Roman Empire was a sacred thing. To defend its frontiers and return it to its proper glory was a holy purpose. Regrettably, too many of their subordinates could not in practice rise to that level. Some, like Mundilas at Milan, did.

For several hundred years emperors had become such by successful insurrection. Belisarius' own emperor could never believe that his most successful general would not do the same. After all, he doubtless would have had their positions been reversed. Furthermore the best imperial troops were household cavalry paid by and loyal to their own commanders rather than to the emperor. Belisarius' most trustworthy soldiers were such and in the years of his command this corps of his personal troops grew to the size of an imperial army. Then too, the bulk of his other troops were foederati, barbarian hirelings who took orders from their chieftains. The loyalty of these was entirely dependent upon success and loot; not the type of men to do daring deeds for the sake of a distant Roman sovereign. It was something like depending on warlords to support the government and not to make their own separate agreements with an enemy, or decide to overthrow the throne; and have these supported by tribal groups from outside the realm brought in by the promise of good pay and pillage. Caesar led the best disciplined legions in the world. Alexander had inherited the Macedonian phalanx against which there was no real defense. Napoleon led 650,000 well trained and loyal soldiers into Russia but returned with 20,000 defeated men.

Belisarius won his victories with outnumbered and unreliable troops, insubordinate officers, and with moderate losses.

The early years of Antonina's life are entirely fictional but a likely conjecture, except the broad details that her father and grandfather had been charioteers in the hippodrome at Constantinople; and that her mother had been a stripper who put her on the stage at an early age - that is, prostituted her. According to Procopius, Photius was her son by a "first husband." That he was a Byzantine official with whom she lived in Alexandria and Antioch, while my fiction, is entirely possible. Somehow she was the friend of Theodora so I have no trouble with somewhat mirroring Theodora's own history in this fiction. (Theodora lived for a time with a Roman official in Libya. After he dropped her she made her way to Alexandria and Antioch where she fell under the influence of the Monophysite patriarch Timothy, a predecessor of Severus.) Procopius claims that Antonina had many other affairs, even hinting maliciously that they continued after marrying Belisarius. But, aside from her affair with Theodosius, he gives no details, only hints. Procopius is always careful to only suggest slanders of which he has no personal knowledge. Personally I believe that if what he says were true, Procopius, being Procopius, would surely have delighted in giving the details. Certainly, he was capable of slander, as is obvious from his valuation of Justinian as a demon. The twins are my fiction to account for Procopius' charge of Antonina having had many pregnancies and abortions, though as I remark in the text, that "fact" in her early life was almost certainly unknowable to him and a supposition. (Just as I've suggested were his details of the second seige of Rome.)

In his history of the wars Procopius does identify Photius as the child of Antonina "by a previous marriage." One suspects, however, that in a book meant for public consumption and published during the lifetime of Belisarius, he may have upgraded her status, making her concubinage something of a common law marriage – just as historians have often done with the cohabitation of Joannina and Anastasius.

We do not actually know how Antonina met Belisarius, or for that matter how she became a `confidant of Theodora. It is possible that she and the empress knew each other from their wilder days at the hippodrome or Alexandria, or Antioch, and many authors assume this. Some believe that Antonina was Theodora's instrument from before she married Belisarius and that Theodora arranged the marriage. Some believe that Antonina accompanied Belisarius at Theodora's behest to keep an eye on him. All this is possible but undocumented and the novelist is free to construct whatever fiction suits his story. I'm not so sure that historians should.

Procopius admits that Belisarius loved Antonina deeply and

certainly Belisarius was no fool. Even if Theodora did put them together, he loved her. That Antonina was also infatuated with Theodosius does not preclude her loving Belisarius, and he her. Even after her affair was revealed he was ready to lose Rome in order to hurry to her defense at Porto (though also to secure his only port on that coast). That public fact is definite since it is revealed by Procopius. The details of their more private lives are a matter of choice by any historian however. I am a mere novelist, but I take issue with more serious historians who put forth their own interpretations as fact. I prefer to believe, and hope, that the fiction I have written is something like the truth though.

I admit that their first meeting in Antioch is pure fiction, as is Antonina's presence at Dara and her father's sexual abuse. Did Antonina and Belisarius marry entirely for love? Who can say? In that age it would have been unusual and it is possible that Belisarius' ambition recommended to him that he wed a close friend of the empress. That has been suggested but it is cynical and I doubt it. If Antonina was looking for a sugar daddy or if Theodora threw them together for her own purposes, it is hard to believe that Procopius would have passed up that juicy bit of gossip, or that Belisarius would have remained in love as he clearly did. One cannot prove a negative, but if a negative is missing in such a slanderous narrative, it is indicative that there was none.

We are as ignorant of Photius' youth and upbringing, though John of Ephesus does say that he was "bred to arms." I prefer to interpret this as referring to his teen years, perhaps even after Antonina married Belisarius, but, of course, it could be otherwise. For what details there are about these things, one should read Procopius' *Secret History* but with a very critical mind. Every subsequent author has his own interpretation, usually based upon a word or two, here or there.

It might be mentioned that the *Secret History* was not discovered until centuries after it was written and a few historians have questioned its actual authorship. However, most believe it to be authentic. *The Wars* recounts in far more detail than I have the history of Belisarius' exploits and the politics leading up to and after his campaigns. This account was published in Procopius' lifetime and is very reliable. Also reliable is his short book on the building projects of Justinian which aside from his account of the construction of the great cathedral of Hagia Sophia is of little interest to the modern reader save for historians. To follow Procopius is not easy. Scholars find him very readable but not everyone will, particularly since he does not write his history in chronological order. It is especially difficult to establish a time line for the romance between Antonina and Theodosius and I cannot but wonder if that is not deliberate on Procopius' part in order to obfuscate the six year gap in Italy. Although the lovers would have been constantly together in Italy, Procopius gives no suggestion of any amours between the business of the slave girl Macedonia's alleged murder and the renewal of their affair. That is: between the Sicilian campaign, and while Belisarius was in Persia fighting his second war there, and while Antonina was in Constantinople.

Finally, I would like to make it clear that with little more than Procopius as a guide any author can attribute what motives he likes to Antonina. Personally I refuse to see her as simply a cold hearted bitch. Certainly she was a strong woman who somehow rose to the highest position open to her. Whether her rise should be attributed to friendship with Theodora, to cold ambition, to luck, or to some combination of these is unknowable, and each historian has his take on it. If she did not behave as some saint, it would be hard to find anyone around her, save possibly Belisarius, who did. Those qualities which are admired in a man are rarely admired in a woman. Procopius hated her for her strength, but many today would praise her for it.

Of Belisarius, himself, Procopius relates the symptoms of his disappointment and clinical depression but fails to diagnose them, seeing our hero as simply a love blind puppy in his relationship with Antonina and weak in the face of Theodora's wrath. But then, what emotion would have been stronger in Procopius' breast other than his own hero worship turned sour?

Was Antonina simply Theodora's tool, as Procopius saw her? He could not avoid mentioning her positive accomplishments, but does so with little grace. It was Antonina, not Belisarius, who stored fresh water bottles for the trip to Africa so that he would arrive in good health. It was Antonina who, instead of remaining safely in Naples where Belisarius sent her during the siege of Rome, instead raised a small army in the Campania. It was she who led these and other reinforcements to the relief of Rome, and even Procopius had to note that it was Antonina who presided over the council of war for that expedition. If I am right that he was jealous that a low-born bitch was so important to Belisarius, not only as a wife but also as a comrade, he may not only have been unable to understand the love between husband and wife, but also been a prig and a prude indeed. I have known women like Antonina who, instead of just supporting some husband, ran successful businesses of their own. (President and Secretary of State Clinton also come to mind.) They are not for every man; it takes a man who is completely sure of himself to love them.

310

Was Bloody John usually on good terms with Belisarius and Antonina, or was he their enemy? That depends on which historian you read. All of them must read between the lines. What we can be sure of is that Belisarius' best subordinates were competent even if as self-involved as Procopius makes them out. Yet, he surely exaggerates. I submit that it is because such men were so competent that Justinian could rule by playing them off against each other, even forgiving treason and assassination plots on more than one occasion. Procopius may, however, have touched upon a common defect in dictatorships. The loyalty of officers is to personal gain before patriotism. Without putting personal gain first, Byzantine officers might not have been able to support their lifestyle and most probably felt no more empathy with their peasant countrymen than do today's wealthy in dictatorial regimes.

What of Procopius' depiction of Justinian, in small part quoted above? Justinian was in his way a sincere Christian and that might have led him to forgive enemies if that virtue was supported by more practical considerations. That Christian virtue was a factor should not be written off as Procopius does. Procopius clearly says that Belisarius would have spared Constantinus, who had tried to kill him - were it not for Antonina's vendetta. So why should Justinian not have behaved in the same way toward ambitious underlings who saw an opportunity to make themselves the ruler?

I saw no great point in using Byzantine military titles and have usually contented myself with such modern forms as general, captain, and lieutenant. The term general is as widely applied today as was strategos, the Byzantine equivalent. Either can signify a theater commander like Belisarius or simply one of his subordinate field commanders. Likewise, as in popular English usage today, "lieutenant" is sometimes used to signify a subordinate regardless of rank.

The exact construction of Byzantine dromons is conjecture, however the rough outline has been supplied by archeology. We know that in earlier centuries the Romans constructed fighting platforms on their galleys, and for these I use the late medieval terminology of castles.

I should clarify my usage of Roman and Byzantine. Byzantium was the ancient name of the village that Constantine the Great replaced with New Rome (Nova Roma) in 330 AD. Citizens of the later empire of the east always referred to themselves as Romans and considered the empire, at least in theory, coterminous with Christianity. I try to follow that usage but for clarity have sometimes varied from it. Especially, I have used Byzantines in the sections about the Gothic wars, reserving the term Roman for the citizens of the city of that name.

When quoting Procopius and John of Ephesus I have made some minor alterations and omissions from the English text for clarity.

Now may I suggest some further readings. Procopius' books on the Persian, Vandal, and first Gothic wars, and of course, his *Secret History* are readily available in print and on line. The second Gothic War does not seem to be on line but is available at least in excerpts in print. His book about the Buildings of Justinian is rarely quoted today except for the section about Hagia Sophia. It can be found on line and I may point out that it gives substantial space to Justinian's constructions on the Persian frontier, including refortifying Dara, Antioch, and Edessa. He built or rebuilt throughout the empire, not only churches, with which everyone credits him, but fortresses, aqueducts, and all those things that Romans considered necessary to city life. It is a short book and probably should be given more attention than it is.

There are many popular books about Justinian and his reign. Generally these owe much to Edward Gibbon's *Decline and Fall of the Roman Empire* and J B Bury's *History of the later Roman Empire*. A Master's thesis by Major Anthony Brogna which analyzes Belisarius' tactics is available on line.

The classic account is that of (Philip Stanhope) Lord Mahon's *The Life of Belisarius* written when he was only twenty four; quite an accomplishment from so young a man but less than entirely critical of Procopius' account. For example, he follows Procopius' judgment on Narses, Bloody John, and John the Cappadocian. Generally I do too, but allow that their actions, while sometimes contradictory, were not necessary as entirely self serving as Procopius indicates. Some historians have tried to more objectively examine their actions. Be that as it may, Procopius' view makes for a good story. Mahon also accepts the legend of Belisarius having been blinded, though few other historians do. I. therefore, do not. Aside from making Procopius a eunuch, I have tried not to actually violate scholarly opinion.

There are two important 19th century works which can be consulted on line: Thomas Hodgkin's volume four of his eight volume *Barbarian Invasions of Italy,* with its asides and poetry, is not only fine history but superb writing, and well worth reading for pleasure. The German historian Ferdinand Gregorovius' *History of the City of Rome in the Middle Ages* is likewise a classic, though this author detects a prejudice against *the Greeks* (as he insists on calling the Byzantine army) even though he certainly knew that few of them were ethnically Greek, or even Hellenistic.

More recently James Allen Evans has written two interesting books about Antonina and Theodora: *The Empress Theodora, Partner of Justinian*, and *The Power Game in Byzantium, Antonina and the Empress Theodora*.

Lastly I could not forgive myself were I to pass over the fictionalized biography of Belisarius and Antonina, *Count Belisarius*, by Robert Graves. Surely, this is the most readable book on the subject, though Graves also had to fill in a lot of detail from his imagination, especially about the youth of Belisarius and how it was that he and Antonina met. Beautifully written though it is, *Count Belisarius* uses far more fictionalized detail than this book. For that reason it may be more readable. Certainly his fiction is historically sound and justifiable, but after the entirely fictionalized early life of our heroine, I have preferred to use a form which is more narrative than imaginative. Frankly, the more imagined dialogue there is, the less authority. I suppose that this makes my *Antonina* less readable, but my modest hope has been, not only to entertain the reader, but to provide a more sympathetic picture of Antonina than has generally been the case, without whitewashing her actions.

This book is not primarily about Belisarius, or about Justinian and Theodora, so it skimps on the details of their lives. It is about Antonina. She lived in a hard age. Antonina could not have been simply the bitch painted by Procopius; she was a strong women in a male-dominated age, a survivor, and a helpmate. To repeat what I wrote in chapter 1: This author chooses to believe that Antonina was less to be faulted than successful businessmen and gossips. She was just unimpressed by the hypocrisy of those who make much of the seventh commandment while ignoring the others. Whether she and Belisarius married for love, or fell in love afterward, it speaks to Belisarius' strong character, that he loved her as she was.

NOTES

(See also the separate Appendices of names and places. Those terms underlined in the descriptions have their own citations.)

Aide de camp – A secretary and personal assistant to a senior officer. Such an aide is far more than a servant however, but himself an officer of high rank.

Anglos and Saxons - After the Roman legions were withdrawn from Britain, the island fell easy prey to a number of Germanic invaders; the most important being the Anglos, Saxons, and Jutes.

Anointed of God – See Elect of God.

Antichalcedon - See Non Chalcedon.

Appian and Latin ways - These roads from the south of Rome were used to supply that city with food from the Campania and Ostia. See the places appendix.

Arabs - In our context, Arab means Moors. The term Arab is rather indistinct. It is neither racial nor religious, but essentially geographical. It can refer to any of many tribes inhabiting North Africa and the Middle East. However, the term "Moor" is restricted to peoples of mixed Arab and Berber blood in North Africa. Since this story is set before the time of the prophet Muhammad, the Arabs of North Africa are Christian. There is still a minority Christian Arab population in North Africa today. The Arabs of Saudi Arabia were Bedouin and like their ancestors before Muhammad, pagan. Their god was called Allah. and he was believed to have fathered three daughters. Muhammad kept the name but ennobled the concept, now considering Allah to be the same as the God of the Jews and Christians, and without children. Although Muhammad revered Jesus as the most important prophet before himself, he did not believe him to be divine. Muslims believe the bible to be inspired just as the Koran was, but to have been corrupted.

Arianism - The Arian doctrine insists that Jesus Christ was not eternal with God the Father, though he might be created before time. Christ as the Logos was formulated by the Father of like, but not the same substance as Himself. Arianism was declared heretical at the first council of Nicaea, called by the first Christian Roman emperor, Constantine I (the Great). The Nicene creed declared that the <u>Logos</u>, that is the Divinity of Christ before His incarnation in time, is "begotten, not made, of one substance with the Father." Some later Roman emperors in Constantinople were themselves of the Arian persuasion. I quote below a letter from one bishop Ulfila who was sent from Constantinople to convert the barbarian German tribes. As described in the letter, his position might be seen as semi-Arian. In any event, the Gothic rulers in Italy did not try to force their Arian beliefs on the orthodox Italian population, and the two churches existed side by side. This Was not so, among the Vandals in North Africa. There the Nicene (<u>Catholic</u>) population were initially left undisturbed in their beliefs, but later were persecuted under Genseric. The letter states: *I, Ulfila, bishop and confessor, have always believed in this, the one true faith, I make the journey to my Lord; I believe in one God the Father, the only unbegotten and invisible, and in his only-begotten son, our Lord and God, the designer and maker of all creation, having none other like him (so that one alone among all beings is God the Father, who is also the God of our God); and in one Holy Spirit, the illuminating and sanctifying power, as Christ said after his resurrection to his apostles: "And behold, I send the promise of my Father upon you; but tarry ye in the city of Jerusalem, until ye be clothed with power from on high" (Luke 24:49) and again "But ye shall receive power, when the Holy Ghost is come upon you" (Acts 1:8); being neither God (the Father) nor our God (Christ), but the minister of Christ ... subject and obedient in all things to the Son; and the Son, subject and obedient in all things to God who is his Father ...(whom) he ordained in the Holy Spirit through his Christ.*

As you show mercy, so shall mercy be shown to you. (Math: 5:7)

Augustus - The original title of the Roman Emperor, replaced in Byzantium with the more inclusive Greek title of <u>Basilios</u>. When <u>Constantine I (The Great)</u> divided the empire administratively between Rome and Constantinople, there were to be two senior augusti and two junior caesars who were to succeed the augustus on his death. The arrangement was not very successful and in time the term augustus was replaced by basilios in common usage. <u>Caesar </u>became primarily an inherited position of honor and little actual power, much as did that of <u>senator</u>.

Aurelian walls - The Roman city walls, still partially intact, had been allowed to decay at the time of our story, because the reduced population of Rome could no longer maintain their twelve mile circuit. See map in the text.

Autocrator - The Greek equivalent of the Roman <u>Imperator</u> or general. From Caesar Augustus the term evolved into the concept of an emperor.

Avoir de l'audacité, toujours l'audacité, encore une fois l'audacité - Georges Jacques Danton rallied Frenchmen against the invasion of foreign armies after the French Revolution with the call: " We need audacity, more audacity, always audacity and France will be saved!"

Ballista - A Roman artillery piece resembling a huge crossbow used to fire darts and stones.

Baptism - The sacrament by which a person becomes a member of Christ's church, and the celebration welcoming him into the Christian community. Whether an infant can be baptised remains a matter of dispute, even today, among Protestant denominations. Whether a baptism by an unworthy priest is valid was also questioned in the early church. Today's Catholic teaching is that any person can validly baptise a person of any age, whether the person conducting the initiation be sinful or pious, a layman or a cleric, in communion with Rome or not, so long as his intent be to make the person to be baptised a member of Christ's church. But that took centuries to establish. It seems that the Arians accepted infant baptism but only by a priest, and one who was of their persuasion.

Barbarian - To a Greek, "barbarian" meant anyone who spoke a foreign language. Romans who used the loan-word may have assumed a folk etymology that it came from the Latin for bearded men. Not till late Roman times did the word take on its modern meaning. (Procopius was likely considering the dual meaning when he refers to Persians as barbarians.)

Basilia – Empress, by virtue of being raised to the throne by the basilios. His wife, an augusta, was not necessarily raised to the status of basilia. It should be remembered, though, that in this usage, as in all terms, meaning changed. The Byzantine empire lasted eleven hundred years from the foundation of Constantinople in 330 AD till the conquest of the city by Ottoman Turks in 1453. The author has fudged the usage a bit. At Justinian's time it would have been more loosely used than later. (See note in Basilios below.)

Basilios - Emperor, King of Kings, God's Anointed. The Eastern Empire is sometimes termed Greek. A more accurate identification would be Hellenistic for it was composed as much of oriental as of Greek traditions; and, of course, of Roman elements. It was in the east that Roman emperors were first deified, and though that did not fit in a Christian state, the emperor as the Elect of God and Equal of the Apostles was the next closest thing. The emperors ruled with a mandate from heaven, for which reason an unsuccessful revolt was sacrilege as much as treason, while a successful one meant that the mandate had passed to a new ruler. Justinian lived in an era of transition between the classical and the medieval world. His authority certainly was considered to have been derived from the Almighty, but he would not yet have been seen as fully endowed with all the semi-divine glow of later emperors. At Justinian's time, the term basilios was probably in popular usage in the eastern empire in imitation of the Persian monarch's identification as "king of kings." However, it was not until a bit later that the emperors were officially identified as basilios. Officially Justinian would have been called by the Latin titles of <u>imperator</u> (<u>autocrator</u> in Greek) and <u>augustus</u>.

Bedouins - Literally "those who live in the desert." Until recent decades Bedouins were exclusively nomadic Arabs, identified by strong tribal relationships and spread throughout the desert parts of the near and middle east.

Berbers - The native mountain people of North Africa. They were extremely poor and without any great culture at the time of our story. Some were Christians (St. <u>Augustine of Hippo</u> was a Berber) and some were Jewish, but most were probably pagan.

Better is the patient spirit than the lofty spirit. (Eccl 7:8)

Bireme - A galley with two banks of oars. In combat the soldiers on the lower level would row, whereas those on the higher would row or fight as necessary. (see also: dromon.)

Blues and Greens - The colors of rival hippodrome teams whose partisans eventually differed also in matter of politics and religion, the Green faction favoring <u>Arianism</u>; the Blues, orthodoxy. While <u>Justinian</u> favored the orthodox Blue faction, <u>Theodora</u> supported the Greens. She did so not because of an Arian inclination but because when her father, who had been a bear keeper for the Blues, died and her mother remarried, the Blue leader refused to appoint Theodora's stepfather to her natural father's old job. This left her and her two sisters and their mother destitute. They begged on their knees for their stepfather to be made the new bear keeper but were coldly refused. Instead, their Green opponents, whose own animal keeper had recently died, showed them mercy and gave his job to the widow's new husband. Such experiences do much to explain Theodora's cynical view of mankind and the cold heart and vindictiveness she is charged with as empress.

Bubonic Plaque - The Justinian plague. The first recorded pandemic, it struck Europe in 541 AD and returned with each generation until about 750. The initial outbreak may have killed one quarter of the population in the eastern Mediterranean. Later outbreaks were less severe, but still very serious. Procopius' description of the plague and its symptoms, which I have somewhat abbreviated here, is considered a masterpiece of its kind. He insightfully notes that the disease first attacked from the seacoast and was not passed on by contact with its victims. Unfortunately for the population of Europe he failed to recognize that it was carried by fleas that traveled city to city on ships' rats. This so-called Justinian plague is well remembered in Eastern Europe where it recurred periodically for centuries. In the west, a fourteenth century outbreak known as the Black Death is better remembered. That outbreak took the lives of an estimated twenty five million people.

Bucellarii - Household cavalry. Each commander was expected to have a large retinue of cavalry loyal to himself who would fight in his wars and accompany him as guards of honor around Constantinople. He would be expected to provide for their sustenance, hence it was necessary that he receive a large portion of the spoils of battle. Belisarius' bucellarii eventually numbered over seven thousand. When they were taken from him in the period of his disgrace it was a disaster for the empire. Without them he had only a few thousand raw recruits with which to fight Totila during the second Gothic war. Had Justinian really intended that he reconquer the devastated peninsula, he should have recalled these excellent troops from where he and Theodora had scattered them.

Bulgars - A group of Asiatic tribes that fought the Byzantines from at least the sixth century.

Burgundians - Probably of Scandinavian origin, the Burgundians occupied the part of France still termed Burgundy. They were frequently at war with their neighbors, the Franks, but at the time of our story they were allied.

Caesar – The later Roman emperors made various attempts to both provide for an orderly transition of power upon their death, and to better administer the huge state. The simple solution was to divide the empire into eastern and western parts and then further subdivide these sections. Each half was to be administered by an augustus, aided by a caesar who would ascend to the position of augustus upon the latter's demise. Sometimes it worked. Of course by the time of our story there was no longer an augustus in the west. That title therefore belonged to Justinian alone, who had been a caesar under his stepfather Justin. In his final days Justin raised Justinian to the rank of a co-augustus. In later centuries the title of caesar continued but lost its original meaning, becoming only a title of dignity for members of the imperial family.

Camp followers - The term is commonly used to refer to prostitutes who follow an army; but properly, it refers to anyone who does. These would include the equivalent of pawn brokers who would exchange battlefield loot for cash, as well as cooks, laundry women, purveyors of local foodstuffs, etc. In other words anyone not properly a member of the army and under military command.

Canon Law – Church law.

Cataphracts - The heavily armed Roman and Persian cavalry, though I use the term in this story only to refer to the Roman, calling their Persian equivalents saravan and dehgans. A cataphract and his horse were armored with scale armor. He carried a lance, bow, ax, and sword; and in battle wore headgear which covered his entire face.

Catholic and orthodox - At the time of our story there were no separate Catholic and Orthodox churches as we know them. As used here both terms refer to those Christians who affirmed the Councils of Nicaea and Chalcedon. I follow historians in using the capitalized term Catholic as the proper name for these orthodox Christians in both the east and west, as opposed to Monophysites, Arians, etc. Of course, the modern "Catholic" church lays claim to authority which it did not have at the time of our story. The emperor was the temporal head of the church, and the doctrine of papal infallibility would not be defined until modern times. That said; even in the sixth century, the popes were granted a status and authority far greater than simply first among equals. Thus the authority to rule as Patriarch of Constantinople depended upon their assent.

Centenaria - One centenary equaled one hundred pounds of gold.

Chalcedon, Council of, Chalcedonians - The Council of Chalcedon repudiated the Monophysite doctrine that Jesus had only a Divine nature, and stated that Christ has two natures in one person. (See also: Chalcedon in the places appendix.)

Chasing after wind - "It is an unhappy business that God has given to human beings to be busy with. I saw all the deeds that are done under the sun; and see, all is vanity and a chasing after wind." (Ecclesiastes 1:1, 23-15)

Chi-Rho - Christ's monogram in Greek. First used by the emperor Constantine the Great on his banner at the battle of the Milvian bridge to encourage the many Christians among his soldiers. This banner, or labarum, continued to be used by his successors.

Christ Pantocrator - (Christ, the ruler of all) The severe image of Christ typically in the dome of eastern churches. Christ forgives, but as with a king one approaches him in fear.

Cistern – There were and are many cisterns in Istanbul but the one mentioned in our text was, in fact, constructed by Justinian, and remains even today a tourist site. Known as the Yerebatan Saryi, or underground palace in Turkish, it is prettily lit and recorded music plays.

Codex Iustianus - the foundation of modern continental law, it was the work of Tribonian on the order of Justinian.

Comes (modern count) - A late Roman military and civil title, a comes reported directly to the emperor. Thus the comes Irenaeus was dispatched from Constantinople, with a troop of Imperial soldiers to arrest the Alexandrian patriarch Severus in Antioch, and bring him to the capital to answer charges of heresy.

Commissariat - The division of an army charged with supplying food, clothing, medical supplies, etc. A nice safe place for a godson until he could be trained, and a position in which he could learn more about the operation of an army than by rowing the boat.

Consul - The most honorable office in ancient Rome where two consuls were elected to administer the state for a year. By the time of our story, however, the office had no real power but retained great prestige. It was also so expensive to occupy that soon after the consulship of Belisarius the office was eliminated by Justinian. Consuls were expected to distribute largess to the populace, provide entertainment, etc. In theory this was out of their own purse, but the cost had become so onerous that the state had to assist.

Convent - A convent for women can also be termed a monastery in Eastern Christendom.

Copts - Egyptian version of Christianity. The Coptic church still survives in the Middle East. The Coptic Church claims descent from the evangelist St. Mark, who founded a church in Alexandria. It was considered heretical by those who fully accepted the decrees of the Council of Chalcedon. In point of fact, the differences were more political than theological and the Copts were persecuted by Byzantine emperors.

Courtesans and concubines - As used in our text a courtesan is a high class prostitute whereas a concubine has a bit more respectability as a man's regular female companion, but without marital status.

Cubicularia (Plural cubiculariai) - Ladies in waiting on the empress. The masculine form, cubicularius (not used in this story), refers to eunuchs waiting upon the emperor or empress. Like Narses, eunuchs could hold important positions in the administration and the military. Narses himself would never have been called a mere cubicularius however. His position was effectively that of a prime minister.

Cuirass or corselette - A breastplate and back covering such as was worn by the cavalry of Napoleon, and is seen embossed to indicate musculature on heroic Roman sculpture.

Curule chair - The seat of important Roman officials, in our case the consul. The tradition remains in the Catholic church today; a cathedral being the place where a bishop's cathedra or chair is kept. Thus the pope's cathedral is the ancient church of St. John Lateran built by the emperor Constantine I in Rome, St Peter's basilica being simply a great church and the center of Catholicism but not a cathedral, the "seat" of the pope as bishop of Rome.

D-day plus two – The term D-day has become so identified with the allied invasion of Normandy in World War II, that it can be forgotten that the term had been in general use for any attack. Using such a term, rather than a specific date, increases security and allows flexibility in planning. Some things have to be done a certain number of days before the attack, others – such as bringing in additional food and ammunition - a certain number of days afterward. The letter H is similarly used to stand for the hour of invasion.

Dalmatic - A loose fitting garment worn over the tunic by both sexes, but mostly by men. Originally fairly simple, during the course of Byzantine history dalmatics became very ornate court dress. Our story is set in a period of transition between true Roman and Byzantine fashions so I use the term rather loosely.

Dates - "The seventh day of September in the 1285th year since the founding of the city of Rome and 533 years after the birth of Our Savior." I have only surmised the exact day that Belisarius landed in Africa. Years are reckoned by our present Gregorian calendar which assumes the birth of Christ as being in the year 1 AD.

Dehgans - The Persian aristocracy from which Chosroes' heavy cavalry was drawn. Traditionally, Persian heavy cavalry had been composed of ancient saravan nobility and it is these that Belisarius faced at Dara. However, after an egalitarian movement in Persian politics after Kobad's death, Chosroes found it advisable to create a new minor aristocracy from among the more successful peasant landholders. These were the dehgans of Chosroes' army. In this story I use saravan and dehgan as synonyms for Persian heavy cavalry (cataphracts) in order to differentiate them from the Roman cataphracts, though the Persians actually employed cataphract cavalry before the Romans did. They differed little in armament from the Roman.

Dromon - A Byzantine warship derived from the Roman. It could use either oar or sail power and carried up to two hundred fifty rowers and fighting men. In later centuries dromons would be equipped with Greek Fire and a mechanism to project the liquid onto other ships. In this narrative I equip the dromons with fore and aft "castles." Although the terminology is from

322

later western usage, the concept of fighting platforms, either fore and aft as in my narrative, or possibly amidships, was developed by the Romans and continued by the Byzantine navy. (See also: <u>Bireme</u>.)

Dux (Modern Duke) - A late Roman military title meaning "leader". Although not the administrator of a province, in practice he held great power in a world collapsing under <u>barbarian</u> attack.

Eagle - I have created the fiction that Belisarius had an iron eagle made, such as the standard which led the legions of the republic and the caesars into battle.

Either he will hate the first and love the second; or treat the first with respect and the second with scorn. (Math 6:24)

Elect of God - Title of the emperor. Byzantine titles have a rather alien sound in translation, so I have generally limited them to <u>Your Serenity, Your Sovereignty</u>, and such western forms as Your Majesty. In Christian political theory, the emperor could no longer be a god as in Roman theory, so the Elect of God was the nearest alternative, together with such terms as the <u>Equal of the Apostles</u>. As in China, where the Elect of Heaven ruled absolutely by Divine right so long as he ruled justly, he had a mandate from heaven, but this mandate could be lost. If a revolution against an emperor's rule succeeded, surely the mandate had passed to the rebel. If it failed (in the Chinese terminology, the rebel had shot his arrows at Heaven) he had not only attacked the state, but God's chosen representative on earth, and was deserving of the most severe punishment. Justinian tended to be merciful but not all emperors were. What might have worried Justinian in his later years is that, although Belisarius had many times proven his loyalty to his oath, he was also subject to Roman law. Were the army and people to demand that he take the throne, and raise him on a shield at the hippodrome, he would have been released from that vow. He would be answering a higher duty, the demands of the Senatus Populusque Romanus (Senate and people of Rome.) In the words of the great historian of Rome, Theodore Mommsen; the empire was "an autocracy tempered by the legal right of revolution."

Ephthalites - So-called "White Huns" from the Steppes of Asia. The Ephthalites had more Caucasian-like features than other "Huns." They may have been of Turkic or Indo-Iranian stock.

Equal of the Apostles (Isapostle) – See note under <u>Elect of God</u>.

Eucharist - Properly the term refers to the Real Presence of Christ under the appearance of bread and wine in the Divine Liturgy (known in the west as the Mass from the closing Latin words: ete missa est.) The Eucharist is also known as Holy Communion to emphasize the social aspect of the service. The term is often used to designate the entire liturgical service however, and I follow this usage in the story.

Eunomianism - This denied entirely the equality of Christ with the Father. It was therefore an extreme form of the <u>Arian</u> family of heresies.

Eunuchs - In accordance with its Oriental character, eunuchs were much more common in Byzantium than in the West. Many were from the middle classes but some were aristocrats. Since they could never hold the position of emperor and had no children to advance, they were considered safe to appoint to high positions. They often held important administrative and even military rank, and very many served the empire loyally and well, though some connived to advance other members of their families. Eunuchs did not necessarily appear more effeminate than others at court as it was normal even for manly and courageous military emperors to wear cosmetics and perfume (at least in later centuries.) It is thought that the elderly man standing behind Justinian in the Ravenna mosaic may be the eunuch <u>Narses</u>, but note that he has a mustache so perhaps men castrated after puberty had facial hair. There is some question too whether all eunuchs were entirely devoid of sexual desire. Supposedly those castrated after puberty could achieve an erection and enjoy coitus, but not ejaculate. There is also the possibility that men who were homosexual from an early age were lumped together with the castrated; the theory being that these were natural or holy eunuchs. (See also the note about eunuchs under <u>cubicularia</u>.)

Fifth column - An irregular military unit such as resistance fighters. The term comes from the Spanish civil war. As the Nationalist general Emilio Mola was approaching Madrid he announced that he had four columns outside the city which would be supported by a fifth column of his supporters inside the city.

Foederati - Troops supplied to the empire by allied barbarian tribes which had been permitted to settle within the imperial frontiers. In other words barbarian invaders in the pay of the invaded. Such troops, as well as mercenaries under their own warlords, were unreliable but necessary since the empire could not raise sufficient troops within the realm. Having said that, they could be effective so long as there was loot to be had.

Fori - Forums in Constantinople, and in Rome at its height, and in other cities, served as centers of politics, religion, business, and trade. They were the shopping centers of the day combined with the capitol buildings.

Franks – A confederation of Germanic tribes; some of whom invaded the failing Western Roman Empire, and others of whom served it. In time, they would control most of modern France and Germany, their greatest king being Charlemagne. (But that is well after our story.) About the time of Justinian the Franks were moving southward and threatening Italy. They occupied parts of Gaul under their Merovingian kings. Three centuries later under the Carolingians they were to control northern Italy and Germany, stop the advance of Islam into Europe at the battle of Tours, and produce Charlemagne, whose reign is considered to have begun the long climb out of the "Dark Ages."

Galley labor - We assume that, as with the Roman navy of classical times, the rowing was done by the soldiers aboard, not slaves. Some professional sailors would have been needed for more complex duties such as handling sails and rigging, however.

Gates of Rome - See the map in the text. In addition to the major gates there were a number of minor sally ports.

Gepids - A Scandinavian Germanic tribe, which after a number of wars and see-saw alliances settled in Byzantine Dacia. There they had to fight Theodoric the Great and the Ostrogoths. They lost and moved east to the area of Belgrade, Dacia becoming a part of the Gothic state. Thus Mundus was fighting a tribal enemy in his own homeland.

Gladius - The quintessential short piercing (rather than striking) sword of the Roman infantry legions. (also see Spathion.)

Golden Gate - The gate near the southernmost end of the triple walls of Constantinople, reserved for use by imperial processions only.

Golden Horn – See places appendix.

Goths - Originally there was one Gothic people which split into two sections - the Visigoths, and the Ostrogoths. The Visigoths were the first to attack Italy but then they moved on to France and Spain. The Goths, with whom we are concerned, are the Ostrogoths who conquered Italy under their great king Theodoric in 493 AD.

Grand Chamberlain – See Praepositus of the Sacred Bed Chamber, Narses.

Great (Sacred) Palace - The palace complex overlooking the Bosphorus and adjacent to Hagia Sophia cathedral and the hippodrome.

Greater love than this no man hath, then he lay down his life for his friend. - John 15:13.

Grecia, Italia, Roma - Greece, Italy, Rome. No attempt is made to be consistent in using obvious Latin and English place names. The author has used what sounded best in the context.

Greek Fire - This was the most effective weapon before gun powder, and often saved Byzantine forces. It was used on land but was especially effective in sea battles, where it would be spewed from "siphons" and could not be extinguished with water. Hodgkin knew that it was a later invention, of course, but romantically imagines Belisarius' boats armed with some primitive form thereof. More likely their armament was of the same flammable materials as had been used for centuries.

Gregorian calendar - The modern calendar created during the pontificate of Pope Gregory XIII; it replaced the Julian calendar of the Romans which had become inaccurate over the centuries. Our dates are according to the Gregorian calendar.

Hadrian's tomb - The present Castel Sant' Angelo in Rome. During the middle ages the tomb was converted into a fortress.

Hagia Sophia - The church of the Holy Wisdom (the Logos, or Second Person of the Blessed Trinity). This beautiful church, now a museum in Istanbul, is the third church of that name on the same spot. The first was built by Constantine the Great, but destroyed in a fire. It was rebuilt but lost to an earthquake. The present building was built by Justinian after the Nike insurrectionists finished off the second building with fire. Since the present structure was completed in six years, it is almost certain that Justinian had already begun the planning. The architect was Anthemius of Tralles. When the great dome collapsed some years later a new higher dome was raised in its place by Isidorus the younger. Built in the late Roman style of architecture, Justinian certainly intended that it be an impressive imperial structure. Later and much smaller churches more truly reflect the Byzantine attitude toward worship. While northern Europe was creating Gothic cathedrals that reached toward the heavens but were fairly monochromatic inside, the Byzantines and Italians preferred less ostentatious exteriors but employed colorful decoration for the worshiper to contemplate inside. Paul the Silentiary sang a hymn of praise: "Above all rises into the immeasurable air the great helmet of the dome, which, bending over, like the radiant heavens, embraces the church. A thousand other lamps within the temple show their gleaming light, hanging aloft by chains of many windings. The night seems to flaunt the light of day, and be itself as rosy as the dawn.... Thus through the spaces of the great church come rays of light, expelling clouds of care, and filling the mind with joy."

Handshake of The Graduate - In the 1967 film *The Graduate* Dustin Hoffman playing Benjamin explains his infidelity with Mrs. Robinson as being nothing more serious than a handshake. Understandably, Mr.

Robinson does not see it that way.

Hashish and mandrake mixed in wine - Anesthesia was not completely unknown in Belisarius' day, but was imprecise and dangerous - and therefore reserved for cases where its use could make a difference in whether a man lived or died from the shock of amputation. Smoking is the best way to get hashish into the blood, but that method had not been realized.

Hellenes - Name by which the ancient Greeks called themselves.

Hellenistic – I am forced to use the term in something a bit broader than its dictionary definition. That has the Hellenistic period extend only from the time of Alexander the Great to that of the early Roman emperors. But then, what term in common usage would describe the period, at least so far as Alexandria is concerned? True, Christian culture had supplanted the classical, but far from completely; and to describe the vibrant culture there as Greek, Roman, or Medieval would be still more inaccurate.

Hephthalites - See Ephthalites, Huns.

Heresies - In this story I have actually downplayed the importance of the early Christological disputes. After all, this is not a theological text. Suffice it that the two important disputes were about the relationship between the Divine and human natures in Christ. These positions were far from monolithic however. There were many variations within the sects and I am indebted to several authors of the Wikipedia for their clarification, from which I often quote in this appendix. See Arianism, Monophysites, Semi-monophysites, Non Chalcedonians, and Nestorianism.

Heruli - Ax-wielding mercenaries from Scandinavia, probably from Denmark. In 512 AD these predecessors of the Vikings settled within the Roman Empire along the Danube and were employed as federates.

Hippodrome (circus) - The racetrack. Used for chariot races and festive occasions in Constantinople, but also a gathering place for political dissenters.

Hira - A tribe of Bedouins. Their chieftain, Alamoundaras, advised Kobad not to attack the garrison at Antioch by the easy road from Amida.

Hittites – A Bronze Age people who inhabited Anatolia from the eighteenth century BC. Such ancient remains, like dinosaur bones, would likely have been seen as destruction from the biblical flood of Noah's time.

Holy - Often attached to the names of saintly persons, alive or dead, or of objects dedicated to religion (holy icons, holy church). It has a broader sense than the English "saint" which is reserved for deceased persons of undoubted holiness. In the Roman church being declared a saint (canonization) has, for many centuries, only followed after a strict investigation.

Holy Orders - The priesthood. While monks were celibate, eastern rite priests were not usually so. Those priests who were also monks were, of course, celibate. Even in the West, where the Roman church was trying to enforce celibacy, priests were still often married at this time. It might be noted that to take a vow of celibacy means to forgo the comforts and distractions of married life. Simple chastity is required of all Christians; but violations, while sinful, were considered to be normal and natural. To avoid excessive division of inherited land, many sons would become clergymen (deacons, sub-deacons, etc.), but not necessarily priests. East or west, this did not have much to do with spirituality and can be said to have lead to the kidnapping of the church by the aristocracies.

Humors, choleric bile - Medical theory from the Greeks and Romans held that the human body contained four basic substances, called humors, which are in balance when a person is healthy. All diseases and disabilities resulted from an excess or deficit of one of these four humors. These deficits could be caused by vapors that were inhaled or absorbed by the body. The four humors were black bile, yellow bile, phlegm, and blood. Each of these humors would wax and wane in the body, depending on diet and activity. When a patient was suffering from a surplus or imbalance of one fluid, then his or her personality and physical health would be affected. This theory was closely related to the theory of the four elements: earth, fire, water and air; earth predominantly present in the black bile, fire in the yellow bile, water in the phlegm, and all four elements present in the blood.

Huns - In our context the term normally refers to the so-called White Huns, otherwise called Ephthalites or Hephthalites. At the time of our story they lived northeast of Persia and were employed by the Byzantines as mercenaries. See Ephthalites.

I adjure you that by eating this precious fruit. - An actual Byzantine incantation that the author found somewhere.

Icon – An image of Christ, the virgin, or some saint; painted on wood but often obscured with silver decoration. In theory it is a simple representation with its stylized art intended more to indicate the character and holiness of the person depicted than his actual appearance. In practice, however, in the popular mind icons have often taken on the character of a link with the actual saint. In later centuries this was to cause a bloody dispute among eastern Christians, some revering the "holy icons," and others wanting them totally banned as graven images. In my novel, *Count No Man Happy*, that time and issue forms the backdrop.

328

Iconostasis - The decorated screen between the celebrants and congregation in eastern rite services. As the name indicates, it bears a number of icons.

Illustrious, Illustrati – A rank of late Roman aristocracy held by Belisarius.

Illyrian divisions - Illyricum (Somewhat the same territory as Dalmatia) was at times held by the Romans and Byzantines, at other times by Goths and various other intruders. It was a major source of Byzantium's best troops. Justin, the magister militum per Illyricum (master of soldiers for Illyricum) was of the same race. The problem with Belisarius' officers was more often insubordination than incompetence. The other best source of troops from within the empire proper was Thrace, where Belisarius himself was born.

Immortals - I don't make much of this term in the text but they were the famous shock troops of the Persians, almost never defeated. However, they were defeated when they met the Heruli Swedes at Dara.

Imperator - Emperor. Originally a Roman military title, superseded by the Greek equivalent, autocrator.

Isapostle - Literally "Equal of the Apostles," a title of the emperor.

Jaws of the lupi (wolf) - There seems to be no ancient definition, but from the name and the fact that the jaws were placed at gates it is presumed that they were a sort of portcullis, a heavy spiked gate that drops into place.

Jews – Since the Jews of Naples took a very active part in resisting Belisarius' siege of that city they apparently preferred Gothic to Byzantine rule. I have passed over the ill treatment of Jews by Justinian and the fact that both Jews and pagans were succored by Persia. It was in the time of Justinian that the Babylonian Talmud was created in Nisbis though no mention of this is made by Procopius when he describes the battles near there. Of Justinian's treatment of the Jews Procopius writes: "The Emperor also exerted himself to destroy the traditions of the Jews. For whenever in their calendar Passover came before the Christian Easter" (that is during the Lenten season), "he forbade the Jews to celebrate it on their proper day, to make then any sacrifices to God or perform any of their customs. Many of them were heavily fined by the magistrates for eating lamb at such times, as if this were against the laws of the state." There were other laws restricting Jews and Samaritans and the usual occasional riots, but Justinian seems to have been more inclined to attempt converting Jews to Christianity by inconveniencing them than by active persecution. It is interesting, however, that Procopius criticizes Justinian for his anti Jewish laws, so even in that age there must have been some sympathy for their plight, if not for what

would have been considered their stiff necked refusal to accept Christianity.
Justinian Plague – See <u>Bubonic Plague</u>.

Khan - A common Asian title with varying importance depending on the time and place. The khan is the military leader of a tribe or group of tribes. In such a context it was not necessarily an hereditary title nor one held in settled times. It was seen as important, however, to have an autocratic ruler during periods of war and migration.
Kontakion - A hymn. In this case one written for the dedication of <u>Hagia Sophia</u>.
Kyrie Elision - Literally, "Lord be with us," frequently repeated in Orthodox chant.

Labarum - A military standard displaying Christ's monogram, the <u>Chi-Rho</u>. It was originally formed as the standard for <u>Constantine I</u>'s army when he recognized Christianity. This standard continued to be carried in successive centuries.
Lamellar armor - Made from hundreds of metal plates and sometimes worn over chain mail, it produced a deflective surface for blades to skim over, rather than strike and pierce.
Lancers – <u>cataphracts.</u>
Latin and **Appian ways** - These roads from the south of Rome were used to supply that city with food from the <u>Campania</u> and <u>Ostia</u>. See the places appendix.
Latrunculi - A Greek and Roman board game of military tactics sometimes compared with chess, which, however, was unknown in Europe before the ninth century.
Lazi - A Christian tribe on the East coast of the Black Sea. The Lazi lived on the isthmus between the <u>Euxine</u> (Black) and the Caspian Seas, north of <u>Mesopotamia</u> in an area known anciently as Colchis, the fabled land of Medea and the Golden Fleece. Their disputed allegiance was the *casus belli* of the Persian wars. Depending on one's inclination, Chosroes can be considered to have beeen fighting one war or two at the same time since while he was conducting operations against the Lazi to his north, he was also fighting the Byzantines on his western frontier. Of the Lazi and the Romans it is appropriate to use the cliché that "the enemy of my enemy is my friend," but that does not mean that their operations were well coordinated. This book being about Antonina, I make little of the Lazi war.
Lemons and oranges - Citrus was well known in the Roman world or at least in the Asian and African part. Most sites indicate that it was then introduced or reintroduced into Europe by returning crusaders, however

they are probably referring to western Europe. Surely citrus fruits would in earlier years have made the short passage from the Near East to southern Greece where they are still cultivated.

L'etat c'est moi - The state, it is I. A statement, probably inaccurately, attributed to King Louis XIV of France, the Sun King. Rightly or wrongly attributed, the expression accurately reflects the absolutist divine right of kings theory.

Lieutenants - In this story I have largely used rough modern equivalents to proper Roman and Byzantine military titles. As with the term general, I use the word "lieutenant" to designate not only lower ranking officers. but also a general's subordinates whatever their rank. Thus a captain would outrank a lieutenant but they would both be subordinate lieutenants of Belisarius.

Life, if well lived, is long enough. – Seneca: *De Ira.*

Logos (Word) - In Greek philosophy, the Divine principle of reason or wisdom. St. John the Evangelist writes of Jesus in his Gospel: "In the beginning was the Word (Logos), and the Word was with God, and the Word was God. He was with God in the beginning. Through him all things were made; without him nothing was made that has been made. In him was life, and that life was the light of all mankind. The light shines in the darkness, and the darkness has not overcome it. … The true light that gives light to everyone was coming into the world. He was in the world, and though the world was made through him, the world did not recognize him. The Word became flesh and made his dwelling among us."

Lombards or Longobards - Literally "long beards". A Germanic tribe from Scandinavia, which invaded Italy after the Second Gothic war. They inherited Italy from the Byzantines because the wars of Justinian had left it too weak to resist them.

Long Wall of Anastasius - Complete with towers, gates, forts, and ditches, the fifth century wall was built (or enlarged) by the Emperor Anastasius. It was forty miles west of Constantinople and intended as an outer defense for that city from invasions by Huns, Slavs, and Bulgars.

Lyre - There is such a thing as a Byzantine lyre but it is not mentioned until the ninth century. Anyway, it was played with a bow. More likely, Procopius is referring to any of several plucked instruments. Of course, he may be more specific in the Greek than in the English translation that the author used.

Macedonians - Macedonia is north of Thrace. Belisarius is making a rude comment about Macedonian ways. The Hellenes of Plato's time had practiced man-on-man sex and the Macedonian phalanx of Alexander the Great was founded on a sexual relationship which paired each young trooper with an older one. This was not necessarily the result of homosexual urges however, and that was why it so horrified Jews and early Christians. True love was considered the love of one man for another and this diminished women, leaving them only the role of child bearing. Of course, to what extent this was simply an aristocratic ideal is debatable. Husbands and wives have a way of falling in love.

Magister equitum (Master of horse) - Commander of all cavalry in a theater.

Magister militum (Master of soldiers) - A theater commander such as Belisarius, Julius Caesar, Eisenhower, or MacArthur.

Magister Militum Per Orientem - Master of Soldiers for the East. A theater commander. The Persian frontier was all important in Justinian's day as it had always been in both Greek and Roman history. Compared to commanding all troops on the eastern frontier, Africa and even Italy were adventures, a fact which students of Justinian's wars sometimes forget.

Mazdan burial customs - See Zoroastrianism, and also Ahura Mazda in the Names appendix.

Monasteries, Monasticism - It has been estimated that perhaps fifty percent of Byzantine men spent at least a part of their lives in monasteries. While lone holy men were very respected in Byzantium, by the time of our story most monks lived a communal life. Eastern monks, particularly in Egypt, were often very political, undisciplined, and riotous, and only nominally submissive to their bishops.

Monophysites and semi-monophysites - Monophysitism, is the Christological position that Jesus Christ has only one nature, his humanity being absorbed by his Deity. A brief definition can be given as: "Jesus Christ, who is identical with the Son, is one person and one hypostasis in one nature: divine-human." Monophysitism is opposed to the Chalcedonian position which holds that Christ maintains two natures, one divine and one human. As Monophysitism is contrary to the orthodox Chalcedonian Creed it has always been considered heretical by the Western and most of the Eastern Churches. Later, a *monothelitist* belief - that Christ was two natures in one person except that he only had a divine will and no human will - was developed as an attempt to bridge the gap between the Monophysite and the Chalcedonian position, but it too was rejected by the members of the Chalcedonian synod, despite at times having the support of the Byzantine emperors and once escaping the condemnation of Pope Honorius I. Historically the term Monophysite is used to denote all Non-Chalcedonians. There were however a number of Monophysite churches, some more extreme than others. To one extent or another, however, they taught that the human nature of the man Jesus was subsumed in the Divine Logos. It followed that not a man but only an image was "crucified, died, and was buried" as is stated in the orthodox Nicene creed.

Moors - See Arabs.

My days are swifter than a runner. They speed by without seeing happiness. (Job 9:25)

Nestorianism - A heresy condemned at the First Council of Ephesus in 431 AD, it held that the human and divine natures of Christ were separate or only loosely connected. Its only interest in this story is that the Monophysites were a reaction to Nestorianism; and the Monophysite, orthodox, and Arian disputants liked nothing better than to accuse each other of Nestorian leanings. After Nestorianism was condemned in the empire, many of its adherents fled into Persia and settled in the city of Nisibis, though that plays no part in our story.

New Africanus - See Scipio Africanus in the names appendix.

New Rome (Nova Roma) - The official name of Constantinople, given to the city by Constantine the Great when he created the city as a second capital for the Roman Empire. The term was usually used only in official documents which would state: "Nova Roma which is Constantinople."

Nicaea, Council of – See Nicene Formula.

Nicene formula - There are a number of English translations of the Nicene Creed. The one given below is that currently used by the Orthodox Church in America. It may be noted that whatever their other differences, adherence to the Nicene Creed unites all the so-called "high churches."

"I believe in one God the Father almighty, Maker of heaven and earth, and of all things visible and invisible. And in one Lord Jesus Christ, the Son of God, the only-begotten, begotten of the Father before all ages; Light of Light, true God of true God, begotten, not made, of one essence with the Father, by whom all things were made. Who for us men and for our salvation came down from heaven, and was incarnate of the Holy Spirit and the Virgin Mary, and became man; and was crucified also for us under Pontius Pilate, and suffered and was buried; and the third day He rose again according to the Scriptures; and ascended into heaven and sits at the right hand of the Father. And He shall come again with glory to judge the living and the dead; of His kingdom there shall be no end. And in the Holy Spirit, the Lord, the Giver of life, Who proceedeth from the Father, Who with the Father and the Son together is worshiped and glorified, Who spoke by the prophets. In one Holy Catholic and Apostolic Church; I confess one baptism for the forgiveness of sins; I look for the resurrection of the dead and the life of the age to come. Amen."

There is one serious difference between the Eastern Orthodox version quoted above and the version used by the western churches. Sometime after our story the Catholic church formally inserted into the Latin text the word filioque, meaning "and Son," after the text: "And in the Holy Spirit, the Lord, the Giver of life, Who proceedeth from the Father." This substantially altered the meaning and remains today probably the major theological stumbling block separating them.

Nike – Literally "Victory". The Nike was doubtless the most serious - and bloody – domestic insurrection ever staged against the Roman throne. There were numerous attempts to seize the throne by dissident generals throughout the history of Rome and Byzantium, but the Nike revolt is unique in that it can be seen as an attempt by the populace to overthrow a totalitarian government. Certainly, the aristocratic historians of the time would not have sympathized with it. There was no call for a return to democracy, or for rule by the senate. The rioters only wanted to replace one emperor with another. That the rioters were a rabble is surely true, but likely low-lifes too poor to be heavily taxed. Therefore, so far as their motivation being anger at the arrest of criminal leaders, Procopius may be telling the truth. (Though that has the disturbingly modern sound of a dictator's propaganda.) However, the rioters were supported by a part of the aristocracy which saw its wealth being taxed away by Justinian.

Ninja - A supposed secret society of Japanese assassins. I use the term here not because Cappadochian John's guards resembled Ninja but to emphasize their skill and purchased loyalty. They were not like the veteran lancers of Dara and Ad Decimum, but a tyrant's shield. The guards surrounding Belisarius, when in Constantinople, were on parade and one might, from time-to-time, place his plumed helmet on a six year old "cataphract's" head and lift the child for a better view of his master. John's guards maintained a security ring around him, watching the hands of anyone who came nearby for any weapon. I did take a bit of liberty with Procopius' description however. He says that John was surrounded by hordes of guards whereas I make it a few ninja-like experts. Our point is the same, however. The guards were to protect him from assassins, not, as in the case of Belisarius, on parade.

No man can serve two masters. - (Math 6:24)

Non Chalcedon - a term now used to identify members of any sect which rejected the formula created at the Council of Chalcedon. In the past these were often less accurately lumped together as Monophysites.

Noncom - The modern term means non-commissioned officer (sergeants, corporals) but soldiers have always been close to their noncom, who shares the danger of battle and is both nursemaid and disciplinarian.
Nuts - Common American slang at the time of World War II, used to express contempt and refusal. During the Battle of the Bulge, General Tony McAuliffe sent this as his reply to the German commander who was demanding the surrender of the American Forces at Bastogne.

Onagra - The onagra was a catapult used to hurl large stones.
Orthodox – See Catholic.
Ostrogoths - The Goths of our story. At the behest of the emperor Zeno in Constantinople, (whom their leader, Theodoric the Great, was intermittently harassing), they had moved into Italy replacing Odoacer, a German in the employ of the Roman empire. Odoacer was the first king of Italy having deposed the last emperor there. In theory he ruled in the name of the remaining emperor in Constantinople, a fiction which Theodoric maintained, ruling his own Goths as king but the local Italians as the representative of Zeno. See also: Goths.

Padishah, Shahanshah - Great king, king of kings.
Palla, Pallium - A Roman cloak-like overgarment for both men and women which could extend to the hem of the tunica, but was often draped over the arm. It could be used to cover the head. In time it became an imperial garment and is now an ecclesiastical garment derived from that usage.
Pantocrator, Christ - Christ, the Ruler Of All; the central figure in the dome of eastern churches.
Patriarch of Constantinople - Originally there were three patriarchates in Christendom: those of Rome, Antioch, and Alexandria. Constantinople was added when that city was founded as a "New Rome." The Patriarch of Constantinople still deferred to the primacy of Rome however. Since the office of emperor no longer existed in barbarian-occupied Rome, but pope did, the emperor (as political head of the church) called and presided over church councils, but papal legates assumed first place among the bishops.
Patrician - An aristocrat. This ancient Latin title originated in Rome during the republic.
Pharos lighthouse - One of the wonders of the ancient world, it was on Pharos Island near Alexandria. The lighthouse was built in the third century BC, was damaged a number of times, and was destroyed by an earthquake in the fourteenth century AD. There were many implausible stories of its

great mirror, such as its light being visible in Constantinople and it being able to set fire to ships at sea.

Philosophy - The Athenian schools of pagan philosophy were closed by Justinian but many intellectuals, including Church leaders, were well versed in philosophy. The orthodoxy of those who tried to reconcile Christianity with philosophy was always suspect however. It seems particularly apt to this author that Justinian, who wanted sectarian peace, closed the schools. The Fathers of the Church seem to me to have been more interested in angry argument and supporting their personal views by dissecting the divinity of Christ according to the methodology of Greek philosophy, than in fostering Christian love, or, if one will, the moral teaching of Holy Jesus the Jew.

Plague – See Bubonic plague.

Political commissars - One of the weaknesses of the Soviet military was that commanders at all levels were shadowed by political commissars, whose duty it was both to indoctrinate the soldiers and to report on officers, if their commitment to the party seemed weak.

Polo horses - Variants on the game of polo have probably existed for as long as men have ridden horses, but the direct antecedent of our game was first played in Persia, from where it was introduced into Byzantium before the time of our story.

Polytheistic paganism - The paganism of early Roman history was essentially worship of the same gods as did the Greeks, with the important addition of Vesta, goddess of the hearth fire. About the same time that Christianity was spreading, however, other cults also were. Although they might sometimes adopt the old Roman names they were very different, like Christianity, emphasizing individual piety and salvation. It is a little difficult therefore to generalize about the remnants of paganism, and to what extent polytheism might still be believed in by simple people. Likewise, to what extent educated pagans saw one god under the appearance of many.

Praepositus of the Sacred Bed Chamber - Justinian's grand chamberlain Narses. In Byzantium all power resided in the emperor but the grand chamberlain was probably as near to being a prime minister as there was.

Pride goeth before a fall – A common misquote. The biblical text is properly translated as Pride goes before destruction, and a haughty spirit before stumbling. (Proverbs: 16-18) The sense remains the same however.

Prostration - In the ritual of the Orthodox Church, at Divine Services most of the time is spent standing; only the enfeebled sit. There is little kneeling as in the west but there is prostration. This is akin to the Muslim ritual. The worshiper kneels on the floor with his hands before him and touches his head to the floor. It is unlike prostration at the ordination of priests in the Western Church who lie entirely flat. I should note here that while there was

336

as yet no breach between the churches of Rome and Constantinople, there were and are differences in ritual.

Resquiescat in Pace - Latin for Rest in Peace.

Romans - The Byzantines never called themselves Byzantine. They considered themselves Roman, by which they meant members of a Christian Roman empire. I usually follow this usage except during the siege of Rome where to do so would mean confusion with the local citizenry. The term Roman was the Byzantines' term for themselves. It came to signify a Christian unity centered politically in Constantinople; and also the Eastern Empire itself: "the Land of the Romans." They never called themselves Byzantine and were offended when called Greek. This is not unreasonable since the empire extended over non Greek territory in Asia and, at times, in Sicily, North Africa, and parts of Italy; all of which were Christian.

Sacred - Often used as an adjective for imperial properties (Sacred Palace, etc.) since the emperor was considered Christ's deputy on earth and the political head of the church and the Christian people.

Santa Maria in Trivio - Though much rebuilt, Belisarius' little church, or oratory, is still extant in Rome. Nothing of the original but the dedication stone is still recognizable however.

Saracen - The term properly refers to Arabs of the Syrian desert and nearby. However in the middle ages it became a synonym for Arabs and Muslims generally.

Saravan - The old Persian nobility. Belisarius and his infantry faced saravan cataphracts at Dara, the new Dehgan cataphracts in the second Persian war.

Sassanid - The Persian empire at the time of our story was ruled by the Sassanid dynasty, (224 AD to 651 AD). It replaced the Parthian empire of classical times and was itself replaced by an Islamic caliphate. The reign of Chosroes (Kavadh I) in our story is considered the Sassanids' golden era.

Scale armor - There are technical differences between the scale armor of Roman legions and the laminar armor of the Byzantines but they both consisted of loose iron plates which could deflect a slash or stop a thrust. Chain mail was also employed.

Scholari - These were not scholars but palace guards more accustomed to fancy dress than actual fighting. They would have received military training, but had little military experience, except, perhaps, for occasional riot control.

Scriptoria - The room, usually in a convent or monastery, where books are recopied.

Semi-monophysitism – As may be imagined, this was not a single group, but any Monophysite sect which tried to compromise Monophysitism with Chalcedonian orthodoxy. (See also: Chalcedon, Council of.)

Senate, senator - By this time the Roman Senate was powerless, however being a senator still carried prestige both in Constantinople and Rome

Sergius and Bacchus, Church of - Still in use as the mosque Kucuk Ayasofya.

Sic transit gloria mundi – Latin for: Thus passes all worldly glory.

Silk - In the story no mention is made of it, but it was in the reign of Justinian that Europe was freed from reliance upon China for silk. In Europe, silk garments were an important sign of prestige among rulers and aristocrats, but in times past the raw material (or when necessary dyed silk) had been brought overland from China. These came via one of the "silk roads" through the Gobi desert and across the 'stans of western Asia (Turkmenistan, Uzbekistan, etc.), or across northern India and up the Persian Gulf. The secret of producing silk had been kept a state secret in China. However, during the reign of Justinian, a pair of missionaries to China returned with silk worm eggs and the secret of raising the worms on mulberry trees. This was made an imperial monopoly and source of revenue to the exchequer. (As a curious aside, I'd like to mention that Syrian merchants had sometimes brought dyed Chinese silk garments to the empire, where some might be bleached and rewoven to be resold again in China as "Roman silk.")

Slavery – Though I make little of slavery in the story, slavery was very much a fact of life in Byzantium. It is recorded that seven thousand slaves were used in the construction of the cistern referred to. Two mitigating things should be noted. First, as elsewhere in Europe, the difference between slaves and free men working farms and large estates was becoming less, as the free were more and more bound to the land or occupation of their fathers. Second, the treatment of the slave was necessarily more humane than in ancient Rome. He was a child of God now, and likely a Christian. The church disapproved of slavery but the institution was never seriously threatened. Parenthetically, the term slave is derived from Slav since the trade in slaves north of the Black Sea was so general. The Latin word was servus from which the English servant descends.

Solidus - The standard gold coin of Byzantium; it was accepted at face value throughout the Western world because it was not devalued for eight hundred years.

Spathion - A long double edged sword intended more for striking than

338

piercing as had been the case with the Roman <u>gladius</u>. In the cavalry version, it was not designed for piercing at all.

St. Nicholas fund - A fictional fund to help poor girls. (See <u>Nicholas, St.</u> in the names appendix.)

Status quo ante bellum - Latin for the state of affairs as they were before a war. An example would be the cease fire at the end of the Korean war, which reestablished the 38th parallel as the border between North and South Korea essentially as it had been before the war began.

Stola - A woman's upper garment that in early Byzantium fell to the waist. In later centuries it became longer and was effectively indistinguishable from the men's <u>dalmatic</u>. Our story is in a period of transition from the classical to the medieval world. For example, Justinian spoke a decadent rural form of Latin as his native tongue, but he was the last emperor to use Latin at all. So too, dress was changing into its quintessential Byzantine ornateness compared with the restraint of classic Greek and Roman clothing.

Strategos - The Byzantine term for a general, though I make only limited use of the word. As with our own usage, it is a generic term. Not all Strategoi or American generals hold the same rank and authority.

Strategos autokrator - The Greek equivalent of the Roman **imperator**; a theater commander. This was Belisarius' title for the first Gothic war. I place this promotion at the beginning of the Vandal war though it was actually slightly later, at the beginning of the first Gothic war.

Superstition, witchcraft, spells, divination, etc. - Amulets and curses were as popular as in pagan times, though I make little of it in the story. Icons were believed to have the power to heal or to have been made "not by human hands." In Constantinople priests riled against foreign superstition, but were blind to it when it had a Christian face. Science was unreliable; the unseen powers, both good and bad, were not. The future might be known to Christians who correctly interpreted the stars which reflected the Divine will, or from dreams. Less respectably it might be made known to those versed in pagan lore who could interpret thunder or the flight of birds. pagan superstition and custom was seen as demonic and evil; yet not fraudulent.

Suzerain - A nation that controls another nation in international affairs but allows it domestic sovereignty; or a feudal lord to whom fealty is due.

Sythian - A rather generalized term that can refer to various peoples from what are now Iran, central Russia, Rumania, and the Ukraine.

Tactical defensive - Belisarius was not one to hide behind walls but he did use them. At Dara he stood on the defensive until the Persians had exhausted themselves and then counterattacked. He stood a year-long siege in Rome but fought sixty nine battles and skirmishes outside the walls, while plague did its worst in the Gothic camp. Only when the exhausted Goths retreated did he begin his march to their capital of Ravenna. **Take therefore no thought for the morrow for the morrow shall take care of itself.** (Math 6:24)

Temples - It might seem at first that with the end of paganism in the Roman empire more temples would have been converted to Christian worship. That didn't happen but not because of revulsion at their previous use. Christians might decry paganism but they often continued its traditions by one excuse or another. However, with their forests of columns, most temples were not architecturally suitable for large crowds to gather in to hear sermons, offer the mass, and commune with one another. They were places for pagan priests to offer sacrifices, or for occasional private visits to ask a special favor of a god. In this they were like Buddhist temples in Japan. Instead, Christians adopted the open basilica form of building which had been developed by the Romans for more public activities. This remains the basis of most traditional Western churches, having a long central section with windows high in the walls and divided by an aisle. Lower roofed sections on either side provide additional light. Later, another two sections were added at ninety degrees to form a cross and in the typical Byzantine configuration a place for a large dome.

Theotokos - Greek term for Mary as the God bearer, or as preferred in the west, "Mother of God." The term is important since the Nestorians would only concede the title Christotokos or Christ-bearer (Messiah bearer). God-bearer is more precise than Mother of God since it avoids misunderstanding of Mary's role. She could not have been eternally the mother of God, but rather the bearer of Christ's human nature. Yet since orthodox doctrine after the Council of Nicaea accepted the perfect blending of Christ's two natures the title of God bearer is permitted. (See Nicene formula.)

Thracians - Thrace is located west of Constantinople. It was on the Thracian-Macedonian border that Belisarius was born. But see the note under Macedonians.

Three Chapters controversy - An attempt by Justinian to reconcile both the Non-Chalcedonian Christians of Syria and the Egyptian Copts, with the Chalcedonians, by condemning certain writings considered Nestorian. It failed at least in part because Pope Vigilius vacillated about signing (or not signing) the agreement. This may be because it was difficult in the Latin translation to comprehend the subtlety of the Greek originals.

340

Third watch – (Midnight to 3:00 AM) Traditionally a watch is a set number of hours that a soldier or sailor stands guard duty. "From the morning watch even unto night let Israel hope in the Lord." (Psalm 130:6) The term "third watch" is sometimes used to emphasize the loneliness of night duty.

Thou shalt not murder - Belisarius would have been familiar with the more accurate Greek Septuagint translation of the Hebrew than our common "Thou shalt not kill." The latter is derived from the Latin Vulgate of St. Jerome. The difference is, of course, all important for a soldier.

Time - The Roman day was divided into twenty four hours: Twelve during daylight, and twelve at night. The length of each day or night hour would necessarily depend on the time of year. There were sundials and water clocks which would, however, be largely inaccurate, if only because the clock would register each hour as of equal time.

Torture and atrocities - It was a rough age. That is what can be said for Byzantine punishment, particularly their inclination to blind wrongdoers, slit noses, and remove body parts. Belisarius was no exception. Though there is no record of him removing parts, he could slit the nose of a traitor. In their defense it can be said that before the modern age long term incarceration was unusual. The usual punishments worldwide were death, exile (including internal exile in monasteries), and mutilation. Having one's hands removed does discourage theft and having one's tongue removed does restrict slander and the spread of seditious plots. None of this was new. Cruel punishments were inherited from the Romans and especially from the customs of Rome's conquered Eastern provinces. The Byzantines did not create cruelty; they simply did not eliminate it. Little by little, however, Christian charity did demand better treatment. It would be wrong to view these punishments only as cruelty. If there was little long-term incarceration in prisons (which might have been a blessing), wrongdoers might be sent to monasteries. At times, prostitutes were offered or sent to group homes which can be viewed as prisons or as rehabilitation centers depending on one's point of view. The blinding of a traitor, rather than his execution, left him alive to repent his sacrilege against the Elect of God, so that he might avoid eternal damnation at the judgment. Justinian tended to be merciful toward his political enemies, though whether it was truly mercy or good politics is a matter of opinion. Procopius accuses Theodora of imprisoning enemies in dark cells under the palace. If that is true - and it may be an exaggeration - this was political or personal spite, not punishment for crime.

Trojan war - The great Greek epic is Homer's *Iliad* in which Greek heroes under Agamemnon defeated the Phrygian city of Troy in modern day

Turkey.

Triumph – In ancient Rome a victorious general or emperor might be granted a great victory parade, called a triumph. He would ride in a gilded chariot leading his troops and captives, through triumphal arches, to be granted the wreath of victory. I use the term a bit loosely here. For one thing, Belisarius walked afoot and, importantly, the parade was not called a triumph. By then, triumphs had for some centuries been reserved for emperors. Of course the important pagan religious elements had been stripped and replaced with Christian ceremonies. Even so, the resemblance was real and would not have been lost on the crowd.

Tunica, Tunic - The undergarment of the upper classes and the only garment of the lower. Men's tunics came to the knee, women's to the ankle.

Twins - There is no record of Antonina bearing twins who died young; but Procopius does charge her with having had multiple pregnancies and abortions. Since he'd have had no way of knowing that Antonina had abortions before her marriage, I split the difference and give her a pregnancy with the children dying young. That, of course, was extremely common in her time.

Van - The vanguard of an army.

Vandals - An East German tribe that entered the Roman Empire in the fifth century. They sacked Rome and their deprecations while retreating through France to Spain, where they set up a kingdom, has linked the name of this tribe with Wanton destruction. Under king <u>Genseric</u> they entered Africa from Spain. They also held Corsica and, for a time, <u>Sicily</u>.

Vespers - Sunset, the eighth canonical hour. The prayers ordained for that time.

Visigoths - Originally the Visigoths and <u>Ostrogoths</u> were united, but as their invasion of the Roman empire progressed, first the Visigoths, and later the Ostrogoths, attacked Italy. Famously the Visigoths defeated the Romans at the battle of Adrianople and, under their chieftain Alaric, sacked Rome. They did not, however, remain in Italy, but moved on to southern France and Spain.

Walls of Theodosius - Built in the fifth century after the city of Constantine the Great had expanded to a population of perhaps as many as one million, the triple land walls - still extant today - were a marvel of medieval defense. They withstood numerous attacks until 1453 AD, when, after a prolonged siege, the Turks finally breached them with artillery.

Whore de jure - I'm just playing with words, although I can certainly imagine some WW II GI in France using the expression.

Wine dark sea - Term used excessively by the poet <u>Homer</u> to describe the Mediterranean in the Odyssey.

Woman caught in adultery (John 53: 8-11) Jesus intervened to save the life of an adulteress, where he famously said to the crowd: " Let he who is without sin cast the first stone," and proceeded to doodle in the sand. When he looked up again the crowd had melted away. He then simply told her to "Go and sin no more."

Your Serenity, Your Sovereignty – See note under <u>Elect of God</u>.

Zoroastrianism - The Persian national religion founded by the prophet Zoroaster (or <u>Zarathustra)</u> in the sixth century BC. The Persians worshiped <u>Ahura Mazda</u> in the form of fire so cremation was a desecration. However Mazdan religion also stresses the need to quickly dispose of the dead, lest disease spread from the corrupting corpses. See <u>Ahura Mazda</u> in the Names appendix.

NAMES

Abandanes - One of the royal secretaries of <u>Chosroes</u>. During the Third Persian campaign, he was sent to Belisarius' camp in order to find out what sort of a man he might be.

Adolius - During the Third Persian Campaign, Belisarius deceived <u>Chosroes</u> by sending two thousand men across the Euphrates who appeared able to prevent Chosroes' much larger force from crossing the river. One of these men was Adolius, an Armenian by birth, who served the emperor while in the palace as privy counselor but at that time was commander of some Armenians. We know nothing more of him. It is interesting to note, however, that <u>Narses</u> was far from being the only person, normally a civilian, who had experience of war and command. Nor, parenthetically, was Belisarius the only man in the ancient world to be given high rank while still young.

Aeschylus - The father of Tragedy (c 525/524 BC - c 455/456 BC) was the first of the three ancient Greek tragedians whose work has survived.

Africanus - Justinian calls Belisarius a "new Africanus" in imitation of the Roman general <u>Scipio Africanus</u>. Scipio received that title as conqueror of Africa (Libya) in 202 BC, when he defeated the Carthaginians under <u>Hannibal</u>, thus ending the Punic Wars with the absolute extermination of Carthaginian power.

Agamemnon - Leader of the Greek force in the <u>Trojan War</u>, seventeen hundred years previous.

Agatha - A fictional friend of Antonina who had taken her under her wing.

Agathias Scholasticus - Byzantine historian who wrote *On the Reign of Justinian,* and continues the history of Procopius. He is the chief authority for the period 552-558 AD and deals chiefly with the struggles of the imperial army in Italy under the command of <u>Narses</u>.

Ahura Mazda - In <u>Zoroastrianism</u>, Ahura Mazda is the uncreated primary god, though not the only spirit. There is a struggle between the good creator (Ahura Mazda) and evil personified in Ahriman. The founder of Zoroastrianism was the prophet <u>Zarathustra</u>. Essentially dualist in theology it is yet monotheistic in that Ahura Mazda is the only uncreated spirit, and in the end evil will be destroyed. Worship is made in the purifying presence of sunlight or fire and the dead are left to be devoured by birds so as not to pollute the earth by burial, or pollute fire by cremation.

Aileen – A fictional friend of both Belisarius and Antonina.

Alamoundaras - Chieftain of the Arab <u>Hira</u> tribe. Loyal to the Persian throne, he led an Arab attack against Antioch from across the Syrian desert, together with Azarethes' heavy cavalry.

Alexander Psallidion - Known as" the Snips" or "Scissors," he was sent to Italy after Belisarius had been recalled at the end of the First Gothic War. He gained the nickname from the dry joke that he could remove a bit of gold from a coin without it being apparent. Alexander headed up an office of tax collection in Italy which plundered the citizens and also cheated the Byzantine foederati and mercenaries. Many of these deserted to the Goths, making it easier for them to return to power. Justinian's short sighted taxation was strictly enforced because Alexander received a twelfth of all the revenue. It is admitted by all that Italy was ravished during the campaigns of the eleven generals, the five years of Belisarius' second command, and the final conquest by Narses. This ruined military morale and turned the Italians against the Byzantines. Alexander was much to blame. If, as Procopius claims, Belisarius unduly enriched himself, it was by excessive withdrawals from the treasuries of Genseric and Witiges, not from his soldiers or the peasant farmers.

Amalafrida - The Vandal king, Thrasimund, had wed the Gothic princess Amalafrida, the sister of Theodoric the Great. After Thrasimund's death she and her six thousand Gothic guards were slaughtered by the new king Hilderic, a near relative of Thrasimund. This act demolished the alliance between the Goths in Italy and the Vandals in North Africa, forcing Hilderic to seek an alliance with Byzantium, by offering his allegiance to Justinian's predecessor. The Emperor Justin.

Amalasontha - The daughter of Theodoric the Great she was especially well educated and could speak Greek and the Gothic languages equally well. She acted as regent for her son Athalaric who, however, died before ascending the Gothic throne. She then married Theodatus, a nephew of Theodoric, but he had her murdered in her bath so as not to share the throne. The regency of Amalasontha is considered a high point of the Gothic kingdom for she generally continued the wiser policies of Theodoric and supported the careers of both Boethius and Cassiodorus.

Ammatas - Genseric's cousin who commanded the Carthage garrison. Genseric required him to kill Hilderic, the rightful king of the Vandals, and also Hilderic's close supporters. Then he was to attack and hold Belisarius at Ad Decimum. His impetuous piecemeal attack cost him the battle and his life, and in all likelihood cost Genseric his throne.

Anastasius - Belisarius' daughter Joannina was betrothed to Theodora's nephew (or grandson) Anastasius. But Belisarius and Antonina put off the marriage and Theodora died before they could be wed. Procopius alleges that Theodora forced the pair to live together and that they then fell in love.

346

According to him, after Theodora died and Antonina returned to Italy, she drove Anastasius away, yet some historians believe they married.

Andreas - In civilian life Andreas had been a wrestling coach. We know nothing else about this champion other than this anecdote from Procopius.

Anthemius Antonius - Antonina traveled to the East as a concubine to a minor dignitary or merchant. Although this much is true, his name and the details in our narrative are fictional.

Anthimus - The Monophysite whom Theodora had managed to have appointed as Patriarch of Constantinople (535-536). After being deposed by Pope Agapetus, the predecessor of Silvarius, he was hidden by Theodora until his death. Neither Pope Silvarius nor Pope Vigilius would restore him, although Vigilius had led Theodora to believe he would if he himself were made pope.

Antonina - Our heroine. The cover image of this book, based on the Ravenna mosaics, is believed to be an accurate portrait, as are those of the other key figures in the mosaic. In the originals Antonina, together with Belisarius' daughter Joannina, is standing next to Theodora, and Belisarius is beside Justinian. Narses lurks behind the emperor.

Appius - Fictional senator who found Antonina nursing the injured of Antioch after that city's multiple disasters, and who played matchmaker between Antonina and Belisarius. We do not know how the famous couple actually met. Historians are inclined to assume that Antonina was a friend of Theodora from their earlier lives in Constantinople. Yet there are problems with that scenario. For one thing, Procopius makes no mention of such a friendship which I think he would have; and there is no report of their paths having crossed in their years as concubines. Besides, it is doubtful to me that Theodora and Justinian would have had friends from the streets surrounding them at court as has been suggested. Theodora did help (or incarcerate) prostitutes who wanted to get out of the business or were too old for the life, but that does not mean such as these were friends at court. Certainly Antonina was special. That does not necessarily mean that they'd been lifelong friends; a coincidental meeting of a senator dispatched to Antioch after the second earthquake and the "widow" of an official of that city and agent of the empire is as probable. No one knows; this is fiction folks.

Archelaus - The Admiral commanding the invasion fleet in the African campaign.

Arnold, Benedict - For non American readers, Arnold, probably George Washington's best general, tried to betray the American fortress at West

Point to the British. Afterward he led British forces against the colonists but fled to England before the war's conclusion. In London he was honored by the king but the remainder of his life was troubled by financial scandal and disrespect from his fellow officers.

Ascan - A friend of Belisarius, who, after killing many of the notables among the Persians, was gradually hacked to pieces and finally fell in the battle at Callinicum. This much can be said for Procopius that, true to then literary tradition, on many occasions he did immortalize heroic men.

Augustine of Hippo, St. - The most important Father of the Church and, together with the much later Thomas Aquinas, the most important Doctors of the Church. In his *City of God*, St. Augustine successfully defended Christianity against those pagans who were blaming the sack of Rome by the Visigoths (410 AD) on desertion of the ancient gods.

Azarethes - With fifteen thousand Persian heavy cavalry, together with Alamoundaras' Arabs, he attacked Antioch across the Syrian desert.

Basiliscus – In 468 AD the emperor Leo I had sent a huge fleet under the command of Basiliscus, his brother in Law, against the Vandal kingdom in North Africa. The Vandals pretended submission, but requested time to arrange details. This was a ruse. As soon as there were suitable winds, they sent fire ships and their galleys against the Roman fleet. Nearly the entire invasion force was killed.

Belisarius - According to one learned guess, the name is a transliteration of the Slavonic "Beli-Tsar," or "White Prince." Procopius elsewhere says Belisarius came from Germania, a village "on the border of Thrace and Illyria." Thus both the Germans and the Hungarians have been able to claim this general as an early hero of their race. But, it is supposition.

Bessas - Himself a Thracian Goth, Bessas was a loyal supporter of Belisarius in the Gothic wars. In fact he intervened physically when Constantinus tried to kill Belisarius. Yet he damaged his reputation by hoarding supplies when Rome was under siege in the Second Gothic War and selling them at exorbitant prices to the more wealthy. How serious the hunger in Rome actually was has been disputed by Lord Mahon. Procopius was not at this siege and his description may be more imagination than real. He may have simply repeated stock descriptions of a city under siege and exaggerated the avarice of Bessas. What cannot be disputed, is that at a time when Bloody John was ravishing southern Italy, Bessas' failure to support Belisarius' attack on Rome cost him an important symbolic victory.

Bloody John - See John, Bloody.

Boethius - It was in Rome in the time of Theodoric that Boethius, the last Roman philosopher to deserve that name, lived.

Bouzes (Buzes) - Bouzes, who was a Thracian, appears many times in Procopius' history. He was at the battle of Mindon, and held the important left cavalry wing at Dara. He succeeded Sittas when that general was killed during the Armenian revolt and brought that war to an end by treacherously killing one of its leaders. For awhile he held command during the Second Persian War until the arrival of Belisarius from Italy. The kindest thing one can say of him in that war was that he avoided combat. According to Procopius he fled the besieged city of Hierapolis taking the best of his troops with him, and took for himself the money that the citizens of Edessa had contributed for the ransom of prisoners from Antioch after that city fell to the Persians. When Justinian and Theodora sought to charge Belisarius with treachery because he did not support Theodora's claim to rule, when Justinian nearly died of the plague, they could find no evidence to convict him. Bouzes, however, was imprisoned as an example. Later he held some minor commands.

Caesar, Thucydides, and Xenophon - Julius Caesar wrote his self-serving *Commentaries* on his victories in Gaul; Thucydides wrote the *History of the Peloponnesian War* in which he was a general, and Xenophon wrote the *Anabasis*, the history of his fighting retreat with 10,000 Greek mercenaries out of Persia. All these classics of western literature, history, and military science were written by fighting participants.

Callista - Antonina's first daughter and the wife of Ildiger.

Cassiodorus, Flavius - Cassiodorus was effectively the prime minister to Theodoric the Great, but is better known for bridging the gap between classical learning and medieval spirituality.

Chosroes (Khosrau I) - King of Persia, also called Nushirvan the Just. Our story is written from the Roman perspective as detailed by procopius, but in Persia (Iran) his reign is considered a high point of their history.

Cicero, Marcus Tullius – Roman Consul for the year 63 BC, Cicero was not only a great orator but is held up as the finest example of the duties and privileges of being a Roman patrician in the time of the Republic. His orations to the Roman senate remain the backbone of a classical education in the Latin tongue. (See: Verres)

Constantine the Great - Constantine I. He founded the eastern capital in 330 AD to split the administration of the unwieldy empire. Ir didn't take long, however, for the two halves to turn against each other.

Constantinus - A competent, if headstrong, subordinate in North Africa and during the siege of Rome, he was executed by Belisarius after he attempted to kill the general. Most texts give his name as Constantine; I keep the Latin and reserve the name Constantine for <u>Constantine the Great</u>, the first of many emperors and kings of that name.

Cosmas and Damian, Sts. - Roman physicians who were tortured and executed during the Roman persecution of Christianity.

Coutzes and Bouzes – Commanders who were charged with supporting Belisarius at Mindon. The battle was lost but Procopius is unclear as to why. Perhaps unfairly, I have placed the blame on these two brothers who, like Belisarius, were young Thracian nobles. <u>Bouzes</u> was to appear elsewhere in our story.

Cyril - A fictional carpenter to whom Antonina apprenticed Photius in Antioch.

Diana - Goddess of the hunt in classical Greek mythology. The classic stories were still very much a part of everyday life throughout the Byzantine era.

Dickens, Charles - British author best known for his depiction of slum life in nineteenth century London.

Diocletian - Roman emperor who first formally divided the empire for administrative purposes. Unlike <u>Constantine</u>, however, he did not found a new city to be a second Rome, but set the administration at wherever the co-emperors were residing at a given time, such as <u>Milan</u> and <u>Ravenna</u>.

Eisenhower, Dwight - Ike, as he was known, was famous for his wide, friendly, and confident grin, although he also showed a famous temper in private. He made it a point to keep in mind that the soldiers who would die on his orders were not just numbers or "the boys." According to Hugh Ambrose, he tried to have as many as possible see the man who would be sending them into combat; and he personally signed the letter of condolence to the family of every soldier who died under his command. It is unusual to see such effort to force himself to empathize in other great conquerors or in dictators. But unlike commanders who were passed over for supreme command in Europe, he'd had no combat experience, and his first command of fighting troops was the less than impressive North African campaign. He enjoyed playing poker with his staff.

Eugenius - A servant of <u>Antonia,</u> to whom <u>Procopius</u> likes to attribute the actual carrying out of the crimes of which he accuses his mistress.

Euphemia - Former empress, wife of <u>Justin I</u>. Also the name of the daughter of <u>John the Cappadocian</u>.

Galen - The most honored physician of ancient Rome whose theories seem to have been wrong about nearly everything, save for some insight into brain and nerve function. He was however a successful physician on the practical level, probably because of his emphasis on a healthy diet, exercise, and hygiene. Not to underrate his ability, the author would compare him with Ptolemy in astronomy. Both were brilliant for their time, and doubtless men who would have held correct theories had they known them, but their opinions became a dead hand on lesser men, who blindly followed in their shadows until the Renaissance.

Gelimer - Vandal king of North Africa during the Vandal War. He imprisoned and later had the rightful king murdered.

Genseric - He had been the greatest of Vandal leaders. He also had been tolerant of Catholic ritual in the North African kingdom.

Gibbon, Edward - Author of the eighteenth century classic but prejudiced, *Decline and Fall of the Roman Empire*. Gibbon bears responsibility for describing the "fall" as the "triumph of Christianity and barbarism." His was a Renaissance view which, because he revered the classic, diminished the medieval. Certainly Christian Europe was a moral, if not a material advance over ancient Roman society; and Byzantium was the highest civilization west of China until it was supplanted by Islam. Even modern medicine and technology descends from the medieval rather than the ancient world where theory was rarely applied to practice. (Slaves were cheap, so why bother with machines?) To his credit, Gibbon was not blinded by religious myths and exaggeration and that was what made his views both critical and controversial, if unbalanced, in the eighteenth century. That said, the golden age of Roman philosophy and rhetoric was already gone when Christianity appeared; the architecture of the ancient world was adapted to the new religion and that can be seen, not as a decline, but as a vibrant change. The lot of the poor had been slavery and it was slave and army labor which built the empire. Nor was life in the Roman army something to be sought after. Discipline was cruel and the term of enlistment twenty to twenty five years. Yet even so, it was no longer able to effectively address the barbarian threat. Certainly medieval life was hard, but so had Roman been if one were not wealthy. Certainly it was superstitious, but the Roman population had been even more so. Much was lost with the end of the empire in the west but what was lost was not lost because of invasion or change in religion. At the same time, a new culture was developing which, at least in theory, valued the individual and would, in time, lead to the enlightenment.

Gilbamundus - A nephew of Gelimer who was instructed by the king to attack the Romans across a salt flat from the south of <u>Ad Decimum</u>. He was prevented in this and his force was decimated by Ephthalite archers.

Gregorovius, Ferdinand - Nineteenth century author of eight volumes on the *History of the City of Rome in the Middle ages.* His work is no doubt thorough but not as enjoyable as Hodgkin's. He is more critical of Belisarius than many authors and constantly refers to the Byzantine army as Greeks, which I do not think he means as a compliment and which is decidedly incorrect anyway. One might not want to follow the Byzantine custom of calling themselves Romans, but they would have been insulted to be identified as simply Greeks. The empire was far too extensive for that.

Hannibal - The guy who tried to take elephants across the Alps - but lost all but one of them. He defeated numerous Roman armies in North Italy, but was forced to return to <u>Carthage</u> when <u>Scipio</u> invaded his homeland. He lost.

Hecebolus of Tyre - Theodora's consort before Justinian. He was a senator and the governor of Cyrenaica. They lived in the city of Sozousa. He did her wrong.

Hector - Greek hero of the <u>Trojan war</u>, immortalized by <u>Homer</u>.

Herodotus – Ancient Greek historian (5th century BC). In his *Histories* he describes the wars between Greece and Persia together with the causes. He is often called the Father of History because he analyzed events and motives and did not simply describe events or attribute the outcome to the gods alone.

Hermogenes - A soldier-diplomat, Hermogenes accompanied Belisarius at <u>Dara</u>, and commanded a part of the Roman cavalry.

Hilderic - **Thrasimund's** successor as Vandal king, he was imprisoned and finally killed on <u>Gelimer's</u> orders. Gelimer's coup was Justinian's excuse for invading Africa.

Hodgkin, Thomas - I cannot but admire Hodgkin's eight volumes with their chapter-long asides (For example:The aqueducts of Rome, the life of St Benedict) and poetic quotes (often from *Horatius At The Bridge,* which at his time all schoolboys learned.)

Homer - Ancient Greek poet. Classical learning was far more valued in Byzantium than in the West. The Byzantines never ceased to study and imitate ancient models in literature and history.

Hypatius - Senator who was persuaded by the crowd at the hippodrome to assume the imperial regalia during the <u>Nike</u> riots. He was aged and he and his brother Pompeius initially did not want the attention. Procopius says that Justinian would have pardoned the old men but that Theodora would not have it so.

Ildiger - Besides being Belisarius' son-in-law, he was a competent subordinate. He was the husband of Antonina's first daughter, <u>Callista</u>. He was Sent to Libya after Belisarius' victory. Later he joined Belisarius in Italy. He prevented a Gothic entrance to Rome through an aqueduct and was responsible for saving <u>Bloody John</u> at <u>Rimini</u>.

Irenaeus – The <u>Dux</u> Irenaeus was dispatched from Constantinople, with a troop of imperial soldiers to arrest the <u>Monophysite</u> patriarch <u>Severus</u> and bring him to the capital to answer charges of heresy.

Isaac of Armenia - A sub-commander who was charged by Belisarius with holding <u>Porto</u>, while he was attempting to recapture Rome. His impetuous attack on a detachment of Goths cost Belisarius the battle.

Joannina - The only child of Belisarius, Theodora wanted to have her nephew <u>Anastasius</u> marry Joannina in order (according to Procopius) to acquire Belisarius' wealth. It is not known whether these lovers married after Theodora died.

John the Armenian - John led the successful dash through <u>Ad Decimum</u> but was accidentally killed while fighting the retreating Vandals at <u>Tricamaron</u>.

John (Bloody John) - A thorn in the side of Belisarius during the Gothic Wars, nevertheless he was an aggressive leader of men. Procopius charges him with caring more about looting easy districts in Italy than achieving strategic success. It was difficult for Belisarius to control John while John's friend the grand chamberlain <u>Narses</u> was in Italy. His impetuous seizure of <u>Rimini</u> gave Narses an opportunity to share strategic decision with Belisarius. During the Second Gothic War, John married the niece of Justinian, and that link with the imperial family further emboldened his, so that he hardly felt any need to obey Belisarius. From a strategic standpoint, however, his constant raiding - while Belisarius was engaged in more strategic warfare - must have relieved some of the pressure on Belisarius. It may be that Belisarius needed his help more than Procopius wanted to admit. In his narrative, because John takes the part of General Sherman in the American Civil War, Belisarius,can remain the unblemished hero. It might seem inconsistent that I have no quarrel with Belisarius enriching himself by his conquests but do with Bloody John (and others) doing so. Belisarius, however, became rich off the Vandal and Gothic treasuries, not from raiding civilians. That might have been acceptable in an enemy country, but Justinian was trying to pacify North African and Italy and return them to imperial control. The actions of John (and Bessas in Rome) have no strategic purpose in a land which one wishes to make friendly. Charges that Belisarius unduly enriched himself could never be made to stick.

John the Cappadocian - Praetorian Prefect. Although John had an excellent legal mind and headed Tribonian's commission that codified Roman law, he is best remembered for his zeal in raising revenue for Justinian's projects. Procopius' account might be considered excessive except that in general terms it is confirmed by other contemporary writers. After Antonina trapped him in treason, he was forced to become a priest and was exiled by Justinian. For awhile he was well treated and allowed to keep a large part of his treasure, but when he was accused of involvement in a plan to murder his bishop his exile was made more severe and his wealth confiscated. Nonetheless John continued to plot to restore his position at court. After Theodora died Justinian did recall his old friend, yet he never regained the power he sought.

John of Ephesus - The source of what little information we have on Photius other than Procopius. Procopius liked Photius; John did not. In his *Ecclesiastical History* he accuses Photius of being excessive in his revenue raising though he makes no charge that Photius benefited personally. Those such as John who held to the council of Nicaea but not Chalcedon, have been termed only semi-monophysites. Under Justinian (who was searching for a formula that would reconcile the orthodox Catholics with as many Monophysites as possible) his heresy was overlooked. Semi-monophysites and the orthodox both accepted the teachings of such church fathers as St. John Chrysostom and St. Cyril. One of the tasks that John performed for Justinian was searching out and persecuting pagans in Constantinople and in Asia. In this he claims to have been very successful, even building monasteries on ruined temples. Two of the names by which he was known in his lifetime were John the idol breaker and John the teacher of the heathens.

Justin - Justin the magister militum per Illyricum supported Narses in his treacherous refusal to follow Belisarius' orders in Italy. After Narses was withdrawn by Justinian his loyalty to the sole commander was restored.

Justin I, Emperor - The uncle of Justinian, himself a rural shepherd from Illyricum (Dalmatia), he became an imperial guardsman and was conveniently positioned to force the senate to make him emperor at the death of Anastasius I. Justin was nearly seventy when he took the throne, and he soon adopted his nephew Justinian as a son. Justin is usually assumed to have been senile in the last years of his reign (he died at age seventy seven), and Justinian is given the credit for most of the achievements of his reign.

354

Justinian - (Born c 482, Emperor 527-565) Justinian was born Flavius Petrus Sabbatius but took the name Iustanius to honor his stepfather, the emperor Justin, who had adopted him as a son. I have not given a physical description of Justinian in the text, but Procopius describes him as having a round and not ill-favored face which showed color even after a two day fast. One cannot see that in the rather horrid figure in the Ravenna mosaics, but it should be noted that he would have been in his mid sixties when that image was created. Fearful and judgmental as he appears in the Ravenna mosaic, according to Procopius he usually affected a mild and friendly visage. The achievements of his reign are too numerous to relate here. I will only mention: the codification of Roman law which is the foundation of European law; the construction of Hagia Sophia and building or rebuilding of many other churches; Belisarius' defense of the empire's eastern provinces against two Persian monarchs; the conquest of North Africa, and conquest of Italy; and the development of a major silk industry. (See Silk in notes.) It should be noted that although much of Belisarius' and Narses' conquests in Italy were later lost, not everything was. The empire retained the large and very important exarchate of Ravenna, Sicily, parts of southern Italy, and had influence in areas controlled by the papacy. Though Procopius paints Justinian as a demon, there was much greatness in him. He strove mightily, if unsuccessfully, to unify the various sects of Christianity. He could be kind and of a Christian intent even to traitors. I think it speaks for the age that Justinian pardoned men who sought his death. (As, Procopius suggests, Belisarius would have done with Constantinus who had tried to kill him.) That Justinian was an often frightened and paranoid person is no doubt true, but unlike others whose avarice and political ambitions are given prominence by Procopius, he was trying to behave as a Christian, at least as Christian behavior was conceived of by contemporaries in a world torn by religious dissent and political ambition. One can excuse and lament his paranoia and look to his achievements; or vice versa, according to the temperament of the historian.

Justus - A nephew of Justinian who served without particular distinction in the second Persian War. He, like Bouzes, hid behind city walls until Belisarius arrived and shamed them.

Kerikos - fictional bishop just mentioned once.

Kobad - Kobad was king when war broke out on the Armenian frontier and Belisarius had his first experience of warfare. He was still king throughout the first Persian war. On his death peace was arranged and it more or less held until <u>Chosroes</u> assumed the crown.

Kyra - Fictional cubicularia and friend of Antonina. Mentioned only once.

Leo I - (Eastern Roman Emperor 457-474) In 468 AD Leo sent a fleet of one thousand ships under the command of his incompetent brother-in-law <u>Basiliscus</u> against the Vandal kingdom in North Africa. The <u>Vandals</u> pretended submission, but requested time to arrange details. This was a ruse. As soon as there were suitable winds, they sent fire ships and their galleys against the Roman fleet. Nearly the entire invasion force was killed.

Macedonia - A servant of Antonina who betrayed her infidelity with <u>Theodosius</u> in Sicily to Belisarius. As witnesses, she also brought two boys of Antonina's bed chamber. Procopius passes on the rumor that they were all killed, mutilated, and thrown into the sea by Antonina's servant <u>Eugenius</u>.

Mahon, Lord (Earl Philip Henry Stanhope) - His Life of Belisarius remains the standard biography of Belisarius. One might complain that he does not sufficiently balance Procopius' opinion of the participants in the wars of Belisarius, but Lord Mahon was only twenty four when he published it.

Marcellus - The commander of the palace guard who accompanied <u>Narses</u> to <u>Rufinianae</u> when <u>Antonina</u> trapped <u>John the Cappadocian</u> into revealing his treasonous plan.

Marcus Aurelius - Roman emperor and stoic philosopher who held off German invaders for eleven winters on the Rhine Danube border. He is greatly to be admired but to a reader of his *Meditations* he must have been a bore.

Mark the Evangelist, St. - One of the seventy disciples that Christ sent forth to preach the gospel. He founded a church at <u>Alexandria</u> to which today's <u>Coptic</u> church traces its origin.

Martinus - A loyal subordinate of Belisarius, he was sent to relieve <u>Bloody John</u> at <u>Rimini</u>, but John refused to leave the city. He was also with <u>Procopius</u> and <u>Solomon</u> when the Sicilian garrison mutinied, and was holding the frontier at the beginning of the second Persian war. When Belisarius was recalled to Constantinople he was given charge in that conflict by Justinian. Martinus did, however, fail Belisarius by failing to relieve <u>Milan</u> resulting in the death of the entire male population and the rape and enslavement of its women.

Maxentius - Roman emperor who shared rule with <u>Constantine I</u> until they feuded. Constantine defeated Maxentius at the battle of the <u>Milvian bridge</u> Maxentius drowned in the river. It was in this battle that Christ's <u>labarum</u> (monogram) was first used as an army standard, Constantine claiming to have had a heavenly vision that he would conquer under it. Constantine went on to legalize the practice of Christianity, found Constantinople as a Christian city, and eventually, himself be baptised.

McAuliffe, (Gen.) Tony - See <u>Nuts</u> in notes.

Mirranes - Not a name but a title of *Perozes*, the Persian commander at <u>Dara</u>.

Mundilas - The Byzantine commander at <u>Milan</u> who tried to motivate his starving troops to die in defense of the city. He failed in this and the Milanese were slaughtered after the surrender of the city.

Mundus - A <u>Gepid</u> barbarian and friend of Belisarius. During the <u>Nike</u> riots he led troops into the <u>hippodrome</u> from the emperor's box while Belisarius did the same from the end. Later he invaded Gothic-held <u>Dalmatia</u> with his <u>Illyrian</u> troops while Belisarius invaded Italy itself. He died in that war.

Nabedes - Belisarius' competent Persian adversary at Nisibis.

Narses - Although Procopius hated him and doubtless slanders him, the eunuch grand chamberlain was a devoted (or superstitious) Christian who asked the Virgin Mary for advise before any of his battles in Italy. Having said this, he and Belisarius were certainly rivals. Narses thought himself to be as important as the Supreme Commander. His pride nearly cost him his head when he deliberately misinterpreted a letter from Justinian explaining that Belisarius was in sole command. The author is reminded that both Generals Bernard Montgomery and George Patton nearly lost their commands for such arrogance and presumption. Montgomery thought himself better suited than Dwight Eisenhower to be in command of all land forces after the Normandy invasion; Patton slapped a soldier. Both these self-important commanders humbly - in fact, cloyingly - appealed to Eisenhower not to fire them. He didn't, although Patton lost the opportunity to lead the invasion of Normandy. Like these two, Narses soon returned to acting with pride and ambition and wanting independent command. Justinian recalled him. That he had strategic ability is not doubted even by Procopius and he was returned to Italy after Belisarius withdrew from the second Gothic war to fight the Persians. He succeeded in Italy, but did so with all the support which Justinian had refused to Belisarius, Unlike Belisarius who had a family, Narses could not be a threat to the throne. Not only was he a eunuch, by this time, though in excellent health, he was aged. <u>Agathias Scholasticus</u> wrote of Narses "He was a man of sound mind, and clever at adapting himself to the times. He was not versed in literature nor practiced in oratory, but made up for it by the fertility of his mind."

Agathias also gave a physical description of Narses. "He was small and of a lean habit, but stronger and more high-spirited than would have been believed." This description and his age is confirmed by his image behind Justinian in the Ravenna mosaics.

Nicetas and Peter - These were young troop commanders who cost Belisarius a victory at Nisibis by their impetuosity during the second Persian war. Later, however, they served him faithfully as they did Martinus after Belisarius was recalled to Constantinople.

Nicholas, St. - Among other things Nick is the patron of poor girls, the legend being that as bishop of Myra he secretly provided dowries for several poor but noble sisters. Of course, he is loved by children for other things.

Odoacer - The barbarian ruler of Italy prior to the Goths. As leader of some Herulian foederati he deposed Romulus Agustulus, the last Roman emperor, and became the first king of Italy. However Zeno, the than Roman emperor in Constantinople sent Theodoric the Great of the Ostrogoths against Odoacer. After some fighting they agreed to share power but Theodoric treacherously killed Odoacer at a banquet. Any alleged corruption by Belisarius in taking an unfair share of the Gothic treasury for himself pales by comparison with the power politics of the age.

Osdas - A Goth commemorated by Procopius as the bravest of the brave for his defense of the bridge barring access to Rome during the second Gothic war. Two hundred Goths died with him when Belisarius' barges attacked with fire bombs and archery.

Pallas Athena - Guardian goddess of Athens, and usually depicted as armed and beautiful.

Pelagius, Archdeacon - A future pope, he tried to negotiate with Totila during the starvation that accompanied the siege of Rome during the second Gothic War. When Totila agreed to treat the Romans kindly but not the Sicilians who had attempted to supply them with grain, Pelagius refused the offer and returned to the city to share in the misery of its citizens. Such behavior shames Bessas who is said to have horded the small supply of grain within the city and only released small portions to those who could pay an extravagant price. As pope, Pelagius was to support Justinian's attempt to reconcile the various religious factions in the empire. This failed.

Peranius - Although little mention of him is made in this novel, Peranius was one of Belisarius' major lieutenants during the first Gothic campaign. He was a Georgian prince. Lest I neglect him (for he obeyed orders), I will quote the details of his career from Wikipedia: "Peranius and his family fled the Sassanid oppression of Iberia into Lazica in the 520s. They placed themselves under Roman protection and left for Constantinople, where Peranius joined the Byzantine imperial army. Later in the 530s, he served under Belisarius in Italy and was in Rome during the siege by the Goths (537–538). During the siege, he defended the Porta Praenestina and led a sally from the Porta Salaria. In mid-538, he laid a siege to Urbs Vetus (Orvieto) which fell in early 539. Early in the 540s, Peranius was transferred to the eastern frontier where he fought the Sassanid Persian armies. He raided Taraunitis in 543 and was one of the Roman commanders defending Edessa in 544. The Persian shah, Khosrau I (Chosroes) (r. 531–579), ineffectively demanded the surrender of Peranius on the grounds that Peranius was his hereditary slave. When a Sassanid contingent under Azarethes threatened to break into the city through one of the gates, Peranius led reinforcements of soldiers and citizens to the spot and averted the danger."

Perozes - The Persian commander at Dara.

Pharas - Commanded the Heruli reserves at Dara.

Photius – Photius is identified by Procopius in *The Wars* as Antonina's son by a previous marriage, but in the *Secret History* he makes no mention of a previous marriage but only of Antonina having lead a dissolute life. I suspect that in *The Wars,* written for public consumption during the lifetime of Belisarius, he was giving legitimacy to Antonina's concubinage. Could she and her consort in Antioch have been wed? Yes, but it runs counter to his portrait of Antonina as a slut. After his imprisonment by Theodora, Photius became a monk and abbot in Jerusalem. Later in life he seems to have effectively served the emperor Justin II, the successor of Justinian, as a tax collector for the throne. Allegedly, he was so villainous in this work that even the emperor upbraided him. John of Ephesus recounts his exploits as a tax collector: "Photius had been bred," he tells us, "to the profession of arms, and had accompanied his stepfather in several campaigns; but finally he had assumed the tonsure, and the monkish dress, though he by no means conformed to their morals, but had put on the appearance of a monk under a borrowed name, by which is meant, not that he concealed who he was, but that his adoption of the profession of a monk was but a pretense. And this soon led him to repent of the step he had taken; for shortly afterward, being unable to quell the savageness of his temper, and bend it unto piety, he betook himself to the king, still clad outwardly in the monastic garb. Now it so happened that the Samaritans were in a state of revolt, and the king therefore sent him with full powers into Syria. As his wish then was to please men, and anger the God who made him, by running on every pretext after impure gains, he gave himself up to the spoiling and plundering and oppressing of mankind, till he became their uprooter and destroyer; and all the regions in the east, great and small, were ruined as utterly as if they had been pillaged by barbarians: and so great was the terror he inspired, that even the bishops and clergy of the cities fled from before him: for if he heard of any one whatsoever, either in the city or the country, possessing in sufficiency his daily bread, he seized them, and plundered them, and imprisoned them, and hung them up, and tortured them, and imposed upon them a fine of a pound of gold, whoever they might be, whether they were worth as much or not. Nor could he be induced to alter his sentence, even though a man had to sell himself and his children into slavery, and his household, and his substance. For when he laid hands on any one, whatsoever, he said, 'Give me so many pounds of gold: for the king has need of gold to expend upon his wars.' And in this way he gathered together hundreds of pounds of gold, and sent them to the king, in order that he might obtain authority and power from him to do whatever he liked to whomsoever he liked, and that no man might stand before him. For he even exacted large sums from bishops; and if any one resisted him, forthwith on the very spot he strung him up to a rope fixed either behind his head, or to his elbows, or to one arm. And in this way, it is said, he served the bishop of Askalon, on whom he levied a contribution of three hundred pounds of gold; and when the bishop bewailed, and begged for mercy, saying he had not so much, he ordered him to be hung up by a rope, and left him hanging, and went on his way, leaving orders that though he should hang for three days, they should not let him down till the money was paid. Nor was he loosed from the rope till the three hundred pounds of gold were brought. And he treated the rest in many instances in a similar manner, till the land trembled before him, and all the magistrates and governors and the rest of the lords. And when many went to the king, and in his presence implored for mercy, he wrote to Photius, saying, 'The money you send us being got by plunder is a sin;' but he wrote in reply, 'Do not you be afraid, my lord, of sin, in respect of the gold which I send you: the sin is on my; head.' In these doings he was accompanied by a crowd of monks fit for such deeds, and members even of the imperial family, and officers of the household troops, and guardsmen, and a host of Romans. And when in this base course of destruction and wickedness and cruelty, devoid of all fear of God, he had fulfilled a period of twelve years, his allotted time overtook him, and he descended to the tomb by a miserable end, and with an accursed remembrance. And there was appointed in his stead a certain Abraham, the abbot of what is called the new monastery in Jerusalem."

I quote this account to balance <u>Procopius</u>. This, of course, is after the events with his mother and it must be insisted does not show any personal gain by Photius. One expects that the author greatly exaggerates because, being a churchman himself, he could not bear seeing churchmen taxed, even if, as is probable, the funds were needed to fortify the frontier nearby them against Persian attack. One must read between the lines. One may suspect that there is more to the affairs described than John wants to reveal. He himself says that Photius was accompanied by monks apparently more loyal to the crown than the author. He also states that the bishop of Askalon, who claimed he had not enough to pay the exaction, somehow found it when under torture. Hmm!

Presidius - A loyal Italian who was dispossessed of his heirloom daggers by <u>Constantinus</u>, then military governor of Spoleto.

Procopius - Procopius might have been likened to a new <u>Thucydides</u> had he not written the *Anecdota* or *Secret History.* Though his *Buildings* is a panegyric it is not inaccurate, and *The Wars* is a masterpiece of reporting to match <u>Caesar's</u> *Bellum Gallicum.* The *Secret History,* however, is so mean-minded that even the details are suspect, though the author is careful not to take personal responsibility for the many rumors that he recounts. Though in this story I have identified him as a eunuch, there is no evidence to support that. I have abridged and edited some of the speeches that he puts into Belisarius' mouth. It is doubtful that Procopius was making literal transcriptions of Belisarius' harangues to his troops.

Psallidion, Alexander – See <u>Alexander</u>.

Ptolemies - Grecian rulers of Egypt until the Roman occupation. These kings were descendents of one of Alexander the Great's generals, his empire being divided between his generals after Alexander's death.

Rhaskos - A fictional eunuch and majordomo in the household of Belisarius.

Roderic - Commander of the Gothic garrison at <u>Ostia</u> unwisely attacked by Isaac, who should have been holding <u>Porto</u> where <u>Antonina</u> was.

Sabbatius - The father of <u>Justinian</u>, though Procopius relates the rumor that his mother was actually impregnated by a demon. It was also Justinian's birth name.

Scipio Africanus - Defeated <u>Hannibal</u> in the last war between republican Rome and Carthage, thus ending Carthaginian power in the ancient Mediterranean and leaving Rome dominant.

Seneca – Roman politician, philosopher, and statesman.

Severus - The Monophysite patriarch of Antioch.

Silvarius - Silvarius was elected pope over the objections of Theodora who wanted Vigilius. Vigilius, she thought, would be more flexible toward the Monophysites. Silvarius refused to confirm the Monophysite patriarch of Constantinople Anthimus. When Vigilius replaced Silvarius however, he proved no more flexible toward the Monophysites.

Sittas - General and friend of Belisarius. His wife was Theodora's sister. Sittas and Belisarius had campaigned together as young officers on the Armenian frontier.

Solomon - Solomon was known as "the Beardless general" because of an accident as an infant that made him a eunuch. He was Belisarius' Domesticus or chief of staff in Africa. He succeeded Belisarius in Africa where his troops mutinied, and with the Vandals, attempted to kill him. However Belisarius returned to Africa and restored loyalty. Later Solomon had the unfortunate duty of implementing Justinian's disruptive policies.

Sunica - A secondary commander at Dara.

Theodatus - The King of the Goths at the time Belisarius invaded Italy. A cultured man, he was also a coward who for a time offered his throne to Justinian. He was deposed by the Goths after the fall of Naples and was shortly thereafter killed by a personal enemy. Also see Amalasontha.

Theodora - Justinian's wife and empress. Some of her early life is quoted from Procopius in my Afterword. Theodora seems to have been a steadying influence on Justinian and a power in her own right. As with Bill Clinton as candidate, Justinian could have claimed that the people would "get two for the price of one." Whether true or not, Justinian presented himself as mild. He was certainly indecisive, condemning a person one day and restoring his honors the next. Theodora is portrayed by Procopius as far more steady and determined which is probably true if his account of the rulers' behavior during the Nike insurrection is typical.

Theodoric the Great - Theodoric is the great Gothic monarch. As a child he lived in Constantinople as an honorable hostage and was even made a patrician and consul. When Theodoric later raided territory of the eastern empire itself, the emperor Zeno urged him to Italy where he established a Gothic kingdom. Although an Arian, Theodoric allowed Catholic worship. He ruled the Goths as their king but the native people as the representative of the empire, and established peace. His tomb in Ravenna is a UNESCO World Heritage Site.

Theodosius - Belisarius' godson and Antonina's paramour. Also the name of one of the greatest Late Roman emperors.

Theotokos – See the notes section of the appendix.

Theudibert - King of the Franks, he sent a force of allied Burgundians to the siege of Milan.

Thrasimund - Vandal king who wed the Gothic princess Amalafrida, the sister of Great Theodoric. Succeeded by Hilderic.

Timothy, Patriarch – The Monophysite patriarch of Alexandria who is thought to have persuaded a young Theodora to that doctrine while she was making her way back to Constantinople after being dumped by Hecebolus, her paramour in Libya.

Totila - One of the most noble of the Goths, he was a man who could be cruel but who never broke his word to friend or foe, and who, like Belisarius, had too keen an understanding of warfare to expect victory through numbers alone.

Tribonian - Jurist and legal scholar credited with formulating the Codex Iustianus, the foundation of modern continental law.

Uliaris - One of Belisarius' subordinates. Together with Martinus he failed at Milan, resulting in a major Gothic atrocity.

Valentine - One of Belisarius' personal guards who was charged with protecting Photius. When Belisarius was surrounded by Goths near the Milvian bridge, he detached himself from Photius and charged suicidally into the Gothic cavalry. He died but in death bought Belisarius and the others enough seconds to disengage and race for the Flaminian Gate.

Valerian - A loyal subordinate of Belisarius, he served in the African, Second Persian, and Italian wars. He assisted in restraining Constantinus when he tried to kill the general. He brought reinforcements during the siege of Rome though, admittedly, too late.

Verres, Gaius – Notorious for his rapacity as governor of Sicily, he was prosecuted by Cicero in 70 BC.

Vigilius. Pope - He succeeded Silvarius. Theodora had always wanted him as pontiff because she considered him malleable. Yet as pope he did not support Justinian's attempt to reconcile orthodox and heretical sects within his realm by formulae that he could not accent to on theological grounds.

Von Choltitz. Dietrich - Though no saint (In the Soviet Union he aided in the extermination of the Jewish population), Von Choltitz did save Paris at the risk of his life by disobeying an order of Hitler's to burn the city, and by negotiating its surrender before it could be damaged by battle.

Witiges (Vitiges) – He was king of the Goths through most of the First Gothic War after Theodatus was dethroned and killed.

Zabergan, khan – This Bulgar khan crossed the frozen Danube, pillaged the Peloponnese, and moved through Thrace to threaten Constantinople itself. Then he met Belisarius in one of the general's smallest, but most important, engagements.

Zarathustra - Prophet of Ahura Mazda and founder of the Zoroastrian religion, the national religion of Persia. (There are still a few adherents.)

Zazo - Brother of Gelimer. At the time of Belisarius' North African invasion, Zaro was attempting to put down a rebellion in Sardinia.

PLACES

Abydos - This important "toll gate" controls a relatively narrow section of the <u>Dardanelles</u> and was therefore important to Byzantine commerce. It was also nearly the first mainland port for naval ships exiting the <u>Aegean Sea</u> en route home to Constantinople.

Abyssinia - See <u>Axsun</u>.

Ad Decimum - Literally: "at the tenth (milepost)" east of <u>Carthage</u>.

Adriatic Sea - Between Italy and the former Yugoslavia and modern Greece, in Roman times the Adriatic separated the east coast of Italy from <u>Dalmatia</u>.

Aegean Sea – Generally south of the <u>Dardanelles</u>, the Aegean separates modern Greece and European Turkey from Asiatic Turkey.

Aemilia - The area around and west of <u>Ravenna</u> and including <u>Rimini</u>, and <u>Piacenza</u>.

Alba on Lake Celano - About seventy five miles east of Rome. The lake has since been drained.

Alexandria - Founded by Alexander the Great as a Greek city in a foreign land, by the time of our story it is the important city in Egypt, and the center of the all-important grain trade that fed Constantinople. The greatest library in the world was located there, and the famous lighthouse, one of the seven wonders of the ancient world, would still have existed on the nearby island of <u>Pharos</u>. It was also the place where the <u>Monophysite</u> theory on the Divinity of Jesus originated.

Amida - (Modern Diyarbakir) Situated on the <u>Tigris</u> River, Amida was within Roman territory in Syria northwest of <u>Dara</u>, but was often fought over.

Anatolia - Asia Minor. The Asian part of modern Turkey. Most of the interior of Anatolia consists of a high plateau that becomes increasingly mountainous as one moves east where it borders the <u>Armenian</u> highlands. Anatolia is separated from the Highlands by the <u>Euphrates river</u>, and from Syria by the <u>Orontes</u> River. Together with the <u>Bosphorus</u> and <u>Dardanelles</u> straits, the <u>Sea of Marmara</u> forms a connection between the <u>Black</u> and <u>Aegean</u> Seas and separates Anatolia from <u>Thrace</u> on the European mainland. Central Anatolia contains the desert moonscape of <u>Cappadocia</u> where the soft stone was dug into to form living quarters for hermits and veritable underground cities for safety from invaders.

Antioch (modern Antakya) - One of the largest cities in the Roman world, Antioch was especially important to Christians. In apostolic times it was visited by Sts. Peter, Barnabas, and Paul. However the city was often troubled by earthquakes and declined in importance during the middle ages.

Apamea - A Syrian city which, like Antioch, is located on the Orontes River. It was a Monophysite center.

Apennines - Mountains forming a north-south spine through central Italy.

Appian Way - The first of the Roman roads, built by the censor Appius Claudius to link Rome with Brundisium on the heel of the Italian boot. Since it runs through the rich Campania countryside, it could be used to carry relief supplies to Rome. Though mostly paved over today, the Italian government maintains a stretch of road outside Rome in its original condition.

Apulia - This area forms the heel of the Italian boot and the area along the coast immediately north of the heel. Although the main presence of Byzantium in Italy after the fall of the Gothic kingdom to the Lombards was Ravenna, it also intermittently held the loyalty of some other areas including Apulia. (But that is for another story.)

Armenia - Armenia is still a Christian nation as it was at the time of our story, Armenia was a pawn in the warfare between Byzantium and Persia. It is located across the Armenian Highlands from Anatolia.

Athens and Corinth - These sites of ancient wisdom and art were still honored but were no longer of any real importance.

Athyras River - Site of the Bulgar encampment only twenty miles from Constantinople.

Axsum - Basically Abyssinia, now known as Ethiopia. Axsum adopted Christianity at about the same time as Constantine the Great did in the Roman Empire. At that time it was considered one of the world powers along with Persia, Rome, and China. It extended over modern Ethiopia, Eritrea, Yemen, Saudi Arabia, and parts of the Sudan.

Babylon - By this time ancient Babylon was but a province of the Persian empire, though one with its own culture, and important religiously to both Persian and Christian sects. This is also where the Babylonian Talmud was written at about the time of our story. The capital of Persia was not far away at Ctesiphon.

Barbary Coast - The Berber coastal regions and cities along the middle and western coastal regions of North Africa - what is now Morocco, Algeria, Tunisia, and Libya.

Black (Euxine) Sea - A short boat ride up the Bosphorus from Constantinople, the Black Sea coast was a place to trade with Asiatic tribes, especially for slaves and furs.

Bosphorus - The narrow waterway connecting the Black (Euxine) Sea to the Sea of Marmara (Propontis). On a point of land jutting into the Bosphorus, Constantine the Great built Constantinople. Besides being an easily defended city, it controlled the trade in furs from the north and the silk road across Anatolia from the east.

Boucoleon district and Harbor - The Great Palace sat here on the shore of the Sea of Marmara. The name Boucoleon was probably attributed in the reign of Justinian when the small imperial harbor in front of the palace was constructed. According to tradition a statue featuring a bull fighting a lion stood there, giving the port its name.

Byzantium – The name of the original Greek village where Constantine the Great built his New Rome (Constantinople.)

Caesaria - In Palestine (modern Israel); at the time of our story, it was a flourishing commercial center.

Callinicum - See Sura.

Campania - The fertile instep of the Italian boot, incorporating the city and port of Naples.

Cape Bon - The site of a Roman attempt in 468 AD to defeat Genseric the Vandal king. A fleet of 1,100 ships and 100,000 men was destroyed when Genseric, after waiting five days for a favorable wind, sent fireships against them ahead of his galleys.

Cape Malea(s) - The second most southerly point on the Peloponnese, it separates the Aegean Sea in the east from the Laconian Gulf in the west. It is famous for the treacherous waters thereabouts.

Cape Matapan - Located on the lowest point of the middle "finger" of the Peloponnese, this was from ancient times considered the gateway to the underworld. An ancient temple originally dedicated to Poseidon, god of the sea, was converted into a church in Byzantine times and remains in use.

Cappadocia – The moonscape of central Anatolia.

Caput Vada (modern Chebba) - An unfortified natural harbor where Belisarius landed about sixty miles east of Carthage.

Carthage – This important city has existed since the first millennium BCE. It was the home of Hannibal and fought the Roman Republic in three Punic wars. However after the defeat of the Carthaginians and the destruction of the city, the Romans found it necessary to rebuild Carthage. At the time of our story it was the urbane capital of the North African Vandal kingdom until conquered by Belisarius. In later years it was an important Muslim city and lair of the Barbary pirates. It exists today as a suburb of Tunis.

Caspian Gates - A pass through the Caucasus mountains that both Persia and Rome agreed must be held secure against invaders from the Russian steppes. Despite their feuding otherwise, there had long been agreement to share the cost of this defense.

Chalcedon - Site of a church council in 451 AD which established the orthodox doctrine of the Divine Trinity and branded the Monophysites as heretical. Chalcedon and its sister city, Chrysopolis, are within sight of Constantinople but on the eastern shore of the Bosphorus.

Chalcis - A desert town located 15 miles southwest of Aleppo on the west bank of the Queig river. It was near to where the battle of Callinicum was forced upon Belisarius by his troops.

Chettos - A village west of Constantinople.

Chios - A large island just east of the Asian mainland in the Aegean. Chios wine was believed to have been the first red wine and was a luxury product even in Greece. It was exported throughout the Hellenistic world. In Rome it was not only a luxury wine; it was also believed to possess medicinal properties.

Chrysopolis - A city on the Asian shore of the Bosphorus within sight of Constantinople.

Cilicia, Cilician Gates - The southeastern coast of Asia Minor bordering Syria and separated from the Central Anatolian Plateau by the Taurus mountains. The mountains are pierced by the strategic Cilician Gates.

Classe - The port of Ravenna.

Colchos - See Lazi.

Constantinople – Founded in 330 AD by Constantine the Great as a New Rome, it soon became popularly known as Constantinople or Constantine's City. It was built on the site of the old Greek village of Byzantium and Constantine's intent was that it be an administrative site for the eastern part of the empire, while Rome (or another town) remained the administrative center in the west. Both had their own emperors who were to work together. Of course, that did not work.

Corinth and Athens - These sites of ancient wisdom and art were still honored but were no longer of any real importance.

Ctesiphon - The capital of the Persian Empire, Ctesiphon is located on the Tigris River and rather distant from the action in our story.

Cyzicus (Artace) - The place of exile of John the Cappadocian, it was located on the East coast of the Sea of Marmara, not far from the Dardanelles (Hellespont).

Dacia – The territorial extent of Dacia varied at times but it consists roughly of the Balkans.

Dalmatia (Illyricum) - A province of the Roman Empire lying east of the

Adriatic Sea. Dalmatia was always a source of fine troops for Rome and Byzantium, but during most of the fifth century it was held by the same Gothic kingdom as Italy. Justinian recovered it for the empire and, unlike Italy, it remained in imperial possession though always threatened by barbarian inroads.

Dara - Dara (or Daras) and Nisibis were forward outposts on the Persian frontier. Nisibis was a major city while Dara was fundamentally a fortress, hence the Persian anxiety.

Dardanelles - See Hellespont.

Dunkirk – Site of the British withdrawal from France at the beginning of World War II after a German victory in the Battle of France was assured. Although a withdrawal, leaving behind most of their weapons, can hardly be considered a victory, it was a brave and dashing affair made possible by the efforts of civilian boat owners who risked their boats and lives to bring the army home; as well as to the bravery of covering French troops who held off the enemy long enough to allow the British and some French units to get to safety.

Dyrrachium - In present day Albania.

Edessa (Turkish Urfa) - This town, lying in the fertile plain of Haran and ringed by limestone hills on three sides, controls the strategic pass to the south through which runs a road from Anatolia to northern Mesopotamia.

Eighth Avenue - In New York City Eighth Avenue, especially around the Port Authority Bus Terminal, is a hangout for drug pushers, prostitutes, male hustlers holding their crotches, thieves, and other lowlifes. The only thing keeping it safe is a constant police presence - much like in Dickens' London and the area around the Hippodrome.

Ephesus - The most important Asian city in the Byzantine Empire, but like Antioch it was troubled by earthquakes and finally lost most of its importance when the harbor silted up. It is now several miles inland but is considered to be one of the great ruins of the Ancient world. It was visited by the Apostles Paul and John and was the city to which Paul's Epistle to the Ephesians was directed.

Ethiopia – See Axsun.

Euphrates - The Euphrates and the Tigris rivers, running roughly north to south from the Taurus mountains to the Persian Gulf, are the borders of classical Mesopotamia, the cradle of western civilization.

Europum - The headquarters of Belisarius on the Euphrates where he hoodwinked Chosroes into giving up his plan to move on Jerusalem.

Euxine Sea - The Black Sea.

Exarchate of Ravenna - Though Byzantium was to lose most of its reconquered territory in Italy, the city of Ravenna and a large part of the countryside thereabouts as well as Sicily and parts of southern Italy remained in imperial hands. The Exarchate of Ravenna was for the next two hundred years a most important outpost of Byzantine civilization and an important cultural link between Italy and Constantinople. Since most of the religious art in Greece and Turkey and other parts of the empire was destroyed after the Turkish conquest, the finest extant Byzantine mosaics are in the city of Ravenna.

Fiesole - A Tuscan fortress town located on the heights above Florence, it was taken by Bloody John.

Golden Horn - The inlet from the Bosphorus forming the northern border of Constantinople. It is one of the world's great natural harbors and, together with the Bosphorus on the east and the Sea of Marmara on the south, protected the city on three sides; the fourth side being covered by the famous triple walls of Theodosius (still extant).

Hellespont - The modern Dardanelles south of the Sea of Marmara. Together with the Bosphorus, north of the Sea of Marmara, they separate Europe from Asia.

Heraclea (Perinthus) - A town just west of Constantinople itself.

Hermione - A pleasant inland retreat in the old Roman North African province of Byzacium, and just four days' journey from Carthage.

Hierapolis - Modern Manbij in Syria.

Hippo (modern Annaba in Algeria) - Located on the North African coast, it forms a triangle with Sicily and Sardinia. This had been the bishopric of St. Augustine, the greatest of Church fathers, honored by Christians both in the east and west.

Iberia - Basically modern Georgia (the country) and not to be confused with the Iberian peninsula (Spain and Portugal), of which the empire also held a small section. Confusing? Confusing too, that so many medieval Greek names start with Theo, and that there were two (or was it three) Narses around at the time of our story, which, however, thankfully only deals with one of them. Not to mention that the Golden Gate was bronze and that there are now two Macedonias, Europum was in Asia, and many places have at times been referred to by two or more very different names. (OK, the author is getting pissy.)

Illyricum - See Dalmatia.

Insula Sacra - This is an island splitting the river <u>Tiber</u> near <u>Ostia</u>, the old port of Rome.

Ionian Sea - Located below the <u>Aegean</u>, it covers the area between the sole of the Italian boot and the western coast of the Greek <u>Peloponnese</u>.

Isauria - A district of south central Asia Minor, chiefly on the northern slopes of the <u>Taurus mountains</u>. Although Constantinopleans considered Isaurians uncouth they were highly valued as cavalry.

Kontoskali - A harbor within the land walls of Constantinople on the Sea of <u>Marmara</u> west of the <u>hippodrome</u>.

Latin Way (Via Latina) - A road from Rome to <u>Naples</u> and therefore important as a supply route during the siege of Rome.

Lazica - The country of the <u>Lazi</u> on the isthmus between the <u>Euxine</u> (Black) and the Caspian Seas; also known anciently as Colchis, it was the fabled land of Medea and the Golden Fleece.

Liguria - The crescent shaped coastal area of northeastern Italy on the Gulf of Genoa.

Lucania - The mountainous area southeast of <u>Naples</u>; between the sole and heel of Italy on the Gulf of Taranto.

Luxor and Thebes - Ancient pharonic sites. To give Antonius his due, these places are not near <u>Alexandria</u> or Cairo, but rather far up the Nile

Macedonia - The northernmost part of modern Greece. In classical times there was disagreement among the <u>Hellenes</u> as to whether it should be considered part of Hellas at all, or whether their northern border was at the extremity of Thessaly.

Mare Nostrum - Latin for "Our Sea." Mare Nostrum was a Roman nickname for the Mediterranean Sea.

Marmara, Sea of – The <u>Propontis</u>, the southern boundary of Constantinople. Together with the <u>Bosphorus</u> and the <u>Dardanelles</u> it separates Asia from Europe.

Melantias - A village in <u>Thrace</u> on the banks of the river Athyras, eighteen miles from Constantinople.

Mesopotamia - The land between and bordering the <u>Tigris</u> and <u>Euphrates</u> rivers, located between the <u>Taurus</u> Mountains and the Persian Gulf. Belisarius' actions mostly took place in modern Syria though the war itself extended northward to <u>Lazica</u> under other commanders.

Methone (Modern Modon) - Belisarius' landing place on the Peloponnese west of the treacherous Cape Malea(s). Belisarius would have sailed directly westward across the Aegean from Abydos, out of sight of land and with the need to keep the ships in close company. From Methone he sailed directly to Sicily and Africa.

Milan - In the far northwest part of Italy within sight of the Alps. It was an easily attacked city for Frankish or Burgundian forces from Trans-alpine Gaul.

Milvian Bridge - According to Procopius this famous bridge across the Tiber river was the only near way for the Gothic army to reach Rome. It is famed as the place of battle where, under the standard of Christ, Constantine the Great defeated his one-time partner Maxentius and became sole ruler of the Roman Empire.

Mindon - The site of a fortress the young Belisarius built on the Persian frontier about three miles from Dara. Lord Mahon believed that the spelling should be Mygdon, a river on which Nisibis was also built, and may refer to a village of the same name on that river.

Mt. Papua - Berber village, the last refuge of **Gelimer**.

Naples - About one third the way up the western coast of Italy, Naples had been a major city since classical times. After the Gothic war it gave nominal allegiance to the emperor via the exarch of Ravenna.

New Rome (Nova Roma) - In 330 AD the emperor Constantine I divided the administration of the empire between Rome and Nova Roma, i.e. Byzantium. It had been the site of an ancient Greek town on the Bosphorus. That name never took and even official documents referred to the city as "Constantinople which is New Rome." Diocletian before him had also divided the administration but what makes Constantinople unique is that the emperor intended it from the beginning to be a purely Christian city without the remnants of paganism which remained in Rome itself.

Nicea – See Nicene Formula.

Nisibis (Nusaybin) - Nisibis is situated north of Antioch on the Görgarbonizra river where it passes through a narrow canyon and enters the plain. Nisibis strategically commands the entrance to the upper Syrian plains from the mountain passes of Asia Minor. Here the disobedience of a young subordinate prevented Belisarius from attaining a strategic victory, though whether the result should be considered a draw, a limited victory, or a loss depends upon one's point of view. Nisibis was a center of Nestorian Christianity.

Orontes - The river on which Antioch (modern Antakya) and Apamea are located. Twenty miles from the Mediterranean Sea, it is the chief river of Syria.

Orvieto - A nearly impregnable fortress on a butte eighty miles north of Rome. It was besieged by Peranius (see in names.)

Osimo - A seacoast town, it was the major city of Picenum.

Ostia - The original port of the city of Rome to which it was connected by road, and by water up the Tiber. By the time of our story, however, Ostia was largely silted up and its defensive walls were in ruin. There was no tow path along the Tiber to tow barges, and the road to Rome was indirect and in poor condition. The preferred port was Porto but at the beginning of Belisarius' second Italian campaign this was in the hands of the Goths.

Otranto - A city on the heel of Italy.

Palestine - During the Byzantine period Syria, Palestine, and Samaria were together named Palaestina which was divided into provinces.

Pavia - On the River Po twenty miles from Milan, Pavia suffered an attack by Franks from trans-alpine Gaul against both the Gothic army inside the walls and two Roman armies besieging it outside. The recall of Belisarius before Pavia fell, prevented his conquest of the whole of Italy in the First Gothic war.

Peloponnese - The southern peninsula of Greece containing such famous ancient cities as Sparta and Corinth. Athens, while on the mainland, is nearby.

Pelusium - The plague is first reported in July 541 at the port of Pelusium in Egypt, a secondary port on the eastern end of the Nile delta. From there it spread both east to the Levant and west to Alexandria. where it hopped a ship for Constantinople and beyond.

Persarmenia - The site of Belisarius' first clash with the Persians.

Petra - A Byzantine fortress in Lazica on the Black Sea. Not the Jordanian site of that name.

Piacenza - Piacenza controls the route: Ravenna - Bologna – Milan.

Picenum - A district on the Adriatic coast south of Ravenna.

Po River - The Po flows west to east from the Alps across the whole of northern Italy till it reaches the Adriatic near Venice.

Porto - The replacement port for Ostia, created when Ostia began to seriously silt up in late imperial times. There was a good road alongside the Tiber from Porto to Rome which allowed barges to be towed to Rome by oxen.

Propontis -   the Sea of Marmara, it forms the southern border of

Constantinople.

Ravenna - The Gothic capital in our story, it was to be important for the next two hundred years as the <u>Exarchate of Ravenna</u>, an important outpost of the Byzantines in the west. Quite pretty. For us, Ravenna is the Gothic capital, but even before the Goths took it, the city had become the seat of the Roman emperors in the west. Like Venice, it was surrounded by swampland and was thus defensible yet easily supplied by sea. Today it retains the finest Byzantine mosaics in the world including two showing <u>Justinian</u> with <u>Belisarius</u> and <u>Narses,</u> as well as <u>Theodora</u> with <u>Antonina</u> and their daughter, <u>Joannina</u>. These are believed to date from roughly the time of the second Gothic war, or slightly later. To this author they seem portraits, not stylized representations. While Antonina is pretty, Theodora who was dying of cancer is thin and wan.

Reggio (de Calabria) - Reggio is on the Italian mainland on the Strait of Messina, a brief ferry trip from <u>Sicily</u>.

Remagen - During World War II, the allies invading Germany were surprised and fortunate to find that the Germans had failed to destroy the bridge over the Rhine river at Remagen, thus greatly aiding the invasion.

Rimini - Rimini is located on the <u>Adriatic</u> south of <u>Ravenna</u>.

Rome – For a delightful survey of the eternal city at the time of our story, read Thomas Hodgin's volume four of The Barbarian Invasions of Italy (available online.) Hodgkin narrates an imaginary walk though of the town by Procopius.

Rufinianae (Modern Kadikoy) - A district across the <u>Bosphorus</u> from Constantinople, it was a private possession of Belisarius. It was a part of <u>Chalcedon</u> where the fourth ecumenical council, the Council of <u>Chalcedon</u>, was held in 451 AD.

Sardinia - A large island located west of central Italy and northwest of <u>Sicily</u>.

Sicily - While most of Italy proper was lost to the Lombards twenty years after our story, Belisarius' conquest of Sicily, as well as North Africa, held until rule was disputed by Arab conquerors in the tenth century and was finally ended by the Norman conquest in the eleventh.

Sisauranum - A Persian fortress on the <u>Tigris</u> taken by Belisarius from which he retired, according to Procopius, at least in part to confront Antonina for her infidelity. Procopius does admit, however, that his retirement was strategically justifiable.

Spolitium – A fortress town through which <u>Constantinus</u> was passing while pacifying Tuscany for Belisarius. It was there that he seized two daggers

374

which he refused to return to their owner. The result was that, feeling insulted, he attempted to kill Belisarius.

St. Cyprian monastery - This is a fictional name. Certainly Ephesus was a center of monasticism in the sixth century, as well as later; but the author is unaware of the names of any monasteries that were there at the time.

Sura or Callinicum - A city on the Euphrates river near where Belisarius' soldiers forced him to fight a useless battle, in which they were defeated.

Syracuse and Palermo - The major cities of Sicily.

Taurus mountains – This rugged chain of mountains extends across southern Anatolia to the border with Persia.

Terracina - A coastal city 18 miles south of Rome via the Via Appia.

Thebes - See Luxor and Thebes.

Thessaloniki - Probably the most important city in the European part of the empire after Constantinople, it is located in the southern coast of Macedonia.

Thrace - The area northeast of Macedonia and west of Constantinople.

Tiber - This river forms a strong western barrier for the city of Rome. It is renowned in song and story. The historian Thomas Hodgkin loves nothing better than to interrupt his narrative with quotes from the poem *Horatius at the (Tiber) Bridge* by Thomas Babington.

Tigris River - The Euphrates and the Tigris rivers, running roughly north to south from the Taurus mountains to the Persian Gulf, are the borders of classical Mesopotamia, the cradle of western civilization.

Tivoli - About 20 miles east-northeast of Rome, the city offers a wide view of the Campania.

Tricamaron - Tricamaron is located only about twenty miles from Carthage, so I had no hesitation in placing Antonina relatively near, yet in safety, at Carthage while the battle was being fought at Tricamaron.

Troy, Trojan war - The great Greek epic is the *Iliad*, in which Greek heroes under Agamemnon defeated the Phrygian city of Troy in modern day Turkey.

Tyrrenian Sea - On the west coast of Italy; the Adriatic being on the east, and the Ionian on the south.

Umbria - The area northeast of Rome, bisected by the Apennine mountains.

Urbino - Inland fortress town a day's march south of Rimini.

Urbs Vetus – Orvieto.

Made in the USA
Charleston, SC
03 October 2013